Tragedy and Truth

Tragedy and Truth

STUDIES IN THE DEVELOPMENT OF A
RENAISSANCE AND NEOCLASSICAL DISCOURSE

TIMOTHY J. REISS

NEW HAVEN AND LONDON, YALE UNIVERSITY PRESS

Designed by Sally Harris
and set in IBM Aldine Roman type.
Printed in the United States of America by
Halliday Lithograph, West Hanover, Mass.

Library of Congress Cataloging in Publication Data

Reiss, Timothy J   1942–
    Tragedy and truth.

    Includes bibliographical references and index.
    1. Tragedy. I. Title.
PN1892.R4   809.2'512   80–10413
ISBN 0–300–02461–4

10   9   8   7   6   5   4   3   2   1

For Jean, Matthew, Suzanna, and Justin

Contents

Acknowledgments

Obviously, anyone who writes on tragedy is indebted to previous writers. Although most of those debts are covered by the bibliographical references, reasons of space have dictated the excision of many acknowledgments and of a more general bibliography. There are several more or less important omissions: my apologies to the authors concerned and a blanket expression of gratitude are therefore in order. In addition, it is a pleasure to thank various friends, colleagues, and students who have read and commented upon various parts of the manuscript and given me the benefit of discussion and conversation on the matters it examines: Pierre Beaudry, Denise Galanti, Georg Garner, Pierre Gravel, Judd Hubert, Georges May, Walter Moser, Jean Paris, Irene Ponomarenko, Sylvie Romanowski, Georges Roque, David Lee Rubin, Eugene Vance, Jean-Pierre Vernant, and Paul Zumthor. I owe particular thanks to the members of the project on "Le tragique et la tragédie dans la tradition occidentale," undertaken at the Université de Montréal; to the Gouvernement du Québec which generously financed it (DGES-FCAC, 1976–1979); to Joy Simmott for her painstaking typing; and to Anne Lunt for her admirable copy editing. Special thanks also go to Terence Cave, who read through and commented upon the entire manuscript, and to Françoise Gaillard, for conversation and encouragement going considerably beyond the matters dealt with here.

In much briefer form chapters 1 and 2 appeared in French in the *Revue Canadienne de littérature comparée* 4, no. 2 (1977); chapter 3 was published in a very different version in *Yale French Studies* 47 (1972); chapters 10 and 11 appeared, also in rather different versions, respectively in *L'esprit créateur* 13, no. 3 (1973) and the *Australian Journal of French Studies* 13, no. 3 (1976). I am grateful to the editors of these various journals for allowing me to reuse the material here. Some of these and other chapters were delivered as lectures at various universities, and I would like to thank the members of their audiences for many useful comments and discussions. I am grateful also to the administration of the Université de Montréal, who granted me a leave of absence in 1977–78, and to the Canada Council, who gave me a leave fellowship in 1978. As always, an expression of profound gratitude is reserved for Jean Reiss, who has again made possible the necessary time and the (relative) peace.

  In conclusion, it is perhaps useful to indicate that many of the matters considered in the present volume, summarily on occasion, have been explored at greater length and in reference to a different corpus (that of science-fictions and utopias) in a completed book that has yet to see the light of day: *Logics of Literature.* This concerns especially such concepts as discursive conflict and dominance, occultation, contract, analytico-referentiality, enunciative power, and responsibility. The two are, in a sense, companion volumes.

1 A Hypothesis and Its Prehistory

Tragedy and Knowledge

The French philosopher Henri Gouhier summed up the ideological grounds for most critical discussion of tragedy since the European seventeenth century in two sentences: "The tragic is a dimension of real existence. Tragedy belongs to literature and to theatre, the tragic belongs to life."[1] This, with the myriad similar statements of other writers, marks the division between literature and life that has become traditional in Western critical thought. It is a division between discourse in general and a lived, experienced reality conceived as *other*, a reality that is signified by discourse, contained within it, and known through it.

The division of literature and life, of the domain circumscribed by the utterance of some self-identity and that conceived as the activity of an other, the separation of the individual and the social, of desire and societal demands, of subjectivity and objectivity, all of these mark the place of a particular ideological order. They indicate a specifiable semiotic field whose functioning is at least partly the result of a development in the discourse of tragedy. These divisions were elaborated throughout the Renaissance and typify our modernity. To that extent any study of tragedy must be retrospective and is obliged to examine the development in question in the very terms of the ideological values for which that development itself is at least partly responsible. One must be aware that one's own analysis participates in those values. For that reason there can be no discussion of a "cause" of this development, and one must start from the simple

epistemic change

observation of its occurrence so as to follow the elaboration of the lines of force that the analyst derives from the manner in which the discourses revealing it function.

I suggest that the formal literary discourse indicated by the name *tragedy* is a discursive type that performs a specific role within the totality of discourses composing what we call "society"—a role important to the intellectual, conceptual, and ideological functioning of a given culture. Some details of this role are demonstrable. Tragedy performs it at certain moments of seemingly abrupt epistemic change and has done so at two such "moments" especially: the fifth century in Athens and the sixteenth and seventeenth centuries in Europe (though this period should perhaps be slightly extended to cover the case of Germany).

The episteme whose development it permits is that organized by—within—what I call *analytico-referential discourse*. By this term I mean a discourse whose syntactic order (conceived eventually as coincident with a rational-logical order) is taken as the analysis of an exterior which it subsumes as its referent.[2] By *discourse*, in general, is understood a particular organizing *use* of language, of a system of signs that *acts* to put in order a "signified" taken as in some way different from itself.[3] By *episteme* is meant that accumulation of discourses whose particular process of producing meaning characterizes a sociocultural domain at a given time and place. The sense given here to both *discourse* and *episteme* therefore derives from the suggestions advanced by Michel Foucault, principally in *The Order of Things, The Archeology of Knowledge,* and *The Discourse on Language.*

My argument, then, will be that at the moment of a shift in the discursive order that rules a society, a shift in what one might call the way in which discursive space is filled (that "space" being the area of the possibility of any and all discourse or thought), tragedy fulfils the role of making a new class of discourse possible.[4] The discourse it made possible for our modernity was one that functions on the basis of analytical and referential *truth*. Tragedy shows, almost in Wittgenstein's sense, the manner in which that discourse which seeks to create a referential truth overcomes all internal questioning (as to how, for example, it can in any sense whatever come to mean anything outside itself—and communicate such meaning). Tragedy eventually becomes the container of a particular knowledge, provides scientific knowledge.[5]

Tragedy appears ultimately as the discourse that grasps and encloses a certain "absence of significance" that may well be common to all discursive acts at the "inception" of the discourse making such acts possible, and that renders *im*possible, before such particular ordering, the meaningfulness of any such discourse. Perhaps this is why Francis Bacon so continually laments the insuperable difficulties he feels lie before the communication of an entirely new way of speaking. Samuel Johnson appeared to feel that this matter of meaningfulness was still a central difficulty even for a writer as late as Dryden: "He delighted to tread upon the brink of meaning, where light and darkness begin to mingle, to approach the precipice of absurdity, and hover over the abyss of unideal vacancy."[6]

This absence of significance, this impossibility of attaining to meaning in discourse, is rendered, at least in the Renaissance, as what we call the tragic. Tragedy is the discourse that at once produces and absorbs that absence called the tragic. In the development of tragedy throughout the European Renaissance we can follow the stages of this production and absorption.

Greek tragedy offers a kind of stripped-down model of this development. In itself it is a corpus too thin and too selective to provide any very complete evidence for what I wish to suggest. What we possess is, after all, a very small part of a far larger number of plays and performances and that small part is itself the accidental remains of a selection made by scholar-critics long after the Athenian fifth century. And what evidence is there that those remains provide us with the "best" or "most representative" portion? What were the criteria accompanying the notion of "best" or "representative"? In reference to what scholarly requirement was the original choice made? Even more important, the corpus lacks its beginning: for us, excepting the fragments of earlier plays, it begins with the few remains of Aeschylus.

For that reason I will not discuss the Greek theatre in any detail. The second part of this chapter merely seeks to show how this abbreviated corpus buttresses my hypothesis concerning the role of

the discourse *tragedy*. It is necessary to do this because the tragedy
of the European Renaissance is reinvented through a reading of the
Greek model (partly directly, partly through Seneca), though this
later tragedy also has a "beginning" that we are able to read: for
example, the neo-Latin tragedies of George Buchanan examined in
chapter 2.

It is often supposed that we deal with two distinct kinds of tragedy
during the Renaissance. The one seeks to draw the spectator almost
physically into the action, to cause the conditions of his life to be
fused momentarily with what is carried out not so much in front of
him as with his participation. It seeks to cause the dramatic activity
to become "his" in full awareness of his own present being and not
simply by the proxy of his identification with a character or a particular situation. This tragedy, which I call *dialectical theatre*, is represented by Shakespeare, Alexandre Hardy, Lope de Vega. There is
here a play of theatrical elements, an interference of several semiotic
systems. Later criticism takes the playwright to task for such interference:

> Many, peradventure, of the Tragical Scenes in *Shakespear*, cry'd
> up for the *Action*, might do yet better without words: Words are
> a sort of heavy baggage, that were better out of the way, at the
> push of Action; especially in his *bombast Circumstance*, where
> the Words and Action are seldom akin, generally are inconsistent,
> at cross purposes, embarrass or destroy each other; yet to those
> who take not the words distinctly, there may be something in the
> buz and sound, that like a drone to a Bagpipe may serve to set off
> the *Action*. [7]

What is revealed by Rymer's disdain is that some other theatrical
form has won the day. Indeed, all other critics answer Rymer not by
arguing that his criticism is misplaced but by asserting that Shakespeare, "closer to nature" than subsequent writers of tragedies,
achieves *the same results* that they do, though in ignorance of the
Aristotelian laws. What is more remarkable, and what reveals that we
are perhaps *not* dealing with two different kinds of theatre, is that
these "dialectical" plays are themselves very often finally "reduced"
from within, as though directed to a point of intersection (of semi-

otic systems) marked by a knowledge imposed from above, on occasion quite literally (i.e., by the use of stage space). This reduction brings this kind of theatre close to the other kind of tragedy to which I have referred, which I call *analytical*, in whose terms Shakespeare, for example, will be recuperated by neoclassical criticism.

Early Renaissance tragedy lays claim to a concern with the nature and power of language and to being an attempt to rediscover and rework the tragedy of Antiquity. From Buchanan, in whose tragedies the use of all and any language for purposes of intentional communication becomes in the end impossible, where failure and unknowing are the marks of discourse itself, the development of tragedy passes through several phases: the metaphorization of that (discursive) unknowing and failure, of the impossibility to order (the tragedies of Jodelle, for example, or Marlowe's *Tamburlaine*), the eventual *performing* of that metaphor as a character (Marlowe's *Doctor Faustus*, Garnier's *Les Juifves, Porcie*), and tragedy as linear history (though told in the margins, not perhaps played as such: Ben Jonson).

Ultimately the character becomes a *person* endowed with psychological depth, and tragedy is taken as a container of certain knowledge showing the moral, psychological, and so forth functioning of society and the individual. In Racine, Dryden, and their contemporaries, the *development* of modern tragedy is concluded: the episteme no longer needs it. The absence of significance has been enclosed and meaning provided in the psychological identity of an individual place in the center of a web of societal relationships. In these writers the discourses that set forth our specific forms of knowledge and truth are (re)produced and represented: they elaborate economic individualism, the political theory and practice of the contractual state, of normative psychology, of the history and society of our modernity.

Tragedy is no longer required to perform an active role in the establishing of the episteme. But that is not to say that tragedies do not continue to be written: Pradon, Otway, Lee, Crown, Southerne, Campistron, Rowe, Crebillon, Addison, and of course Voltaire spring immediately to mind. I suggest that there is no further *development*, save in the direction of an ever-increasing realism that leads directly to the naturalist drama of the late nineteenth century and to the

Brechtian critique of the so-called Aristotelian theatre. What seems specific to tragedy, the *act* of overcoming unmeaning, the "treading on the brink of meaning," the approach to "the precipice of absurdity," has become a true description of man in society. And tragedies continue to be written because now they are needed in some degree to *maintain* the ordering relations that have been established. In the tragedies of the eighteenth century the production of order is no longer, as Raymond Williams puts it, "in solution in particular works," it is rather a "precipitate."[8] Tragedy now confronts a ready-made order, an order to be shown and maintained, a justice poetical that is also a moral and social order in the world. Tragedy now shows social man's response to the inevitability of that order, and it deals now with suffering of any kind associated with a degree of mental or psychological anguish—no longer does it have to strive to overcome that radical "suffering" that is the impossibility of utterance. Tragedy now helps to confirm the exactness, correctness, and certitude of a known world order. As such it has become just one of a series of *literary* discourses whose difference from other types of discourse will be sought not in the domain of action but in that of the mysterious "aesthetic."

Tragedy by then—like the rest of "literature"—has become a particular form of the representation of nature. But nature is not simple, and tragedy re-presents it in two ways. For on the one hand nature is everywhere and at all times one and the same, yet on the other it is also dependent on the particular conditions of a given society. That is why tragedy must follow the rules laid down by Aristotle at the same time as it shows a keen observation of life in the time and place for which it is written. On the one hand, "the Rules of *Aristotle* are nothing but Nature and Good Sense reduc'd to a Method,"[9] and for that reason a tragedy ordered according to them has the authority of nature itself and is equivalent to it: for in this aspect its order depends (as Johnson will write a century later concerning Dryden's general critical precepts) "upon the nature of things and the structure of the human mind."[10] Here the *order* of tragedy is coincident with the order of nature (and the human mind). On the other hand, the author of tragedies must also take account of the specific religious, political, and even climactic conditions familar to the audience for

whom he is writing: in that, tragedy is a representation to the life.[11]
Here the *content* of tragedy is nature. Thus, Dryden writes in *The
Grounds of Criticism in Tragedy* (1679) that the fundamentals of
tragedy (i.e., the rules) should be copied from the Ancients, "those
things only excepted which religion, customs of countries, idioms
of language, etc., have altered in the superstructures."[12]

It is essentially this double aspect of tragedy that Lisideius appears
to have in mind when he gives his well-known "definition" of a play
in the *Essay of Dramatic Poesy* (1668): "a just and lively image of
human nature, representing its passions and humours, and the changes
of fortune to which it is subject; for the delight and instruction of
mankind."[13] The existence of this double aspect (corresponding to
an analytical "syntax" and to referentiality) is what makes it possible
for some critics of the period to argue that literature in general and
tragedy in particular is now *better* than it was in ancient times. For
while the basic syntax is common to the productions of both periods,
"natural causes [are] more known now." This means that plays can
now give a truer representation of reality and, Neander remarks, those
plays which "best fulfil that law" by which they are a lively imitation
of nature must "be esteemed superior to the others."[14]

Yet in Dryden there remains that ambiguity which accounts for
Johnson's comment on his "hovering over the abyss of unideal vacancy." It proceeds from just that dual nature of all literature and,
again, of tragedy in particular as the most sublime literary genre:
tragedy "is indeed the representation of nature, but 'tis nature
wrought up to an higher pitch."[15] It is as though tragedy were and
were not a "representation." On the one hand it does imitate elements of nature, but on the other it *is* nature, because the proper
order of tragedy, of mind, and of the world are all identical: they
are *one* order. In 1677 Rymer expressed the same view: "Like good
Painters [writers of tragedies] must design their Images like the Life,
but yet better and more beautiful than the Life."[16] It is as though
there remained a tension between tragedy as a discourse intent upon
making sense, *composing meaning*, and tragedy as in some way a
mirror image of the "real." This tension will explain Dr. Johnson's
discomfort with Dryden, as it recalls what Gerald Else has shown to be
present in Aristotle's *Poetics* itself: the tension between *poietike*

and *mimesis*.[17]   Like the Stagirite, the critics at the end of the seventeenth century in Europe are trying to define tragedy after a recent and radical change in its nature.

Under the influence of his arguments with Sir Robert Howard about the suitability of rhyme in tragedy, Dryden's attitude changes subtly. He is very soon writing that the aim of the playwright must be "to heighten the beauties of some parts [of nature], and hide the deformities of the rest." And a few pages later he remarks that "poesy must resemble natural truth, but it must *be* ethical. Indeed the poet dresses truth, and adorns nature, but does not alter them."[18] He had not previously been overly concerned with any ethical dimension. But now this ethical exigency becomes increasingly common. It corresponds to Rymer's notion of "poetical justice," first advanced, I believe, in *The Tragedies of the Last Age* (1677), of which two recent historians of criticism remark, with particular reference to André Dacier's commentary on the *Poetics* of Aristotle (1692):

> Dacier seems here to be pointing to a new kind of sensibility, that there is justice in the universe and if man wills himself to adhere to the moral law, he will benefit from that justice. Good will come out of good and evil come from wickedness. Essentially man is master of his fate. The idea of 'poetical justice' (a phrase coined by Rymer long before Dacier's work was published) suits the temper of the new age.[19]

Nature itself is endowed with an ethical imperative. By this means the rules by which tragedy is ordered and its representation of the cultural "superstructure," as Dryden calls them, have come together. The tension has been resolved. It is as though tragedy has created a meaningful order which has in turn been transferred into the world itself. The order is no longer one of discourse: it belongs to the "real world."

Analytical tragedy, then (the dialectical, too, albeit with more ambiguity), already acts within that classification of the human (eventually due to become a general taxonomy, as Foucault has shown) which begins to be imposed at least from the beginning of the European sixteenth century. Characterized by *distance*—both within discourse, which will now speak *of* something instead of simply *speaking,* and without discourse, since the spectator will have become an observer—this tragedy is the sign of some supposed knowledge, a knowledge already half consecrated. A measure has been taken; an order has been elaborated that would not be possible without the supposition of the possibility of "knowledge." The very fact that an elaborated discourse of tragedy is possible suggests that the absence of meaningfulness, its impossibility, the "unknowing" now called the "tragic" has been enclosed and thereby "cast out." And this must be the case even when tragedy is acting out the very failure of discourse, as it does in Buchanan, though tragedy had not yet acquired an exterior social referent, and though that acting out remains within the discourse, tragedy.

TRAG. = THE SIGN OF KNOWLEDGE

By the late seventeenth century tragedy has become the ideal ordered and instructive model, the highest of the literary genres. If properly constructed, tragedy is a kind of machine for attaching the right and true meaning to the activities of man in society and of man in nature (though society and nature are only obscurely distinguished from one another, as if one could not conceive of man except within society).[20] Thus, Rymer is able to write:

> Something must stick [to the spectator, for his instruction] by observing that constant order, that harmony and beauty of Providence, that necessary relation and chain, whereby the causes and effects, the vertues and rewards, the vices and their punishments are proportion'd and link'd together; how deep and dark soever are laid the Springs, and however intricate and involv'd are their operations.[21]

Such a claim is inconceivable, I suggest, until tragedy has secured a specific domain of meaningfulness. On the other hand, while tragedy does now take as its particular domain the psychological activity of men and women in ordered society at crisis, the activity of tragedy as a "machine to order" is certainly not the invention of Thomas Rymer and his contemporaries. Nor does it derive simply from Aristotle. It proceeds from the practice of the writers of tragedy and is already to be found in the remnants of the Greeks, to whom Rymer (like Racine and the French critics) pays so considerable attention.

For if we ask the apparently simple question, "What is tragedy?" we are constrained to answer that it is first and foremost a particular *defines tragedy = ordered discursive system*

kind of discourse, intended for stage performance, presenting an action of some kind that generally involves a potentially disastrous crisis and that concerns people whom the spectator can deeply respect. Unless we want to start talking immediately about its "meaning" we can do no more than note that tragedy is an orderd discursive system. In doing so, we repeat Aristotle: for that "definition" does indeed answer the question, though it tells us nothing about what tragedy *does*.

I do not seek to deny that tragedy does have certain effects when read, seen, or heard. But such effects come *after* the existence of tragedy qua discourse; they are the consequence of the development of that discourse. The meaning of tragedy itself—the answer to the hypothetical "why?" that it poses depends on the episteme in which the interpreter is functioning. That episteme is the sum of its discourses, of which tragedy is one. Our dismay and pity inspired by the majestic suffering conveyed by Aeschylus, the individual disasters set forth by Sophocles, the almost unredeemed brutality of humans and the near frivolously haphazard deeds of gods portrayed by Euripides are the result of the "machine" of tragedy: our emotions are not to be confused with that machine.

The meaning that tragedy clearly provokes us to discover in the cause of such pity or dismay is not a kind of excrescence on the body of tragedy. Far from it. But nor should we place the cart before the horse. The "real situations" of which we take tragedy as "making sense" do not precede tragedy: they come into existence with it. That Euripides makes his plays a commentary upon life in Athens while Aeschylus had remained aloof from such social immediacy is, as I will try to show, a function of the development of the discourse tragedy, in terms of which we may perhaps say that the compassion and terror in Euripides are for Athens itself. But the *meaning* we give to tragedies is the result of that particular ordering process we call "tragedy," and of the way of its development.

We talk about the "tragic action" in a tragedy, in which at least one "tragic hero" participates. It is tragic because of some ignorance, some flaw—some lack of knowledge in any case—on the part of the principal protagonist. But from whose point of view are we speaking? Is it possible to participate in a "tragic action" and to have at the

same time an *idea* of the tragic? If what is tragic can be *said* to be so
then it has been fixed, it has become meaningful, and if that is so
then one can no longer actually participate in it: the lack of knowledge has been canceled out. As something *named*, the tragic is the
creation of the discourse, tragedy. To be in a position to show the
tragic presupposes an analysis which, in providing the terms in which
human activity is to be deemed possible, circumscribes the domain
of the meaningful. If this were not so the tragic could not be shown.

The spectator, provided with a measure of the limits of the protagonist's knowing and doing, may perceive the situation as tragic, but
the protagonist himself cannot apply the word to his own situation
because to do so would provide the missing meaning. For the spectator tragedy itself provides a standard by which it is possible to
measure, to classify the "failure" of the character in terms of an idea
of the gods, of fate, of some particular tragic flaw or more general
human blindness, of some absolute of perfection that has not been
attained, of what Walter Kaufmann calls "man's radical insecurity," [22]
or of *the order of tragedy itself which allows us to grasp the protagonist's incapacity as a failure of discourse* (as will be the case for the
earliest tragedies of the Renaissance). As a recent author has written:
"The answer to the problem Hamlet confronts is *Hamlet* itself." [23]
The answer is for the spectator/reader, of course, not for Hamlet, to
whom Horatio's story has not been disclosed. Tragedy shows *us* the
limits of meaning and knowledge, and *this* showing presupposes a
human capacity for order: that of this discourse itself. The tragic, the
tragic action as some extradiscursive reality of which tragedy is taken
as speaking, is an extrapolation from the naming that occurs through
the discourse, tragedy.

In everyday parlance nowadays we tend to apply the word *tragic*
to some suffering that someone has undergone "undeservedly," implying that it was not that person's fault or that its extent surpasses
what might have been expected as the result of his or her actions.
We give the word a meaning, precisely, in terms of "what is to be
expected" and thus we mark some occurrence or condition as escaping from the order of "everyday reality." [24] In doing so we under-
score the reliability of that everyday reality as a form of the *known*.
To say something is "tragic" is a means of recuperating a situation

that would otherwise remain unaccountable, of relating it to the known. We have transferred the idea of the tragic from the realm of discourse into that of the real. We have made the tragic a piece of reality, as numerous volumes on the subject attest: tragedy, they say, seeks to explain the tragic.

Such a hypostatization of the tragic has been given the increasing weight of tradition from Johnson, Hume, and Lessing, to Hölderlin and Hegel, Schopenhauer and Nietzsche, Bradley and Unamuno, and the majority of recent writers on the subject. The point I wish to emphasize is that when this transference of the discursive to a separate reality has been achieved then there is no more *need* for tragedy: the "impossibility" that discourse had confronted of making meaning has been named as a knowable condition within an overall ordering of the real. It is no longer a difficulty within the very activity of *knowing*. It is but one element of the known. Tragedy and the tragic have been separated.

This hypostatization of the tragic is, then, a modern development. It would have been nonsensical for Aristotle to ask Walter Kaufmann's question: "What is tragic about tragedy?" And for the Greeks the modern philosopher's answer to his own question—"The emotions it evokes in the spectator"[25] —would have been hopelessly reductive. For such emotions are merely one part of what is involved in the *technique* of writing tragedies. For Aristotle *tragic* is simply the adjective corresponding to the noun *tragedy*, and it can therefore mean no more than "what appertains to tragedy."[26] Our calling some event or situation tragic is simply the result of that hypostatization of some element that, since the neoclassical interpreters of Aristotle, we take as what is essentially expressed in and by tragedies.

This has led to rather pointless disputes concerning different readings of tragedies and to theories that neither the texts themselves nor criticism until quite recently can support, such as the widespread and now quite traditional view that "any realistic notion of tragic drama must start from the fact of catastrophe. Tragedies end badly."[27] One difficulty with such statements is that the catastrophe is a technical device that does not have to terminate the play (and certainly does not in the case of the early tragic trilogies of Athens), though it is of course essential to all tragedies. To accept the idea that tragedies end badly we must either exclude a very large part of extant Greek tragedy or redefine *tragedies* or *badly*.

No doubt it is of less importance that the view expressed here flatly contradicts Aristotle on the subject, since definitions suitable for the Greeks are not of necessity suitable for us. Nonetheless, Aristotle's refusal to consider an unfortunate ending as more than one possibility in tragedy, and that not the most preferable,[28] is significant. Misfortune, evil, a bad ending, unhappiness, cruelty, and other elements of the same paradigm are not *primary* in tragedy: they are possibilities that must be taken into account when *constructing* a tragedy. What is primary is the fact of an order, the paradigm of harm is a possible element of such order, even a necessary one; but it is just one element. To emphasize that paradigm above all the other elements of composition, as the neoclassical tradition has, is to make a fundamental of what is but a *particular reading* of the system of tragedy. It supposes that a specific answer was being sought and has been found to the special problem of human suffering for which tragedy can be supposed to permit the revelation and resolution of those secondary questions that turn about it: "the 'who,' the 'what,' and the 'how' of the action."[29] The posing of such questions is the result of a discursive development that tragedy itself helps to make possible.

The emphasis, then, on a particular kind of action that can be said to be tragic, and that is conceived as some condition *represented* by tragedy, is the result of a particular development of discourse. It is a reading of tragedy dependent on the separation of tragedy from the tragic. It confuses a reading of tragedy with the function of tragedy. Just as Aristotle does not choose to single out the paradigm of harm, of final misfortune, so he does not ask (unlike the majority of his successors) *why* the protagonist suffers such misfortune. Much modern criticism, indeed, has felt this to be so serious an omission that it seeks to explain it by declaring that Aristotle was able to omit such considerations from the *Poetics* because he had dealt with the matter elsewhere. But the point is that the Stagirite is content to try and examine tragedy as an already given construct. He does not look at tragedy to discover what it "should" be but rather to show what it is, and then to discover what elements are essential and common to those which most please him. These last are the ones whose example he most uses, but by no means exclusively so, for if *Oedipus the King* is his favorite it nevertheless does not fit in with his preference for tragedies that do not end badly. His point is that final misfortune, while by no means essential in tragedy, is quite simply a fact of many tragedies, but it is no more than that: it is part of the technique that goes into their construction, part of the machine.

The question asked by Aristotle, therefore, is not a general one concerning the nature of human suffering, but the much more particular and technical one as to how such misfortune can be "adjusted" to the kind of character who seems most pleasing in the preferred tragedies. It is for this purpose—and this purpose alone, if we follow Else's reading of the *Poetics*—that Aristotle brings in the term *hamartia*. If the word merely means an ignorance of some details essential to the satisfactory performance of some action carried out by the protagonist, or even if it means some more general ignorance, then it is clear that no "why?" is answered. What we have is simply the expression of some *fact* about how to construct a tragedy.[30] To translate the word as "tragic flaw" is to make of a later particular reading of some tragedies a Principle of Tragedy, it is to make a general explanation concerning all tragedy out of the meaning which that particular reading is able to ascribe to some tragedies.

Not only Aristotle but the Greek tragedies themselves, in the text, do not seek to suggest, in accordance with what that Principle would demand, that they deal with a suffering of which they show how it is deserved. Not seldom, indeed, they show the contrary: at Colonus Oedipus convincingly argues his own innocence (*unwittingness* might be a better word), and in *Electra*, both that of Sophocles and that of Euripides, the protagonist argues to the same end. This would not be possible if *hamartia* meant some moral flaw, something other than mere ignorance.

It is spectators, readers, and critics who have sought to provide causes, and that activity tends to emphasize once again that we have not in fact derived the meaning of tragedy from what tragedies *say* so much as from what they *do*, in the sense of the effects they are supposedly intended to induce. The vast majority of writers on the subject have read the plays from the viewpoint of these supposed effects and have then claimed that they say things that are demonstrably absent.[31] Yet we have, by and large, paid little attention to the fact that it is the way in which the discourse of tragedy functions that has *created* the "meanings" we have then said to be the purpose, the cause, the *telos* and so on, of tragedy. The *effect* of the enclosure of "ignorance," of the lack of significance, has been to make possible the ascription of a meaning to the protagonist's "suffering," to provide a reason for human catastrophe.

Tragedy in itself does not reveal any cosmic law. It does not show the impossibility of overcoming fate; it does not settle or unsettle the place of man in a divine order. Tragedy is a theatrical (or simply textual) machine that enables us subsequently to make such readings. We need to learn to look at tragedies, then, not in the light of what they supposedly say, nor even in that of the broad elements of their construction (as Aristotle and the majority of his Renaissance successors did), but rather in terms of how they *organize* their saying, of the way in which they use sign systems. Once we look at tragedy first and foremost as a particular way of ordering language and producing meaning, we will necessarily perceive certain hoary "problems" in a quite different way. We have already seen what such a changed perception may do to the notion of "tragic action" and to that of the "tragic" itself, as well as to such explanatory devices as "fate," "tragic flaw," and the like. It has consequences that some might consider even more dismaying.

If one takes the view I am suggesting, the notorious catharsis of Aristotle will not then appear as some "purging of the emotions" when faced with the overthrow of a hero in a concluding resolution.[32] Whatever may be meant by such a "purging"—whether an abrupt voiding of passion or a kind of general numbing of the passions that will enable us to function more calmly in life situations (as Heinsius claims in his *De Tragoediae constitutione* [1611], thus expressing a view that was to be extraordinarily influential upon subsequent criticism)—it must always remain external to tragedy itself as a discourse. Aristotle, however, seems to be using the term *catharsis* in order to express some factor in the *construction* of a tragedy: that is why Gerald Else argues at length that catharsis is the presentation *within* a tragedy of a "purification" of the "tragic act" of the protagonist (in a moral and religious sense).[33] That is once

again, of course, a reading for meaning, and one may feel free to
choose whether one accepts it or not, but its importance is that it
places catharsis back where it belongs, in tragedy as a discursive
activity. [34]

What all these readings of the term *catharsis* have in common with
one another, with Aristotle, and with what the texts *do* may be
summed up in some concept of *equilibrium*. What occurs is a kind of
balance of ambiguities through their immobilization, their sealing
in an ordering discourse. Such a balance or equilibrium is possible
only through the awareness of "causes." It is indeed what we call
"knowledge." When it remains unavailable to us, then the tragic
might exist as a "dimension of life," as Gouhier and Unamuno would
have it, and there it would remain by definition inexpressible—the
mark, the presence there of chaos, of the impossibility of order: "Le
silence éternel de ces espaces infinis m'effraie." During the action of
a tragedy this may be the case for the protagonist, but not for the
spectator. [35] When Aristotle writes that the two most efficacious
devices in the construction of the "best" tragedies are peripety and
recognition, it is to an entire situation that he is referring; the two
devices together do not mean the revelation of a particular identity
(though the European critics frequently placed the emphasis on such
recognition), but the unveiling of a general condition up till then
unavailable to understanding. [36] That "general condition" is, in the
first place, simply an *order*.

The equilibrium of which one may speak when the term *catharsis*
is used is not external to the particular tragedy we see performed—
though it may well provoke an emotion and an interpretation that
are. In itself the equilibrium is not of such a kind, that is to say, as
will place us, having seen the "right" and "wrong" of Antigone and
Creon, in a position to "solve" the conflict that has seemed incapable of any but a fatal solution. If we were speaking of some such
equilibrium we would no longer be speaking of a discursive type
called "tragedy"—we would have in mind some reality to which we
would be supposing tragedy to refer. Tragedy, at the outset, does
not explain or even indicate such an external solution; which is why
my "equilibrium" is not to be confused with "reconciliation" due
to tragedy's "vision of eternal justice," as we find it in Hegel. Tragedy

performs the equilibrium in its own action, it resolves the ignorance of a protagonist, the insolubility of a conflict between mutually exclusive ethical or social imperatives, or the more general absence of meaningfulness *by the order of its own performance.* Catharsis, writes Else, is "a process, not an end-result, and a process operated by the poet through his 'structure of events.'"[37] *Tragedy is a discursive process that creates order and makes it possible to ascribe meaning to that order.* This volume will follow the development of that process between 1540 and 1700.

The space that will be called "the tragic" is open, unresolved, and has no possible resolution. It supposes an endless dialectic between a system of human signs and a meaning never to be reached, a referent never to be grasped. At best, grasped in an ordering discourse, it tends to destroy that discourse from within because it denies the very possibility of meaningful discourse (the case, perhaps, of all discourse conscious of its inescapable "subjectivity"). If one retains the sense I am suggesting for the terms, then *tragedy* (once available as discourse) will be a sign process in permanent quest for some totally adequate signification, which, in the form tragedy itself permits and in a well-circumscribed time and place, it will succeeed in finding. The history of, say, Renaissance tragedy is the history of the rediscovery of a discourse and the performing of that quest. The tragic destroys that goal from within by tending to make of tragedy a sign that will never find an unambiguous referent. Hence the ambiguities that Johnson both admires and criticizes in Dryden. But as thus expressed the tragic is brief indeed. As it is gradually enveloped, the tragic itself becomes transformed into an element whose meaning is specifiable and that is endowed with an extradiscursive reality. When that has happened tragedy can be read as a discourse of knowledge and truth.

Notes on Greek Tragedy: The Signs of an Order

The tragedy of the Renaissance started its development largely as a philological exercise. To a considerable degree it is a rhetorical and stylistic teaching device, a practice of translation and a re-creation first into Latin and then into the vulgar languages (though it is a very

[handwritten margin notes: "good for Hermeticism the king orders the structure of the world"]

long time before the Greeks are put in their entirety into a vulgar tongue). Senecan tragedy was no doubt the most stylistically and thematically influential because of the belief in the superiority of the Greek language (see below, especially beginning of chapter 2).

It was because of this formal perfection that the humanist scholars thought it useful to translate and copy the Greek model and in no sense because they looked to it as an "origin"—unlike Thomas Rymer, for example, for whom the fact that tragedy originated with the Greeks is the basis for his arguments in *A Short View of Tragedy* urging that every element of Greek tragedy is good and modern tragedy is corrupt because it has forsaken so many of them. Nor are the humanists much interested in discussing what the origin of tragedy itself might have been. For us this attitude of the humanists with regard to the formal aspects of Greek tragedy is of considerable interest, for in both cases, that of fifth-century Athens and that of sixteenth-century Europe, tragedy makes an abrupt appearance; and in each case it seems to fit into a set of discursive changes whose characteristics reveal remarkable similarities.

[handwritten margin notes: "?? states his purpose"]

What I will now seek to do is indicate some of the discursive relations of tragedy and their context in Greece and draw a parallel between the implications of such relations and the theoretical pattern indicated in the first part of this chapter. It will be worthwhile recalling that, in France at least, the first appearance of tragedy in the vulgar tongue is contemporary with the earliest translations of the Greeks (into Latin and French), although printed editions of Seneca had been available from the earliest days of the printing press.

[handwritten margin notes: "Foucault stuff"]

In Greece, tragedy is part of a general development toward a particular order of rationality. Prior to the "Hesiodic rupture," as Marcel Detienne has termed it, the Greek would have lived in a world of analogies, of sympathies between the material, the divine, and the human in many ways comparable to the multiple discourse of the European Middle Ages, indicated by Michel Foucault in *The Order of Things* under the name "Renaissance."[38] F. M. Cornford has noted how, during this same archaic period, the notion of the individual/king as ordering the structure of the world gradually replaced the older notion of *moira*, posed as indifferent to any particular interest and as a natural order to which everything submitted and in which all participated, including the gods.[39] T. B. L. Webster adds that the development from a kind of all-pervasive divineness (by definition inaccessible to human *commentary* or order) was a very long process and remarks, speaking of the form of certain divinities shown on Mycenean artifacts:

> In all these cases the Mycenean seems to be somewhere between a stage in which birds, trees and stones are gods, and complete anthropomorphism in which gods in human form have birds as attributes or trees and stones which are sacred to them: and *in popular belief this double view lasted long after the time of Homer.*[40]

With Hesiod this development can be seen as the "arrival" of a mind which *sees itself* and which understands itself as different from a certain exteriority, instead of being incorporated in it (though in the latter case the notion of "exteriority" would be very different, if it could even be called such). Thus Marcel Detienne, writing of the changeover from the Greek "Middle Ages" to the "Renaissance" of the fifth century, can note that "the entire behaviour of Hesiod's worker betrays a profound disquiet, a veritable anguish. The peasant of the seventh century leads a hide-bound existence, haunted by innumerable rules whose precise and correct application is indispensable."[41] For all these rules that served to maintain the essential relationship between physical, social, and religious life are now losing their reference to any "experience of totality." Detienne remarks that "the relations of a proprietor to his land form a set at several levels, a series of experiences which are lived in a global way," a way indeed that was that of a "religious experience." This participation in a natural order has now been lost.[42]

This period, then, is one in which there begins what appears to be the deconstruction of a traditional form of life and thought. The individualization of the inheritance of land, for example, in a straight line of descent necessitates a *division* of property and replaces a more communal process that refused any such division. In Hesiod this is represented as a movement away from the land and toward the city, necessitating a reorganization of relationships among men and between men and gods for which the "instruments" are lacking.

It is then that the notion of *hubris* occurs, the mark of a sense of injustice installing itself between the human *dike* (law, right, justice, balance) and the divine *Dike*.[43] There appears a gap between a purely social order, a simply human system characterized by "innumerable rules," and everything that escapes from and weighs upon that order without its being able to grasp it. A sense of injustice appears, compounded of ignorance, fear, unfulfilled desire, and suffering, the mark of an "absence" which of necessity escapes organization. It is this that will be in question in the discourse, tragedy: the "tragic" that is the trace of the inevitable gap between the human known and knowable and all that escapes discourse.

The "anguish" noted by Detienne in Hesiod, which would be the sign of this dislocation, is accompanied by a whole series of analogous and absolutely fundamental "distancings." Thus, for example, the king, who loses those divine attributes which placed him among the gods, is replaced shortly after the fall of the Mycenean civilization by the priest: a special mediator between man and gods.[44] This transformation, like that which afflicts the peasant in Hesiod, is quite representative of those which lead toward the constitution of the city and its laws, toward a new economic basis and the invention of coinage, toward philosophy itself, in part made possible perhaps by the discovery of alphabetical writing, toward the concept of an interpretative science of nature developed by the Milesians.[45] Of this immense series of dislocations that occurs roughly between 1100 and 600 B.C. Webster has written: "The essential here is perhaps a belief in human reason, in human capacity to reduce things to simple and clear patterns so that they become manageable—a purely human operation when all the mystery and magic of the King had failed.[46]

This, then, is the context within which the discourse of tragedy appears for the first time. It does so simultaneously with that of historiography, and it is assuredly no accident that both Plato and Aristotle feel it necessary to compare the two and that the latter in particular finds himself obliged to define the relationship between history and tragedy. History can be argued easily enough to be a true rendition of the real activities of men with regard to one another and their place in the world: it is a didactic and essentially ethically utilitarian *record*. It makes order from chaos in just the same way as do science and the ordering of property, of social life, of religious experience, as does the use of a token of value in the economic sphere or a token of sound and meaning for the writing down of thought. The new discourse of history does not create any difficulty of explanation.

But what does tragedy do? Perhaps by its mere existence, it underlines a moment of "rupture": *the moment of accession to referentiality.* The other discourses to which I have referred take for granted the possibility of a discursive ordering of chaos, of the as-yet unknown. Tragedy *performs* the overcoming of that "absence" in discourse of which I spoke as "injustice."

"Tragic drama," George Steiner has informed us, "tells us that the spheres of reason, order, and justice are terribly limited and that no progress in our science or technical resources will enlarge their relevance."[47] This can be so, only in so far as tragedy may be supposed to contain, to *show* some reality (for example) that tragedy itself is not; in so far, that is to say, as it is taken as a representation of something which is not itself the product of discourse. In this case, tragedy is taken as representing the breaking, as Steiner puts it, of the tragic personage "by forces which can neither be fully understood nor overcome by rational prudence." This, as we saw in the first part of this chapter, is to privilege a particular reading as giving us the very fundamentals that tragedy can then be said to be all about. But tragedy itself, as an ordering process, *does* overcome these mysterious "forces." It situates them in a rational scheme of things. The personage who himself composes a part of that ordering process may be "broken" unknowing (and even this is debatable), but the spectator is not. It is only when viewed *primarily* as representation that tragedy can be seen as such a "telling." And, one may feel prompted to ask, if tragedy is a *negation* of the possibility of a systematic order of knowledge, how is it that it is itself one of the finest examples of this supposedly impossible order? Tragedy is rather affirmation than negation, and the notion of representation upon which depends the view of tragedy as a pessimistic commentary on human affairs is a consequence of later developments made possible in part by its very existence.

For, one may ask, why is it that the appearance and flourishing

of Athenian tragedy coincides so precisely with the period between
the victorious wars against the Persians and the disastrous campaigns
of the Peloponnesus—with the moment of the very strongest faith
in systematizing reason (political, legal, social, ethical, economic)?
Why does original tragedy largely disappear with the failure of these
imperialist campaigns, the demonstrated fallibility of human systems, and the consequently visible weakness of their claims to dominion, to the imposition of the self, to knowledge?

It is certainly not unimportant to this whole matter that Thucydides, commenting upon the breakup within Greek life at the time
of the Peloponnesian Wars, stresses the denaturing of discourse.
Whereas before the "codification" was taken as "natural," where
language was taken as an ordered presentation of the real, now its
arbitrariness not only appears but is put to use: "The ordinary accep-
tation of words in their relation to things was changed as men thought
fit." This leads to the dissolution of all ordering discourse during the
wars and to a general disturbance of society itself.[48] The later chapters of Thucydides' history are a long illustration of this. A similar
significance is suggested by the fact that Hobbes translated Thucydides and thereafter proposed a theory of the State avowedly dependent on the human discursive ordering of all systems human, precisely
at a moment coincident with the culmination of tragedy in England
and France and just prior to what I have already referred to, after
Raymond Williams, as its "precipitation," its "decadence."

In so far as the "disappearance" of tragedy is concerned, the collapse
of normative discourse seems more important than the disturbance
of society as such that accompanied it. Indeed, since the Peloponnesian
Wars were not followed by any complete collapse of society, of the
state, it does not seem possible to ascribe the passing of the old forms
of tragedy simply to social, material, or practical causes. There was no
barrier of any such kind placed before the creation and performance
of tragedy—rather the contrary. The singular *power* of Athens was de-
creased but the form of the city-state remained as before, and would
continue to do so certainly until the Macedonian invasion. Tragedy
was, we are told, succeeded and "replaced" by philosophy. But *why*
were there no successors to Aeschylus, to Sophocles, to Euripides?[49]

It would clearly be naïve, foolhardy, and, in view of the volumes

expended on the subject, somewhat impertinent to seek an unequiv-
ocal answer. But I suggest that a partial one is to be found in the
direction of a tight correspondence between the formal system of
tragedy and the structures of mind (thought) that formulate it—and
that it helps formulate. Thus, for example, Jean-Pierre Vernant has remarked that as a result of extensive analysis of the vocabulary and
structure of the Greek tragedies Louis Gernet was able to show that
"the visible material of tragedy is the social thought belonging to the
city, especially juridical thought in the very process of elaboration."[50]
The conflict Vernant notes, at the very center of social experience,
between a politico-legal discourse and a heroi-mythical one is produced, possibly re-produced, within tragedy, where the "gap" itself
is, so to speak, played out.

If the schema proposed in the first part of this chapter, and toward
which I am working here from a different historical viewpoint, is
exact, then it provides a fairly peremptory answer to the question
just proposed. The reading of Thucydides strongly reinforces it and,
though the corpus is itself too slight to provide a field for corrobora-
tive exploration in detail, the extant Greek tragedies do furnish more
than a few supporting indications. Greek tragedy occurs as a commentary not upon the world but upon the current "idea" of the
world *in the very terms and form of that idea*, of the forms of discourse that make that idea possible. It is not a "mimetic" representation, it does not simply repeat that idea; it produces and makes
possible the idea, its ordering and its systematization. In doing so it
remains ambiguous because it encloses the mark of the impossibility
of system: "If tragedy thus appears, more than any other literary
genre, rooted in social reality, this does not mean it is a reflection of
it. [Tragedy] does not reflect this reality, it puts it in question."[51]

Its "content" would be a kind of warning, an admonition, repetition of the ambiguity of all system. Its content would be an admonition, but nothing more than an admonition *just because* it is tamed,
contained in the strongest sense. Tragedy encloses the ambiguities in
a kind of exorcism, through and in discourse.

The Greek enlightenment is the period of which Husserl and so
many others speak as that in which the Western "mind" confirmed
its fundamental belief in the powers of isolated human reason, in

its limitless capacity to impose a system on things; and this aspect was reaffirmed from the European fifteenth century on. Such a moment is very likely to be that in which the feeling of the "tragic," as a name given to a necessary and definitive ignorance, to a kind of bottomless impossibility of will and power, of knowledge and action, disappears. And it disappears as the very consequence of its naming. Tragedy, as a discourse, would therefore be at once the creation of the "tragic," its sign and *at the same time* the sign of its disappearance.

This is no paradox. On the contrary, the capacity for an ordering discourse must presuppose that what is ordered is something known, and something known as an operational "truth": we can *act* upon it. What tragedy "tells" us, then, is that man *can* know. The protagonist may remain "in the tragic" but not the spectator, not the one who constructed the code:

> If the ancients admired them, if a modern public is as over-whelmed before some [other tragedies] as it is before *Oedipus the King*, this is because tragedy is not bound to a particular type of dream, because the tragic effect does not reside in some content [*matière*], even oniric, *but in the way of putting that content into form.* [52]

I am not concerned here, therefore, with any search for an Origin, whether of Greek or of Renaissance tragedy, but rather with the function of the repeated use of a certain type of discourse. I do not wish to repeat after Nietzsche that tragedy can be explained as the result of an interference of the Dionysiac and Apollonian spirits, nor that it is the result of a certain development of a tragico-lyrical chorus, of the dithyramb, of the mysteries of such and such a secret sect. Certainly there has been since Antiquity a biased reading (Jones) of Aristotle, who himself often invested the *Poetics* with a political intention. [53] This has led directly to the more recent excesses of the same tradition (of which the very *idea* of a discovery of origins forms a part) based on the philosophical authority of a Nietzsche and the academic authority of a Gilbert Murray, whose theory of the *eniautos-daimon* is not without its adherents even today. Such theories no longer carry the weight they once did, [54] but in a general way they

continue to inflect our understanding not only of the Greek but of
all theatre, which we are only too willing to view as a kind of popular
ritual—and that in an era that otherwise emphasizes its secularity.
The consequence of the search for origin is profound and far-reaching.
I suggest a quite different but, I would affirm, equally historically
oriented view not of the meaning of individual tragedies but of what
tragedy *does*.

In view of the historical circumstances of the appearance of tragedy,
rather than seeking an origin and its explanation, it is no doubt safer
to assert simply that what we call tragedy exists in the form we know
it because certain needs of a particular era created it, using for that
purpose the materials ready to hand. Saying that, one says nothing,
but it is certainly preferable to inventing causes. I do not deny the
possibility in theory of an evolutionary history of tragedy: I do deny
that such a history would tell us anything significant about tragedies
themselves. In any case, until now lack of evidence external to the
tragedies themselves has made all such histories tautological. All we
know is the simple fact of the existence of tragedy. What are its
functional structures? What *are* the needs to which it responds? Such
questions run the risk of becoming normative. The most recent work
on the matter (e.g., Vernant, Vidal-Nacquet, Vickers) suggests that
the exact description of the discourse of tragedy can only be achieved
by contact with that of other contemporary discourses, and that its
role is understood better by means of such a "synchronic" analysis,
which breaks with the idea of a diachronic continuity as an explicative necessity, than by trying to insert tragedy in some kind of objective history—actually anything but objective.

All the writers who search for origin come up against a serious difficulty: indeed, one could say that the search is carried out *because* of
that difficulty, which is to overcome the seeming fact of the abrupt
appearance of tragedy; without warning, as it were. One example will
suffice: Nietzsche argues that the chorus of Greek tragedy is *developed*
from the Dionysiac dithyramb, but in doing so his own argument
reveals that the break between the two, the *discontinuity*, is in fact
definitive. He notes the difference between the spectators who, he
claims, allow themselves to become *actors* in the performance, and

the chorus, which represents them, the spectators, at the same time as symbolizing the "votaries actually spellbound by the god." He then tries to argue that "all was one grand chorus of dancing, singing satyrs, and of those who let themselves be represented by them."[55] Nietzsche is attempting to have it both ways, to overcome the great abyss "created" by systematizing discourse, the great transformation of a new order, by showing a development. To do so he is obliged to contradict himself.

The only solution is to treat tragedy in terms of the very suddenness its appearance has for us, to assert like Gerald Else that tragedy is "the product of two successive *creative acts* by two men of genius. The first of these men was Thespis, the second was Aeschylus."[56] Else suggests simply that tragedy can only be considered as a discursive system analogous to the others of the time—social, religious, political, and so on. Kitto agrees that tragedy per se was the invention of the tragic poets.[57] With such viewpoints one can only agree. It is not to say that tragedy appeared ex nihilo, merely that in its effect for us it did.

There are many signs that the formalization of tragedy is characterized by the distancing process of a systematic (and systematizing) "commentary." Jean-Pierre Vernant, for example, in talking about the way in which the tragic mask serves to place the protagonist (a professional actor) in opposition to the collective character of the chorus (a group of citizens), remarks that

> the mask situates the tragic character firmly within a clearly defined social and religious category: that of the hero. It makes of him the incarnation of one of those exceptional beings out of whom legend, sealed in the heroic tradition sung by the poets, constitutes one of the dimensions of their past for the Greeks of the fifth century. It is a distant past, and now long gone, which contrasts with the city's order but which nonetheless remains alive in civic religion, where the cult of the hero, unknown to Homer and Hesiod, occupies a select position. There is, then, a polarity in the technique of tragedy between two elements: the collective and anonymous being of the chorus, whose role is to express through its fears, hopes and judgements, the feelings of the spectators who compose the civic community; the individualized

character, whose action forms the drama's centre and who appears as the hero of another era and is always more or less foreign to the ordinary condition of the citizen.[58]

To perform, to "incarnate" even the hero of myth, whether or not unconscious for a condition that may never have existed,[59] to put in order a sign of the city (or the city itself as sign)—all that can refer only to the systematization of a structure already considered known. As Vernant has shown, the *performance* of tragedy repeats the "code" of the text. Webster, too, notes how the metrical and thematic differences, the textual distinctions made between the activity of the individual actors and the passivity of the chorus, and the like, are actually played out spatially, when he comments on the fundamental and visible physical gradation composed in the arena from spectator to chorus to character.[60] A system is made visible *as* a system, and the increasingly individualized role of the tragic character (from, say, Aeschylus to Euripides) marks the gradual seizure within discourse of the elements that would otherwise make the ordering of the city impossible.

The performance of the discourse in space provides yet another sign of the way in which it sets the limits of a *known* order:

> The drama of antiquity was an *act* and not a spectacle. That act gave body to the crowd's insatiable desire in a beneficent way. The high stage wall did not hide anything: it was not a curtain but a *limit* voluntarily placed between act and desire.[61]

The stage itself, in this reading, shows the limits of what can be ordered, of the known and the unknowable, of what can become a meaningful social act and what must remain but a vaguely felt desire beyond act. The rear wall, through which alone can occur the entrance and exit of the proscribed character, makes visible the enclosure that is all discourse. The front wall, the height of the stage itself, marks the limit of the discourse of tragedy. The proscribed is thus circumscribed within (and by) the code. Ajax's madness is the sign on this side of the rear wall, the silence of Oedipus after departing Thebes would be the sign on the other. There is no question here of some punishment of Destiny (for example): *both the proscription and the circumscription are the very conditions of existence of the social system.*

We may perhaps add that the difference apparently able to be made between Thespis and Aeschylus confirms the fact that tragedy is essentially a discourse marking a distancing and delimiting process. If it is correct that a rhapsode such as Homer *recites* his poem (at the same time as "composing" it, to be sure),[62] even if he "imitates" his characters to some extent, this is clearly utterly different from what happens when the event is divided into two parts (whatever may have been the precise "development"), when a Thespis installs himself as *tragoïdos* playing the protagonist opposite a chorus, and playing him in the mask of his invention. For then the difference between the real and the "artificial" system seeking to show some *comprehension* of that real has been definitively underscored. At first one might suggest that what is above all important is simply the fact of difference: that is, the awareness that the system offers itself as a schema that parallels the real but is not to be taken for it. From the moment when a second (and then third) actor is used, however, for which Aeschylus (and possibly Sophocles, for the third) are responsible, then the order of discourse begins increasingly to take on that mimetic, representational character that will eventually be fundamental to Western discourses. The *awareness* of discourse begins then to disappear as a function within discourse, which will, after much development, acquire the pretension of being the transparent medium of the declaration of truth. With Aeschylus, the hypocrite (*hupokrités*) —he who reflects, who answers, who plays what he is not—has arrived on stage.[63] The development is a long one and is indeed never completed by the Greeks.

Even in Aristotle himself, recent commentary suggests, the idea of representation, in the modern sense, is not available. Mimesis, suggests Walter Kaufmann, is best translated as "make-believe, pretend, ways of pretending." Pierre Gravel emphasizes that it connotes "unveiling," "evocation."[64] This changed interpretation of the term *mimesis* results from a more attentive reading of Aristotle. For when the emphasis was placed on the grandeur of the individual hero, then clearly the temptation was very great to read tragedy as an imitation of the psychology of such an individual caught up in a web of various

activities. But it is just that grandeur that is *not* of primary importance: on the contrary, if the hero so strikes us it is because of his
reaction to the *order* in which he must function. The performance
itself, in which alone such reaction can occur, is no more than the
staging of the ordering discourse. The latter has precedence, and that
is why Aristotle insists that the reaction to tragedy should be the
same for the reader, listener, or spectator.[65] Where mimesis is of
urgent concern is in the "plot" (*muthos*) of tragedy. It is to be found,
writes Gerald Else, "not in the performance or presentation, when the
poet's work finally reaches an audience, or even in the linguistic composition of the poem in words and verses, but specifically *in the
drafting of the plot*, the 'making' of the over-all form of the action."[66]

Aristotle emphasizes that tragedy is an evocation not simply of
human beings, but of human beings *in action*, and it is above all important to render the order of such action.[67] Particular men and
women are, so to speak, the variables of an action whose constants
are unaffected by them. That is why it is always an error to use the
extraordinary activities of certain historical or legendary individuals
for other ("fictional") characters, because individuals vary in their
reaction to similar situations and unfamiliar reactions are to be
avoided—unless they are known (or believed to be known) historically to have occurred, the *order* will disappear from view.

A mere copying of human life would suppose the nature of that
life to be fully known—what Aristotle urges is that tragedy reveal *the
order underlying human action*. That order involves the exclusion of the element provoking disorder. A bad tragedy, in Aristotle's
view, is one that does not lay primary emphasis upon such order
but displaces it onto spectacle, or diction, or thought, and so on. The
plot, *muthos*, of tragedy is the ordered evocation of action, *praxis*,
and that ordered mimesis of action is, he asserts, the very soul, *psuché*,
of tragedy. It is the basic structure that animates bodies that may
themselves vary from one another in detail: "Tragic action," writes
John Jones, "presents the translucent and vital quiddity of a life event;
it makes sense of experience."[68] Else, in his commentary, emphasizes even further that this order is the creation of the originator of
the particular discourse, the poet, the delegated representative of the
city:

By "plot" Aristotle means primarily the *shaping* of the structure of incidents, the forming process which goes on in the mind (soul) of the poet: in other words *muthos* really signifies a working part of the *art of tragedy*. It is the *archē* of the poem just as the idea of the house in the builder's mind is the *archē* of the house.[69]

One would say, then, that at the outset (and in Aristotle still) tragedy appears "consciously" as a codifying system. For Aeschylus there can be no confusion between the order of tragedy and some reality conceived as exterior to it. Indeed, posed thus with regard to Aeschylus the problem does not really exist, for it *can* be posed in such terms only within an episteme whose basis is representational. In Aeschylus the discourse is sufficient to itself, but it also corresponds to an order that is that of other discourses contemporaneous with it. Thus the concluding decision of Athens at the end of the *Oresteia* is the mark of the final imposing of a social, legal, and moral order, upon all, including he who was until immediately before the "tragic hero." And that decision is not ambiguous. The knot cut by the goddess marks a point where ordered knowledge would cease, for knowledge is revealed in and corresponds to action; and without Athene's decision no action, no further movement at all, would be possible. The judgment brought in denotes an order that overcomes that unknowing, that rejects ambiguity.

During the process of an individual tragedy its order contains, for this very reason, a profound ambiguity: but it is an ambiguity of "referent" not of the order itself. Vernant, once again, has convincingly shown how there is in Greek tragedy a constant fluctuation of key words among several semantic fields. The spectator would be constantly aware of an ambiguity of a kind such that (for example) two characters may give the impression at a given moment of understanding one another perfectly though in fact their identical terms belong to different vocabularies: "religious, juridical, political."[70]

For tragedy does not *represent* the social and legal order—it *shows* what is necessary for it to exist. It also shows that the advent of an order can only be abrupt—nothing prior to that order can explain the fact of its coming into being.

In the same way, therefore, what characterizes fundamentally Oedipus's search is the demand for a totally rational structure that

will permit the ethico-social world to be ordered. Bernard Knox has
shown how strongly the straight, linear motion of the new "scientific"
spirit is marked in *Oedipus the King*. He notes in particular the importance of such words as *heúrein* (to find out), *phaíein* (make visible,
known), *saphés* (clear, true) and their cognates, which fill the text of
the play and which are but three samples of a paradigm of "learning"
and "teaching" that rules this example of Sophoclean discourse. [71]
Despite the apparent success (as knowledge) of Oedipus's quest,
Knox, like everyone else, has been able to maintain that the tragedy
of *Oedipus* shows the *failure* of its protagonist. [72] But in what way?

When Oedipus finally blinds himself physically it is precisely
because he is *no longer* blind mentally. And it is meaningless to
ask *why* the gods have condemned Oedipus to his "fate." It is meaningless because the "gods" mark the limit of the order that is that
of human knowledge. One may well ask, What is "that full, complete knowledge which Oedipus *tyrannos* thought he had," and which
the gods *do* possess? [73] The only "knowledge" they have is that of
the pattern in which Oedipus is caught: they know the logical space
in which we must function. Of this Oedipus himself does go from
ignorance to knowledge, while the gods are said to know it from the
outset. But so too do the spectator, the reader, the listener, or the
author. And that is precisely the reason Knox is able to speak of the
"recurrent pattern of character, situation, and language which is
strongly enough marked to be called characteristic of Sophoclean
tragedy." [74] The hero may act "in a terrifying vacuum" (the space
of the ambiguities of vocabulary, for example, pointed out by Vernant) but not, once again, the spectator, who is in position to supply
the limits of that vacuum (to cut the knot) and to enclose it within
the bounds of sense.

The knowledge thus given is essential to Western man, whether
hero or critic—it is a balance that would not exist without the certainty of this system:

> An Oedipus who discovered that he had become his father's
> murderer and his mother's husband through nothing but a series
> of coincidences which are inexplicable in any terms outside
> themselves would be a spectacle too terrible to contemplate. He
> would be simply a hideous product of erratic circumstances,

comparable to a biological sport, a freak of nature, a monster. His incest and patricide would be as meaningless as the indiscriminate mating and killing of the birds and beasts; his cry of agony an echoless sound in an indifferent universe. Fortunately for his sanity, and ours, there *is* an echo; what he has done can be referred to something outside himself, indeed outside all human understanding—the prophecy. [75]

But to make such a decision, as in the case of Orestes, is to subsume the unknown within the limits of discourse, to place it inside the known. Otherwise, as King Lear will cry: "O, that way madness lies: let me shun that" (act 3, scene 4). And when the critic adds straight away that the prophecy represents the expression of destiny, he utters that "knowledge": for the critic as well needs to make the order of discourse into an absolute, for the reason he himself gives. The lack of such an absolute would open the door to madness, for us as for Oedipus, as for Lear. It is now almost a cliché to speak, in the case of Sophocles, of the mathematization of human, moral, political, and social relationships, of the very organization of tragedy. It is a mathematization that aims at the tranquil knowledge represented by the tautological balance of any equation. [76]

In Sophocles, and even more Euripides, the discourse of tragedy *appears* to become more easily open to interpretation in terms of representation. Yet Kitto can write of Aeschylus and Sophocles that "both are constructive rather than representational" and add that the moment when a complete naturalism would be achieved, when the order of discourse would become the exact expression of reality, would also mark the end of the theatre of tragedy. [77] The very fact that Greek tragedy in its heyday was obliged to obey certain ludic rules, rules of the game, so that the dramatist/competitors would start as equals, in itself emphasizes the systematic and constructive nature of a discursive form that is *willfully* stylized. This is no less the case for Euripides, and it is no doubt a "fact" that the notion of literary discourse as a representation of the real does not play much of a critical and aesthetic role until the Alexandrian readings of Aristotle—as far as we can tell, at least.

Another commonplace tells us of the increasing pessimism of tragedy from Aeschylus to Euripides. And yet, as to the fact of order itself, I am not so sure that this is the case. In Euripides the situation in which man finds himself may be quite devoid of "justice" other than that of his own manufacture (when he avoids falling into the trap of "dog kill dog"), yet tragedy still shows man coming to terms with it as a stable system, however revolting it may be and however uneasily he may do so. As Heracles says of his arms: "They must be borne, but in pain I bear them."[78] And what is perhaps terrible about Dionysos's trick on the doomed Pentheus in *The Bacchae* is not so much the horror of it as its necessity: two orders could not coexist, for chaos would ensue, but *an* order is essential. Both Pentheus and Dionysos, being each in one order, are blind to the meaning of the other, and the stronger must finally cut the knot, as Athene did in *Eumenides*. It is significant that *The Bacchae* is Euripides' last play, for if we, the audience, can no longer make a decision, then possibly tragedy is no longer available to us.

With Euripides tragedy is showing not merely order but also some of its implications: as the Athenian order itself is beginning to come apart, tragedy shows that the price of reason is the turning of a blind eye, the cultivation of one's own garden. Euripidean tragedy shows the order of human activity to be such as to make that an impossible choice; it shows order (and therefore tragedy itself) as an island in the midst of general chaos. Is that, too, a lesson of *The Bacchae*—an attempt to make an order out of chaos itself? Perhaps it is because his tragedies show both the necessity and the accompanying untenability of a reasoned order that Euripides in his life time was, as Richmond Lattimore puts it, "parodied more often and more brutally (and more intelligently, too) than any other literary man in Athens."[79]

The great days of Greek tragedy come to a close with the full outbreak of the Peloponnesian Wars because its myth of reason had become untenable: untenable not because tragedy showed reason to be limited but because *events* showed it to be so. At this point tragedy's paean to reasoned order becomes the anguished but necessary choice played out in a play like *The Bacchae*. Of this Heracles, too, is a most remarkable demonstration: the old scheme is undone and reversed in madness, the old order of the first half of the play is overthrown and revealed in all its precariousness, reduced by the threat of a world of unreason. In doing so all the more emphasis is placed on the necessity of *some* order. It is in that sense that one can understand Heracles' cry of pain. For as before, the order is by no means necessarily apparent to the protagonist (and he might not like its dependence on himself even if it were). Thus, he may very often cry out against the disorder and unreason of those very gods who, in Aeschylus or Sophocles, were creative of order. So Orestes:

> Dreams, lies, lies, dreams—nothing but emptiness!
> Even the Gods, with all Their name for wisdom,
> Have only dreams and lies and lose Their course,
> Blinded, confused, and ignorant as we. [80]

The spectator, like the author, knows this accusation to be unfounded: for Apollo has brought Orestes to Tauris in order that both he and Iphigenia may be saved. As William Arrowsmith writes in his introduction to *Hecuba*, "Man continues to demand justice and an order with which he can live," and without the visibility of such order and such justice "he forfeits his humanity, destroyed by the hideous gap between his illusion and the intolerable reality." [81] Hecuba strikes out in anguish, lost in the abyss of utter meaninglessness. But *we* see, as before, and as before we *know*. It is because humanity would otherwise be given over to chaos that at a certain strategic moment in the development of an episteme the order of tragedy is *essential*.

Tragedy has broken with mythical thinking, awkward and confusing for an analytical logic; it has replaced it with a thought of individual and causes placed in the context of the social and ethical process of exchange that marks the city. That supposes a victory over a certain type of "ignorance" concerning a specific *place* occupied by man in what is now *his history*. The spectator of a tragedy is judge and organizer of a commentary that, to him, is anything but confused. While the chorus is a passive and half-knowing element, while the protagonist plays his role blindly but actively, the spectator is at once conscious of his capacity to know (since he knows more than the chorus itself) and of his aptitude to action: the Greek must have been just as aware as we are that there are to be found obvious parallels between the meetings of the [parliamentary] Assembly on the Pnyx and the performance in the theatre half a mile away: the involvement of the mass audience, the active participation of a large number of the citizens, the eloquence of the orators and of the actors.[82]

The distance between the spectator and the protagonist already indicates an ordering, the performance itself shows the spectator his control over and responsibility for that ordering. The play does not pose any dilemma for the spectator. It confirms his order.

Tragedy thus appears as an essentially optimistic art in its development.[83] The "pleasure" received from it has, in this sense, a certain complacent aspect about it, even if much tragedy seeks to prevent such complacency. If the protagonist continues to pose something of a problem it is because he alone cannot make out the order in which he must needs occupy a place. But for the spectator the protagonist's fall (if and when it occurs) only confirms the truth and justice of the discursive order presented in tragedy.

What counts then in tragedy—at least at the outset—is not its reference to outside events and conditions. What counts is the simple fact that it finds a way to set in order a certain "ignorance" within its own signifying process. Eventually patterns of different types of discourse may all come into agreement with one another (as occurs in European neoclassicism), but at first tragedy works out the way in which such processes of signification may function at all. The discourse of tragedy may be ambiguous internally, but that is just the point: it is an ordered and enclosed ambiguity. Its very existence implies that, seen from the outside and as a finished discourse, tragedy is *not* ambiguous. It presupposes a knowledge. For the first time perhaps man has a discursive model that will enable him to grasp its objects *as his own* instead of being a means of fitting himself into a universe over which he has no control.[84]

What I am proposing, therefore, is a research that sets out to discover what tragedy *does* in relation not so much, or not simply, to the individual (or even collective) recipient as to the other discourses that form its epistemic, its socio-cultural, context. I wish for that reason to remain relatively indifferent to what we might choose to read as the particular meaning of a single example of the discourse, tragedy, in order to emphasize the role of the discourse as a whole. It will then appear irrelevant to speak, for example, of the "death" of tragedy, a notion that seeks to endow a literary discourse with a kind of nostalgic reality going far beyond discursive and epistemic use, and that seems due precisely to regarding tragedy from the point of view of its *reception* rather than from that of its *production*.

Clearly these two are part of a single process, but what I am seeking is a possible elucidation of the discursive role of tragedy within an epistemic development, before being concerned with its effect upon spectator or reader. For this effect is created by the role thus performed by tragedy. Such effect must change from occasion to occasion, from individual to individual, above all from cultural context to cultural context—and with it our idea of what tragedy *is*, so long as that idea is sought in terms of the specifiable "meaningful" content of individual tragedies. The effects generally and vaguely indicated by the common use of such words as *catharsis*, *pity*, and *terror*, seem to a considerable degree subsumed in the view that seeks first to examine tragedy in terms of a discursive role. Such emotional effects could all be explained, for example, as the ("psychological") reaction to a discourse that visibly encloses the mark of the potential impossibility of *any* discourse for which knowledge is the true expression of reality: the reaction to tragedy, that is, would be at once the fear of a lack of all order and the pleasure at seeing such lack overcome.

In such a reading the "moral uplift" traditionally argued as the benefit of the tragic emotion (and the reason, of course, why its "death" could be bemoaned) is no more than the result of tragedy's affirmation that a knowledge of the kind just indicated *is* possible. If one starts from the discursive principle the various psychological, moral, emotional, and metaphysical explanation of tragedy all come to resemble one another rather strangely: for they are all produced by the very role that tragedy plays in the production of a particular episteme.

The re-creation of tragedy during the Renaissance is even more marked than is the Greek by a process permitting a "search for truth." There one can follow a gradual *enfolding* of a particular trace within discourse of the impossibility of signifying, of ordering something supposed as outside it. The earliest stage can be seen in the tragedies of George Buchanan, whose study is the more interesting because that stage is "lost" so far as Greek antiquity is concerned (it would have preceded Aeschylus). This enclosure permits the tragedy of neoclassicism and its avatars to become referential and veridical: for the enclosure is also a distancing. And such "impossibility" *must be* enclosed, it must be—as it is—given a meaning within the order of that discourse; it cannot be permitted to lie somewhere on the outside, so to speak, a beast waiting to spring from the jungle, a mark of some space exterior to that of this discourse.

One would not, of course, propose that tragedy alone made possible an episteme of analysis and referentiality, nor that, under different conditions, another discourse (or several) might not fulfill an analogous function. For I am speaking of a process of "coming to signify" epitomized by tragedy but which, at least in its final form, is characteristic of all the discourses of the society in question. Where these others do not appear to function in the same way as tragedy is in the original, fundamental questioning of the act of producing "meaningfulness." The act accomplished by tragedy, though the evidence of this moment is lost for Greek tragedy, is the enclosing of this questioning, the endowing of it with a particular truth function within the entire reality sealed by (within) the episteme. Tragedy makes it possible for its companion discourses to take the possibility of referential truth as a given. It makes possible the very idea of knowledge based on a principle of truthfulness to what is not discourse. And it does so as a discourse whose very premise, both internally among different "speakers" and externally between those speakers and their spectators, is the possibility of discursive communication. *That* premise, whatever the surrounding discursive or perhaps ideological conditions, is the second thing that remains specific to tragedy (and other drama),[85] and it is the production of that specificity which needs to be examined.

Having said all this, having sought to indicate the "pre-history" of my hypothesis both as a general theoretical premise and as it will be applied hereafter particularly to the tragedy of the European Renaissance, I should warn the reader against a misunderstanding. I am suggesting that the discourse, tragedy, has performed a specifiable role in the establishment of the episteme of analysis and referentiality. I have claimed that it had already performed an analogous role in fifth-century Athens. I would like to note at least one crucial difference between Greek and Renaissance tragedy; crucial because it is the mark of an essential societal difference, and therefore, too, because it indicates that the order which tragedy helps make possible will not necessarily be just the same at each of its appearances.

There can, I think, be no question but that Greek tragedy was a collective experience, and that the complex relations of chorus, actors, and spectators that are peculiar to it play an integral part in the kind of discursive order tragedy can then help to establish:

> The dramatic form embodies, in a unique way, both the history and the presence, the myth and the response to the myth. The known history is enacted by the three masked actors, who have separated out from the chorus but, as their sharing of roles and their formal relations with the chorus make clear, not separated out altogether. [86]

And the chorus's status as a group of citizens serves in turn to bind them to the audience.

Renaissance tragedy, on the other hand—even when it possesses a chorus (often a rather empty gesture to form that provokes Dennis's mocking reference to a chorus of Rymer's imagining: a group of ladies "dancing a Saraband to a doleful ditty")—is an ineluctably individual process. Meaning in the Greek practice is produced in terms of an interplay of discourses, as Vernant has shown; it *is* in a sense that play of relations. From the time of the Renaissance in Europe "meaning" fills the absence at the center of all discourse as some kind of absolute: whether it be the referential truth of the new science, the absolute Truth to be attained in religious or mystical belief, or the ideal essence of an Hegelian totality. *This* truth has to be fixed by a subject, at first individual and later collectivist—but collectivist as a kind of occulted individualism. [87] As Hegel remarks in this context:

> To genuine *tragic* action it is essential that the principle of *individual* freedom and independence, or at least that of self-determination,

the will to find in the self the free cause and source of the personal act and its consequences, should already have been aroused.[88]

The Greeks had no such solution available, any more than the Renaissance could have sought to adopt a Greek collectivism. That distinction is identical to the one that must be made between classical theories of natural right, for example, for which the *polis* itself is the origin of all right, and modern theories, starting with Hobbes, for which the individual is the origin. In fifth-century Greece and during the Renaissance tragedy performs an analogous discursive role, but the discursive relations and the overall context into which each is inserted, in which each is produced, are not the same. The Greeks lack that very notion of willfulness which is essential to analysis and referentiality.[89] The role will be the same, but the elements of which the discourse can make use in its performance of that role and the details of that performance will necessarily be different.[90]

2 Buchanan, Montaigne, and the Difficulty of Speaking

[handwritten margin notes: "Isn't it a recreation of life?" / "failure of order" / "speaker trapped in life" / "the why of reappearing"]

Renaissance tragedy is at once a reworking of classical tragedy and a self-conscious creation of its own language. In a way one may say that *tragic* and *tragedy* are initially inseparable in the early Renaissance, for the failure is that of order itself. The failure of the principal speaker does not proceed from a hero's defeat at the hands of Destiny or of some gods, or from his inability to surpass his humanity, or whatever. What happens rather is that discourse cannot be translated into action, that no socialized meaning can be given to an individual's utterance. The speaker is sealed into his language in spite of all efforts to break the seal—and the sealing occurs to a considerable degree just *because of* those efforts. It is the search to express a general and ordered meaning that is itself abortive.

The tragic of this Renaissance theatre, from Buchanan's *Baptistes* to Marlowe's *Tamburlaine*, is fundamental in a particular sense then. The "why?" of human ignorance or suffering (to take one interpretation as indicative) cannot be answered, because the discourse posing the question cannot change the rules of its logic so as to give the answer. It cannot get outside its own ("conceptual") limits. The question is posed as a particular function of its own discursive structuring and not as some exterior element of which the discourse could then be said to speak. The *why* in question, that is to say, *is* that of discursive ordering.

Renaissance tragedy initially reveals the failure of discursive system. At the same time it sees itself in terms of at least two other systems whose success as ordering processes could be seen in the past and might be foreseen in the future: those of classical tragedy and language itself. Renaissance tragedy provokes from the start, therefore, a permanent question concerning the relationship of these systems. The first question, before any conclusion can be hoped for, will be that of situating any "final" system. If an answer can no longer be sought in a divine logos then what is initially at issue will be the very assumption of order itself—and that issue will at first be fought out within the very formation of discourse. Renaissance tragedy begins as a search for language, as an attempt to escape from the "injustice" of disorder. For one may say, I think, that the discourse that shows itself inoperant in Buchanan's original tragedies takes up once again the *absence* that is experienced in Hesiod. As we find it in Buchanan, discourse shows itself quite inefficacious for any speaking *about*.

Thus, too, we may say that the history of Renaissance tragedy at one level is that of a particular development. At first the discursive order called tragedy, as it is presented in individual tragedies, is preoccupied with the working out of a text, with its own rhetorical patterns; then it will be concerned to generalize by reference to a genre, tragedy; and finally it will conceive itself to be playing out the imitation of an exterior reality going beyond the mere concerns of a literary genre. At that point Renaissance tragedy will be called "neoclassical." Obviously one of these concerns does not disappear when another appears; there is a gradual building-up, so that a tragedy by Racine may appear more complex to us than one by Buchanan. It is the accumulation of these preoccupations, perhaps, that makes one of the chief distinctions between, say, Renaissance and Racinian tragedy.

Yet we do find from the outset an ordered discourse that recognizes itself as tragedy: we should never forget the explicit reference to Greek tragedy. Indeed it is this interior and explicit germ that will eventually permit the "tragic" of discourse to be absorbed in the genre *tragedy*. It can already be seen in *Tamburlaine* or in Garnier's *Les Juifves* where the "tragic absence" begins to be symbolized in metaphors that may readily be inserted into the Greek system: Apollo, Phaeton, Prometheus. Once it has received such a metaphorical naming, the impossibility of finding meaning (which, needless to say, could not previously have been considered as an *element* of discourse) may easily become a failure of human action. And that is a distancing that already leads toward neoclassical tragedy, because it constitutes a setting into system of just that element of discourse which, before, could not be situated, let alone named. In a sense the metaphor creates the element that it is taken to metaphorize: it makes meaning possible and provides not merely *a* narrative but a whole accumulation of narratives all ready to expand such meaning.

For this reason it is an essential fact that the effort to create a tragedy written in the vulgar tongues toward the middle of the sixteenth century in England and France especially was accompanied by an effort to "improve" those languages, to make of them instruments of expression and communication capable of withstanding comparison with Latin and particularly Greek. The importance of that comparison is that it will eventually concern the relative precision of the referential bond taken as obtaining between the order of language and that of concepts and phenomena. The creation of tragedy and the development of a language form two projects that are narrowly associated with one another, indeed, they can come to be seen as a single project: we are familiar with the rather cavalier remark made by Du Bellay concerning the usefulness of writing tragedies and comedies in the classical manner "pour l'ornement de [la] langue."[1]

Comments made concerning the work of Robert Garnier, the writer considered then (and now) the most important tragedian of the French Renaissance, will suffice to emphasize this point. Among the various liminary poems preceding *Porcie* (1568) and repeated in the complete edition of his works in 1585, the majority refer continually to these two aspects. Jean Dorat and Robert Estienne, in Latin, Greek, and French, consider it enough praise to make a favorable comparison of his work with that of the three Greeks, while Estienne in yet another poem (three of the liminaries are his) repeats the comparison with reference to Rome. Ronsard remarks in his sonnet that Garnier "bastit Athènes en la France" while du Baïf compares his inspiration to "la muse grégeoise." Estienne says that Garnier is surpassing the admired "language antique" of Aeschylus himself, du Baïf speaks of his "grave chanson," and Belleau affirms that Garnier

is one of those "divins esprits / Fertiles de discours et de doctes escrits."
In his commendatory verses placed before *Cornelie* (1574) Ronsard,
once again, compares Jodelle and Garnier in terms of "le vieil arti-
fice des Grecs," saying that in subject matter, in "le parler haut" and
"les mots bien choisis," it is Garnier who takes the prize.

Garnier's ye

   The advantage thus given to Garnier is, of course, of less significance here than the terms in which the comparison is made.[2] In his
Art poétique, published in 1605 though apparently begun as early
as 1574, Vauquelin de la Fresnaye will conclude that the accomplishment of surpassing the Greeks both in tragedy and linguistic
perfection has been achieved:

> Et maintenant Garnier, sçavant et copieux,
> Tragique a surmonté les nouveaux et les vieux,
> Monstrant par son parler assez doucement grave
> Que nostre langue passe aujourd'huy la plus brave.[3]

the vernacular

> [And now Garnier, learned and prolific, (as a) tragic (author) has
> overcome the moderns and the ancients, showing by his sweetly
> solemn diction that our language surpasses today the finest.]

   Donald Stone has also noted the particular importance of the
Greeks, and most especially of two plays of Euripides: *Hecuba* and
Iphigenia in Aulis. He is quick to add, however, that the difference
between the Latins and Greeks (particularly Sophocles and Euripides,
Aeschylus being but poorly known) was probably not overly apparent
to the later Europeans.[4] To some extent such may indeed be the
case, but a remark made by Roger Ascham in *The Scholemaster*
(written c. 1563, published in 1570) is not inapposite here; the more
so because it makes a clear distinction between a formal ordering of
action and discourse, of the "matter" of the play (showing "how
[what is done] is done"), and a rather superficial glitter of fine language, a good arrangement of verses that only serve to "lay before
you what is done." It is with assurance that Ascham gives all the
advantage as far as the first is concerned to the Greeks, while in the
second Seneca is allowed to have done at least no worse:

> In Tragedies, (the goodliest Argument of all, and for the vse, either
> of a learned preacher, or a Ciuill Ientleman, more profitable than

> *Homer, Pindar, Virgill,* and *Horace*: yea comparable in myne
> opinion, with the doctrine of *Aristotle, Plato,* and *Xenophon*,)
> the *Grecians, Sophocles* and *Euripides* far ouer match our *Seneca,*
> in *Latin,* namely in οἰκονομία *et Decoro,* although Senecaes elo-
> cutiõ and verse be verie commendable for his tyme.[5]

Both are models for the proper use of language, Greek is the best for
the imitation of tragedy as a formal ordering process.

The attention to Latin and Greek as *the* languages of excellence
and to the theatre of Antiquity as the epitome of formal perfection
raises the specter of translation and transposition. In the humanist
treatment of this matter, too, we find a particular development at
this time that raises the same set of difficulties. At the beginning of
the sixteenth century rhetorical theory still considered translation
a particular and independent poetic genre. In France this still remains
the case for Sebillet in 1548. Yet by 1540 Dolet, in his *Art de bien
traduire,* already reveals a quite different attitude: for him translation
is a poetic exercise, it is *practice* (an apprenticeship in the use of a
particular type of discourse), it is a means to raise the level of the
poet's other verse productions. Peletier argues the same way in the
preface to his translation of Horace's *Art poëtique* in 1545.[6] This
development suggests that the system being translated, unfamiliar
as it had been, is now being seen as a particular stylistic problem
within the writer's own discourse. No longer is he transposing something *different,* now he is dealing with an element of his own discourse, something that is the *same.* It remains a problem—indeed, an
even greater one—for now it is not a matter of the application of
technique in a particular poetic genre, but merely part of a general
questioning concerning poetic communication itself. Obviously
tragedy is not alone in being translated, but because it is one of the
most novel of forms it does pose these problems with particular
acuity. It also does so just because the fact of social communication
is fundamental to its accomplishment.

In any case, that literary production for several decades was inseparable from the question of linguistic "amelioration" suggests
that a—possibly *the*—principal difficulty confronted by the writer
of the period is quite simply that of *speaking,* of uttering meaning.
No doubt this is as much the case for the reader or spectator as it

is for the writer. Why does Grevin insist upon the purity of his language? Why does Jodelle find it necessary to excuse himself before his *Eugène* for having overstepped the bounds of comic verisimilitude by choosing too serious a language, in order, as he puts it, to overcome the difficulty of having to use a "langue encor foiblette de soymesme"? What can account for a play such as the anonymous *Tragédie du Sac de Cabrières*, whose supposed object is the massacre committed by the Catholics on the inhabitants of Cabrières but whose real object appears rather to concern the power of language—much as we will see it in *Baptistes*?[7]

It is in fact this preoccupation with the power and possibilities of language that seems to mark the principal interest of both spectator and author. This is why tragedy does not produce an historical or psychological action played out at a distance upon the stage so much as what one might call a linguistic or stylistic action. This may appear to be a rather peculiar sort of action (even though, in our own time, we are once again accustomed to the stage performance of such preoccupations), but it would no doubt engage the attention of the scholars who were chiefly involved at first: for the problems dealt with are central to the advance of humanism.

It may be (and has been) objected that all theatre presupposes a preoccupation with language and a reflection upon its powers, and that one may hardly claim that there is anything special about Renaissance tragedy on these grounds. However, setting aside the palpable fact that certain forms of theatre neither use nor are about language, what is clear is that what must be considered is the manner and "meaning" of such reflection. It will, I hope, become clear that the use of language revealed in the tragedies of Buchanan (among others, obviously, but the time of his writing and the language he selected to do it in endow his plays with particular significance), in conjunction with a few indications we will draw from the writings of Montaigne, differs completely from what will be found, for example, in the tragedies of Racine.

In Racine language acts *as though* it were transparent. He seeks to hide the fact of discourse. Such transparency, it is intended, will permit the spectator to be in direct contact, so to speak, with the "spirit" of the *person* who is speaking: the means by which this is achieved must not appear. As Pope remarks in his prologue to Addison's *Cato* (1713), the object of the "Tragic-Muse" is to "wake the soul by tender strokes of art," and to make the spectators "be what they behold."[8] In the same way, in a well-known passage of his *Art poétique*, Boileau remarks:

> Que dans tous vos discours la passion émuë
> Aille chercher le coeur, l'échauffe, et le remue.
> Si d'un beau mouvement l'agréable fureur
> Souvent ne nous remplit d'une douce *Terreur*,
> Ou n'excite en nostre ame une *Pitié* charmante,
> En vain vous étalez une scène sçavante:
> Vos froids raisonnemens ne feront qu'attiedir
> Un Spectateur toujours paresseux d'applaudir,
> Et qui des vains efforts de vostre Rhetorique,
> Justement fatigué, s'endort, ou vous critique.
> Le secret est d'abord de plaire et de toucher:
> Inventez des ressorts qui puissent m'attacher.[9]

> In all you Write, observe with Care and Art
> To move the Passions, and incline the Heart.
> If, in a labour'd Act, the pleasing Rage
> Cannot our Hopes and Fears by turns ingage,
> Nor in our Mind a feeling Pity raise,
> In vain with Learned Scenes you fill your Plays:
> Your cold Discourses can never move the Mind
> Of a stern Critic, naturally unkind;
> Who, justly tir'd with your pedantic Flight,
> Or falls asleep, or Censures all you Write.
> The Secret is, Attention first to gain;
> To move our Minds, and then to entertain.
> [*The Works of Monsieur Boileau* . . . , to which is prefix'ed *His Life, Written to Joseph Addison, Esq; by Mr. Des Maizeaux. And some Account of this Translation by N. Rowe, Esq.* (London, 1712), I.106–07. This translation is far from faithful to the sense of the original, but is sufficiently close for us to allow the advantage of using a contemporary translation to overcome the disadvantage of its unfaithfulness.]

In a poem addressed to Racine, Boileau praises the playwright for

having been able to "enchanter les coeurs et les Esprits." Though
one would not necessarily wish to argue that Racine and Boileau's
ideas on this matter are identical, it is clear that their common
intention is to conceal the *tool* of language in order that the supposed sensibility of its user may appear directly: the critic's perplex-
ity when faced with the "récit de Théramène" in *Phèdre* merely
serves to underline this (see ch. 11). Elsewhere Boileau praises those
tragedies where "l'Auditeur . . . se croit voir lui-même au milieu du
péril," according to the expression he has taken over from Longinus
and translated in a way to emphasize the central idea (*Traite du
sublime*, ch. 22).[10] All that is very different from a theatre that is
determined, deliberately and continuously, to bring its use of language, *as an instrument*, to the awareness of the spectator.[11]

But the reason for this crisis in language, and for the consequent
emphasis placed upon it in the tragedy of the early Renaissance,
also owes much to tradition. The kind of study made of the written
text in the schools, in which as much emphasis was placed on the
language as on the thought, on the medium itself as on the message,
had been a central part of education for hundreds of years. The
construction of texts (or spoken discourses) in accordance with well-
established rhetorical rules was perhaps *the* principal way of teaching
and learning from the Middle Ages: whence a profound awareness
of the formal nature of one's language (Latin, of course, in this case).
As a result of the Reform and its threat to ecclesiastical authority,
for example, this awareness must have been sharpened even further.
One could mention the technique of glossing old texts (whence
comes, initially, the knowledge and "understanding" of the theatre
of Antiquity?); the care with which a Buchanan must seek to avoid
ambiguous terms in his texts that touch on religious matters (he is
not completely successful and finds himself in the hands of the Por-
tuguese Inquisition); the consciousness that a small error of language
could really be a matter of life and death: and Dolet, who has the
misfortune to translate Plato, having written that after death one
will be "rien du tout," goes to the stake. . . .

Montaigne criticizes in all this linguistic preoccupation what he
considers a false profundity. Like many of his contemporaries at the

end of the sixteenth century, he views this concern with language as something of a red herring, and wishes to get rid of it once and for all: to repeat, in fact, the gesture of Athene in *Eumenides*, and with many similar implications (not a few of our own contemporaries would strongly agree with the gesture!). Montaigne proposes to use a "simple" language, a language that, according to him, permits an absolute correspondence between what he writes and what he is (in the essay *Du Repentir* for example). Elsewhere, in the essay *De l'expérience,* like Rabelais before him, he explicitly criticizes all these linguistic quarrels. It is a criticism aimed both at the medieval method of the gloss, still popular among theologians and jurists of his time, and at that particular aspect of the literary movement (closer to the medieval spirit than its practitioners claim) which is to enlarge the language by the use of neologisms, various subtle distinctions and nuances, new figures of speech, and the like:

> Nostre contestation est verbale. Je demande que c'est que nature, volupté, cercle et substitution; la question est de parolles, et se paye de mesme. Une pierre c'est un corps. Mais qui presseroit: "Et corps, qu'est-ce? —Substance. —Et substance quoy?" ainsi de suitte, acculeroit le respondant au bout de son calepin. On eschange un mot pour un autre mot, et souvent plus incogneu. Je sçay mieux que c'est qu'homme que je ne sçay que c'est animal, ou mortel, ou raisonnable. Pour satisfaire à un doubte, ils m'en donnent trois: c'est la teste de Hydra.[12]

> "Our disputes are purely verbal. I ask what is "nature," "pleasure," "circle," "substitution." The question is one of words, and is answered in the same way. "A stone is a body." But if you pressed on: "And what is a body?"—"Substance."—"And what is substance?" and so on, you would finally drive the respondent to the end of his lexicon. I know better what is man than I know what is animal, or mortal, or rational. To satisfy one doubt, they give me three; it is the Hydra's head. [Montaigne, *The Complete Works, Essays; Travel Journal; Letters*, trans. Donald M. Frame, London, n.d. (1958), pp. 818–19.]

This criticism will be answered only by the work of the grammarians and writers of the second half of the seventeenth century—and with how very different an attitude! For they find themselves able to take the external referent for granted as an ultimate goal of their researches (though with what ambiguity Louis Marin has recently shown),[13] whereas Montaigne, as we will see, will find himself driven back into the "interior" of language, driven to view language as essentially creative of its object. In this he is like Rabelais, whose search for a "paradigmatic use" of language marks his reaction to the same problem.[14] Writers like Henri Estienne, Du Vair, and above all Ramus and his many disciples, all of whom make the same complaints, will seek a language capable of expressing with precision a reality exterior to the human mind, or at least a series of sensations that may be seen as such. The present chapter examines the rather more restricted question of the presence of this crisis in the two original tragedies of Buchanan and in the commentary I will draw from Montaigne in so far as the preoccupations of his writing coincide with those of the tragedies and form a kind of interpretation of them. My argument is, of course, that the *performance* of this crisis in tragedy will at least partially allow later philosophers and grammarians to provide a formal solution.

Buchanan's enormous influence as a teacher is well known. It was an influence felt particularly by the young humanists of the years between 1540 and 1555, including Montaigne himself and the members of the *Brigade*, which was soon to be transformed into the *Pléiade*. Through his relations with Antoine Muret in Bordeaux, and later in Paris, Buchanan's pedagogy (of which his theatre formed a part) gained many adherents.[15] His two original plays, *Baptistes* and *Jephthes*, not only reflect the effort to create a new theatre, that reworking of the tragedy of Antiquity, but are an integral part of his pedagogical method. They mark at one and the same time his own preoccupations as a professor and humanist, the thought he is teaching, his style. The mechanisms of his thinking will be thoroughly implicated in this discourse, will coincide with it. One should remember, too, that a rather unique sympathy must have been created between stage and spectator (reader): the plays were seen, but they were also examined particularly closely in other ways. In school disputes, they would have been studied for their style, their structure, their rhetorical organization. Exemplary as they were, they would have been above all examples to be followed, models to a point where reading and writing might almost coincide. As a rhetorical practice, they were exercises in the problems involved in the use and ordering of language.

The very subtitles of the plays are an indication that we should look there for a dispute upon the power of language. Indeed, even for us (at least in *Baptistes*), this dispute forms both the structure of the play and its principal theme. Can it be indifferent that these two subtitles refer directly to notions that are inseparable from a certain conception of language as a barrier?[16]

In the prologue to *Baptistes* we are told that men are like Proteus because, subject as they always are to the calumnies of the envious, the only being (or "becoming") they have is enclosed in the discourse of the other:

> Seseque vertant in figuras quaslibet:
> Subjecta quorum maxime calumniis
> Fortuna semper scenici est spectaculi.   [p. 219, 12–14]

> [They turn themselves into various forms: their fortune, subject to all conceivable calumnies, is always matter for theatrical spectacle.]

The author paints a picture of such speakers of calumny as retail some old story with all kinds of sinister implications: "Omnia in pejus trahunt [They change everything for the worst]." In fact they create in language a man who has no other existence than that of their discourse. Doing nothing themselves, he says, they spend their time looking for the minor errors of others (victim himself of religious intolerance, perhaps Buchanan speaks here with some bitterness), in order that they may create a long invention with no reality but that of the language which bears it; which becomes its own object. The tragedy is thus presented at first as an example to the just man, though the protagonist will shortly discover that language is always, and by its very nature, a calumny.

This tragedy, continues the prologue, is going to show us an innocent man, John the Baptist,

. . . quondam ut regia libidine,
Et invidorum subdolis calumniis
Oppressus, indignam innocens subiit necem.   [p. 220, 39–41]

[. . . who once, oppressed by royal lust and by the subtle calumnies of his enemies, innocently suffered an unmerited death.]

The prologue can then conclude that calumny and fraud will always
be ready to defeat the good and the just:

Nam donec hominum genus erit, semper novae
Fraudes, novaeque suppetent calumniae:
Livorque semper improbus premet probos.
Vis jura vincet, fucus innocentiam.   [p. 220, 48–51]

[Because for as long as humankind exists, new frauds and new
calumnies will always be prepared: unjust malice will always vic-
timize the just, force defeat right, deceit defeat innocence.]

Next follows a scene that puts this calumny into action while at
the same time getting under way the *narrative line* of the play, the
progress of the action. The priest Malchus comes in complaining
about the present condition of the Jews and above all about John
the Baptist, who is winning over the populace by condemning the
priests. He comments that John's power comes most of all from
his use of language; he has some sort of intimate contact with the
crowd's *ears*:

                    . . . ut furore facilius
Vulgi fruatur, omnibus probris patres
Laceret, secundis plebis usus auribus.   [p. 222, 102–04]

[So that he may more easily enjoy the rage of the crowd, he
injures the fathers with every insult, winning over the favorable
ears of the masses.]

Gamaliel, who will take the other side of the argument, tries to
calm Malchus and make him more "reasonable," suggesting that he
should first of all judge himself, and noting that John could just as
well come as a representative of God as Moses or David. Malchus
insists that the preacher should be put to death. Gamaliel suggests

that instead of using words to calumniate John, Malchus should meet with him in a public dispute:

> Si peccat ille, quin palam redarguis?
> Quin lumen ingenii exeris illic tui?
> Rudem peritus, doctus indoctum, senex
> Aggredere iuvenem.   [p. 224, 185–88]

> [If he sins, why do you not refute him in public? Why do you not show there the light of your mind? An experienced, learned, old man go up against an ignorant, inexperienced, young man.]

He adds that before setting out to kill John, Malchus should first try to help him, always supposing the Baptist to be what Malchus asserts him to be: "sit ille, qualem *dicis*." And with this word and this subjunctive he emphasizes the purely discursive nature of the monster fabricated by the priest, who now goes off to seek the help of the king while Gamaliel and the chorus discuss what has just occurred.

The entire presentation of the narrative line is absorbed in the problematics of language, seeking to place in question its ability to express "truth." Referring back to what was said earlier concerning the notion of action (*praxis*) in Aristotle, then we may perhaps say that what forms the soul of the plot here is precisely this questioning. How is it possible to turn aside the *other's* language, since that language necessarily falsifies what I feel myself to be? Or what a third person feels me to be? (Which last merely complicates the matter: for that, too, will be a "calumny," in the sense of being a distorted view). How, too, can I avoid being false to myself in using language? For language, if it can communicate at all, does so in just those elements which are public, which are not particular to myself. Do I not in fact commit a clumsy tautology if I accuse someone of "making a calumny"? For in one sense language will always betray the singular "essence" which it tries to speak: unless, and only unless, that essence is discursive, is the use of language itself. But that "solution" merely brings the difficulty full circle. Indeed, as we shall see, the play can never escape the set of problems it creates.

When Gamaliel, as Lebègue puts it, next "reveals the deceitfulness of his colleagues" to the chorus by speaking of the various maneuvers

they undertake against those they call their enemies, these problems
invade all the several signifying levels of the play:

> Contra instituta nostra si quid audeas,
> Conamur auro evertere adversarios,
> Tollere veneno, subditisque testibus
> Opprimere; falsis regias rumoribus
> Implemus aures; quicquid animum offenderit,
> Rumore falso ulciscimur; & incendimus
> Animum furore turbidum, & calumniis
> Armamus irae saevientis impetum. [p. 225, 231–38]

> [If you dare anything at all against our institutions, we try to
> overwhelm our adversaries with gold, to kill them with poison,
> and to overthrow them with false witnesses: we fill the king's
> ears with false rumors; we avenge ourselves on whomsoever will
> offend (his) mind by means of a false rumor; and we furiously
> set alight (his) already disordered mind, and we arm the violence
> of his anger with savage calumnies.]

Leaving aside the rather brutal commentary contained in this passage of a somewhat Machiavellian political practice, let us insist for
the present upon the semantic and signifying level of this longish
sentence. The three "methods" of distracting one's adversaries are
quickly enumerated: what follows is little more than a series of
complements that confirm the last of these methods and, because
of their cumulative effect, serve to bring the first two into the same
paradigm. The "false witnesses" are indeed repeated four times:
"Falsis . . . rumoribus," "Rumore falso," "incendimus/Animum,"
"calumniis." Moreover this sentence is directly followed by a description of what Malchus will say to the king, in which the further
metaphor of "aliud saevius telum [another more vicious spear]"
will be added. Gold and poison are thus brought into the same system: and not only by the cumulative effect. The play on *aurum*
(line 232) and *auris* (line 235) permits a linking that is further reinforced at the end of the conversation when the metaphor of the
poison is explicitly linked with the idea of calumny: "Haec in regias/
Stillabit aures toxica ingenii sui [He will distill the poisons of his

mind into the king's ears]." It seems to me characteristic of the development we will be following that *Hamlet* will rejoin the same set of problems through the same metaphor, but in the form of a piece of stage business. By being posed visually, at a distance, the question will be quite changed in its implications.

Here, the question of language is caught up in discourse itself, and there is such lack of distance that the subject cannot even fix himself in his own function as enunciator of the sentence. The mixture of tenses, modes, subjects ("audeas," "conamur," "evertere," "offenderit") in the passage indicates a kind of defeat, as though the utterance itself had taken charge. The subject here possesses no other temporality than the quite provisional one of the verb that is uttered at any particular moment. The very existence of that subject is made vague by the crisscrossing of active and deponent verbs that it applies to itself ("conamur," "implemus," "ulciscimur," "incendimus," "armamus"), and whose fluctuation tends to remove from the signified of these verbs all the force we might otherwise grant them. Furthermore, if Benveniste is right in asserting that "*I* is 'the individual which utters the present instance of the discourse containing the linguistic instance *I*'" and that "*you*" would thus receive "a symmetrical definition" (see, here, the first two verses quoted), but that "*he*" represents "the only possible mode of utterance for those discursive instances which must not refer to themselves, but which predicate the process of anyone or anything besides that instance itself,"[17] then it can be seen that the passage appears to follow strictly the schema of normative utterance, or at least of habitual statement form.

In doing so, however, the utterance in question is driven to leave aside any possibility of following a referential logic, for the objective referent of the verb "offenderit" would have to be the same as that of "audeas." Their form opposes this identity: the rules of discourse themselves overwhelm whatever might have been the reference of that discourse. It is an internal necessity of discourse that rules the activity of the enunciating subject, who is unable to overcome its constraints. Just as he was blocked at the metaphorical level (the repetitions of the metaphors of calumny), so, too, is he sealed in at the syntactical level. In this sense, the ultimate failure of John the Baptist's speaking (of which Gamaliel's is a part) is prepared for from the very outset, when Gamaliel declares himself to be crushed under his own speech from that point. In such conditions he is evidently unable to impose his discourse on others: *he* is quite unable to utter calumnies. But by avoiding such imposition, he risks being unable to speak at all.

It is, of course, well known that the image of poison trickled into the ear had become a more-or-less general symbol of the Fall of Man. While humanity had been created by the divine logos, it had fallen through the speech of the devil. One may say that although the division of tongues did not occur until Babel, the multiplication of languages had been made possible from the time of Eden itself. In effect the division marks nothing else but the individual given up to his own discourse. The *I* is speaking instead of God. Such a notion implies the possibility, even the necessity, that this *I* can impose itself, it implies a constant attempt to reduce the other's discourse to *my own.* That is the sense of this poison:

> Le péché, qui dans les os
> Du serpent couvoit enclos,
> Se glissa par une pomme
> Dans le crédule cerveau
> D'Ève, épreinte de nouveau
> Des costes du premier homme.
>   Si tost ce poison ne fut
> Dedans son oreille chut
> Qu'il s'épandit en son âme,
> Et qu'Adam, qui le sentit,
> Aussi tost se repentit
> De la faute de sa femme.[18]

[Sin, which in the bones of the serpent lay concealed, slipped by means of an apple into the credulous mind of Eve, new created from the ribs of the first man. No sooner had this poison fallen into her ear than it spread throughout her soul, and then Adam, who felt it, straightway repented the fault of his wife.]

The Fall is the mark of the other's utterance, which has taken over "my will," which has replaced *my* place as enunciating subject within my own discourse. In that sense the Fall is an essential fact of all socialized discourse, because such discourse can never be entirely within *my* possession. Gamaliel (and John) see this as making of language an essential calumny and tend to fall into the opposite extreme, which is never to escape from the order of discourse itself. While Malchus and Herod will try to seize hold of John in their discourse—to make of him simply the predicate of that discourse—Gamaliel, at least, cannot get to the point of situating "himself" in discourse as enunciating subject.

This opposition of the two extremes suggests that some kind of compromise would be necessary, that some such concept as that of a "discursive contract" will have to be worked out. Such a concept will not be possible for a long time: it is a task carried forward most particularly by the logicians of Port-Royal and by Locke. The means will eventually be found to make room for the "individual" enunciating subject within a socialized discourse of referential truth. (I have given some indication of this in *Logics of Literature*.) Until this is achieved the implacable confrontation of the two extremes represented in *Baptistes* by Malchus and Gamaliel, by calumny on the one hand and by the impossibility of speaking oneself as the subject of enunciation on the other, is an integral part of the tragic of discourse. In Gamaliel discourse cannot utter meaning because it contains no definite mark of the speaker who would grasp it; in Malchus discourse can only utter the meaning invented for it by the mark of the enunciating subject.

Thus the tragic that is of language itself has straightaway become the principal line of the play, the soul of its action. It is clearly presented here in a use of language (Buchanan's) fully conscious of itself and its means. The syntactic uneasiness at which we have glanced, the metaphoric claustrophobia, is soon transposed into the dialogue when, in the very next scene, a conversation takes place between Herod and his queen in which she calumniates John the Baptist. Here the constraints of the single sentence are carried over into a wider field.

When John enters, Herod dismisses his wife and tells the Baptist how much he is hated by the queen, the people, the priests, and the nobles. He accuses him of a series of faults of which not a single one is other than a certain use of language, of speech: which should not surprise us, since we are clearly dealing here with the priests' calumnies. John, asserts the king, insults "omnes ordines" in his public preaching, he deceives the masses who are unfamiliar with the ancient laws; he is spreading a new dogma, he is overthrowing the state and its peace through his speaking; he instructs the army to disobey its orders, promises "nova regna" to the crowd and vows to free them from the foreign yoke, encourages them to "spe . . . vana," prevents the nation from settling down by stirring up the people against the Romans, has been accusing Herod of an incestuous marriage, is inciting to revolt, and has been trying to abolish the ancient rites. Quite a lot for one man. And the king recognizes that the whole affair is a matter of words, for he says that he is willing to listen to John's justification for all this. If these accusations had any reality outside discourse they would be unanswerable. Nor is it just anyone who makes them: it is the state itself, in the person of the king.

As in Gamaliel's statement which I have just examined, it is as though the sign had here been freed from all bond, whether artificial or essential, with any exteriority whatsoever. The sign represents only itself, it "exteriorizes" itself. Instead of any referent in phenomena or worldly events it accumulates (here as in Gamaliel's proposition) a series of homologous formulae whose "sense" is the accumulation itself. We are dealing here with something utterly different from the imposition of the order of discourse upon some materiality exterior to, and different from, that order. As in Montaigne's *Essays* the sign is self-representative: if, in the case of Montaigne, the "reality" of the self is nothing other than the very activity of writing ("Je suis moy-mesme la matière de mon livre"; "Je peints le passage"), in *Baptistes* that same "reality" is the production of discourse. And this discourse seeks no other confirmation of the real (such as would be referential meaning, truth) than such as is provided, produced by its own process: the character called "John the Baptist" has no reality outside the conflict of speeches, just as his "crimes" *exist* only because the king *names* them. Neither now nor later will there be any attempt to "justify" these accusations by means of some interpretation foreign to language itself. What is necessary, then, if the preacher is to continue to "live," is to maintain the series of speeches. If the speeches opposing balance out the speeches supporting, he will live. If not, he will disappear.

Clearly a crime characterized only by words can be expiated in the same fashion, and the congratulations of the chorus when Herod asks for John's verbal response indicate that the chorus is as well aware of this as anyone. However, the affair will not be so easily laid to rest. After a long speech in which the Baptist replies in turn to each accusation (thus maintaining symmetrically, at this level, the equilibrium), Herod decides to show his teeth. The chorus responds by imploring God's help.

This entire demonstration falls naturally into an order: the Queen's calumny and her efforts to move the king, the latter's accusation against John, followed by John's refutation. The queen's attempt is then balanced by her husband's monologue and the decision that ensues from it. From the rhetorical point of view the two middle terms (Herod's accusation against John and its refutation) cancel each other out: the queen's calumny thus remains alone, and will convince the king. The episode is closed by the chorus's prayer—another rhetorical formula, which satisfies the episode's equilibrium by a persuasive effort opposed to that of the queen, which opened the episode. This last effort, however, must remain without effect upon the opponents within the play because it appeals to a term exterior to its equation: a divine, instead of a human, discourse. The prayer nonetheless suffices to leave an *impression* (upon the spectator/reader) that the debate remains equal.

The equilibrium is maintained during the third episode, which begins with the lamentations of Malchus. He feels isolated and hated by the people, because he alone has dared raise a voice against John. Following the advice of Gamaliel, he now says he is willing to seek reconciliation, if possible; if not, he will seek the preacher's death. At this point John himself appears, in the midst of one of his speeches to the throng. When he sees Malchus he launches into a long and vehement accusation against him. There follows a dispute in stichomythia between the two adversaries that concludes, after John's departure, with a series of threats shrieked by the priest, beside himself with rage.

Once again, if one excepts the general commentary of the chorus
which bears on hypocrites—and which lies outside the principal conflict—we have the appearance of an equilibrium. John's speech and
the threats of Malchus situated on either side of the central dispute
cancel one another out, while the latter's monologue of the beginning
leans toward reconciliation: yet this monologue, as we have seen,
contains a scarcely veiled threat. And once again, the chorus's generalizing reflection upon hypocrisy sets itself into a different discursive context from that of the conflict between John and Malchus.

The fourth episode serves only to reveal the final dissolution of
any and all balance: in effect we see only the opposition to the
preacher. Malchus complains of Herod's hesitation and convinces
the queen that she must persuade the king to kill the dangerous
individual, counseling her to use a strategem if necessary. The praises
that the chorus thunders out in the Baptist's favor have no effect
upon this upset equilibrium, for they lead us, as before, into a quite
different discursive space. They here introduce the next episode in
which the chorus submits to God after John has shown that death
represents only a natural term of life and entrance into eternal life.
The chorus's farewell and John's description of the eternal happiness
of the innocents clearly represents a victory for calumny (just as the
discussion itself represents a victory for John at a different level, in
a different discourse, outside the play—the divine). It is not only at
the level of the signified, as might appear from what we have just
said, that this change occurs: John and the chorus go off into prayers,
into a sort of *te deum*; they perform a kind of Mass that emphasizes
by the change of speech formulae that a different class of discourse
altogether is being spoken. We are immediately shown the way of
Malchus's victory.

Under pressure from the queen, Herod has promised to reward his
daughter for her dances. She, following her mother's direction, will
demand the head of John the Baptist. Confronted with this fait
accompli, the king tries to wriggle out of it. The queen reminds him
that it is question of a promise, which binds him (pp. 248–49). He
affirms that he is resolved to carry out this promise, if he must, but
nonetheless deeply regrets this *vow* which makes him at once guilty
and impotent:

> Sicne oportuit
> Jurasse temere? sic puellae me meam
> Obstringere fidem?   [p. 249, 1246–48]

[How had I the temerity as to make such an oath? To bind my
faith thus to a girl?]

The equilibrium has changed, therefore, from the moment when
the speech that is hostile to John's party no longer encounters opposition but, on the contrary, receives a docile response or flat refusal to
become engaged in such a conflict. The play can then conclude with
an epilogue in which the victim's death is announced and which thus
accomplishes the promise of the prologue to show the fatal effects
of calumny. In spite of this equilibrium of the external form of the
play, we should note that its first part (the proposition concerning
calumny and its demonstration through a series of *disputationes*) is
almost twice as long as its second (the resolution and final proof).
Since the demonstration of calumny's efficacity is concluded from
the fourth episode, there remains only to show its results. To these
results we may well apply the fine sentence written some few decades
later by Ben Jonson, a writer who shared many of these preoccupations: "For a lying mouth is a stinking pit, and murthers with the
contagion it venteth."[19]

These discursive disputes, characteristic of all levels of the play,
take the place of purely spectacular action. Each sentence, each
episode, each series of episodes, the whole play accords with a particular equilibrium to produce a conclusion decided from the beginning. "The plays are not just a series of 'set pieces'; each play, in
itself, is a kind of mammoth 'set piece' in which diverse elements
must balance," Richard Griffiths has written of Montchrestien's
theatre.[20] The same applies to the plays of George Buchanan. From
a rhetorical point of view, however, victory remains in doubt until
the retreat of the forces of John the Baptist: the opposition of the
conflicting speeches can last only so long as they remain equal.
Baptistes functions then by virtue of an opposition *in* discourse. As
in the case of Montaigne, discourse cannot make contact with phe-
nomenon or event, all effort in such a direction is bound for failure,

as we saw in the case of Gamaliel. The simple fact of speaking seems to be all that can take the place of any referentiality.

Baptistes is, in that sense, nothing but "text," it has no "meaning" beyond that. For that very reason, however, in the conditions of a theatrical situation where the spectators' interests coincide with those of the author and the actor, the problems of a discourse blocked in upon itself by its very nature would have been felt the more deeply by such spectators: what is *performed within Baptistes* is the difficulty, perhaps for the present the impossibility, that is the discursive expression of anything other than discourse. Such a difficulty is not only an impediment to any kind of *knowledge* whatsoever: it would also place an almost insuperable obstacle before all social exchange and any form of communication. That is why, while it can be *discussed* in other types of discourse, it can only be actually *played out* in some such discourse as that of tragedy. That, it seems to us, is what *Baptistes* does.

Even there, however, there is one "privileged" kind of utterance able to make all discourse impossible, leading directly to silence: if Gamaliel and John continue to battle against the discourse of the opposition, it is because their battle is not really rendered useless until the moment when the promise is made. From that moment all saying is sealed in the past. For the promise, the vow, can only make room for *what has already been said.* Any subsequent process is impossible. No doubt that is why John switches into another class of discourse altogether. That is the only "solution" remaining open to him; but in doing so, he yields the other to Malchus and the queen. *The vow thus presents the death of discourse*—the only possible boundary, an absolute one, to this discourse whose continuation would present, in turn, the only possible kind of *being.* The vow *necessarily* draws after it the death of John. In that sense, dying and ceasing to speak are the same thing.

Buchanan's second original play responds like a kind of challenge to his first. Indeed, it seems quite clear that this conclusion of *Baptistes* provided its author with the point of departure for his new play, which he entitled *Jephthes sive votum (Jephtha, or the Vow).* This play was published before *Baptistes*, but it was written second.

The closed domain of the vow is spread out before the listener, who is confronted with an impression of the immobile and the ineluctible from the very first verses of *Jephthes*: "Magni tonantis huc minister aliger, / Coeli relicto" ("I am the winged messenger of the great Thunderer, come from the heavens" [p. 181, 1–2]). This appeal to a mass of established formulae, which leave only a restricted and well-defined series of choices in the Latin (and Greek) theatre, to an impression of closure, forces the spectator/reader directly into the restricted field offered by language, according to what we saw in *Baptistes*, to all subjects of enunciation.[21] From the start, then, the speakers of the plays are situated within the restrictions of a particular discursive space.

The angel informs us that although the Israelites have been brought back to their God through the suffering He had imposed upon them, He has been obliged (following His custom) to send them a man of courage, Jephtha, so that they should not be inclined to attribute their forthcoming victory in war to their own devices: for each time He relaxes his vigil the Israelites return to false gods. Unlike the Greeks, if we follow the suggestions of Aeschylus in *The Persians*,[22] the Jews have sufficient hubris to believe that such a victory could be gained through their own strength. The angel goes on to add that in order to prevent Jephtha, in turn, from becoming too prideful, he will himself receive injury:

> Etenim arma in hostes perfidos quum sumeret,
> Belli secundus si daretur exitus,
> Quodcunque primum se obviam ferret sibi,
> Promisit aris se daturum victimam.   [p. 182, 56–59]

> [For when he took up arms against the faithless foe, he promised that if a favorable outcome of the war were granted him, he would give as a victim on the altar whatever he should meet with first (upon his return).]

It will be his own daughter whom he meets. Immediately after saying this, the angel announces the arrival of this eventual victim on stage accompanied by her mother, Storgé, who is troubled by a dream that appears to concern Iphis: "haeret vox in ipsis faucibus, / Nec ora verbis

pervium praebent iter" ("My voice sticks in my throat, nor do my
lips present an unobstructed passage for my words" [p. 183, 74–
75]).

All speech is and will remain futile, confronted as it is with Jephtha's vow which forms an absolute boundary of discourse and forbids any dispute. (In theological discussion of Buchanan's time, it
was the absolute nature of the vow that provoked argument as to
its legitimacy, linked, as the question could easily be, to the matter
of free will.) Everything upon which the vow can bear here appears
beneath the sign of a *barrier* ("Quodcunque primum se obviam ferret
sibi"; "Nec ora verbis pervium praebent iter"). From her own point
of view it is perfectly logical for Iphis (who has not yet spoken, and
so does not "know" this barrier) to suggest to her mother that the
means to escape such gloominess is to utter a few joyful words. That
suggestion appears to propose that a confrontation of two kinds of
discourse is possible, similar to what we saw occur between Gamaliel
and Malchus, between Herod and John. In this case, though, Jephtha's
vow made at the outset (through the angel), like Herod's promise at
the end, has already seized hold of the others' discourse (any discourse, that is, that might have been capable of responding to it). All
speech is blocked; and that fact provokes Storgé to a cry of despair:

> IPHIS: Quin ominare cara mater laetius,
> Vanasque causas abjice aegritudinis:
> Et ista mentis turbidas ludibria
> Secura sperne, spretaque obliviscere.
> STO.: Utinam liceret!   [p. 183, 84–88]
>
> [IPHIS: Dear mother, why do you not more joyfully cast off fore-
> bodings and vain causes of suffering: and free from care
> put afar off these mockeries of a disturbed mind, forget
> these things that should be scorned.
> STO.: Alas, would that I could!]

This scene affirms the inevitability of the outcome of the play in
the accomplishment of the vow. In a sense, therefore, the play is
"finished" as soon as it is begun: but only if one insists on finding
in all theatre some process, "psychological" or other, leading from

a given situation to a later and different one. This theatre is based in a circular movement of language whose interest focuses upon the discursive means at the disposal of the subject of enunciation: its chief concern is not story, not some lively progress of narration. Indeed, because any discussion is "forbidden," we might well expect the play to be composed of epic and lyric elements even more developed than in *Baptistes*. And such is the case. The stanzas given to the chorus are more extensive, the laments of the three principal speakers are almost continuous, we listen to Storgé's dream, to two long speeches by a messenger who first announces the Jewish victory and then relates the death of Iphis, to two long discussions upon the nature of the vow.

The scene in which the messenger presents his first speech straightaway shows us the only means remaining that are capable of at once marking the inevitable closure of discourse and permitting the continuation of speech. Victory, he cries, is ours:

> Nempe istud ipsum missus huc sum ut nunciem.
> Fusis, fugatis hostibus, victoria,
> Re, laude parta, salvus est exercitus.
> Haec summa.   [p. 186, 229–32]

> [Truly am I sent to this place to report that the enemy has been put to flight and scattered afar, that victory, the battle, and glory have been won, our army is safe. Our affairs are at their height.]

These last words do not lack irony. Further, the accomplishment of the vow will be made possible just because the chorus joyfully urges Iphis to make herself beautiful and greet her father. The irony is thereby further emphasized. It is prolonged throughout the next scene, in which Jephtha, alone, thanks God and gives praise to Him:

> Tuis tremendus, & severus hostibus,
> Tuis amicis lenis & salutifer,
> Irae timendae, sed tamen placabilis,
> Amore fervens idem, & irritabilis. . . .   [p. 190, 434–37]

> [Terrible and stern to Your enemies, mild and benevolent to Your friends, of anger fearful, but nonetheless easily placated, easily enraged and at the same time warm with love. . . .]

This expression of gratitude is followed immediately by his renewal of the vow, succeeded by his daughter's entrance. Jephtha turns away from her, avoiding her anguished questions with ambiguous answers. She cannot understand why he should act in this way, she complains, but exhorts her father to send up prayers to God even in prosperity and to accomplish his vows. That is really twisting the knife, and serves to emphasize again that any possibility of a real communication (an *exchange* of speech) has been removed by the utterance of the vow. This "nondialogue" continues in the same vein. It is impossible not to feel the cruelty beginning to be provoked by this irony, permanently settled within discourse. One might mention further the beginning of a conversation between Symmache and Jephtha (p. 194) in which the former blames the general for his grief, asserting that he should rather praise God for His generosity than lament. The technique is continuous.

The irony that fills the play, added to the evidence of Storgé's dream and the vow's repetition, underlines the absolute and insurmountable closure of discourse. Two speakers seek to prevent the vow's accomplishment (Symmache and the priest, who undertakes a long and tightly organized, somewhat casuistic, dialogue with Jephtha), but we have already seen how the first expression of the vow has served to interdict any dispute that might be carried on at the same level. The priest's discussion of the fifth episode is obliged to remain quite abstract, almost as though it were not dealing at all with a most pressing and concrete case. That very abstraction is criticized by Lebègue, for whom the outcome is by no means assured. [23]

But I suggest that the conclusion is not in doubt. The generalized discussions upon the nature of a vow, like the passages referred to by Lebègue as "digressions antipapistes," clearly belong to another discourse (just as did the commentaries of the chorus in *Baptistes*), and thus remain foreign to the precise case proposed in *Jephthes*. Such passages do not seek to influence the outcome; by their very ineffectiveness as "dialogue," they serve to confirm the inevitable nature of the barrier, of what has *already been said*.

Unlike *Baptistes*, in which an exchange of discourse is possible, in *Jephthes* the vow is announced in the prologue and shuts off all subsequent process. That this settles once and for all the nature of the play does not seem to me a matter for doubt. Storgé's dream emphasizes the barrier, the continuous irony underscores it yet further; such discussions as there are must always return to this beginning. In *Baptistes*, until the moment when the promise is made, until the moment when John switches his discourse, so to speak, everything could change: there are two equal discourses opposed to one another, that of Malchus and that of John himself. Here is only one, invested with all the value of incontrovertible *fact*, coined by the *other*, against which the victims' speech ceaselessly and futilely returns. (The victims are plural because not only Iphis but every other speaker is constrained by the vow.)

In a way, then, we might say that the "system" of tragedy (or a part of it) has been well and truly turned against itself. The dialogue between protagonist and chorus, for example, though it clearly recalls the Greek "dialectic," more immediately turns in upon itself. What is in question between Gamaliel and the chorus is the very possibility of dialogue: blocked at every level, the speech of John the Baptist's party appears to indicate the individual's effort to speak *himself* to the other and to predicate that other, without denying himself and without falsifying that other (the first, because he must use a discourse that is not his own, the second, because he might seek to use a discourse entirely his own—a calumny). That effort appears as a negation of speech, to the extent that speech always appears as a lie, to the extent that speech is always a generalization of the particular utterance (Locke's problem, later, of the conflict between language as private expression and as public communication). John's effort will be vanquished by that discourse which fully accepts its public character, though it "misuses" it: that of Herod and Malchus—or the vow.

In Buchanan's tragedies the vow thus becomes the only possible *public* means of performing an expression of the enunciating subject as an act of will. It is the only possible (and absolute) means of imposing the *I* of discourse, permanently as it were. It marks the installing of an "irreducible subjectivity" which makes all subsequent progression "strictly impossible."[24] There lies the "tragic" of which we have been speaking all this time. On the one hand the movement

of discourse denies any attempt to provide a meaning lying outside
the particular instance of discourse that may be seized at any given
moment, as it also prevents the subject of enunciation from situating
itself other than as the (doubtful) subject of that fleeting moment
of discourse, and thus prevents the grasping of a kind of zero point
of consciousness. On the other hand, any positive attempt to fix
such an *I* leads either to silence and "death" of the subject itself (in
the case of John, who leaves the discursive space in which he had
been battling), or to the interdiction of discourse altogether (in the
case of Jephtha: all movement being utterly aborted). That is no
doubt the reason a Montaigne cannot stop writing and rewriting.
Like John the Baptist in Buchanan's play, he could well say: "Scribo
(dico), ergo sum." Or rather, no doubt, since the space marked by
the *ergo* is not yet there: "Scribo sum."[25]

Since Montaigne offers in some ways what is almost a commentary
on Buchanan's plays as we have been looking at them, it will be
worthwhile to take a glance at this "exegesis." The *I* expressed in
the *Essays* marks little more than the process of a discursive syntax.
The only "knowledge" (consciousness?) this *I* can be said to possess
is that of its own writing. The enunciating subject defines itself as
an act of writing:

> La constance mesme n'est autre chose qu'un branle plus languis-
> sant. Je ne puis asseurer mon objet. Il va trouble et chancelant,
> d'une yvresse naturelle. Je le prens en ce point, comme il est, en
> l'instant que je m'amuse à luy. Je ne peints pas l'estre. Je peints
> le passage: non un passage d'aage en autre, ou, comme dict le
> peuple, de sept en sept ans, mais de jour en jour, de minute en
> minute. . . . Je pourray tantost changer, non de fortune seule-
> ment, mais aussi d'intention. . . . soit que je sois autre moymesme,
> soit que je saisisse les subjects par autres circonstances et con-
> siderations.[26]

> [Stability itself is nothing but a more languid motion. I cannot
> keep my object still. It goes along befuddled and staggering, with
> a natural drunkenness. I take it in this condition, just as it is at
> the moment I give my attention to it. I do not portray being: I
> portray passing. Not the passing from one age to another, or, as
> the people say, from seven years to seven years, but from day to

day, from minute to minute. . . . I may presently change, not
only by chance, but also by intention. . . . whether I am different
myself, or whether I take hold of my subjects in different circumstances and aspects.]

The sign here has value (discourse itself) not through what it might
be taken as meaning, for there is no single and set meaning, but
through the very process of signifying. It has no referent beyond
itself, but it contains—within itself so to speak, by the very fact of
its own existence—sufficient "certainty" that the process of enunciation may become the definition of the subject. It is no doubt the
certainty of a tautology. The *I* is defined (here) by its graphic form:
it is a *passage,* a *narration,* subject of its own writing, a kind of recording. And there is the reason Montaigne must turn away from the
exterior world in order to hollow out his "private existence." He
does not—cannot—seek to define man in some relation with a material
world, but only in terms of his own discourse, *as a function of that
discourse*: "Les autres forment l'homme; je le récite et en represente
un particular bien mal formé" ("Others form man; I tell of him, and
portray a particular one, very ill-formed" [p. 782; Frame trans.,
p. 610]). Or again: "Icy, nous allons conformement et tout d'un
trein, mon livre et moy" ("In this case we go hand in hand and at the
same pace, my book and I" [p. 783; Frame trans., pp. 611–12]).

The anguished ambiguity of Rabelais's *Tiers Livre*, wandering into
a gulf of *non*-sense, of non-significance, has disappeared. It has been
replaced by the ideal, or at least the process, of a tautological significance: "I signify I." Repentance (to take the essay from which
we have been quoting) is the sign of a *difference*, an absence, a lack
of coincidence between a sign and something it was supposed or
intended to signify, something *other* that a proposition already
stated "ought" to have said. Just as calumny cannot be avoided,
so too repentance would be a necessary mark of all socialized language: for a gap will always be found between (private) expression
and (public) comprehension. The *Essays* seek to avoid this difference
by detaching themselves from an exterior, by avoiding all attempt
at a socialization of discourse. It is later criticism that has claimed
that in making a study of himself Montaigne is claiming, or intending,
to make a study of all mankind. The writer marked in the text of

the *Essays* never expresses anything of the kind: on the contrary, the text constantly commiserates with its reader for obliging him to remain always with the *I* of the text.

It is thus that Montaigne responds to the impossibility that marks the tragic in Buchanan's tragedies: the socialization of discourse, the attempt to provide it with some kind of reference outside discourse that would permit the speaker to participate in a discourse shared with others, is precisely the point where the discourse is blocked because it finds it can only say *itself*. And if, on the contrary, the speaker allows that discourse to be imposed as the *will* of some other, then indeed it is death—as in the cases of John the Baptist and Iphis, frozen by Herod's promise and Jephtha's vow. A speaker can discover some meaning only to the extent that what he speaks can be grasped by some interlocutor. Once thus grasped, however, it is the end: order is imposed, but it is always an order that belongs to someone else. In that sense, John's opting for a divine order is nothing other than an escape from a human dilemma. In *Baptistes* two other equally unattractive alternatives are offered: Gamaliel's initial descent into a domain of "nonmeaning," Malchus's and the queen's choice of calumny. It would appear that the only other alternative to an absence of meaning or an imposition of silence is, for the moment, to continue to speak.

The difference between a socialized sign and its signified (here, the supposed real intention of the individual who is making the utterance) indicates a trap from which it is the whole aim of the *Essays* to escape—and to show that they have so escaped. That difference is mark of a lie simple to accept and impose. In one sense, according to the speaker (writer) of the *Essays*, any sign at all that has been consecrated by social discourse occupies the same boundary with regard to *my* discourse as does the vow or promise. Only, because that boundary comes not from my discourse but from outside, as part of a more generalized system, it blocks only that part of my discourse which preceded its entrance: it does not seal my discourse in itself (*I* can go on), but only whatever of it is transferred into the domain of the social. That is the very question that is dealt with by the eighth essay of the first book, "That intention is judge of our actions."

A verbal commitment is the sign of an act of will; it is indeed the only sign for society of such an act of will. The discourse that reveals the intention *is* the intention, says the writer of the *Essays* in a not wholly astonishing prefiguration of the Austinian concept of "performative." "Il n'y a rien en bon escient en nostre puissance que la volonté" ("There is nothing really in our power but will" [p. 32, Frame trans. p. 20]), it is written in the essay: but that *volonté* can only be its expression. The fact that discourse is both public and private permits this *volonté* to be hidden (it is a part of *my* discourse), precisely because of the distance that lies between the discourse of the *I* and that of others (*we* or, better still perhaps, *they*). We can communicate only by adopting others' discourse but, unless we could make this discourse entirely and essentially our own (which is impossible), it must necessarily falsify the individual, betray the "private." The intention contained in *my* discourse may therefore not be the same when it is caught up in others'. To make public one's discourse, to socialize it, is to give it a referentiality over which one no longer has control: on the contrary, it controls its own speaker. And that is the source of Gamaliel's difficulty when he tries to control that speech which is that of the priests. That, too, explains the constant repetition, by everybody, of Jephtha's vow: it has taken over all *saying*. And yet if an intention is always and only coeval with its expression, then it can never be merely a part of private discourse: an act of will can then be said to have existence only in the exchange of socialized discourse. The expression of intention is the essential point of contact between my and others' discourse.

It is just that point which Montaigne emphasizes in the essay on intention. Whereas the "Comte d'Aiguemond [tenait] son âme et volonté endebtée à sa promesse" ("the Count of Egmont, consider(ed) his will and soul in debt to his promise"), the king of England, who had promised not to kill the duke of Suffolk, "faillant à sa parole par son intention, ne se peut excuser pour avoir retardé jusques apres sa mort l'execution de sa desloyauté" ("in intentionally breaking his word, cannot be excused merely on the grounds that he delayed the execution of his dishonest plan until after his [own] death" [p. 32; Frame trans., p. 20]). Actions, Montaigne is arguing, can only be judged in accordance with the discourse to which they correspond, and not to the contrary. If society is to function at all, discourse (written or spoken) must be taken as a sign. The promise is here taken as an exemplary form of such a sign. It must coincide with, it must *be* the will of the individual if the needs of a just exchange are to be met, and if the only kind of human knowledge possible is to be achieved. The lack of coincidence in the king's discourse between sign (the promise) and what it signifies (an intention opposite to the expressed commitment) is criticized because it destroys the exchange. At the same time it renders the king's own discourse a nonsense, for it fails at the very point of confirmation: its contact with that of others.

What Montaigne would appear to be appealing for here, then, is some kind of contract between the individual and the social, such that neither suffers. This will not be achieved for more than a century. Its eventual accomplishment will be due in part to what tragedy will have performed. For the moment, Buchanan shows us all that is "tragic" in this appeal; Montaigne reveals that it is utopian: in everyday reality the conflict is used for betrayal, in the *Essays* the difficulty is avoided.

In fact, what permits the writer to continue with the *Essays* is the inversion of the equation suggested before. Instead of bringing the individual and the social to a bond of equals, the exterior must *become* the interior. If "I" cannot be said except within the discourse of which that *I* is an instance, then whatever is predicated within that same discourse must be elements, and *only* elements, of *that* discourse:

> Les choses, à part elles, ont peut estre leurs poids et mesures et conditions; mais au dedans, en nous, elle [l'âme] les leur taille comme elle l'entend . . . chacune est Royne en son estat. Pourquoy ne prenons plus excuse des externes qualitez des choses: c'est à nous à nous en rendre compte.[27]

> [Things in themselves may have their own weights and measures and qualities; but once inside, within us, she (the soul) allots them their qualities as she sees fit . . . each one is queen in her realm. Wherefore let us no longer make the external qualities of things our excuse; it is up to us to reckon them as we will.]

Any communication that might claim to lead toward objective and referential knowledge is out of the question. This exterior which is cut to the measure of *my* discourse cannot be made a part of any public exterior, save only factitiously. The writing (always of the "self") can place in the public domain only its own form; which may be confused with the social. Malchus's deception is thus *necessary*; so too are the stutterings of Gamaliel. They present us with two sides of the same coin.

   "Montaigne will say for example that not only is the word inadequate to the thing, but that it is also ambiguous. . . . What circulates continuously in the word is the incessant transformation of intellectual life."[28] The critique of knowledge, of social exchange, of consciousness itself, always returns to the words that have the appearance of expressing such conceptual predicates:

> Oyez dire metonomie, metaphore, allegorie et autres tels noms de la grammaire, semble-t-il pas qu'on signifie quelque forme de langage rare et pellegrin? Ce sont titres qui touchent le babil de vostre chambriere.[29]

> [When you hear people talk about metonomy, metaphor, allegory, and other such names in grammar, doesn't it seem that they mean some rare and exotic form of language? They are terms that apply to the babble of your chambermaid.]

If the meaning of writing is writing, and if that writing is yet the only pathway to whatever knowledge we may have and the only form such knowledge may take, then it is clear that the meaning and the activity of discourse itself are one and the same thing: a very different idea of "knowledge" from our own.

   Montaigne (or, at least, the expressed writer of the *Essays*) denies the availability of any knowledge of phenomena beyond our own discursive process itself:

> Il y a des autheurs desquels la fin c'est dire les evenements. La mienne, si j'y sçavoye advenir, seroit dire sur ce qui peut advenir. Il est justement permis aux escholes de supposer des similitudes, quant ils n'en ont point.

[There are authors whose end is to tell what has happened. Mine, if I could attain it, would be to talk about what can happen. The schools are justly permitted to suppose similitudes when they have none at hand.]

Nor is there any different kind of knowledge open to experience: "Les discours sont à moy, et se tienent par la preuve de la raison, non de l'experience" ("The reflections [*discours*] are my own, and depend on the proofs of reason, not of experience").[30]

This is a hierarchy that will be maintained in "De l'experience," where he speaks of such experience as "un moyen plus foible et moins digne" than reason (p. 1041). The mind is like an empty box awaiting the fullness of discourse:

Je ne pense point qu'il y ait tant de malheur en nous comme il y a de vanité, ny tant de malice comme de sotise; nous ne sommes pas si pleins de mal comme d'inanité; nous ne sommes pas si miserables comme nous sommes viles. [31]

[I do not think there is as much unhappiness in us as vanity, nor as much malice as stupidity. We are not so full of evil as inanity; we are not as wretched as we are worthless.]

The passing of the pen thus becomes the only consciousness possible, and whose sole foundation can be but the *I* that composes its passage. Beyond that is nothing that can signify "*for me.*" Others' discourse becomes a false wisdom, a false wealth ("valeur," as Motaigne writes), an obligatory lie and calumny. "Their" discourse differs always from "me": whence the source of his critique of the notion of plagiarism, of his defense of his innumerable quotations ("Je ne dis les autres, sinon pour d'autant plus me dire" ["I do not speak the minds of others except to speak my own mind better"]),[32] and so on. Discourse is only dangerous when it attempts to approach communication—then it is fatal.

There, clearly, we come back to Buchanan, whose plays themselves found a particular process of exchange—and thus contradict, by composing such an order, the very undermining of the possibility of order they themselves perform. In this they carry out the role of tragedy as I explored it in chapter 1. The plays were written for students, to be studied, commented upon, glossed, and performed by them: the main "justification" for their existence is the role played in humanist teaching.[33]

At this period, it was above all a question of creating a language, of inventing a new kind of thinking. The ultimate hope of these educators was to achieve that use of language which was indeed to be characterized not much later (by such as Estienne, Pasquier, and so on) as particularly subtle, supple, "praecellent," as able to carry or contain new ideas in such a way as to give way to the "expressive needs" of such ideas, to give the impression of effacing itself before them, of being transparent to the interplay of human "sensitivity" and its perception of the world, its visualization of objects. The vow and the promise confront us with the apparent impossibility of such an achievement. In Buchanan, as in Montaigne, we are brought face to face with a permanent absence of such meaningfulness, situated in the "tragic" space of nonorder, placed before language as some kind of monolithic obstacle to expression and communication, the denial of the hopes of later humanists.

This, it seems to me, explains the choice of subject and the manner of composition of Buchanan's two original tragedies. Their theme of the power of language, of a discourse that creates its own exigencies, is central to the preoccupations of this moment within the Renaissance: an often anguished interrogation of its own premises. The very choice of the vow as the end of one of these plays and the beginning of the other reflects an awareness of writing in Latin for a French public (and more generally a European one), at a moment when the vulgar tongues were beginning to win their victory over the use of Latin. I would suggest that the success of the plays (which was considerable at the time)[34] is due largely to such awareness and to the consequent coherence we have seen of all levels of the play, but above all to their questioning of *their very medium of communication*. It is in that sense that René Radouant was able to write, speaking of the situation in France, "that in this Latin form, it is in fact the future of French prose and of French eloquence that is being decided."[35] Clearly we must extend this statement to take in all the vulgar tongues.

The implicit criticism of the Scottish playwright is aimed first of all at Latin, incapable of "translating" a new and increasingly "precise" human view of the world. Worse, since this new view involved the disappearance of the individual human "sensibility" before the "reality" of the world being studied, Latin was, however familiar, a *foreign* language unable to be effaced in favor of what it claims to express. Thence, too, comes the questioning of stylistic rhetoric itself, here in the form of the vow, which has become goal rather than instrument. In the tragedies, however, the anguish of the speakers does not come from the Latin (how could it? It is, after all, *their* language). It comes from the fact that for them language in use, discourse, is *always* an obstacle, is *always* the mark of an absence of meaningfulness outside its own activity.

This critique of discourse, performed in the tragedies of Buchanan, is made formerly explicit in the *Essays* of Montaigne. Vow, calumny, promise, and lie, which are the only forms of a truly socialized discourse to appear in these plays and which are offered as exemplary of all speech. They are the bearers of a past closed to all change. What the writer of the *Essays* has in view, however, is *all* discourse of society in its relationship with private discourse. Calumny, fraud, and lies are the essence of any effort to fill that distance and that difference. The tragic in Buchanan is to be placed in an impossibility of communication, in the failure of an unequal struggle: John's discourse gives way before the given of the promise, Jephtha's (and everyone else's) is sealed in by the vow. For Montaigne the nature of language, and therefore of discourse, prevents the success of any communicating function and of any objective understanding, whether that be "knowledge" or "consciousness." What one might term the "social obligation" of John the Baptist in Buchanan's play (i.e., this need to communicate with a public) provokes of necessity the lying discourse of the opposition—but, in view of what we have seen played out in *Baptistes* can it not be said that his discourse (*any* discourse) is as much a "lie"? In Montaigne it is the resolute retreat of the subject to being simply the expression of the act of enunciation that permits writing to continue.

It is thus in the wake of these tragedies that much of the Renaissance as it draws toward its close discovers it own tragic: that of a discourse that blocks itself, of a discourse the limits of whose signifying possibilities are set by the imperatives of its own functioning. Such a constraint must be absolute: the system can "see" not at all beyond its own process of signifying. Nonetheless, as in ancient Greece, once placed within a discourse such as tragedy these constraints which would seem to make an ordered process of meaning impossible have been set into an order that overcomes them. For while the speakers of the plays cannot get beyond them, the spectators can: we can se the "effect" of yielding to them. Once performed *in* discourse, they have been exorcised. The tragic has been named.

Once the distinction has been made between society and the individual, once "their" discourses have been situated with regard to one another, then an ordered process of expression and communication become possible. What has been marked by Buchanan (and Montaigne) is the necessary "absence" at the center of any signifying system, such as language. What is shown is the hole within the sign and the questions it provokes: How can the "*I*" be other than the mere mark of enunciation? How can it become, for example, a "knower" and a "consciousness"?. At the same time it has traced out an emptiness "beyond" the sign: this last being marked by the search for a *real* referent. The place of the tragic would thus be the space interposed between the *cogito* and the *sum*, but a space that has not yet been spanned by the *ergo* (and whose interposition "closes up" such space). Once the *cogito* and the *sum* become interdependent, then there will no longer be any absence within discourse. That absence, then, would perhaps be nothing other than *madness* admitted at the very moment of the *cogito*, an essential and constant un-order in "thought," but which will be refused once continuity and process become the very definition of thinking: cogito *ergo* sum. [36]

It is thus that Derrida can affirm, in commenting upon Michel Foucault's remarks about the Cartesian *cogito*, that

> if the Socratic dialectic is reassuring, in the sense Foucault intends, it is because it has already expelled, excluded, objectified or, what is curiously the same thing, has assimilated to itself and mastered as one of its moments, "enveloped" the other of reason, and because it has tranquilized itself, reassured by a pre-Cartesian certainty, by a [*sophrosyne*], a wisdom, a reasonable prudence and good sense. [37]

The tragic, like madness, would be this central danger to all utterance of meaning. The Cartesian *cogito* will be our way of overcoming it definitively and formally. In the development of tragedy it will be overcome performatively.

Racine's attempt will be to *contain* the tragic as a kind of object, to exhaust the danger in discourse and reject it once and for all from civil society as something monstrous. And what marks the end of the development in question is that there there is a particular *bearer* of the tragic, a bearer who brings into the discourse of civil society the threat of a lack of order *from the outside*: whether it be the Cretan Phèdre, the Trojan Andromaque, the Palestinian Bérénice, the "étrangère partout" who is Eriphile. The threat is no longer *within* discourse. The bearer of the tragic in Racine confronts a *logos* that is already working: she does not, and cannot, make it in any essential and lasting manner. That is entirely different from the Greek situation; and if Derrida has been able to demonstrate to what an extent such an "absence" is inherent within the Platonic texts,[38] it is no less the case of tragedy: in the tragedies of Athens as in those of the early Renaissance the danger is a kind of hole in discourse, lying in wait for the subject of enunciation itself. The only escape would be to give up the struggle, to fly discourse entirely. That is the "solution" of John the Baptist: the solution of silence.

At the end of the period of development another solution will be possible, however: that of Racine. It is to surround and cast out the "absence," not to recognize it as an absence at all but as some thing (or someone), to treat it as a *presence*. By then the difficulty of making meaning, having been performed, will also have been named. It will have been hypostatized as a signified able to be located within a discursive order. Montaigne's fear of madness marks a retreat back into the permanence of a tragic such as we have seen in Buchanan: it would be a negation of the subject's *decision* to keep writing. The existence of tragedy says that that tragic has been enclosed. It has been made an element of the order of a text that *shows* how it functions, and that thereby indicates why it is necessary to exorcise this tragic element if there is to be possible an expression and communication of what we, like the humanists and their successors, call knowledge.

3 Jodelle's *Cléopâtre* and the Enchanted Circle

At the beginning of act 2 of Jodelle's *Cléopâtre*, Octavian enters for the first time.[1] He pronounces a series of "words" (as his companion, Agrippe, calls it) in which he seeks to situate himself, Antoine, the political state of affairs, and the general condition of mankind. To achieve such a situation, Octavian makes himself the master of all possible discourse:

> En la rondeur du Ciel environnee,
> A nul, je croy, telle faveur donnee
> Des Dieux fauteurs ne peult estre qu'à moy
> Car, outre encor que je suis maistre et Roy
> De tant de biens. . . .

> [In the surrounding roundness of the Sky to none, I believe, can such a favour be given by the favourable (or "mistaken") gods but to myself: because, even besides the fact that I am master and King of so much wealth. . . .]

Heaven, he goes on, "qui tout sous son empire enserre" ("which grasps everything in its power") has dispatched him from its vault so that he may wield heavenly power on earth, which is a "boule" of small weight for one such as he:

> Il semble ja que le Ciel vienne tendre
> Ses bras courbez pour en soy me reprendre,
> Et que la boule entre ses ronds enclose
> Pour un Cesar ne soit que peu de chose.   [2.109]

Christ's painting in the circle of discourse *v. Met. notes*

[Now it seems that the sky is holding out its curved arms to take me back into itself, and that the ball enclosed within its rounds (circles) is of little moment to a Caesar.]

Octavian, then, like Shakespeare's Richard II, expresses himself as the representative on earth of the gods: he is their microcosm, he says, and wishes to speak as their equal. He also announces himself here as the microcosm of the world itself. This metaphor will prove perhaps of most importance for this play. The world, a round ball, in the usual Renaissance cosmology, is surrounded by the "rondeur du Ciel," the whole forming a sphere containing man. Octavian expresses the mistaken belief that he can escape this sphere, to be not merely the representative of the gods but a god himself. The difficulty is that such a claim merely endows with a false reality what is but a matter of "mots": Octavian is in fact doing no more than laying claim to the control of discourse. And the ambiguity, the simple presumption, of such an attempt as this is itself expressed by a play on words: the dual meaning of the word *fauteurs* applied to the gods. On the one hand, the speaker can (and does) control his own discourse (it is "favorable" to the expression of its own enunciating subject): on the other hand, it is an error to presume to control that of others.[2] The circle, then, the "radiant vault" (1.99), as Cléopâtre calls it, marks the bounds of discourse, beyond which is only silence. Within these bounds is the life of expression, outside them is the death chosen by John the Baptist and imposed upon Iphis.

As far as these bounds are marked in the actual performance of Jodelle's play their limits are fixed by a single and all-powerful subject of enunciation: the presence of the king. *Cléopâtre* is correctly considered—in effect, if not in chronology—the first French tragedy. Its first performance took place in the Hôtel de Reims, the Paris residence of Charles de Guise, Cardinal de Reims. If, as is possible, the performance took place at the beginning of 1553, it did so before a royal Court that was celebrating the return to Paris of the victor of the siege of Metz, the duc de Guise, the cardinal's brother.[3] In such circumstances, the overwhelming fact is the presence of the king, Henri II, and Jodelle makes that presence central to his play.

In his prologue, the poet presents the king in a setting of appropriately

Roman mythology, makes him the mightiest of kings, ruler of the earth, the sea, the sky; the man responsible for having brought the Muses back to France (the present play, needless to say, being an outstanding example of the result). Indeed, adds the poet, he is not so much singing the praises of a king, "ains d'un Dieu dont la place / Se voit au Ciel ja monstrer son espace" ("as of a god whose place / is already designated in heaven" [Prologue, 93]). The entire play becomes the ordered sign of the king's majesty, at once due to him and representing his presence: the tragedy is an exemplary manifestation of the king's discourse. It is hardly necessary to emphasize the similarity of what is here expressed in the prologue and what we saw expressed by the speaker, Octavian, at the beginning of act 2. The play is a kind of discursive world (say both the poet and Octavian). The name of the king provides at once its center and its circumference. Literally present at the edge of the space in which the play is to be performed, the king is presented *by the play itself* as its point of reference *and* as its point of origin. He is its point of reference, because the tragedy is aimed at him:

> Ici les desirs et les flammes
> Des deux amants: d'Octavian aussi
> L'orgueil, l'audace et le journel souci
> De son trophee emprains tu sonderas,
> Et plus qu'à luy le tien egaleras;
> Veu qu'il faudra que ses successeurs mesmes
> Cedent pour toy aux volontez supremes,
> Qui ja le monde à ta couronne voüent,
> Et le commis de tous les Dieux t'avoüent. [Prologue, 94]

[Here the desires and burnings of the two lovers: and of Octavian, too the pride, courage and daily care for his victory set forth will you sound, and you will set yours even above his; seeing that even his successors will yield to the supreme will(s) in your favour who are already ordaining the world to your dominion, and confessing you the representative of all the Gods.]

He is at the point of origin, because it is "le triomphe et le nom" (Prologue, 93) of Henri that have caused this tragedy to be written.

It is the king who makes possible the ordering activity of this discourse:
he is the supreme (and only) master of speech.

The king can be such a master, obviously, only to the extent that
there *is* discourse: the tragedy is every bit as essential to the power
of the king as the king is to the order of tragedy. Language itself,
therefore, the *French* language of the play (as Jodelle insists), the
medium of the discourse, of the performance, will take its place as
of equal importance to its enunciator.[4] It will also be represented in
the metaphor of the circle. Jodelle, as he emphasizes the supremacy
of the king, does the same for the language of the play *and* for its
formal system, its "machinery" (taken over from the tragedy of
Antiquity):

> Nous t'apportons (ô bien petit hommage)
> Ce bien peu d'oeuvre ouvré de ton langage,
> Mai tel pourtant que ce langage tien,
> N'avoit jamais dérobbé ce grand bien
> Des autheurs vieux. C'est une Tragedie
> Qui d'une voix et plaintive et hardie
> Te represente un Romain Marc Antoine,
> Et Cleopatre, Egyptienne Roine. . . .   [Prologue, 94]

[We bring you (how small a homage) this work done in your language, meager indeed, but such nevertheless that this your language, had never before taken this great wealth of (from) the
ancient authors. It is a Tragedy which in a voice at once lamenting
and bold represents for you a Roman, Mark Antony, and Cleopatra, the Egyptian Queen.]

The amelioration of language and the reproduction of the system
of tragedy of which we wrote earlier are, in this way, both provided
with a single master of enunciation: the king himself. We will not
here go into the political implications of such discursive control,[5]
but it is clear that as a solution to the problems raised in *Baptistes*
and *Jephthes*, and "commented" by the *Essays* of Montaigne, this
can only be unsatisfactory for all other potential discursive subjects.
We will see how the speakers *in* the play twist and turn like caged
animals, in an always vain attempt to take control of a discourse

whose limits are marked by the presence of the king *outside* the
tragedy. Their activity is here *visibly* restricted to the space of the
particular discursive order of tragedy: presented to us as such.

For the poet language has all the ambiguity inherent in any medium of mediation; just as does man himself—and, more particularly,
man as king. Of that last ambiguity it is Octavian (after Antoine)
who will be the exemplar. However, though the play cannot speak
of the king "outside" it, the limits *shown* to be those of Octavian's
activity will be seen to be those of all enunciating subjects—however "supreme." Man is caught between the gods and the world
(between, we might say, the discourse in which he is predicated and
that whose subject he is); language plays between the expressing
and the expressed. As we saw it in Buchanan, discourse seeks somehow to utter the "individual's" presence at the same time as making
possible generalized communication and the social exchange. It is
at once container and contained. The nature of the "escape" that
will have to be made by the "successful" speakers of *Cléopâtre* will
underline this ambiguity essential to all discourse, which was so
much a preoccupation of the humanists.

Jodelle begins his narration at the very end of Plutarch's *Life of
Antony*, after the death of Antony himself and just before the last
visit made to Cleopatra by Octavian. In the prologue, the poet tells
us that Cléopâtre is planning to kill herself so as to avoid being borne
in triumph through Rome. Such a triumph would give Octavian the
entire victory he seeks, putting the cap on his success, and it is significant that the poet, having now indicated the failure of Octavian's
project, concludes his prologue by repeating the same praises of
Henri as those with which he began. The play is Henri's triumph, but
as I have suggested, it bears an element of warning.

The order of the prologue is, then, already circular: its conclusion
repeats its beginning. Within this prologue the circular order of the
play itself is put into motion. Clearly, the end can only repeat Cléopâtre's death. As in the case of Buchanan's tragedies, however, we
must be clear what is meant by the term *action*, for in the Renaissance it can only indicate the discursive process of a "plot line." In
Cléopâtre captive it is the progress followed by the spectator/reader
from the moment of Cléopâtre's discussion of her captive situation

to the relating of her death by Proculée in act 5. Death in this tragedy is not a visible physical act, but its statement. From the moment of its announcement in the prologue to that of its announcement in the last act, Cléopâtre's death indicates the limits of the discourse that is tragedy. Beginning and end are strictly identical, and it is within this circle that the play's speakers will be enclosed and the meaning of their situation suggested: just as the limits of Henri's condition are enclosed by the prologue. Indeed, as Balmas and others have suggested, the entire play offers itself as a meditation on the limitations of both kingship in particular and the human condition in general, with special emphasis upon the fatal rewards of too much pride. It is very much in terms of such limits that Cléopâtre's "victory" in death (a silence outside discourse) will be the mark of Octavian's failure in life (his claim to control all discourse).

Because such discursive boundaries are set up from the very outset, it is clear enough that all speakers will be more or less consciously the victims of discourse: they will all be objects rather than subjects. This is so even for Octavian, who from his first appearance reveals a hesitancy that, in view of what has been said of him in the prologue, in the following scene by Antoine's ghost, and then by Cléopâtre herself, would otherwise seem rather strange. In act 2 he first speaks with the exaltation one might expect of the conqueror, but this quickly changes to a kind of depression accompanied by a noticeable generosity toward the defeated. Under the influence of his companions, Proculée and Agrippe, this in turn changes to a harsh severity. In act 3, when Octavian actually confronts Cléopâtre, his language is a mixture of sarcasm, that same harshness and generosity, together with a sort of benevolent condescension (he announces, after all, that he is sure of winning his "trophée"). It is as though, like Gamaliel in *Baptistes*, he is unable to discover a means to control his own discourse—let alone that of others.

As we say, this ambiguous situation is marked from Octavian's first appearance by the ironic nature of his praise of the gods. For those who participate in a discourse aimed at their present activities the grasp of those activities is always unclear. Such ambiguity does not apply to such as are outside the discourse: the prologue is able to make a commentary upon the play to follow, and because the tragedy is, so to speak, itself in a different "space," it can make a commentary upon what is said in the prologue. It is thus that it becomes a commentary on the conditions of kingship and of humanity, and in that sense that it becomes a setting into order. The relationship of discourses (a "commentative" relationship that will eventually make a "knowledge" possible) suggested here is emphasized by the long speech uttered by Antoine's ghost immediately following the prologue.

Now that he is no longer a participant, Antoine can see how little control he had. He insists throughout upon the involuntary nature of his love for Cléopâtre, on its having been inflicted upon him by some "god," jealous of his power (a "pride" to be echoed by Octavian), and he affirms repeatedly his role as a victim. He views himself as a "hunted prey," as "condemned." He compares himself to "vieil Promethee" both of them "blinded by this fatal fire" ("ceste ardeur fatale" [1.96]). The wordplay is significant: partly because its "equation" of love and technical knowledge ("fire") as discursive predicates suggest, first, that we are dealing here with a problem concerning the relation of speaker to what is spoken and of speaker to whomever is spoken to, and second, that power (Antoine's over the world), desire (his relations with Cléopâtre), and knowledge (the theft of fire) are above all a matter of specifying such relationships; and partly because, as we have earlier indicated, the development of the Promethean simile forms an important element in the general development of tragedy.

In this particular instance, the name of Prometheus is simply used as a simile for one who has broken out of the circle and been punished for it. Later on such similes will become metaphors identified with a particular kind of active person: the tragic personage will almost always be "Promethean" (certain of Corneille's heroes will be exceptions to this characterization), but he or she will always, then, be *re*presented as a psychological type familiar in our own reality. For Jodelle, the name of Prometheus is a passing reminder of another discourse (from the ancients, though not necessarily tragedy, of course), and a means of fitting Antoine, Cléopâtre, and Octavian (also, by extension and potentially, Henri II himself) into the same discursive paradigm.

For Antoine death is an escape, it is both a remedy ("remede") and a cure ("guarison," [1.97]) brought on by the venom ("venin"), poisons ("poisons") and pleasures ("plaisirs" [1.96]) of love. As for Prometheus, so for Antoine: at once dead and yet not dead (after all, in Antoine's case, his ghost returns to speak this second prologue), death is both a shame and a glory, a victory (the memory of their love will remain forever; so will the knowledge brought by Prometheus) and a failure (neither one can benefit from the memory or the knowledge). Antoine recalls that his death occurred in the small, enclosed room in which his lover had taken refuge and emphasizes that this enclosure was a foretaste of its final result: to thrust him *for his punishment* ever deeper into the center of the circle, into the shadowy valley ("le val tenebreux" [1.95]). Cléopâtre's death will be compounded of the same ambiguity.

In this "second prologue" presented by Antoine (actually the first scene of act 1) we are next reminded of the queen's death. The ghost tells us that he has appeared to Cléopâtre in a dream demanding that she come and join him. Now in the name of neoclassicism, realism, naturalism, psychologism, or whatever, it is apparent that we are provided with no further information here. Nor does this scene in any way further the action of the play. The speech offers a rhetorical expansion of the few lines of the prologue addressed to the king that speak of the love of Antony and Cleopatra. Addressed now to the public at large, the speech is proffered as a kind of elegy emphasizing the circularity of the play's movement. It retells a little of the past, it foretells a little of the future. That past and that future are elements in the present instance that is the ghost's discourse. The whole play is contained here, and will be a rhetorical expansion of his particular utterance. In that sense the dead Antoine perhaps does control the others' discourse in a way he could never do alive: but within the discourse he controls he is silent, to him it is always a "past" or a "future." Furthermore, in the same way, the discourse he enunciates is controlled by the utterance that is the prologue addressed to, and which exists only as a function of, the king's presence in the audience.

We are presented here with a kind of hierarchy of discourses, each of which makes possible the next as it is made possible by the one

before (including the "king's": after all, it is written by the poet),
but each of which is excluded from all the others as elaborated even
though the potential of each is contained in the one preceding.
The listener/spectator cannot enter the utterance (as the "participant" claimed by later tragedy), though it can be commented upon
from outside, as it were: from another discourse. In that way, any
particular utterance is, for its speaker, a portion of a discourse from
which there is no escape: it is a portion of a circle to be given the
name of "destiny." Or it will be given the name "the gods," who will
then be able to play about the *person* of the speaker, to prevent an
escape from his or her destiny, to make him or her into their "victim." As soon as names are given in this manner then what is a limita-
tion of discourse will begin to be hypostatized, made into elements
of a (for the moment "literary") reality. Such naming depends upon
the discursive hierarchy of which we have been writing, for the names
cannot be provided from within the discourse whose elements are
being named—they come from the one next to it.

Knowledge, then, depending as it does on the naming of its components, cannot possibly do without the discursive hierarchy that is
here performed in tragedy. It will be essential to the analytical and
referential discourse whose instauration is shortly to be worked out
and proclaimed, though that discourse itself will not formally proclaim its necessity. Perhaps, indeed, it could not: because to describe
thus the activity of analytico-referential discourse would constitute
a "naming" itself indicative of a passage into a different discourse. No
doubt that is why it was only at the moment when analytico-referential discourse was itself in crisis, when a further development was
absolutely necessary, that the concept of discursive hierarchies was
elaborated in detail as an essential element of knowledge—most
notably in the work of Bertrand Russell from the beginning of the
present century. Russell is simply formalizing what had always been
essential to the functioning of the discourse in question. It could
not, however, be stated if the discourse was to be claimed to be functioning "objectively," "transparently." If it were to be stated it
would reveal that knowledge is the production of discourse itself:
Descartes's doubt, for example, would then be insoluble in any terms
when available.

The hierarchy of discourses, essential to the kind of knowledge in process of being invented, thus comes into existence as a condition of communication and as the way in which "speaking relationships" are organized, not as the result of a formal elaboration (say, in a scientific or philosophical discourse) but because it is performed, played out. This is the next step after that which saw the containment of the absence of signification. Of course, if we state these discursive activities in this manner, we are speaking retrospectively: we cannot really say that these developments occur *in order that* analytico-referential discourse should be developed, and so on. All we can say is that they *did* occur and that the discourse of analysis and referentiality was the eventual result. Just because the relationship between these developments and their outcome is not teleological is the reason why no formalization was necessary—or in fact could have occurred. Because no formalization *did* occur, the invention of modern "scientific" knowledge was possible. Discourse is a trap, but there is more than one discourse, and *that* makes possible explanation, description, meaning, and all communication.

In *Cléopâtre captive* the closed nature of the discursive circle of a given level (demonstrated here by the level of the narration of the play's action itself, expanded from the speech of Antoine's ghost) is immediately confirmed in the stichomythic dialogue between Cléopâtre, Eras, and Charmium, whose very first term indicates the vanity of discourse (being at once the circle, the container, and the fruitless expression of the attempt to escape it, the contained): as Cléopâtre cries out, "Que gaignez-vous, helas! en la parole vaine?" (1. 97). Within the circle of discourse the only possible activity, it need scarcely be said, is that of words; and words are vain because they cannot change their properties and break from the circle: they cannot pass into the next "higher" discourse in order that the speaker of *this* discourse may name her situation.

Yet it is only the use of language that *seems* to offer these characters the possibility of change. To them, language use alone appears to be under their control in a situation where all other activity has been foreordained. The artificial click of the stichomythia seem to offer a kind of activity, a possibility of situating the identity of the speaker. Yet the discussion of the stichomythic dialogue seems nonetheless to bound and rebound off invisible, but impassable, walls; walls that are provided, as we saw, by the limits of the "next" discourse to that of these speakers. Antoine is mentioned by Cléopâtre, and in doing so her discourse is reabsorbed. The passage into Antoine's discourse would be Cléopâtre's "death."

At the moment when Eras concludes the dialogue, telling the queen that she should follow her "desire," the latter's discourse becomes that of Antoine's ghost and takes up all its terms in turn: she considers her "fatal attractions," the gifts he had given her and which had caused the resentment of the Romans, their voluptuous life together and finally his suicide (1.100. Cf. 1.96). The elegiac form of her speech repeats that of Antoine, the content is identical. It is as though the discourse had accepted the vanity of all attempts at "activity" and been forced into the necessary resumption of its own boundaries: called the passive acceptance of destiny. Cléopâtre —now in dialogue, to be sure—describes her dream of Antoine, how he looked, what he demanded of her, and her decision to die rather than be led off in triumph by Octavian. This decision is conceived as a victory for the queen: "Non, non, mourons, mourons, arrachons la victoire,/Encore que soyons par Cesar surmontees" ("No, no, let us die, let us die: let us grasp the victory, even though we are overcome by Caesar." [1.103]). And it will be a victory, in the same sense as John the Baptist's in Buchanan's tragedy: a passing out of discourse, out from under the control of the other—hence the ambiguity of the statement that the women (in *Cléopâtre*) would still be "overcome" by Caesar, for, in his discourse, so they will.

The long lamentation upon which the chorus now embarks is by no means a mere ornament. By generalizing the present situation into a commentary on the changeable nature of the human condition and the ephemerality of good fortune, it applies the lesson to *all* speakers of discourse, not just the apparent "victims," here Antoine and Cléopâtre and the queen's two attendants. The commentary made by the chorus extends to Octavian and to the king of the prologue. It is a commentary proceeding from the next discourse up, so to speak: that of the poet himself, the final arbiter here of order.

At the beginning of this chapter we saw the manner of Octavian's entrance into the pattern of discourse at this point (i.e., immediately after the remarks made by the chorus). One might expect him to be *outside* the circle, in so far as he wishes to present himself as the chief representative ("general commis," 2.109) of the gods, their principal instrument on earth: not, therefore, a participant in the troubled discourse of other humans. On the contrary, he is well and truly within it. The very expression of his aspirations reveals his own role as captive: "Or'je desire, or'je desire mieux, / C'est de me joindre au sainct nombre des Dieux" ("But I desire and I desire even more, and that is to be joined with the sacred number of the gods" [2.109]). The reason for this desire he makes clear: on earth no fortune is constant. Yet so to express it emphasizes his situation within the circle, he wishes to jump the limits precisely because he is a prisoner within them. He wishes to *name* ("*nom*bre") himself among the "gods": but that is impossible for the reason we indicated earlier, that to do so the speaker would already have to be outside the bounds of *his* sense, in the space of a different discourse.

It is indeed on just those grounds that Proculée justifies César for having sought Antoine's death (Octavian had momentarily regretted it). He argues that Antoine had attempted just such a naming of himself, he had striven to vie with the "gods," and the reward of that must be death: the exclusion (in this case) from the arguments of humanity. This is the counterpoint of Antoine's own ambiguous affirmation in his earlier speech: in death, in his silence to the discourse of Cléopâtre and Octavian as it goes on in the play, he has achieved something godlike—now he may compare himself to Prometheus. Octavian is now doing the same thing, though Proculée will not make the connection until the very end of the tragedy, after the death of Cléopâtre: "César verra, perdant ce qu'il attent, / Que nul ne peut au monde estre contant" (Caesar will see, by losing what he expects, that no one in this world can be happy" [5.146]). Now, within discourse, *this attempt to jump the bounds of sense will be given a name*: pride (though it will only be after Cléopâtre has "left" their discourse, thereby changing its terms, that that name will be able to be ascribed to Octavian's activities within it).

The proud man, continues Agrippe, César's other companion, is the very epitome of the normal condition of all men, of every individual who "ne cesse point de courir et glisser, / Virevolter, rouler et se dresser . . ." ("Does not stop running and slipping, twisting, rolling and raising himself" [2.110]). This image of man is precisely that already performed by the stichomythia mentioned before. It is an image on which Agrippe insists as he emphasizes the futility of all activity within this circular trap:

> Ainsi ceux-là que l'orgueil trompe ici
> Ne cessent point de se dresser ainsi,
> Courir, tourner, tant qu'ils soyent agitez
> Contre les bords de leurs felicitez.   [2.110–11]

[Thus those whom pride deceives here do not stop raising themselves thus, running, turning, so much are they bestirred against the bounds of their fortunes.]

The very movement of the play's discourse further emphasizes the view of human activity being built up: it constantly returns to the same series of tropes. Agrippe now returns to the notions of Antoine's blindness, his disorders, and so on, to which so much attention has already been paid. This time it is exaggerated even further by a commentary on all the omens that Antoine and Cléopâtre had ignored: their "crime" is such that Agrippe wishes to push his master to destroy their very names: "Racle leur nom, efface leur memoire,/Poursuy, poursuy jusqu'au bout ta victoire" ("Scratch out their name, efface their memory, pursue, pursue your victory to the end" [2. 112]). To destroy a name would indeed be a victory, but it too would be a victory at the price of passing beyond the boundaries (just as to make a name is). Octavian responds, therefore, *within* the limits: his victory must be to make those names his possession. Agrippe's exhortation reminds his leader of his potential triumph in Rome and of the efforts necessary to obtain Cléopâtre's presence there. If he could achieve that he would be the equal of a god, but without leaving the discourse: he would be its master, and the master of all other speakers of that discourse.

The theme of the triumph has by now become central. Its every mention is juxtaposed with that other principal theme, launched by Antoine's ghost (but already indicated in the prologue), which is that of the irresponsible love of Antoine and Cléopâtre. For all three speakers, these indicate "goals" that represent a means to a power over discourse, a means to "escape" limits over which they have no control. Just as Octavian envisages the triumph as raising him so, too, did the lovers conceive of themselves as raised beyond the ordinary run of humanity: that is why their love must also be called "exceptional" and "memorable." And yet, as they must, Octavian and his companions seek always to reduce it to mere lust and luxury, exceptional only because of its disastrous political effects and not at all because of the individuals indulging in it. In its defeat, therefore, this love has already thrust Antoine deeper still into the contraining circle: and he has invited Cléopâtre to join him. The memory of the love will defeat the fleetingness of its initial expression, but at the cost of the death of its initiators. Memory is precisely its naming in another's discourse.

Meanwhile the debate continues. Proculée urges that suicide threatens to liberate the queen from their hands. Agrippe replies in such a way as to make the protection of Cléopâtre's life a goal equivalent to the triumph itself. Her future within the discourse represented by the triumph is that of a possession: but we have already seen her drawing closer to the discursive space presented by Antoine's ghost, and we have seen her placed by the poet. All efforts so to seize the other are in vain. Agrippe emphasizes that in order to prevent her untimely death they will have to "dessus elle veiller. / Sonder, courir, espier, travailler . . ." ("watch over her. Probe, run, spy, work": whatever one may say of this translation, it does serve to indicate that the exact sense of the passage is less important than the feeling of hurrying, anxious, and vain activity that is imparted by the rapid sequence of infinitives [2.113]). Convinced, Octavian says he will take the appropriate steps. *We* know that all activity in this direction is doomed to failure in advance. Octavian's captivity, not altogether unmarked in his discourse, is as absolute as is hers. Where two discursive opponents are concerned a possession of the one by the other does not appear to be possible: the one can always defend itself. Such was the case in *Baptistes*. The one can possess discourse only when the other leaves it: but then it is empty and possession is vain. If the other passes into a discourse "higher" in the hierarchy, however, then this new discourse can contain, can "know" the other in a way it cannot know itself. The "superior" can give new names

to the activities of the "inferior." The *use* of this hierarchy as an
ordering device did not occur in Buchanan.

For the moment the debate is inconclusive; a fact underlined by
Proculée when he returns to a reflection upon the ephemerality
of things human and of glory, upon the horror of death. This meditation is reinforced by the chorus, equating man with his pride and
placing both of them within the circle:

> De la terre humble et basse,
> Esclave de ses cieux,
> Le peu puissant espace
> N'a rien plus vicieux
> Que l'orgueil, qu'on voit estre
> Hay du ciel, son maistre.   [2.115]

[The weak space of the humble and lowly earth, slave of its skies,
has nothing more vicious than pride, which we see is hated by
the sky, its master.]

The proud are hated for the same reason as the Titans, as Prometheus
in particular, and as Icarus (2.116–17). They attempt while yet living
to break out of the bounds of their "humanity." César, they add, is
courting the same danger (2.119).[6] In Buchanan the word "pride"
referred to the comportment of a speaker towards another speaker:
it named the discursive relationship itself, by its very nature outside
any given instance of discourse. In *Cléopâtre* an element of discursive
activity has been named as "pride" by means of the hierarchy of
discourses. It has received a status that is no longer simply the activity
of the enunciating subject seeking to control its own discourse. Other
discursive elements can receive names in a similar fashion.

The passage of enunciation is itself given a name and that, together
with "pride," hypostatizes the whole matter as the natural (real,
material) condition of mankind. In Buchanan "being" had been
nothing other than the continuation of speaking. In Montaigne, only
the passage of discourse, only the activity of writing assured any
existence whatever: "meaning," "self," "life" were no more than
the passing of the pen over the paper—and no less either. That "passage" is now given a status outside what can speak of it: "Le temps

peut tout faucher;/L'orgueil qui nous amorce,/Donne à sa faulx sa force" ("Time can cut down all, and pride, which lures us on, gives force to its cutting edge" [2.120]). It is no longer the movement of speaking itself that supplies the limits of the human, but "time," which, once named, can become explanatory of the human situation and an object of knowledge as the mere movement of discourse could not.

At this point, then, "time" and "pride" become two of the "forces of destiny" that will infallibly cause the failure of the love of Antoine and Cléopâtre and of Octavian's triumph. "Pride," picked up again here by the chorus, had already been named in the poet's prologue. Provided with an extradiscursive reality, it can be presented to the king as a warning in a way it could not be if it issued only from the king's own discourse—one could not criticize the king, but one can comment on the general condition of humanity to the extent that it is shared by him. But what the poet has had to show is the *meaning* of such pride: it has been performed as the attempt to control discourse as a private possession, as the attempt to go beyond its limits, to make oneself a "god," and thereby invent the discourse others are to use. It is the individual speaker's attempt to lay down the law for others. The *meaning* of the word *pride* is thus derived from a particular set of activities, but once it has been thus derived it can become a piece of reality. The same can be said to apply to the word *time* (derived from the linear, "forward" movement of discourse), to *destiny* (the limits provided by discourse), and so on.

Obviously I am not suggesting that such words as *time, pride,* and *destiny* are new. What I am suggesting is that the concepts they signify, developed out of a new discursive context, are a new invention (though, equally obviously I think, they are not developed in one discourse and in one small time span). For example, once time has been derived from a discursive process it is then available to a subject, just as discourse itself is: mankind can then take charge of its own history. History is no longer the attempt to interpret a divine order, nor the recounting of the exploits of some significant individual; it is the comprehension of man's own ordering of himself and the world.[7] The same kind of thing can be said of the other terms.

What is occurring in this discursive development is a whole new conceptual orientation. Jodelle's *Cléopâtre* provides some of the evidence for it.

Act 3, the turning point of the play in so far as its eventual outcome is here given an explanation, is the only one where the imprisoned struggle of words is permitted to become physical—albeit extremely briefly. Yet this action, in view of what we have so far seen, appears to adopt the aspect of a metaphor for the rhetoric rather than the other way round—which is only to be expected, given that such terms as *time, pride,* and the rest themselves appear, for the present, as metaphors for what remain in this play activities of discourse.

We join Cléopâtre and Octavian, in fact, in the very middle of a dispute; a dispute whose futility is, once again, made quite clear at the very outset. César poses to the queen the question that has become almost a leitmotif: "Voulez-vous donc vostre fait excuser?/ Mais dequoy sert à ces mots s'amuser?" ("Do you wish to justify your action?/But what use is it to waste time in words?"[3.121]). Cléopâtre, who wishes to lure Octavian into complacency as regards her own intentions, first offers various apologies to provoke his pity, but he interprets her lamentations as so much pretense. Next she shows him the letters she has from his father proving Caesar's love for her and arguing that he should spare her out of deference to that love—and she consequently blames Antoine and her love for him. But Octavian merely brushes aside these tokens: words are utterly futile. She finally appears to give in and offers Octavian all the treasures of her dynasty. At this point Seleuque accuses her of misusing language, of in fact having hidden most of her treasure and of offering the Roman a mere fraction of it.[8]

Having offered various kinds of "empty" words, Cléopâtre has now offered the lie on which we saw Montaigne comment. It fails because Seleuque knows the intention to be different from what is seemingly expressed. Cléopâtre appears to realize that there is no way she can "defeat" Octavian so long as she accepts the argument in his terms. At Seleuque's unexpected accusation she flies into rage. She jumps on the unfaithful servant, kicking him and beating him with her fists. Octavian stands by uninterfering and passes half-

amused remarks on her fury: her failure here could be understood as
a victory for him.

No doubt her fury can be ascribed to the fact that she had been
wishing to win a certain amount of liberty in order to avenge herself
and Antoine (an idea previously advanced by Agrippe), and that she
wishes to save her children (the reason she later gives for having
wished to retain some of her wealth, whereas Seleuque had indicated
that her lie was merely a dishonorable trick). But what seems above
all made clear by this outburst is the closed nature of the circle and
Cléopâtre's final awareness of it. What has been most evident throughout the tragedy is not so much her desire for vengeance as her concern to avoid the triumph being prepared by the Romans.

She has a double reason for allaying Octavian's fears. If she could
live perhaps she could gain some kind of victory for herself by killing
or bribing César (and the mere avoidance is vengeance enough, because
it would be the indication of her escape from his control), or, failing
life, if she could find a way to be alone she could kill herself and avoid
the triumph that way. The first alternative is destroyed by Seleuque's
treason, which almost does away with the second at the same time by
putting the emperor on his guard against the queen's trickery. She is
saved only because Octavian takes the deception itself as an indication
that she wishes to live. The treason has, however, taken from Cléopâtre the last possibility of escape (in life). She finds herself once
more up against the wall, and the physical outburst against Seleuque
is the result, unique in this play.

From this moment the play races toward its conclusion: the last
two acts together barely make up the length of each of the other
three. The inevitability of the conclusion is emphasized in a discourse
whose repetitiveness tolls the bell of destiny, indicates that *it is*
destiny, underlines the queen's captivity and, now, her acceptance
of it within *that* discourse:

> Penseroit doncq César estre du tout vainqueur?
> Penseroit doncq César abastardir ce coeur,
> Veu que des tiges vieux ceste vigueur j'hérite,
> De ne pouvoir ceder qu'à la Parque dépite?
> La Parque, et non César, aura sus moy le pris;
> La Parque, et non César, soulage mes esprits;

La Parque, et non César, triomphera de moy;
La Parque, et non César, finira mon esmoy. . . .   [4.135]

[Would Caesar then think he could be victor over all? Would
Caesar then think he could debase this heart, considering that I
inherit from an old race this strength, to yield only to the spiteful Fury? The Fury, and not Caesar, will win over me; the Fury,
and not Caesar, can calm my spirits; the Fury, and not Caesar,
will triumph over me; the Fury, and not Caesar, will put an end
to my trouble. . . .]

The repetition of these phrases, with their continuous *p*'s and *v*'s, not
only emphasizes captivity: it also creates a sense of exaltation. Cléopâtre seems to have come to the realization that she can, in fact,
break the circle. She can do so by means of silence, death itself. She
can do so by stepping out of "Roman" discourse into that of the
dead Antoine. And Charmium takes up the cry in her turn (with an
"Encore que . . ." repeated seven times), to hand it on to Eras: "Ha
mort, ô douce mort, mort, seule guarison/Des esprits oppressez d'*une
estrange prison* . . ." ("Ah death, sweet death, death, the only cure/
For spirits oppressed by *an incomprehensible prison*" [4.136]. The
italics are mine).

Yet the escape from the prison is only possible through a discourse
that is entirely that of others: the tragedy itself, which makes a memory. The subject itself here, by the very nature of the case, cannot, if
it continues to speak at all (as does the ghost of Antoine), escape the
discourse it must use, and seek to order in using. The end of the play,
therefore, is Cléopâtre's silence. As Antoine goes further into the
circle for his punishment, so the queen goes into his tomb to die (4.
139–40), and Proculée will find her "en ceste chambre close" (4.145).
Antoine becomes indeed for Cléopâtre the desirable image of death,
as she echoes the structure of Eras's phrase to return us to an idea
first set forth by her beloved's ghost at the beginning of the play.

Antoine, ô cher Antoine! Antoine ma moitié!
Si Antoine n'eust eu des cieux l'inimitié,
Antoine, Antoine, helas!   [4.138]

[Antony, dear Antony, Antony the half of me! If Antony had
not been hated by the heavens, Antony, Antony, alas. . . .]

When Proculée discovers the suicides in the following short act—or
rather, when he relates that discovery—it is natural that he should not
so much bewail the deaths of the three women as the fact that their
deaths will prevent Octavian's complete triumph. That is as it must
be: for this triumph, which would be the symbol of his complete possession of others' discourse and of all possible "acts" open to them,
would have made of him the sole master of discourse. Even the king
present outside the text of the play cannot, it would seem, achieve
such untrammeled mastery: within discourse, if it is not to be frozen
once and for all (as it was by Herod and by Jephtha), an exchange
must be permanently at work. César's "pride," because it leaves him
quite alone with a discourse that can indeed be *his* but that leads
nowhere, has made of his discourse a trap from which Cléopâtre has
been able to escape: "nul ne peut au monde estre contant," as we
have seen Proculée assert at this moment. The chorus, after a brief
lament, insists on this theme:

> Ta Cleopatre, ainsi morte,
> Au monde ne perira:
> Le temps la garantira,
> Qui desja sa gloire porte,
> Depuis la vermeille entrée
> Que fait ici le Soleil,
> Jusqu'aux lieux de son sommeil,
> Opposez à ma contrée,
> Pour avoir, plutost qu'en Romme
> Se souffrir porter ainsi,
> Aime mieux s'occire ici,
> Ayant un coeur plus que d'homme.   [4.147]

[Your Cleopatra, dead in this way, will not die in the world: time
will maintain her (memory), which already bears her glory, from
the bright entrance which the Sun makes here, to the place where
it sleeps, (at an) opposite (end of the world) to my country, because, rather than allow herself to be thus borne in Rome she

preferred to kill herself here, having a heart more than a man's (or, "more than human").]

This last line seems to suggest that in some way Cléopâtre has indeed escaped the discourse of the human. We are brought back to the beginning of the play, full circle: back to the death of Cléopâtre, back to the glory announced for Henri with all its ambiguity, back to the notion of the sun's circle used here to denote the overcoming of time. It is indicated, therefore, that the queen has in some way fled the discourse installed by the play, as though that discourse had been a constant constraint upon her—as, indeed, to her, to Octavian, to Antoine, it was. Still the uncertain nature of this "escape" is emphasized: Cléopâtre's memory survives, but at the cost of her own suicide. The tomb may be magnificent, but it is no less closed. Such is the price of *separating* the members of the hierarchy of discourse into conflicting and mutually incomprehensible units.

The chorus finally allows itself to be caught in the same trap. It repeats the proposition that if such is a victory for the queen then its nature emphasizes its own (and our) captivity in a discourse that defeats mutual comprehension and communication. The members of the chorus cannot follow Cléopâtre's way out: they can but envy the death of "ces trois miserables" (5.147): henceforth they will have to obey "les loix d'un vainqueur estranger" (5.147). For though their discourse is a commentary upon Cléopâtre's and as such in a "space" outside it—the next in the hierarchy—it is for just that reason dependent upon it: the choric element cannot make names for silence. Or not for long. Each member of the hierarchic set is necessary to every other and to the whole if the discourse is to continue to function: the silence of the one will swiftly be followed by the silence of them all.

Death in silence may be the only means by which the individual can escape a circle where all human struggle is characterized by vanity, by pride, by the futility of submission to a destiny that escapes description. For that individual such escape might be considered a victory just because the other enunciators of discourse are left literally speechless. But that is at the cost of that individual's silence also, and her victory can only be *said* to be such by whomever is left. If they are not speechless (as they are not until the last expression by the chorus of their acceptance of "Cléopâtre's place" in Octavian's order, which concludes the play), it is because the space left by the absent protagonist has been sealed up, so to speak. The tragic absence then becomes *named* as a memory, of glory or of despair, it is no matter: the element of conflict will have been absorbed within what had been the "secondary" discourse. Now it has become the first in the hierarchy, taken as being up against, as expressing, reality. Perhaps that is why, at the end of the development we are discussing, at the end of the seventeenth century, tragedies will not so much emphasize the tragic personage as the group from which he or she is to be excluded (I am thinking especially of Racine). Here the end of the play laments a past and an individual, there it will look to a social future.

In *Cléopâtre captive* we remain very far from the results of that development. The considerable ambiguity of an enunciator's relation with discourse and of enunciators with one another, the ambiguity of the hierarchic elements of the discourse of tragedy, the struggles of enunciators to escape capture, all emphasize a certain oppressiveness, accentuate the practice of discourse as essentially problematic. What we have been shown in this tragedy is a condition with no conclusive exit. And yet we have come a long way from Buchanan.

It was fashionable until not very long ago to call such tragedies as this one failures, because the spectator's interest is not retained by "dramatic suspense," by spectacular action. To thus apply criteria drawn from later predilections misses, it seems to me, the entire point of such tragedies. The emphasis of *Cléopâtre captive* lies in a series of problems proceeding partly from its own experimental nature,[9] and partly from the general preoccupations of the humanists (though the one is doubtless the consequence of the other). The play deals with matters of communication and expression, with the bounds of sense. In the hierarchical placing of its four levels of discourse (that of the protagonists, that of Antoine's ghost, that of the chorus, and finally that of the prologue)[10] and in the disputes of the first level, the tragedy acts out the nature of discursive relations among speakers. Within that acting out it asks a number of questions about meaning and knowledge.

"Que gaignez-vous, helas! en la parole vaine?" ("What do you gain, alas! by useless speech?") asks Cléopatre (1.97): "Mais de quel lieu ces mots?" ("But what is the purpose of these words?") asks Agrippe (2.109). Can we mean what we say (how can, as Montaigne might put it, the intention match the verbal commitment)?—"Quoy! Cesar pensoit-il que ce que dit j'avois/Peust bien aller ensemble et de coeur et de voix?" ("What! Did Caesar think that what I had said could well proceed from both my heart and voice?") exclaims Cléopâtre again (4.135).

Yet despite the final exclusion of Cléopâtre and the seeming defeat of all the protagonists (as Octavian puts it to Cléopâtre, "Dequoy sert à cest mots s'amuser?" ["What use is it to waste time in words?" (3.121)]) the conclusion is by no means entirely pessimistic or negative. Because of the hierarchical functioning of discourse within discourse in general it becomes possible to name, to describe, to situate as predicates of discourse elements that had before been unknowable obstacles within its very functioning. In Buchanan "they" led to the decay of discourse or to the affirmation of the obstacle itself as a permanent block to action. Here, named (as *destiny, time, pride, memory*, and so on), they have become the necessary foundation of action.

After the death of Cléopâtre and her confidants, Proculée demands of "Jupiter" whether he is going to allow the continuation of such horrors as those we have just witnessed: "Tant que le tour de la machine tienne/Par contrepoids balancé se maintienne . . ." ("For as long as the turning of your machine is kept up by balanced counterpoise" [5.145]). The answer is provided by the question: what we have also just witnessed is the functioning of a "machine" whose potential is to overcome such horrors. So far as this tragedy is concerned, the machine is the king's: it is Henri II who had been named as Jupiter when, in the very first line of the prologue, he had been called "Roy des Rois." It is the king's . . . and the poet's. And at the end it is also Proculée's, for it is he who speaks to the king as Jupiter.

That does not indicate a collapsing of the hierarchy and a consequent failure in the creation of order. Rather is it shown that the various levels must all function together if the model is to produce meaningful communication, that there must be a kind of internal dialectic if the model is to produce a stable exchange of discourse and, consequently, a stable organization of society. Except for those speakers who cannot use the levels other than as quite separate domains of activity, those who are cogs in the machine (Antoine, Cléopâtre, Eras, Charmium, Octavian, Agrippe), the whole can now function as an instructive model—for writer, speaker, spectator, reader, and king. A machine to order is being prepared, capable of containing and expelling the horrors of nonmeaning and powerlessness, of rejecting the elements preventive of stable communication, able to produce true knowledge (ethical, for the present) and a well-ordered society.

That development still has far to go. For if we are able to speak of the tragedy's reference to some ethical "knowledge," the object of such knowledge acts as though it were (is made to act as though it were) in some obscure and untouchable way outside the bounds of discourse, as though the speaker could in no way take responsibility for it. It is, that is, "ethical" in terms of a pattern that yet remains beyond the speaker's control, within the space of an order called "the divine" and forming an absolute constraint to human action *for itself.* It still remains the mark of, indeed the metaphor for, discourse as obstacle, not as exchange and habit, use and function.

Though a way has been found for discursive naming to take place, for objects of knowledge to be created, through the *under*-standing made possible in the discursive hierarchy, the subject of discourse has yet to take responsibility for it (*within* a process of exchange, not so as to crush such a process). That responsibility will be called the "will," and the exchange in question together with the place ("power" and "right") of the individual within it will one day be called the "social contract." Once *this* naming has been achieved, the responsibility of enunciation (as I have termed it in *Logics of Literature*) can once again be ceded: no longer to some divine order, but in the name of the "real nature" of a permanent human society and of a scientific truth the proof of whose correctness is that it permits humanity to manipulate phenomena. Before that change in the conception of the *limits* of discourse can occur, there will have to have been a moment when the speaker "entered into" discourse, took charge of it in full awareness that it was his or hers to manipulate. That is the next step in this general examination of the limits and manner of discursive meaning, of the limits and possibilities of communication and, therefore, of human action.

4 Power and Fallibility
(*Tamburlaine* and *Faustus*)

Cléopâtre captive suggests that the responsibility of enunciation will require the recognition both of power and of fallibility. The concept of *contract* will eventually give both name and form to that recognition: a reification of the individual enunciating function and of the collective interaction of speakers involved in all discourse. In *Tamburlaine* and in *Doctor Faustus*, though differently, the first function is all-important, the second utterly neglected. Tamburlaine in particular appears as the successor to Octavian, and he fails for similar reasons. He neglects the fact that he is surrounded by other speakers who, though passive before his speech, are its ultimate judges. Tamburlaine seeks to make his discourse all-consuming, to compete, so to speak, with the world itself. He has remade the map of the world in the image of his own speech: saying is, visibly, doing —and being. But he is tied by the identity he has forged between discourse and the world. As soon as a fault appears to widen between them then the efficacy of the discourse of power begins to wane.

In *Tamburlaine* the death of Zenocrate is the beginning of the end.[1] When the emperor cries out: "Live still, my love" (part 2, 2.4.55),[2] it is the first of his commands to fail, and it is only then that what Judith Weil has called the "framing landscape" becomes a reminder that "his power falls far short of his hopes and that it does enormous damage to other men."[3] It is then that *other speakers* remind him that power alone is not enough, that that power must be seen by others to function and a moment will come when a fault appears. Then the judgment of others upon his discourse will come into play. As Theridamas now says: "Ah, good my lord, be patient!

She is dead, / And all this raging cannot make her live" (part 2, 2.4.119–20).

The "enormous damage" reverses the direction of its effect and Tamburlaine becomes aware for the first time that he is as vulnerable to the words of others as they are to his: "For she is dead! Thy words do pierce my soul: / Ah, sweet Theridamas, say so no more!" (part 2, 2.4.125–26). At this point we recall a remark made long before to Theridamas by Mycetes, a remark that at the time had perhaps seemed without any "objective correlative" and quite simply ironic: "Go, stout Theridamas, thy words are swords" (part 1, 1.1.74). We recall it now as a double irony. His words are indeed swords, because Tamburlaine will have forgotten that he is not alone in speaking. When his own discourse fails to impose itself, the gap is instantly pierced and enlarged by another's. Any "dialectic" has long since been excluded and Tamburlaine consequently discovers himself to be utterly isolated—just as the speakers of *Cléopâtre captive* had been. And Theridamas will, of course, say much more.

A key to the role played by *Tamburlaine* in the development we wish to show is perhaps found in a scene I consider the central one of the first part, a scene in which the future of the world is to be decided (and which, in point of lines is literally the central one of the text). Tamburlaine and his officers are already proclaiming themselves victors over Bajazeth, whose defeat is said by Theridamas to be a foregone conclusion. Tamburlaine exclaims:

> Well said, Theridamas! Speak in that mood,
> For *will* and *shall* best fitteth Tamburlaine,
> Whose smiling stars give him assured hope
> Of martial triumph ere he meet his foes.   [part 1, 3.3.40–43]

Not yet do words "pierce the soul" of Tamburlaine. Theridamas, the man who started as an opponent in war and who will conclude as a more subtle opponent in speech, is here the very speaker who expresses the *efficacious* power of language which, from the start, had been the source of Tamburlaine's active success. The entire play is a demonstration of that willful discourse (one might equally well say "discursive will") in its power over the world of men and in its eventual fallibility.

Tamburlaine's first conquests are always through speech. As David Daiches has pointed out, from the very prologue on, what comes first is the act of "threatening the world with high astounding terms," and only afterward the act of "scourging kingdoms with his conquering sword."[4] Tamburlaine is from the beginning the victorious creation of his own act of speaking. He calls himself the "scourge of God" before he "becomes" it. "Words," as Mycetes tells Theridamas, "are swords," swords words. The one, *sword*, contains the other, *word*; and Tamburlaine scourges kingdoms with his conquering word.

If Tamburlaine's first conquests are through speech, his final defeat marks the limits of speech. Those limits were set when he sought to conquer death on behalf of Zenocrate. Between that time and the moment of his own death we are made aware of a kind of desperate race of "impatient words" (part 2, 5.3.55) against silence, until at the end it is just that silence which is confronted: "In vain I strive and rail against those powers . . ." (part 2, 5.3.121). His son, Amyras, who is to succeed Tamburlaine, exclaims that he accepts the succession reluctantly and only because of that silence: "If the unrelenting ears / Of Death and Hell be shut against my prayers, / And that the spiteful influence of Heaven / Deny my soul fruition of her joy" (part 2, 5.3.192–95). True, Tamburlaine himself does not accept the limit until the very end, but then he accepts it in all the abruptness of its absolute nature: "For Tamburlaine, the scourge of God, must die. (*Dies*)" (part 2, 5.3.249). We do well to take note of that most uncharacteristic "must" directed against himself: the sole occurrence in the entire ten acts.

Once again, as in the scene of Zenocrate's death, it is Theridamas who makes the first commentary on the approach of Tamburlaine's death, or rather on Death personified making its attack against Tamburlaine, noting that if this attack is successful the natural wonders "created" by Tamburlaine's poetry will be "disgrac'd":

Weep, heavens, and vanish into liquid tears!
Fall, stars that govern his nativity,
And summon all the shining lamps of heaven
To cast their bootless fires to the earth. [part 2, 5.3.1–4]

Heaven, adds Usumcasane, "will lose the honour of [her] name"
(part 2, 5.3.28). Throughout the play its realities have been entirely
the product of Tamburlaine's act of naming. It is thus fitting that as
he dies Tamburlaine should *rename* himself the "scourge of God."
In view of what he and his entourage have been saying in this last
scene, the term becomes ambiguous, to say the least: must he die
because the instrument chosen by God to punish others brings like
punishment upon himself (as in the case of Jephtha)? Or is it that
he has been a scourge turned against God Himself, in that he sought
to make the world in the image of his own words, to impose his own
speech on all others and create a world in his own discourse?

Tamburlaine, who was at first emperor only in his own willful discourse, did succeed in constructing a world according to the order
of that discourse. He is thus the scourge of *all* those who would speak
against him, be it human *logoi* or divine Logos. He is a new Prometheus arrogating to himself a life-infusing speech, a creating fire. Thus
the final despairing cry of Amyras:

> Meet heaven and earth, and here let all things end,
> For earth has spent the pride of all her fruit,
> And heaven consum'd his choicest living fire!
> Let earth and heaven his timeless death deplore,
> For both their worths will equal him no more!
>
> [part 2, 5.3.250–54]

Indeed not, for his successor will be Amyras, already confronting, as
we saw, the silent limits of discourse. Or it will be the doctor of
Wittenberg who will be saying to himself: "What art thou, Faustus,
but a man condemned to die?" (*Doctor Faustus*, 4.5.42).

Confronted with these limits at the end of Tamburlaine, the
emperor feels it necessary to warn Amyras about the possible failure
of power. Two reasons impose such a warning—Amyras's confrontation with silence, Tamburlaine's own approaching death:

> So, reign, my son: scourge and control those slaves,
> Guiding thy chariot with thy father's hand.
> As precious is the charge thou undertak'st
> As that which Clymene's brain-sick son did guide,
> When wandering Phoebe's ivory cheeks were scorch'd,

And all the earth, like Aetna, breathing fire.
Be warn'd by him, then, learn with awful eye
To sway a throne as dangerous as his;
For, if thy body thrive not full of thoughts
As pure and fiery as Phyteus' beams,
The nature of those proud rebelling jades
Will take occasion by the slenderest hair
And draw thee piecemeal, like Hypolitus,
Through rocks more steep and sharp than Caspian cliffs.

[part 2, 5.3.229–42]

The prospective failure is made clear through the simile of Phaeton, a naming of what had been unnamable. In this tragedy the naming, to be sure, is recognizably metaphorical: Amyras is only *like* Phaeton. But there is nonetheless a distanciation, the provision of a name for what had been a failure of discourse, a grasping at the end of the play of a "tragic" that is, metaphorically, an *explicable* (describable, namable) failure in human action.

Furthermore, the metaphor rebounds onto Tamburlaine himself: it is in vain that he has tried to become a god after having compared himself to one. Though in the speech just quoted he seems to be considering himself as Apollo (Phyteus), he has just previously called on that selfsame Apollo asking the god to cure him (part 2, 5.3.61–63). As in the case of Phaeton, so for Tamburlaine: heat is beyond his control. Thus the physician says: "Your veins are full of accidental heat" (5.3.84); Amyras speaks of "his burning agony" (5.3.210), and it is of course the "choicest living fire" that is gone: "earth droops" (5.3.16, 41) after his departure. In a sense the entire ten acts will have been about the passage of a Phaeton too close to the earth, leaving behind death, "desert," and nonetheless glory. It is no doubt an ugly and awesome glory: it leaves the blackened desert of a Guernica: it is not entirely inappropriate that J. B. Steane, speaking of *Tamburlaine*, talks of the "fascist spirit" of its hero's condemnation of peace and glorification of war.[5] Discourse here is naked power—until it is confronted with the very reality it has created, and until it is pierced by the voice of another.

The metaphorical personification of the failure that could not be named, only suffered, in *Baptistes* is made possible by the accession

of the enunciator to full possession of "his" discourse. That that
possession leads to a different kind of failure is a consequence of
a blindness to the fallibility mentioned at the beginning of this
chapter. That blindness is the reason why a particular paradigm of
metaphors becomes so important in the tragedy of the time—that
of the individual (Phaeton, Prometheus, Icarus) who, in setting himself outside the pale of the collectivity, also sets himself against it,
and does not heed the others' voices. After a while, of course, we
will be dealing with a metaphor no longer: the metaphor will have
been taken as a true description of the human condition. In Dryden, the individual desires of Antony and Cleopatra will compete
with the political needs of Rome; in Racine, Phèdre opposes the
inception of a legitimate civil order, the expulsion of Eriphile (in
Iphigénie) permits it. The metaphors will have performed a job
as a "bridge of naming."

In *Baptistes* we saw that the *tragic* is a name (we give) for the
functioning of discourse as an essential obstacle to expression and
communication, condemned—especially in the case of Gamaliel—
to approach meaninglessness. The *necessary* absence of meaning
(and "knowing") apparent in *Baptistes*, the obstacle to all discursive
process performed in *Jephthes*, the impossibility of willful discursive
imposition played out in *Cléopâtre captive* and resulting there in a
passage into silence, are here replaced by a clear and well-defined situation of the speaker; we can find an adversary able to be possessed
because that adversary is the speaker's own unopposed creation.
Tamburlaine's triumph is as much due to the initial retreat of others
from a participation in his discourse as it is to his own act of speaking. The obstacle to power and knowledge, therefore, is no longer
discourse itself, whether one's own or another's. The obstacle now
is whatever can be named, whatever can be predicated: it is therefore
no longer insurmountable (as it was in both Buchanan and Jodelle).
Tamburlaine defeats country after country because he says he will,
he makes others his by speaking to them: his words are swords.

The successive victories over the kings and emperors show a particular development. Each of the victims makes a different kind of mistake having to do with his use (or misuse) of speech with regard to

Tamburlaine. From the continuous retreat of Mycetes to the continuing threats of Orcanes they are also accompanied by a particular development in the metaphorical distancing of Tamburlaine himself, a distancing that increasingly undermines his power and shows its fallibility. To demonstrate the failure of a particular kind of discursive use is possible only through the metaphor that actually makes such a demonstration. The metaphor at once prevents Tamburlaine from finishing as a Herod, and makes it possible in future for tragedy to describe that failure (in speaking, in naming, in communcation) as a failure of specific kinds of *human activity*. The activity is that of an individual who seeks to overcome an obstacle (conceived as "external," though with psychological, emotional—internal—effects upon the individual in question) which can henceforth be put into speech and known as "real" and recognizable to all, though its particular power or intensity may be "unusual."

Mycetes is first in line of Tamburlaine's victims and from the first, as all critics have remarked, he makes a verbal retreat. He opens a play that is, at one level, all about the use of language by admitting that he does not know how to speak:

> Brother Cosroe, I find myself agriev'd;
> Yet insufficient to express the same,
> For it requires a great and thundering speech.
> Good brother, tell the cause unto my lords:
> I know you have a better wit than I.   [part 1, 2.1.1–5]

He is obliged to have others speak for him. "Declare the cause of my conceived grief," he says to Meander a few lines later on (1.1.29)—though, having made the request, he himself goes on to indicate the cause: Tamburlaine. For Mycetes discourse fails continually. Cosroe, for him, is anything but "good brother." The king seeks to give a command and concludes it by asking for approval: "if so like you all" (1.1.51–55). He sends Theridamas off to fight Tamburlaine likening his departure and return to the rape of Helen by Paris, concluding with the disjointed and irrelevant moral: "Our life is frail, and we may die today" (1.1.65–68). Judith Weil justifiably refers here to the "ironically inept and fatuously expressed moral."[6] The king concludes his farewell with a misplaced hyperbole, equally ironic in view of the fact that Theridamas will not be returning: "Theridamas, farewell ten thousand time" (1.1.82).

Mycetes is incompetent in discourse. His speech neither creates its own reality nor appears to correspond to any. It cannot express his kingship, nor any control whatever. He can communicate only his own fallibility. He suffers, one might say, from the same "tragic sentiment" as innumerable dramatic heroes of the time. For him language cannot offer an unambiguous means of situating himself in the world and with regard to other men. He cannot affirm even his own position as subject of enunciation: whence, "I refer me to my noblemen" (part 1, 1.1.21); "I *might* command you to be slain for this;/Meander, *might I not?*" (1.1.23–24); "*I mean it not,* but yet *I know I might.*/Yet live; yea, live; Mycetes wills it so" (1.1.26–27).[7] Later, on the point of sending his troops into battle, he expresses similar hesitations: "Would it not grieve a king to be so abus'd, /... I think it would: well, then, by heavens I swear . . ." (part 1, 2.2.5–9). That he is himself a king and therefore should not have to use the conditional is but one aspect of these hesitations. We may also note the patent contradiction between such hesitations and the phrases "Mycetes wills it so," or "I swear." Small wonder that in the latter case it is once again swallowed up in the request that another speak for him: "Tell you the rest, Meander: I have said" (2.2.13). These hesitations, contradictions, conditionals, expressions of will undercut even before they are uttered, differ radically from Tamburlaine's discourse. Meander suggests this opposition from the start: "Oft have I heard your majesty *complain*/Of Tamburlaine . . ." (1.1. 35).

J. B. Steane's view that this Persian king "is a cowardly nincompoop, more ridiculous because the accident of birth has placed a crown on his head: and the speech ['Accurs'd be he that first invented war!' (1.4.1)] is there for laughter" avoids the principal question.[8] The syntactical hesitations, the subject's failure to order its own utterance, the inefficacy of *any* discourse put into Mycetes' mouth, all are directly responsible for his defeat: "Ah, Menaphon," exclaims Cosroe, "I pass not for his threats!" (1.1.109).

By the second act of *1 Tamburlaine* the spectator/reader is well

aware of Tamburlaine's power with words and with arms; not Mycetes' and Meander's. Meander now produces a lengthy description
of the Scythian's army that bears no relationship whatsoever with
what we have already seen, and the speech concludes with an exchange of which critics have made much:

> MEANDER: . . . Like to the cruel brothers of the earth,
> Sprung of the teeth of dragons venomous,
> Their careless swords shall lance their fellows' throats
> And make us triumph in their overthrow.
> MYCETES: Was there such brethren, sweet Meander, say,
> That sprung of teeth of dragons venomous?
> MEANDER: So poets say, my lord.
> MYCETES: And 'tis a pretty toy to be a poet.
> Well, well, Meander, thou art deeply read. . . .
> [2.2.47–55]

The *naming* proposed by Meander is so suspect in its propriety that
even Mycetes doubts it: "Was there . . . ?" David Daiches, commenting
on a note by Una Ellis-Fermor, remarks on the "irony" that lies in
the king's incapacity to appreciate poetry, accompanying as it does
his inability to speak or to act: he "shows his lack of understanding
of the relation between language and action by his contemptuous
remark about poets."[9] Perhaps. Certainly that "contemptuous" is a
fine word. The difficulty is that if we have become aware of any
feeling in Mycetes' attitude toward his own discourse it is rather one
of regret than contempt: Tamburlaine can express contempt with
ease, Mycetes lacks the discursive power to do so. While he might
wish to show contempt for poetry, he acknowledges that Meander
has a certain superiority over himself because he knows the poets:
he is a "jewel" (2.2.56) *because* he is "deeply read" in the poets.
Mycetes had no poetry and cannot use words; Meander has a certain
capacity for both, but neither comes naturally to him—they are the
result of book learning. Thence, we would argue, Mycetes' doubt as to
the efficacy of Meander's metaphorical naming. The difference of this
from Tamburlaine's creativity is immediately apparent. Mycetes' last
irritated shout with which the scene is concluded merely emphasizes the
point: "Drums, why sound ye not when Meander speaks?" (2.2.75).

The difference in question is, of course, acted out when Mycetes and Tamburlaine actually meet. Mycetes has been seeking to hide his crown, the physical symbol of kingship: he has not the discourse, so why should he have or how can he *use* any other kind of sign? All the signs should correspond to something—with Mycetes they are empty, they do not work: Tamburlaine *makes* his do the job. Before the Persian can properly conceal the crown, Tamburlaine enters and contemptuously defeats him in a minor skirmish of words, concluding by taking the crown and then, with unexampled scorn, handing it back:

TAMBURLAINE: Are you the witty king of Persia?
MYCETES: Ay, marry, am I: have you any suit to me?
TAMBURLAINE: I would entreat you to speak but three wise
    words.
MYCETES: So I can when I see my time.
TAMBURLAINE: Is this your crown?
MYCETES: Ay: didst thou ever see a fairer?
TAMBURLAINE: You will not sell it, will ye?
MYCETES: Such another word, and I will have thee exe-
    cuted.
    Come, give it me.
TAMBURLAINE: No, I took it prisoner.
MYCETES: You lie; I gave it you.
TAMBURLAINE: Then 'tis mine.
MYCETES: No; I mean I let you keep it.
TAMBURLAINE: Well, I mean you shall have it again.
    Here, take it for a while: I lend it thee,
    Till I may see thee hemmed with armed men.
    Then shalt thou see me pull it from thy head:
    Thou art no match for mighty Tamburlaine.
Exit.
MYCETES: O gods, is this Tamburlaine the thief?
    I marvel much he stole it not away.

[2.4.23–41]

Before Tamburlaine, even more than before Cosroe, Mycetes is all retreat, and in the very next scene (which follows hard on the battle sounds succeeding Mycetes' "marvelling") the Scythian is handing the crown to Cosroe. We have already seen Tamburlaine do exactly the same thing in connection with the verbal joke played upon Mycetes; we are warned of what is to happen.

If Mycetes is all discursive retreat and acceptance of the traps laid for him by Tamburlaine, Cosroe is (apparently) all advance. But Cosroe does not use the "will" and "shall" of Tamburlaine. His technique is sarcasm, to slide, so to speak, into the interstices of his brother's discourse. "Is it not a kingly resolution?" asks Mycetes. "It cannot choose, because it comes from you," responds Cosroe, with obvious implications (1.1.55-56). Nor does Cosroe, again unlike Tamburlaine, himself impose his word. It is Ortygius who comes to proclaim him emperor *"in the name of* other Persian states / And commons of this mighty monarchy," because all "openly *exclaim* against the king" (1.1.137, 149). Furthermore, just as Mycetes' "swearing" is empty, so here it is vows, oaths that are being broken, and Mycetes is quite right to ask, "O where is duty and allegiance now?" (1.1.101). At the beginning of *2 Tamburlaine* oaths are sworn between Sigismund and Orcanes, and the consequence of their breaking is the rout both of Christians and of Turks. We may well recall *Jephthes* and the various comments of Montaigne. Unlike Cosroe, it is because Tamburlaine always does exactly what he says that he is victorious: for Tamburlaine all speech has the import of a vow or an oath. As we saw in the case of Zenocrate's death, it is when speech can no longer so "seize" what it has uttered that the end begins for Tamburlaine: when it becomes apparent that his kind of discursive power is not enough alone.

Until that moment arrives, however, and despite one or two warnings as we will see, Tamburlaine does not waver at all. The scene in which Cosroe is named king by others is followed by a special piece of irony. "God save the king!" they all cry—and as they leave the stage Tamburlaine comes on.

Daiches notes a progressive heightening of the terms in which Zenocrate names Tamburlaine—"shepherd," "my lord," "mighty emperor"—and remarks that that heightening is "produced entirely by Tamburlaine's way of speech."[10] Zenocrate has been defeated by Tamburlaine's takeover of *two* processes that produce meaning: that of language, and that of external conventional signs—crowns, rings, flags, titles, colors, and so on—though they too depend on language for their efficacy. It is through a combination of the two that the future empress's defeat is initially marked: it is her father's, the sultan's, *seal* and his letters that have been taken by Tamburlaine: "Bearing his privy-signet and his hand/To safe conduct us through Africa" (part 1, 1.2.15–16). One of her courtiers even sees fit to emphasize their efficacy:

> And, since we have arrived in Scythia,
> Besides rich presents from the puissant Cham,
> We have his highness' letters to command
> Aid and assistance, if we stand in need.   [1.2.17–20]

Unfortunately—again unlike Cosroe—Tamburlaine neither needs nor recognizes the discursive power of others. He will control all "working words," all that can produce sense and action:

> But now you see these letters and commands
> Are countermanded by a greater man,
> And through my provinces you must expect
> Letters of conduct from my mightiness,
> If you intend to keep your treasure safe.   [1.2.21–25]

We are reminded of the importance of this writing of the "self" later on when Tamburlaine tells Bajazeth that he will overwhelm all the garrisons of Greece and Africa: "Those walled garrisons will I subdue,/And write myself great lord of Africa" (3.3.244–45). The point will form a kind of refrain—when he is telling Zenocrate he will not cease his conquests in favor of her father he uses the same expression:

> Zenocrate, were Egypt Jove's own land,
> Yet would I with my sword make Jove to stoop.
> I will confute those blind geographers
> That make a triple region in the world,
> Excluding regions which I mean to trace,
> And with this pen reduce them to a map,
> Call the provinces, cities, and towns,
> After my name and thine, Zenocrate.   [4.4.79–87]

It is certainly no accident that at the end of 2 *Tamburlaine* the dying emperor traces out the limits of his achievement and commands the future of his sons *on a map of the world* (5.3.124–59).

The equivalence of "pen" and "sword" in the passage above is made in a different register from the similar equivalence we saw made somewhat ironically by Mycetes. From the very first time that we see Tamburlaine he is all force: the sword is a manifestation of power, the word *is* power. We see it first in performance. The frequency with which the words "shall" and "will" occur in Tamburlaine's profession of love to Zenocrate is remarkable: "shall buy," "shall be made," "thou shalt," "will be," "shall we all" (1.2.86, 93, 95, 99, 101, 104). Tamburlaine mocks the companions of Zenocrate by suggesting that they think his words mere "prattle" (1.2.62), a mockery we remember later when two future victims refer to Tamburlaine's wars as a mere "bickering" (3.1.4: Bajazeth) and to his talk of them as a "rattle" (3.2.45: Agydas). Discourse is power and, though offered as an alternative to a battle with more solid weapons, in fact dispenses with the need for them. Thus, before the battle with the Persians, Tamburlaine asks: "Then shall we fight courageously with them?/Or look you I should play the orator?" (1.2.128–29). Techelles replies in the negative, but in doing so he merely reverses the pattern: "*Our swords shall play the orators for us*" (1.2.132).

Tamburlaine, in choosing to talk first (thereby dispensing with advice that other rulers in the play find essential), utters a warning that reinforces the equivalence we saw when Mycetes told Theridamas that his words were swords. We will parley, says Tamburlaine, but "if they offer *word* or violence" (and the order is significant), then "'gainst the general we will lift our swords,/And either lance his greedy thirsting throat . . ." (1.2.142–46). Stabbing the enemy's throat is the favorite method of killing for those on Tamburlaine's side: thus they prevent speech at the same time. This, too, we will recall when we see Agydas seeking to arouse Zenocrate against Tamburlaine by mocking his discourse ("Leave to *wound* me with these words/And speak of Tamburlaine as he deserves," she warns (2.2.35–36); and again when, in the face of this "belittling of his language" the emperor remains "wrapt in silence" (3.2.71), simply sending a dagger a little later as mute suggestion that Agydas kill himself.[11] He does so.

Tamburlaine, speaking of the future when his *"name and honour shall* be spread/As far as Boreas claps his brazen wings" (1.2.205–06), of course "defeats" and wins over the Persian sent by Mycetes:

> THERIDAMAS: Not Hermes, prolocutor to the gods,
>   Could use persuasions more pathetical.
> TAMBURLAINE: Nor are Apollo's oracles more true
>   Than thou shalt find my vaunts substantial.
>   [1.2.210–13]

Usumcasane remarks that in the future the sign of their victories will be when "hosts of soldiers stand amaz'd at us,/When *with their fearful tongues* they shall confess . . ." (1.2.221–22). Theridamas admits himself "won with thy words" (1.2.228), and Tamburlaine seals the issue *with a vow*:

> Theridamas, my friend, take here my hand,
> Which is as much as if I swore by heaven,
> And call'd the gods to witness of my vow.   [1.2.232–34]

The motif of discourse as power and its accompaniment of the progress of Tamburlaine's increasing might runs parallel with the slow filling out of a metaphor that, by the end of *2 Tamburlaine*, will have become all-important. The metaphor—Tamburlaine as Phaeton—is at once ambiguous and increasingly complex: it proceeds from a simple though implicit naming in verbal discourse through a symbolization in another sign system (that of flags and colors) to an acting out upon the stage and an explicit naming. Its initial ambiguity is a matter of precision, not of implication, for it is never really clear whether Tamburlaine is competing with Apollo or with Jupiter, whether he is Phaeton striving to take control of the sun's fire or Prometheus stealing fire. At the first it is certainly the metaphor of Phaeton that is in question, but as *1 Tamburlaine* proceeds it increasingly becomes both at once: we saw above how, when affirming how he will rewrite the world, Tamburlaine begins by belittling Jove.

From the outset Tamburlaine asserts himself ruler of the world in terms of a comparison with Apollo. He "means to be a terror to the

world, / Measuring the limits of his empery / By east and west, as
Phoebus doth his course" (1.2.38–40). He and his army will shake
the world as do the "windy exhalations" of volcanic movements
"within the earth" (1.2.50–51). These windy exhalations are at once
the scorching of fire and discursive utterance.[12] We might compare
Bajazeth's use of the adjective "breathless" to indicate the death of
the beseiged Greeks (3.1.15) or his observation of his army's strength
with the phrase "And all the trees are blasted with our breaths," or
his comment that their cannons are *"mouth'd* like Orcus' gulf" (3.1.
55, 56). Even before Tamburlaine's persuasion of Theridamas in which
he likened his own words to "Apollo's oracles," the Scythian shepherd sets out to play the role of the sun: "Lay out our golden wedges
to the view, / That their reflections may amaze the Persians" (1.2.139–
40). In his courtship speech to Zenocrate he expresses her beauty as
heat; she will melt "the icy mountains' lofty tops" (1.2.100–01), just
as he will shake their foundations. She is at the same time a sign of
a more lofty competition, "lovelier than the love of Jove."

Zenocrate herself, before she has actually declared her love to Tamburlaine, will proclaim it to Agydas in terms of both metaphors:

> As looks the sun through Nilus' flowing stream,
> Or when the Morning holds him in her arms,
> So looks my lordly love, fair Tamburlaine;
> His talk much sweeter than the Muses' song
> They sang for honour 'gainst Pierides,
> Or when Minerva did with Neptune strive:
> And higher would I rear my estimate
> Than Juno, sister to the highest god,
> If I were match'd with mighty Tamburlaine.   [3.2.47–55]

In the next scene Tamburlaine requites her, virtually term for term.
She is Tamburlaine's only equal and must therefore be incorporated
in the same metaphor(s):

> Zenocrate, the loveliest maid alive,
> Fairer than rocks of pearl and precious stone,
> The only paragon of Tamburlaine;
> Whose eyes are brighter than the lamps of heaven,
> And speech more pleasant than sweet harmony;

That with thy looks canst clear the darken'd sky,
And calm the rage of thundering Jupiter;
Sit down by her, adorned with my crown,
As if thou wert the empress of the world.   [3.3.117–25]

It is not yet explicit that a metaphor of Phaeton (or Prometheus) is involved at all. That metaphor would inscribe eventual failure into Tamburlaine's words and deeds, and for the present that is not in question. All we have at the first is a simile: Tamburlaine is *like* Apollo, or he is *like* Jupiter. But no sooner has the simile been proposed than it begins to play a role in his victory. Theridamas marvels: "His looks do menace heaven and dare the gods;/His fiery eyes are fix'd upon the earth" (1.2.157–58). The Scythian is quick to confirm it for him: "Sooner shall the sun fall from his sphere/Than Tamburlaine be slain or overcome (1.2.176–77), and though at this point he appears to see Jove not as a competitor but as a helper ("Jove himself will stretch his hand from heaven" [1.2.180]), he will not hesitate to change that relationship: he has started as a shepherd and even in that he is like the chief of the gods, who sometimes came down to earth "masked in a shepherd's weed" (1.2.199).[13] Tamburlaine wishes to be "immortal like the gods" (1.2.201).

Henceforth the simile in question and the more general use of language both become identified with Tamburlaine's increasing power. Mycetes was overborne entirely by language. Cosroe, however, is not utterly devoid of a certain discursive power: it takes a certain naming to defeat him. Like Theridamas, but without understanding its present implication aright, Menaphon accepts Tamburlaine's evaluation of himself as godlike and so describes him to Cosroe (2.1.7–30). Tamburlaine's head, says he, is "a pearl more worth than all the world," his eyes are "fiery circles [that] bear encompassed/A heaven of heavenly bodies in their spheres." The hint of ludicrousness in Menaphon's choice of words here is an indication of their inferior use of language as compared to that of Tamburlaine and his companions. Cosroe then makes the irretrievable error of agreeing that the Scythian is

His fortune's master and the king of men,
That could *persuade*, at such a sudden pinch,

> *With reasons* of his valour and his life,
> A thousand *sworn* and overmatching foes.   [2.1.36–39]

Cosroe appears to want to do away with the simile (as offered by Menaphon) and bring things back to the "more fundamental" level of the simple use of language. Unfortunately we have already seen the effects of that, and we know, too, that far from being "sworn," Cosroe is already forsworn. Moreover, he has accepted Tamburlaine's own evaluation: "Even as from assured oracle, / I take thy doom for satisfaction" (2.3.3–4). Yet Cosroe does have a certain way with words, and Tamburlaine reverts to the simile. Their weapons will be "like Jove's dread thunderbolts," they will "threat the gods," and the army will be awesome:

> And with our sun-bright armour, as we march,
> We'll chase the sun from heaven, and dim their
>   eyes
> That stand and muse at our admired arms.
> THERIDAMAS: You see, my lord, what working words he hath;
> But, when you see his actions top his speech,
> Your speech will stay, or so extol his worth. . . .
>   [2.3.22–27]

This exchange is interesting for several reasons. First of all Theridamas appears to remove from Cosroe all possibility of answering Tamburlaine when the latter chooses to take his crown from him. We will see in a moment how this is indeed the case. Second, the use of the verb *see* to refer to Tamburlaine's "working words" is noteworthy. It suggests a kind of objectivization of those words in a way another verb (*hear*, for example) would not: one sees things outside oneself, they have a certain "massiness" (to use a Marlovian term). The whole point is, as Cosroe learns to his cost, that Tamburlaine's words *do* create a situation as real for others as for Tamburlaine himself.[14]

A third point regarding this exchange proceeds from a line not yet quoted: when Tamburlaine likens their "bullets" to "Jove's dread thunderbolts," he qualifies the simile with the words, "Enroll'd in flames and fiery smoldering mists" (2.3.20). The general has already likened himself to Apollo—the only circumstance in which this line could be used to qualify the sun occurred when Phaeton "took charge" of Apollo's chariot and caused the earth to be scorched. The reference here is perhaps only distant, a far-off glimmer of what will be a progressive strengthening of the metaphor: brought on by Tamburlaine's working words themselves.

It is interesting that it should be Theridamas who emphasizes these words of Tamburlaine. We saw at the outset that it will be Theridamas who reproves Tamburlaine for his outcry at Zenocrate's death and who points out the first obvious failure of his discursive power, just as he will do at Tamburlaine's own death, upbraiding him for "these impatient words, / which add much danger to your malady!" (part 2, 5.3.54–55): the danger of visible fallibility. It is Theridamas who is the only "enemy" openly admired by Tamburlaine ("Noble and mild this Persian," [part 1, 1.2.162]); the only man whom Tamburlaine even suggests could be his equal ("Then shalt thou be competitor with me, / And sit with Tamburlaine in all his majesty" [part 1, 2.2.208–09]); the only one of the Scythian's major companions initially to say he is not interested in kingship (part 1, 2.5.6); the only one whose "sworn oath" likens him to his emperor and distinguishes him from the other now tributary kings (part 2, 1.5.10); the only one who competes with Tamburlaine in trying to have a mistress (part 2, 4.2.: Olympia).

To be sure, in all of these he is Tamburlaine's inferior. He is a lesser king, and that by the grace of Tamburlaine; he *does* after all accept such a kingship; he keeps his oath to Tamburlaine only after having broken it to Mycetes; he loses Olympia (interestingly enough because she is able to trick him with words and mockery into stabbing her in the "naked throat," [part 2, 4.1.68–82]). Nonetheless, to Tamberlaine the first defection of Theridamas was essential for his future victories—and he showed himself well aware of it in his comments to the Persian. We might well be inclined to suggest that it is Tamburlaine who, in not making him his equal finally, *has broken his word*. It is the only time throughout the entire ten acts when one could say such a thing of Tamburlaine. It is fatal in that it will be Theridamas who, in all the major conjunctures of Tamburlaine's progress underlines the fallibility of this *individual* power over discourse—at the moment of Zenocrate's death, at that of the emperor's own, and earlier, as we have just seen, at the moment of the consolidation of Tamburlaine's power. He does this here by means of the first hint of the Phaeton metaphor: a metaphor whose "working" will undermine the power of discourse as it puts a name to Tamburlaine's eventual failure (to compete with the gods, to be lord of the whole earth, to remake the map, to make Theridamas echo his own discourse).

For Cosroe, to whom we return, all this is far too late. To be sure, he takes up the terms of the metaphor when he discovers that Tamburlaine is after him as well. He argues against Tamburlaine's "presumption" who "dares the force of angry Jupiter," and he wishes to "burn him in the fury of that flame / That none can quench but blood and empery" (part 1, 2.6.32–33). But this kind of thing is already the property of his opponent, and Cosroe underlines it with a threat that can only be interpreted as a mistake. Successful soldiers, we have seen, always direct their swords at the throat—death is above all the inability to speak. Not Cosroe: "Direct my weapon at his barbarous heart" (part 1, 2.6.38). It is thus only fitting that when he dies he does so as a victim of Tamburlaine's success: "And death arrests the organ of my voice" (part 1, 2.7.8).

An error of like kind is made by Tamburlaine's next opponent, Bajazeth. The king of Fez suggests he threaten Tamburlaine, "as from the mouth of mighty Bajazeth" (part 1, 3.2.20), but Bajazeth does so only by sending someone in his stead, to tell the Scythian that he "wills and commands" that Tamburlaine stay put where he is, adding: "For say not I entreat" (3.7.21–30), a remark strangely akin to certain terms uttered by Mycetes. Tamburlaine's response to this bit of proxy work is entirely predictable: "Tush, Turks are full of brags, / And menace more than they can well perform" (part 1, 3.3.3–4). This will be borne out when Tamburlaine comes to outface Bajazeth and his companion kings and to mock him. Here Bajazeth makes *his* mistake, and Fez realizes it immediately: "What means the mighty Turkish emperor, / To talk with one so base as Tamburlaine?" "Leave words," adds the king of Argier (3.3.87–91). Tamburlaine will later underline the "reason" for this defeat when he orders Bajazeth to act as his footstool or be torn apart as though "struck with the voice of thundering Jupiter" (part 1, 4.2.25). In the same act he remarks to Zenocrate about Bajazeth and his wife, Zabina: "I glory in the curses of my foes" (4.29), for their defeat has after all *shown* their words to be useless. It is in their final curses (part 1, 5.2.151–66), calling for his enemies to strike Tamburlaine, not in the organ of speech, but in the "body" and in the "breast" that they mark the identity of their failure with that of Cosroe.

It is, then, after the defeat of Cosroe that the simile (Tamburlaine *like* a god) is consolidated. Tamburlaine sees a "precedent" for his activities in those of "mighty Jove " when he "thrusts his doting father from his chair" (part 1, 2.7.12–17). Usumcasane takes up the simile:

> For as, when Jove did thrust old Saturn down,
> Neptune and Dis gain'd each of them a crown,
> So do we hope to reign in Asia,
> If Tamburlaine be plac'd in Persia.   [2.7.36–39]

And at the end of the act, Tamburlaine can challenge the Furies and the gods (particularly Mars), saying that the crown is now "more surer on my head / Than if the gods had held a parliament, / And all pronounc'd me king of Persia" (part 1, 2.7.53–67). All around him have now *proclaimed* him king, but it is he whose words and subsequent acts have *made* him so.

I mentioned earlier that Tamburlaine had accompanied the verbal production of reality with a physical symbolization of it (seals, crowns, flags) from the beginning. I also suggested that the increasingly complex metaphor was symbolized in another signifying system than that of words alone. It is complex chiefly because that other system is offered as a *visible* manifestation of Tamburlaine's power, whereas the metaphor suggests rather an undermining of that power.

After the defeat of Bajazeth, which occupies act 3 of *1 Tamburlaine*, the conqueror lays seige to Damascus and attacks the domains of the sultan of Egypt, Zenocrate's father. He has a new device to indicate his power and the unwavering nature of his force, to demonstrate that he will not be forsworn. The messenger to the sultan tells how Tamburlaine lays seige for three days. For the first day the whole camp is in white ("to signify the mildness of his mind," [part 1,

4.2.53]); the second day all is "red as scarlet," to signify that sur-
render is now possible only at the price of the death of all "that can
manage arms" (4.7.58); the third day all is black, to signify "death
and hell" and complete destruction of the entire town (4.1.62–64).
The act then shows us the progress through this sequence (scene 2,
white; scene 4, red; 5.1., black). At one point Zenocrate begs him
to show leniency even if the city does not yield at the right time:
"Not for the world, Zenocrate, if I have sworn" (part 1, 4.2.125).
That "not for the world" is meant quite literally: his discourse has
created the world that corresponds to it, and that depends on the
constancy and stability of that discourse—to break his word would
be to lose the world (which is why the mere hint of his having done
so in his not making Theridamas his equal may be so fatal). The
sequence of colours is an oath sworn, it is a "custom" not open to
reversal: "They have refus'd the offer of their lives, / And know my
customs are as peremptory / As wrathful planets, death or destiny"
(part 1, 5.2.63–65). "That which mine honour swears," he asserts,
"shall be perform'd" (5.2.44).

   In a very real way, now, Tamburlaine is bound by his own discourse: he can allow no slippage between the two, he has *said* that
the sequence lasts three days, that it cannot be reversed, and that
the meaning of the three colors—white, red, black—is clemency,
carnage, and death. He is as much bound by the limits he has set
as others are—witness the stage direction for the third day (5.2):
"Enter Tamburlaine, all in black and very melancholy." Tamburlaine would fail if others are able to perceive (as Theridamas will)
some flaw, however small, between discourse and other orders—
including that of the world as seen. They *must* agree. Clearly, others
fail for just that reason: Mycetes with his stuttering discourse which
does not, as Cosroe observes, correspond to his kingship; Cosroe
and Bajazeth, who retreat from speech when confronted with Tamburlaine (having overflowed with threats); Sigismund, who breaks
his vows; Orcanes and Callipine, who claim titles already possessed
by Tamburlaine; Callipine, who finds himself being placed second
to Tamburlaine by his own supporter,[15] and Orcanes, who finds
himself submitted to the bridle, the limits of his speech fixed by
Tamburlaine:

Well, bark, ye dogs: I'll bridle all your tongues,
And bind them close with bits of burnish'd steel,
Down to the channels of your hateful throats.

[part 2, 4.1.184-86] [16]

Tamburlaine himself does not suffer this failure for long; and then it is at the very limits of discourse, when confronted with death and silence. He suffers rather the consequences of his own success: he is bound by his discourse as Jephtha and those around him were bound by his vows. It is certainly deliberate that "oaths," "swearing," and "vows" are such an important part of *Tamburlaine*. Part 2, indeed, begins with two scenes that show the swearing of treaties between Orcanes and Sigismund, another that shows the breaking of allegiance by Almeda, a fourth scene in which Tamburlaine tests the loyalty of his sons and concludes by saying, "For I have sworn by sacred Mahomet" to defeat the "Turkish crew" (1.4.109), and a fifth, already mentioned, that shows Theridamas's swearing. The first three scenes of the second act show us the consequences of the breaking of oaths between Sigismund and Orcanes. Tamburlaine does not suffer the failure for as long as *he* controls the vows, the sealing of discourse, for as long as his discourse can succeed in making the world in its image.

Yet the sequence of colors instituted by Tamburlaine does show indications from the first of getting away from him. It is just after we have learned of this institution that Bajazeth finally seems to realize his failure and utters the only well-directed curse of all those he offers. He calls on the priests of Mahomet to stain the altars with their blood and

Make heaven to frown, and every fixed star
To suck up poison from the morrish fens,
And pour it in this glorious tyrant's throat!   [4.2.2-7]

This curse in turn narrowly precedes the first explicit reference to the Phaeton metaphor in the context of Tamburlaine's "competition" with Apollo:

For I, the chiefest lamp of all the earth,
First rising in the east with mild aspect,
But fixed now in the meridian line,

Will send up fire to your returning spheres,
And cause the sun to borrow light of you [the stars of his nativ-
ity].

. . . .

But ere I march to wealthy Persia,
Or leave Damascus and th'Egyptian fields,
As was the fame of Clymene's brain-sick son
That almost brent the axle-tree of heaven,
So shall our swords, our lances, and our shot
Fill all the air with fiery meteors.
Then, when the sky shall wax as red as blood,
It shall be said I made it red myself,
To make me think of naught but blood and war.

[part 1, 4.2.36–55]

We will see more of these meteors and of this fiery sky.

These two "speech-events" occur exactly between the messenger's announcement of the use of the three colors and our seeing them in action. Is it too much to read in the progress of the colors, now that we have the appropriate curse and, even more, Tamburlaine's own reference to the fiery and blood-red fall of Phaeton, the symbolization of the progress of Clymene's son? White is then the color of the sun in its right place: Tamburlaine speaks of the "gentle beams" (of Mercy) signified by his "milk-white flags" (part 1, 5.2.5–6). Red is the color of blood and fire, of scorching and burning; black is that of the ashes and death left after Phaeton has fallen and Apollo has regained control over his chariot. Such an interpretation is further urged by some of the words uttered by Zabina in her madness after the death of her husband: "The sun was down—streamers white, red, black.—Here, here, here!—Fling the meat in his face—Tamburlaine, Tamburlaine!" (5.2.252–54).

Immediately after this Zenocrate appears. In lamenting the fate of "the Turk and his great empress," she warns Tamburlaine of his own fallibility (5.2.286–310). It is now, too, that Tamburlaine openly casts himself as Jove's rival: "Jove, viewing me in arms, looks pale and wan,/Fearing my power should pull him from his throne" (5.2.391–92). He marries Zenocrate: "As Juno, when the giants were suppress'd,/That darted mountains at her brother Jove,/So looks my love . . ." (5.2.449–51). In celebration of his victories, of his marriage, of peace, Tamburlaine now instructs his companions to "put on scarlet robes" (5.2.463). Scarlet is the color of carnage, of the moment when Phaeton, out of control, scorches up the earth and makes the sky "wax as red as blood." It is as though Tamburlaine's will were now being undercut by the metaphor he has himself mounted.

One is tempted to say that it is this moment that rules the whole of *2 Tamburlaine*. He is no longer the *rival* of Jove, nor even of Apollo: they are now above him, observing him:

> If all the crystal gates of Jove's high court
> Were open'd wide, and I might enter in . . .   [part 2, 1.6.26–27]
> . . . .
>   Jove shall send his winged messenger
> To bid me sheathe my sword and leave the field;
> The sun, unable to sustain the sight,
> Shall hide his head in Thetis' watery lap. . . .   [part 2, 1.6.39–43]

When Tamburlaine kills his son Calyphas for cowardice, he *calls on* Jove to "receive his fainting soul again" (part 2, 4.1.113). He notes that he will not stop fighting "till by vision or speech I hear / Immortal Jove say 'Cease, my Tamburlaine'" (4.2.201–02), and adds that until that time he will continue "making the meteors" (4.2.204). He foresees for himself a translation:

> If Jove, esteeming me too good for earth,
> Raise me, to match the fair Aldeboran,
> Above the three fold astracism of heaven,
> Before I conquer all the triple world.   [part 2, 4.3.60–63]

Besides reminding us of the death agonies of "all-powerful" Hercules, this last case, marking Tamburlaine's inferiority to Jupiter, further emphasizes the theme of failure. For Tamburlaine is telling the king of Jerusalem that his sons will continue his conquests should he himself die before they are completed.

The death of his equal, Zenocrate, is a failure of the sun, exclaims Tamburlaine, in the last vision of himself as rival of the gods:

> Black is the beauty of the brightest day;
> The golden ball of heaven's eternal fire,
> That danc'd with glory on the silver waves,
> Now wants the fuel that inflam'd his beams,
> And all with faintness and for foul disgrace,
> He binds his temples with a frowning cloud,
> Ready to darken earth with endless night.   [part 2, 2.4.1–7]

The remainder of the play is colored with the red of Phaeton's fiery failure. It starts with the advice of Zenocrate herself who, as she is dying, tells Tamburlaine to live, "And sooner let the fiery element/ Dissolve, and make your kingdom in the sky,/Than this base earth should shroud your majesty" (2.4.58–60). He will bring fire to the earth and march under a "bloody flag" now that "amorous Jove has snatch'd my love from hence" (2.4.116, 117). He will burn the town where they are in her memory and she, along with him when he dies, will have (he says) "one epitaph/ *Writ in as many several languages* / As I have conquer'd kingdoms with my sword" (2.4.134–36).

It is now, too, that Theridamas makes his first overt reproof to Tamburlaine ("all this raging cannot make her live"), underscoring the limits of even Tamburlaine's discourse. The epitaph by the Scythian is therefore most aptly a kind of Babel, for her death does indeed mark Tamburlaine's first failure.[17] And the emperor now adopts the posture of falling Phaeton in full:

> So burn the turrets of this cursed town,
> Flame to the highest region of the air,
> And kindle heaps of exhalations,
> That, being fiery meteors, may presage
> Death and destruction to the inhabitants!
> Over my zenith hang a blazing star,
> That may endure till heaven be dissolv'd.
> Fed with the fresh supply of earthly dregs,
> Threatening a death and famine to his land!
> Flying dragons, lightning, fearful thunder-claps,
> Singe these fair plains, and make them seem as black
> As is the island where the Furies mask. . . .   [part 2, 3.2.1–12]

And Amyras adds that they will place a "mournful streamer" (3.2.19), recalling once again the sequence of siege colors.

Now that the Phaeton metaphor and its implications are in full possession of events, the threats of the last conquered kings can become effective. Except for Bajazeth's warning threat, it is the two kings who outlive Tamburlaine who make the only effective threats of the entire ten acts (Callapine also outlives him, but he is put to flight and thus deprived of his chance to curse). Orcanes cries out to Tamburlaine: "This sword shall lance thy throat!" (part 2, 3.5.78). The king of Jerusalem tells him that "shortly heaven, fill'd with the meteors/Of blood and fire thy tyrannies have made,/Will pour down blood and fire on thy head,/Whose scalding drops will pierce thy seething brains" (part 2, 4.1.143–46). As we saw, Tamburlaine will indeed die "full of accidental heat." The two kings attack him with a curse on the power of speech and a curse in the terms of Phaeton's failure. They are victorious over Tamburlaine certainly in that they outlive him: and the more so in that it is they who pull his chariot when he dies.

I said earlier that the Phaeton metaphor progressed from a verbal naming, through symbolization in another signifying system, to its actual performance as an *act* on stage.[18] Tamburlaine, after a long verbal dispute with the kings, remarks that he will soon stop their chatter by putting bits in their mouths (part 2, 3.5.58–174). The kings, that is, have made the same mistake as Bajazeth: they have accepted an exchange of words with Tamburlaine. In consequence they become the "horses" made to pull the conqueror's chariot. On the other hand, however, the metaphorical naming has specified the emperor's failure and it is now undermining his posture as victor and providing us with terms in which we can "explain," "understand" that failure: it participates in a familiar paradigm. Once Tamburlaine has the kings of Trebizon and Soria harnessed to his chariot he makes the reference explicit once again:

> The horse that guide the golden eye of heaven,
> And blow the morning from their nostrils,
> Making their fiery gait above the clouds,
> Are not so honour'd in their governor
> As you, ye slaves, in mighty Tamburlaine.   [part 2, 4.3.7–11]

The king-drawn chariot shows his victory over them, but it also marks the undermining of the willful process that made that victory possible. The metaphor, gradually crystallizing before the spectator, is no longer Tamburlaine's to control (if it ever was.)[19]

It is now, too, at the very moment of this apparent victory that he makes explicit the possibility of his failure, telling the king of Jerusalem, who has just cursed his son, that it is Celebinus who will have to complete his, Tamburlaine's, conquests should he die first (4.3.57–63). Tamburlaine's insistence on driving the chariot of the sun ("Through the streets, with troops of conquer'd kings, / I'll ride in golden armour like the sun" [4.3.114–15]), and even that of Jupiter ("in my coach, like Saturn's royal son / Mounted his shining chariot gilt with fire" [4.3.125–26]), takes on an almost frenetic aspect: as though he were warding off the swiftly approaching moment when his "soul, dissever'd from his flesh, / Shall mount the milk-white way" (4.3.131–32). It is surely the greatest sign of his failure that Callapine should get away from him entirely—Callipine who is in every way as weak with words as was Mycetes. (See note 15.)

At the siege of Babylon we see the last reminders of the color sequence. This day is the "last day's dreadful siege" (part 2, 5.1.29) and all is black. Nonetheless Theridamas and Techelles arrive to persuade the governor to yield, saying that lives will be spared if he does. He refuses, and Techelles carefully notes the slippage of the colors' meaning: "we offer more / Than ever yet we did to such proud slaves / As durst resist us till our third day's siege" (5.1.57–59). Tamburlaine himself, in upbraiding the governor for not yielding earlier, insists, not on the black with its fatal meaning (and at which stage they presently are), nor on the white, which would have meant no penalty but submission, but on the red. Why? Surely not because yielding on the red would have been better than the white, while for those fighting there is no difference between the red and black. But red is the colour of Phaeton, and the images are again the same:

> Sirrah, the view of our vermilion tents
> Which threaten'd more than if the region
> Next underneath the element of fire
> Were full of comets and of blazing stars,

Whose flaming trains should reach down to the earth,
Could not affright you.   [5.1.86–91]

The correspondence between the system and the "achievement of
the meaning" controlled by Tamburlaine is visibly falling away; the
sequence of colors is becoming ever more closely associated with the
Phaeton metaphor. So much so indeed that Tamburlaine himself
appears compelled to accept that *other* signification, and when he
cries out in rage against Mahomet it is as though he were accepting
to play the role of Phaeton in another key. It is in that sense that
I interpret the fact that Tamburlaine falls ill at the end of this scene.
As he feels the approach of death he chooses the very form of the
last stage of the color sequence that had been his in order to indicate
the failure of control: "Set black streamers in the firmament,/To
signify the slaughter of the gods" (part 2, 5.3.49–50). For Tamburlaine, of course, this is a call to lay siege to the heavens, echo of
his earthly sieges; for us it is the mark of the ashes of a singed earth
and of Phaeton's scorched body. "Earth droops," say both Theridamas and Usumcasane. Tamburlaine's body is "parch'd and void of
spirit," says the physician (5.3.95); "this subject, not of force
enough/To hold the fiery spirit it contains," adds Tamburlaine
ambiguously (5.3.169–70). Amyras, we saw, speaks of Tamburlaine's
"burning agony"; Tamburlaine himself reminds us once again at the
end of "Clymene's brain-sick son." The acting-out of the metaphor
does indeed say that Tamburlaine "must die."
     This final (and unique) ascription of the word "must" to Tambur-
laine is the certain mark that he has been taken over by a metaphor
that the spectator/reader can "control": the "tragic" failure of Tamburlaine is not one of discourse (which would condemn us too), it
is one of hubris, of *hamartia.* And so on and so forth. The tragic has
been *placed* as the performance and failure of a particular kind of
human activity. The metaphor of Phaeton offers a bridge between
the tragic of the impossibility of meaningful discourse and the tragic
of catastrophe not unmerited but "incomprehensibly" enormous.
But such catastrophe will be the result of certain human activities
entirely comprehensible in themselves and comprehensible in so
far as the obstacle to their achievement is concerned; and that means

that they can be contained and controlled within a suitably ordered discourse, within a rightly organized civil society.

Tamburlaine falls because it is not he who controls the "proud rebelling jades" (5.3.239) against whom he feels constrained to warn his son. A discourse that sought to be all-powerful is shown flawed by a metaphor that grew, as though accidentally, along with it: and that metaphor eventually revealed an essential disparity between the world and controlling utterance. At that point, when Tamburlaine is forced to see the failure of a discourse upon which he has staked his power and all activity, he "must die," no further speech is possible. Silence and death are synonymous: for Mycetes, for Agydas, for Zenocrate, for Tamburlaine himself. The inappropriately talkative Mycetes dies in silence between two scenes; Agydas kills himself with a silent image of speech; the silence of Zenocrate is the first sign of a disparity in Tamburlaine's discourse. Her silence is alone sufficient to provoke Theridamas to the words that "pierce the soul." Tamburlaine is powerless if the other does not requite him, if the other does not respond: Zenocrate is gone in spite of, not because of, Tamburlaine (unlike the deaths of his various conquered victims, which were requital).

For the first time Tamburlaine becomes aware that the power of discourse depends on the acquiesence of a respondent, on the acquiescence of the world. The gradual growth of the Phaeton metaphor emphasizes Tamburlaine's failure to recognize the essential role of such a respondent and provides the spectator with a paradigmatic explanation of that failure. (See note 19.) It indicates that not only is discursive power necessary to a speaker but also the recognition of the fallibility of that power inasmuch as it *requires* the other. Discourse cannot be self-sufficient to its enunciator, it must find a way to compromise with the world and with others. From that necessity the late seventeenth century and the eighteenth will develop the concept of the *contract.*

There is no compromise, no mark of fallibility in Tamburlaine's speech: it is undermined by a metaphor drawn from another discourse than his own, that of the Greeks, which appeals to an order of which the speaker can "take charge" when Tamburlaine himself cannot. It is that lack of compromise which is perhaps responsible for a certain discomfort on the part of some critics, who feel the language to be overly strained and too bombastic. Wolfgang Clemen writes: "The most characteristic attitude that is revealed in Tamburlaine's speeches is his anticipation of the future. . . . For the most part this future of his has no existence in the real world, but only in a dream of his imagination."[20] This is an odd pair of sentences in more ways than one. No doubt the first sentence is accurate enough, though it expresses in one sense at least a truism: discourse, as a logical *progressive* system, always aims at its own discursive future. (For the subject of enunciation the very problem is the control of that "future.") Clemen's second sentence is palpable nonsense. What is remarkable in *Tamburlaine* is the way in which the principal speaker *does* succeed in controlling the future, does bring into existence the situation that subject has *named* (even, for example, the love of Zenocrate). Even after the Phaeton metaphor is already confirmed in its growth (part 1, 4.2.) and has begun its sapping process, Tamburlaine continues victoriously with his creation of the future he names.

In one way the paradox expressed by Clemen suggests the reason for its author's apparent distaste for the naming/making in question: the future "has no existence in the real world." Indeed not. The "real" world is *what is present to us now*: it is our present structuration of the (to us) otherwise unavailable world of phenomena that composes our "knowing" it. Tamburlaine fishes forms from his mind and imposes his pattern on the world. He is a creator of experiments that become truths. His schema do indeed become those of the real world. His will, *essentially* embodied in his discourse, does dispel contradiction, doubts, all lack of coincidence between word and event —for a while. So, too, did the Ptolomaic cosmology (for example), for nigh on two thousand years. The difference with Tamburlaine is that like a Galileo, the speaker takes responsibility for what discourse creates.[21] And now we, the spectator, can see what Tamburlaine is doing, we can take *him* over in the metaphor that distances and explains. Once he is so situated, he is frozen into the posture of familiar knowledge.

So Tamburlaine passes the future precariously on to his son, Amyras. "Precariously," because his "birth" as ruler is under the sign of Phaeton, under the sign of a fallibility which in this case is a failure of power. And Amyras "becomes" the satanic Doctor Faustus, whose power becomes (is) knowledge, and whose death bitterly emphasizes the inadequacy of discourse to correspond to or even report the structure of events in the world (inadequacy for Faustus, that is; not for us who can watch and judge the terms of that inadequacy and, what is more, see the reason for it):

> . . . or let this hour be but
> A year, a month, a week, a natural day,
> That Faustus may repent and save his soul!
> *O lente, lente currite, noctis equi!*
> The stars move still, time runs, the clock will strike,
> The devil will come, and Faustus must be damn'd. [5.2.149–54]

For Faustus, discourse can no longer control time, as it seemed to throughout *Tamburlaine*. *That* inefficacy is indicated to the spectator by the stage device of the clock striking the hour of eleven, the half-hour, midnight. Furthermore, if Faustus's speech cannot force time to stand still by its own compulsion, no more can it correspond with its passage: the stage sequence visibly and audibly lacks synchronicity with what is familiar to the spectator as "real" time. This is not accidental: there is constant reference to the twenty-four years granted to Faustus, time is telescoped in various ways—the devils who summon up Helen or fetch grapes in the twinkling of an eye; the "*consummatum est*" pronounced at the signing of the pact which is also its end.[22] The spectator can now *see* in action (and is deliberately so shown) the presumption of Faustus which is most brought out just because he cannot impose himself: he "manipulates neither space nor time but himself."[23]

The failure of Faustus is not marked by the growth of a metaphor which, from within the play itself, grows out of and corresponds to the problematic of a relationship with language. For the spectator, the distancing of Tamburlaine into a "familiar" space where we can understand and no longer be dismayed by what is "tragic" for him proceeds from Tamburlaine's own naming. This is no longer the case in *Faustus*: the doctor is given a name before he so much as appears upon the stage. The chorus informs us that Faustus had sought to attain the level of the gods:

> Till swol'n with cunning of a self-conceit,
> His waxen wings did mount above his reach,
> And melting, heavens conspired his overthrow.
>
> [Prologue, 20–22]

Faustus is named as Icarus from the start, just as Amyras was able to
be named as Phaeton at the end. From now on the tragic hero could
always be named as one of the monstrous failures of the myths of
Antiquity. In that way his or her failure is made recognizable, open
to both explanation and prevention. Many changes can be rung up
on the speaker once so named, of course: for he will have become a
character, a personality, and the naming may be used to indicate a
multitude of different relationships (Icarus crops up again in the
person of Hippolyte in *Phèdre*, with implications both similar to and
dissimilar from the present).

This development is further marked by the fact that Faustus never
needs to name himself "Apollo" as Tamburlaine did. Faustus *is* Apollo:
finest healer (Prologue, 12–22), more profound than earthly law-
givers, founders, and protectors of cities (Prologue, 21, 27–36), despiser
of god (Prologue, 48), who is but a Jupiter to be displaced (2.3.89).
He has all the attributes of the Greek Apollo but one—what he lacks,
what he can never have, but what the play is all about his attempt
to acquire, is the "last" and most important of Apollo's attributes:
immortality (1.1.23–25). That is what he most desires, and it is
wittingly to make himself "as great as Lucifer" (1.5.52), the fiery
angel, the Apollo of the Christian pantheon and rival of his god, that
Faustus binds his soul. But that bond limits him to twenty-four years
and his aspiration is thus denied at the very moment when he deludes
himself into believing he starts toward its fulfilment. That it should
be Apollo (and Phaeton, Prometheus, Icarus are all associated with
that figure in one way or another) who provides the half-concealed
master figure forming the metaphorical bridge between the chaos of
nonmeaning and its hypostatization into human error is not without
significance in itself.

We may perhaps be reminded that what is important for Nietzsche
in *The Birth of Tragedy* is less the matter of an origin than it is that
of the simultaneous presence within the text of tragedy of "Apollo"

and "Dionysos," of reason and not-reason. When Nietzsche speaks of the Greeks and of their pantheon he writes:

> The fact that among [the Olympian gods] we find Apollo as one god among many, making no claim to a privileged position, should not mislead us. The same drive that found its most complete representation in Apollo generated the whole Olympian world, and in this sense we may consider Apollo the father of that world. [24]

Apollo is the "necessity" of illusion, the "desire to remain on earth" whose realization demands that the "terrifying" incomprehensible remain hidden. [25] The "illusion" in question is that of singular truth, of sure meaning, of firm and knowable reality. The Renaissance renames Apollo in tragedy. The presence of Apollo, suggests Nietzsche, conceals the truth behind the illusion of rational codes—and that truth may be simply that depth, meaning ("revealed religion," say, or psychological being, or indeed any "life within"), is but the illusion that must be created by ordering discourse if civil society, knowledge, technology, and the rest are to be possible. Perhaps the perennial fascination of tragedy is just that: instead of touching some "deep well-spring of human feeling," it presents us with the risk of the opposite—the knowledge that "man" is but the creation of a particular kind of ordering discourse. "Man" may be no more than the production of a particular episteme (as Foucault suggested at the end of *The Order of Things*), and tragedy both hints at it and conceals it.

From the outset of *The Tragical History of Doctor Faustus* we see the falseness of the doctor's belief that he can create a system to control the world. Faustus's belief in the power of words to control things (by means of magic incantations and the like) is shown to be presumptuous from the start. He is Icarus, he is a flawed Apollo (Phaeton once again): because he *cannot conceal* the lack of adequation between his discourse and the world, between his discourse and his activity *in* the world. Faustus, like Tamburlaine (who does, however, approach partial knowledge of his situation at the moment of Zenocrate's death), remains unaware that this is the case. Now, however, the spectator/reader *is* aware from the beginning. And

in being so we become increasingly *un*aware of the inadequacy of our
own systems: we are now superior to the "tragic hero." We can watch
Faustus's failure and take warning from the demonstration: Faustus
aspired to fly beyond the limits, the proper bounds of mankind. He is
an Icarus who misuses technique (in Faustus's case, his various attain-
ments).

But Daedelus succeeded. And so do we. Judith Weil, commenting
upon Brueghel's *Landscape, with the Fall of Icarus*, observes how
one of the peasants, ignoring the drowning Icarus, "apparently stares
up at an invisible Daedelus flying into the darkness where we, the
innocent onlookers, watch."[26] But the onlooker is never "innocent."
His very choice of observational object is a judgment on the part
of Brueghel's peasant. At the end of *Doctor Faustus* the chorus
provides us with the space for a similar "detachment" on our part,
where "fallibility" and "discursive responsibility" both start to
slide away, to be suppressed:

> Cut is the branch that might have grown full straight,
> And burned is Apollo's laurel bough,
> That sometime grew within this learned man.
> Faustus is gone. Regard his hellish fall,
> Whose fiendful fortune may exhort the wise
> Only to wonder at unlawful things,
> Whose deepness doth entice such forward wits,
> To practise more than heavenly power permits.
>
> [Epilogue, 20–27]

Weil remarks: "But the warning comes too late. Marlowe has already
enticed us far beyond mere wonder. He has killed his hero, then
passed Apollo's green laurel on to his audience."[27] Still, the knowledge the audience can go after will be of a different order entirely. The
"green laurel" can be a "wise" learning, a learning within the limits of
the possible. Daedelus was not tempted to follow Icarus, though he was
not deprived of the warning. The limits of discourse have been transformed into the limits of human action. What was a metaphor in *Tamburlaine* has been embodied in the *person* of Faustus—even though we
still need a chorus to show us the way to discover its meaning. We are
Daedelus and, here, the system of tragedy is our technique.

5 *Les Juifves:* Possession and the Willful Eye

With the development suggested in *Tamburlaine* and *Faustus* we begin to see with increasing clarity how tragedy is becoming a particular way of ordering reality. A gradual change is occurring in a relationship that was at first entirely intradiscursive (the "relationship" of an enunciating subject to the *act* of enunciation, at once its own and that of others) but increasingly distanced. First a hierarchy has been introduced within discourse, which had made naming possible but which at the same time increased the difficulty of relating subjects to one another, just *because* a *distance* has been opened up. Second, both subject and discourse have been provided with an extradiscursive reality. In *Tamburlaine* the subject can eventually be named as Phaeton, and the imposition of *his* discourse (as such ultimately impossible in an earlier tragedy like Jodelle's *Cléopâtre*, for example) is played out as a political and military *possession* of the other.

When it fails it does so because it ignores other speakers. The subject of that possession, the speaker Tamburlaine, has himself been *named* as object in another (metaphorical) discourse. At one level (that of the language available to him for his use) Tamburlaine remains successful, and he can confidently expect Amyras and Celebinus to continue his conquest in his name. At another—that of the naming language offered to the spectator/reader—the speaker Tamburlaine is himself possessed: there is of course no dialogue with the spectators, but neither is there any with Theridamas, whom we have seen as Tamburlaine's subtle opponent, and who *does* warn him of his prospective failure—to no avail, for Tamburlaine views the Phaeton metaphor as a threat to others, not to himself.

READ for
Fourself

Faustus, however, does not see himself as *like* Apollo. Faustus, who is "but Faustus and a man" (1.1.23), also *is* Apollo, and is possessed of all the principal attributes of that god. Faustus *embodies* a particular kind of activity that was merely *named* by Tamburlaine. In *Doctor Faustus* it happens that this embodiment is made more clear by the device of framing it (i.e., the role of the chorus). Now the spectators can begin to take their distance from a speaker who increasingly, therefore, takes on the attributes of a "person," and of a person whose difficulties can be understood and solved. The difficulties confronted by a John the Baptist, a Jephtha, a Cléopâtre or an Octavian, even a Tamburlaine, concern expression and communication, possession in discourse, utterance of a meaning shared by a wide community. What was found in Montaigne and in my indications regarding the widely shared assumption that matters of speech, of discourse, needed urgent attention suggests that we are dealing here with preoccupations of immediate concern to the humanists.

The development of tragedy suggests that the helplessness of Gamaliel (or a John, or a Jephtha) which proceeds from a difficulty perhaps best expressed by the phrase *meaning is what discourse does*, is overcome by a metaphorization of that helplessness (the names "Phaeton," "Icarus," "Prometheus," "Apollo"). And that metaphorization can then pass easily into a personification: so Faustus *is* Apollo, and Apollo in a Christian context would be Lucifer—that Lucifer who also failed to overthrow his opponent. Faustus is also, and in the same way, Icarus. The personification allows such discursive difficulties as the making of meaning, the situating of the subject, the expression of the other, and so on, to be transformed into their human counterpart. The subject becomes the thinking self (and then desiring, feeling, etc.). The expression of the other can become a (political, social, moral, economic) possession or some other kind of interactive relationship. The making of meaning can be any kind of productive activity. The difficulty of situating the enunciating subject and its consequences, a problem absolutely central to early Renaissance tragedy, becomes, once its metaphor has been personified, a matter of the relationships among individuals: political, social, psychological, familial, and so on. The individual subject's failure to leap the limits of discourse becomes the superior individual's inability to go beyond the limits of his humanity

or those set by society. At the same time the overt reference to tragedy as a system may become increasingly strong within the plays.

Such is the case in Garnier's *Les Juifves*, a play written and published in 1583 and thus some four years the predecessor of *Tamburlaine*
and six to nine that of *Faustus*. *Les Juifves* occupies the same transi-
tional moment in the development of tragedy that leads through metaphor to personification. Garnier's play (like most others) uses the
same mythical terms of reference as Marlowe's and distances the system further yet from the reader/spectator by the deliberate reminder
both of Greek tragedy (especially *Hecuba* and *The Trojan Women*)
and of Senecan (particularly *Troas* and *Thyestes*). As in the framing in
Doctor Faustus this helps to distance the speaker from the spectator/
reader and to place him in a particular "codification of the knowable:"

> NABUCHODONOSOR: Pareil aux Dieux je marche, et depuis le
> réveil
> Du Soleil blondissant jusques à son sommeil,
> Nul ne se parangonne à ma grandeur Royale.
> En puissance et en biens Jupiter seul
> m'égale:
> Et encores n'estoit qu'il commande
> immortel,
> Qu'il tient un foudre en main dont le coup
> est mortel,
> Que son thrône est plus haut, et qu'on ne le
> peut joindre,
> Quelque grand Dieu qu'il soit, je ne serois
> pas moindre.
> . . . moy je commande aux hommes,
> Je suis l'unique Dieu de la terre où nous
> sommes.   [2.181–92][1]

[Like to the Gods I walk, and from the rising of the brightening
Sun to its setting, none competes with my Royal grandeur. In
power and wealth Jupiter alone is my equal: and even then, were
it not that he rules as an immortal, that he holds in his hand a
thunderbolt whose blow is mortal, that his throne is higher and
one cannot reach it, howsoever great a God he might be, I would
not be less. . . . I command men, I am the one God of the earth
whereon we are.]

The reference is, of course, to Atreus's entrance in the fifth act of *Thyestes*. It is by no means an isolated instance in this play: "Dieu fait ce qu'il luy plaist, et moy je fais de mesme" ("God does what he wishes, and I do likewise" [3.928]), says the Assyrian king, and he is encouraged in such expression by his very opponent Sedecie: " . . . vous êtes en ce lieu,/ Le temple, la vertu, la semblance de Dieu" ("In this place you are the temple, the force, the likeness of God" [4.1465–66]); though Sedecie makes the important qualification suggested by the words "en ce lieu." There is an obvious appeal here to the kind of stock speaker of whom Tamburlaine and Faustus are both examples—a speaker absent from *Baptistes*, but beginning to be indicated in Jodelle, who glories in his difference, in that very distance from others that enables him to take possession and to lay down the law (i.e., successfully to force others into the shape of *his* discourse). Tamburlaine and Nabuchodonosor have obvious affinities, but there is nonetheless a difference, possibly an important one.

Tamburlaine conceives power as a re-forming of the world on the basis of what he says and of how he speaks, Nabuchodonosor as a particular way of *manipulating* the situation as (he thinks) he finds it. Tamburlaine was quite unaware that others might be able to name as well as he, that by itself his discourse is fallible in its very isolation: hence the gradual undermining of his position and his eventual failure. Nabuchodonosor, on the contrary, makes full use of the presence of others—indeed, he employs a verbal trick in the middle of the play to calm the fears of Amital that works only because he can consider her (and the others) as equal users of discourse. He tells her that Sedecie will never see himself in chains and that the children will not be slaves (3.1194, 1200–02): they, of course, will be dead and Sedecie blind. And Amital, after initially calling the king a "parjure" (5.1878), finally realizes he has made use of her own wishes: "Est-ce ainsi qu'ils devoyent demeurer en hostage,/ Et le Roy leur seigneur delivrer de servage?" ("Is this the manner in which they were to remain hostage, and in which the King their lord deliver them from bondage?" [5. 2039–40]).

She refers to his "lying words," to his "deceiving promise" (5.2043). But they were not a lie, nor was the promise false (actually it was not a promise at all): in fact Nabuchodonosor uttered the truth, and had

Amital not been seeking to develop some other order she would have
seen it immediately.[2] Unlike the Assyrian king, she does *not* take his
speaking into account: she it is who in the play suffers from an ignorance of the limits of discourse, and it is she who is tragic. Indeed
one could say that the fault for which God is punishing the Jews is
precisely the result of that ignorance.

From the moment of his first entrance, even as he utters his most
presumptuous speech Nabuchodonosor recognizes both his power
and its limits ("encores n'estoit qu'il commande immortel"). Savage,
cruel, and overbearing he may be, but that particular "ignorance" is
not his, and in this tragedy it is not he who occupies the space of the
tragic: though, in his anger, he comes close at least once. In talking
about Nabuchodonosor in this way, implying that he is a character
with some psychological attributes and considering the name as indicating a "him" who can make a mistake, we should recall that the
stock "character" is in point of fact a stock series of speeches, a set
of discursive conventions. Nabuchodonosor is not yet entirely an individualized personality, he is a manner of speaking.[3] But the change
in the relationship of speeches begins to cause the development of a
"self," and that of course carries with it repercussions of another
order entirely. The "human" can now begin to become an *object* of
observation, a piece of knowledge, eventually able to be situated and
controlled in a known order (my broad concern being to discover
how that development occurred and what are some of the consequences of the manner of that occurrence).

The change in the relationship of the speaker and what he speaks,
the concern for *other* speakers, means that the world and the other are
able to be viewed as terms of an exchange between actual and potential speakers. No longer will a speaker be struggling (in vain) to get
out of his own discourse, no longer will there be that kind of muffled
tension within language we saw in *Baptistes*. Rather will there be an
open confrontation between speakers; *my* power against that of the
other. As soon as the matter is posed in terms of such a confrontation then it is also exteriorized—for the other speaker is always
"over there." The discourse that confronts *me* (once the emphasis is
placed there and not on the situation of the subject in its own discourse) becomes an *exteriorization* of *its* subject: something (some-

one) lies behind it. All kinds of "distances" are being opened up and the subject of enunciation itself becomes the expression of a *will*, and of a will to dominate (as the subject sought to control its own enunciation).

It is a will that is nonetheless typically expressed by a vow: "Je *jure* qu'il verra sa lascheté punie" ("I swear he'll see his disloyalty punished" [2.212]). Yet even here the change apparent between *Baptistes* and *Tamburlaine* is again in evidence. In Buchanan's plays the utterance of a vow or promise was sufficient to set up an insurmountable obstacle. In *Tamburlaine* there were two kinds of vow: the failed oaths of the conquered and the imposed swearings of Tamburlaine himself. While his vows do indeed prevent further action by his victims, they remain but a part of Tamburlaine's forward-moving activity, they are a part of his rewriting of the map. The difference is that for Tamburlaine *the vow depends on his own use of power*: in Buchanan's two plays it depends on another (Herodias; God). In Buchanan the vow blocks the subject of enunciation itself because it is unable to situate the limits of its enunciation or, to put it another way, in misplaced psychological terms: the character is unaware of the limits of his own power and as a consequence he finds himself a victim of his own attempt to make use of such power. Like Tamburlaine, Nabuchodonosor makes a vow that will increase his *visible* power *because* he alone is responsible for its accomplishment. It is typical, however, that this new "freedom" should be expressed by means of a vow, through a set form of speech-act. "*Je* luy *veux* bien donner autre punition" ("I fully mean to give him some other punishment" [2.218]), adds Nabuchodonosor, as though to make clear the importance of the expression of a personal will.

Of course, we are reminded that like Faustus Nabuchodonosor does not control the "last" level in the hierarchy of discourse—the prophet pointed it out at the beginning of the tragedy and will do so again at the end. The chorus recalls for us that even if, as I suggest, the Assyrian does not break any promise in the tragedy, he has done so in the past when he attacked Jerusalem and killed Joachim "contre sa foy promise"("against his promised oath," [2.431]). Sarree will later recall the concept of the scourge of God for us, as he remarks to Sedecie that in God's eyes regal glories are like a reed played with by

the wind (4.1317–18). This remark comes during a discussion between these two in which they are considering their own sins and (as
they think) coming deaths, so that we may not immediately interpret it as applying to their conqueror. However, during Nabuchodonosor's discussion earlier with his queen, she had actually reminded
him that as Sedecie is to him so is he to God, and that he does not
control a discourse in which he is caught and named (as scourge of
God, and hence again part of a familiar paradigm).

As we saw was momentarily the case with Tamburlaine as regards
his awareness of the metaphor which eventually allows us to name
and place him, Nabuchodonosor, too, appears to be aware of his fallibility. For he replies to the queen: "Laissons-là ce discours, il est
plein de tristesse" ("Let us leave off this speech, it is full of sadness"
[3.947]). Nabuchodonosor does not simply dismiss her words ("ce
discours") by suggesting they have nothing to do with the case; rather
he suggests that they refer to a level of discourse that would contradict *his* power and glory ("plein de tristesse"). This awareness is emphasized by the reason he gives for acceding to her request: he will
save Sedecie's life not from fear of God (3.943) but entirely to
please the queen. By placing his decision in these terms he deliberately brings the discussion back to the terms of a dispute concerning
the prerogatives of kingship, a level the queen had left when she
started speaking of God.[4]

It is deliberately, then, that the Assyrian king refuses her reminder
that he is part of a more-embracing discourse of power: for to accept it would be to accept restraints. His eventual failure will come
from the denial of fallibility, which denial demands that its possibility be confronted as it is here. But that eventual fall will occur only
outside the time of the tragedy—as in the case of Tamburlaine, it is
the spectator who is made judge of it. And in that wider picture we
might well find ourselves inclined to consider not Amital or Sedecie
but Nabuchodonosor as filling the tragic space. For there Sedecie
jumps the limits and joins the voice of the Divinity, whereas for Nabuchodonosor *those* limits will always be an obstacle. Still, the passage between him and the queen suggests that he is aware of that
"higher" level in the hierarchy, and that it is by willful choice that he
refuses to be dominated by it.

There are other signs that he sees and sets the limits to the space in which his power holds. For example, Nabuchodonosor refuses to accept Amital's argument that the father's actions can reprieve the son (Josie, she argues, had always supported the Assyrians, had fought and died for them [3.1110–70]). Each is responsible for his own actions, responds the king, and must set his own limits. Tamburlaine had played the same part and when he dies it is in the midst of instructing his sons to take such responsibility and use it wisely. It is indeed in regard to such responsibility that Nabuchodonosor makes his one mistake, or at least acts very ambiguously: for in slaughtering the young princes he deals with them unjustly in terms of his own discourse; just as Sedecie could not be excused on the grounds of his father's actions, so his sons should not be punished for his. Of course, we may object, Nabuchodonosor is using the princes to punish Sedecie and not the princes themselves, which is why his speeches so often recall those of Atreus. Once again, in any case, this is a *choice* deliberately made by Nabuchodonosor, just as he made a choice with regard to the divine order of discourse proffered by his queen.

Within the tragedy, then, the Assyrian sets his own limits to his power and can then use the fallibility of the situation of the individual *I* to the end of confirming that power. At one level the play is "about" an exchange of discourse that enables Nabuchodonosor to develop the verbal device that takes in Amital and confirms his blinding power. He allows his discourse to be adjusted by that of others in a way that Tamburlaine never does. The first of these exchanges occurs between the king and Nabuzardan, his "lieutenant general." It is the commonplace of a dispute concerning mercy versus punishment and the rights, duties, and obligations toward one's enemies entailed by kingship. In this case the discussion is about whether Sedecie should be put to death or not. Now the question may be a commonplace within the political theory of the time, but in view of what we have been saying two aspects need perhaps to be emphasized. First of all Nabuchodonosor has made his vow ("je jure") in such a way that he can fulfill it in various ways: any punishment will satisfy its apparent fixing of future action. The Assyrian's use of power depends on a certain flexibility of expression—to avoid being taken over by the others, and *just because of the "recognition" that others also use the discourse I use.*

The second point I wish to make concerning the discussion with
Nabuzardan emphasizes this *use* of discursive exchange yet further and
reminds us that Nabuchodonosor does see power itself as the outcome
of such an exchange. For he does eventually allow the series of discussions to formulate his decision concerning the disposition of the
Jews: he will not kill Sedecie. In this the queen is his equal. In her
discussion with Amital (2.587–814), though with less forcefulness
than the king, she argues the point of punishment with Sedecie's
mother, pointing out the seriousness of the crime ("mais le crime est
de rebellion" [2.654]) and the necessity of punishment ("Un Roy
vainqueur n'a point de borne en sa vengence" [2.647]). She allows
herself to be persuaded to try and soften the victor. The discussion
is shortly renewed again between the queen and her husband: this
time she takes the role earlier played by Amital, while he starts by re-
newing his vow (but as flexibly as before [3.899–902]) and concludes
by accepting that Sedecie not be put to death (3.896–974).

These discussions have been teaching the king something we will
later see to be of importance for the control of discourse and power.
Nabuzardan was first to remind him that "l'ennemy qui meurt sort
de nostre puissance" ("the enemy who dies escapes from our power"
[2.228]). Amital will later twice assert the same thing to the queen:
"Ce n'est pas nous mal faire, ains nostre mal guarir"; "La mort aux
affligez vient toujours trop tardive" ("It is not to do us harm, but
to cure us of harm"; "For the suffering death always comes too
late" [2.662, 684]).[5] Amital remarks that the worst thing is to see
the misery one has caused (3.1063). She asks Nabuchodonosor
whether he will be content only with the deaths of the young princes
(3.1069–70)—something not hitherto mentioned, though it will be
repeated later by Sedecie in his discussion with Nabuchodonosor
(4.1482). Amital it is, too, who provides the opening for the discursive trick I have already mentioned (3.1191–1202).

All this provides the conqueror with a way to accede to the various
requests of the queen, of Nabuzardan, and, later, of Amital and
Sedecie at the same time as it permits him to fulfil his own need to
show his power. After his discussion with the queen his oath can be
made more precise: "Je jure le ciel que vostre felonnie / Sera plus
griefvement que de la mort punie" ("I swear by heaven that your

crime will be more grievously punished than by death" [3.963–64]).
His first idea is to kill his friends and the priests before the eyes of
Sedecie (3.966–70): but the discussion with Amital and with Sedecie
himself gives added certainty to his decision to execute the children.
Amital remarks of Sedecie that "sa faute est infinie" (3.1148), and at
the end of the play the prophet will acknowledge that Sedecie's misfortune is also "infini" (5.2101).

By means of a certain give and take, then, Nabuchodonosor succeeds
in marking the limits and extent of his power—it is not limitless, as he
clearly recognizes and as Tamburlaine did not. He can accept (or his
words on occasion imply a recognition of) a higher discourse capable
of sealing him into its system, and he acknowledges the right of
other speakers to make use of discourse. He has to do so in order for
communication to occur at all and therefore for the power of his own
use of such discourse to be effective: he thus resolves a problem of
power that has remained insuperable in earlier plays. The difficulty
he then must confront is that of setting a limit upon the "discursive
right" of others. Those limits are suggested by Sedecie in a question
that implies that either all respondent discourse is an offense (by virtue of the fact that it necessarily puts another speaker into opposition with the first) or no speech is (because all speakers are equal and
none can control all). Sedecie admits that he had committed an offense against Nabuchodonosor, but, he implies, given that the Assyrian rules a system that any can use and that in order to use it the user
must in some sense "control" it, then anyone who tries to do so
must *necessarily* be committing an offense: "Or vous ay-je offensé, je
confesse ce poinct, / Je vous ay offensé: mais qui n'offense point?"
("I have committed an offense against you, I admit the fact, I have
committed an offense against you: but who does not do so?" [4.1413–
14]).[6]

For a speaker who seeks to control discourse, another's use of that
same discourse is always an affront to that control. Nabuchodonosor's
difficulty (and he is partially successful in solving it, whereas for Tamburlaine or Faustus the question scarcely arose) is to strike a balance
between his power, his recognition that that power depends on other
speakers as much as on himself, and the limits placed upon other speakers. Sedecie poses his question as though he were just any other

speaker, but the point is that one can distinguish between such speakers. During her discussion with the Assyrian king, for example, Amital had exclaimed against him with a force that would certainly have provoked him were he really the tyrant he is supposed to be. He merely responds: "Je pardonne à vostre âge." She is in fact *trying* to provoke him, she does not want a pardon but to exchange her life for Sedecie's. That will not work, he says, for she is innocent (3.1067–91).

In what way is Amital innocent and Sedecie guilty? Surely it is that Sedecie posed a *deliberate* threat to Nabuchodonosor. Amital's discourse has no power and expresses no will—its success or failure depends entirely upon the queen's or king's response. This is not the case with Sedecie: he had both power and will. Perhaps that is why he does not appear until the fourth act: by then Nabuchodonosor has almost made his final decision and taken an inflexible oath, one by which Sedecie will be reduced to powerlessness. There was no accident in the Jewish king's offense. He set himself up as an equal opponent to the Assyrian. He has sought to break the restraints that bind him within Nabuchodonosor's speech. The number of times he is called an "oath-breaker" is certainly important: a sequence of six lines during his discussion with his Assyrian opponent gives us, for example, "parjure" ("oath-breaker"), "faulser ta parole" ("break your word"), "parjurer ta foy" ("betray your sworn oath," 4.1379, 1383, 1385). When Sedecie asks, "Qui n'offense point?" he seeks to suggest that it is all an unavoidable accident, and Nabuchodonosor responds shortly by suggesting that that would now merely be an avoidance of the responsibility for having "mis le glaive en la gorge de ceste multitude" ("placed the sword against the breast of this multitude" [4.1420])— to seek power without responsibility.

Unlike his opponent, Sedecie does not take account of others, and like Mycetes or Callapine in *Tamburlaine* he does not know how to use language appropriately. For he now seeks to enter the same discussion with Nabuchodonosor as have Nabuzardan, the queen, and Amital before him. For him to attempt this is to find another way of suggesting his innocence: a speaker who has sought to control discourse and failed is now claiming that the victor should relinquish *his* control because he is the victor. In effect he is saying his position is no different from that of Nabuchodonosor's other interlocutors. The

Assyrian is quick to replace Sedecie in the position he had unsuccessfully maintained before:

> SEDECIE: Cela depend de vous, qui estes le *vainqueur.*
> NABUCHODONOSOR: Voire il depend de moy, qui suis ton *adversaire.*   4.1430–31]

> [SEDECIE: It depends on you, who are the victor.
> NABUCHODONOSOR: Indeed, it does depend on me, whom am your adversary.]

At the end of the discussion, the victor finally puts Sedecie in his place: his *words* (those of a breaker of his word) are useless, "Ce n'est de tes propos que parolle perdue" ("Your speeches are just a waste of words" [4.1472]). Sedecie rounds on him with a violent outburst in which he tells him to do his worst. At this Nabuchodonosor launches a few more telling blows: "Tu parles bravement, mais devant que bouger,/Peut-estre on te verra de langage changer" ("You speak boldly, but before you move from here, we will perhaps see your language change" [4.1489–90]), suggesting that he is going to be forced into using the order willed by Nabuchodonosor. Finally, just before telling the soldiers to remove him, the Assyrian suggests that Sedecie's defeat is absolute, because he can no longer speak properly: "Tu sembles un mâtin, qui abaye et qui grogne" ("You are like a mastiff, barking and growling" [4.1495]). The next time we see Sedecie he is blind.

Both the blindness and the lack of speech (which disappears at the end, with implications we will see later) are the result of his unsuccessful opposition to Nabuchodonosor. The latter is seeking a discursive order of such a kind as will allow him to maintain the singular power of his expression of will while recognizing its dependence on others' similar expression, and without being overly threatened by such other users. This suggests a rather precarious balancing of powers. It is precisely the overstepping of the imprecise boundaries of such power as can be allowed to others (at the wish, we may add, of Nabuchodonosor himself)[7] that is expressed from the moment of the conqueror's first appearance on the stage:

> S'eslever *contre moy?* se distraire de *moy?*

Contre ma volonté se penser faire Roy?
C'est faire proprement aux Estoiles la guerre,
C'est *vouloir* arracher de Jupin le tonnerre.   [2.213–16] [8]

[Raise himself up against me? Amuse himself with me? To think
of making himself King against my will? That is truly to make
war against the Stars, that is to wish to rob Jupiter of his thunder.]

The sequence of oppositions between third and first persons, the emphasis on the opposition of *ma volonté* and the *vouloir* of the third
person is worth noting. Certainly the *I* here has the power of the utterance in which it occurs (cf. chap. 2, note 19), but it marks itself
as essentially in opposition to a third person which (who), while now
under control, appears as a threat by virtue of the very opposition: a
threat now contained, but which *has had to be* contained.

Sedecie, then, is considered as though he had sought to be like
Nabuchodonosor, to take his place. A man like Faustus, Sedecie has
sought the place (here) of Jupiter. It is in that that he is the competitor of the speaker called Nabuchodonosor. We are no longer dealing
here with a difficulty in discourse itself or with a solution that is the
absolute control of discourse by a single speaker and a permanent ignorance by the others. The confrontation of speakers has now become
unavoidable: it shows itself as Nabuchodonosor's maneuvering with the
other, and as Sedecie's revolt. An individual consciousness and a
knowledge of power have come together as proceeding from the same
discursive source. Winning or losing in this relationship will be the result of the reading one makes of a system we may call political, and
which depends on the knowledge of the limits, prerogatives, and possibilities of the relationships that hold between speakers. Nabuchodonosor has such knowledge (revealed only as successful *practice*).
Sedecie and the now defeated Jews do not. As the tragedy draws
toward the moment when Sedecie will finally be brought up brutally
against the limits he had refused to acknowledge (and tried to break
out of) he implies a growing awareness, apostrophizing peoples who
take the *laws* of God "pour ordonnances vaines" (4.1280).

Power and will, then, are expressed in terms of *distance*. The wielder
of power not only accepts distance as the necessary form for the
expression of power, but he *uses* it precisely because it is his closing

of the various distances of which I have already spoken that allows
that wielding of power to be *seen*. The manipulation of distance permits a speaking to become visible, a seizure by an enunciating subject to become the imposition of a willful self:

> Je le *tiens*, je le *tiens*, je *tiens* la beste *prise*,
> Je jouis maintenant du plaisir de ma *prise*,
> J'ay chassé de tel heur que rien n'est eschappé.   [3.887–89]

> [I have him, I have him, I have the captured beast, now I rejoice
> in the pleasure of my capture, I have hunted with such fortune
> that nothing has escaped.]

The first person seizes and seals the third person. But the interesting
thing about Garnier's adaption of the speech given to Atreus by Seneca (*Thyestes*, 3.2) is not simply its brevity or its changed context.
Atreus is about to confront Thyestes in person: his image is immediately followed by a visible confrontation of the two brothers. Nabuchodonosor is telling his queen of how this verbal power ("pareil
aux Dieux") is being made visual. Atreus uses the verb *see* in his
speech literally—his brother is indeed coming to meet him. The Assyrian king uses it to express rather his understanding and his will:
he remarks that the hunters have done their job well ("je le voy"),
that it is only fitting they should share in the spoils because he "sees"
that success, and because, moreover, he *wills* it ("au surplus je le
veux," 3.893–95). *Seeing* and *willing* come together in this grasping
of the other, in this expression of the fulfilled power of the *"je"*
(which occurs five times in the three lines that open Nabuchodonosor's discussion with the queen).

For the master of speeches who is called Nabuchodonosor personal
will is fully effective only inasmuch as those effects are visible: "La
volonté d'un Prince est conforme au pouvoir" ("The will of a Prince
is identical to power" [3.926]). This concept is the object of the various discussions he has with Nabuzardan, the queen, Amital, and Sedecie. His power in this case is concerned with his treatment of the
rebels, which treatment alone can make visible the extent of his power:
for the treatment must be visibly inscribed on the body of the Jews.
Such is the reason why he at first dismisses the queen's reminders
that he must not overstep the limits ("Un Prince qui peut tout ne doit

pas tout vouloir" "A prince who can do anything must not wish to do everything" [3.925]). But he will find a way to stay within the limits and make his power visible: by means of the distinctly symbolic punishment of literally depriving Sedecie of his sight.

As we saw before, the deprivation of sight is accompanied by a loss of speech (Sedecie reduced to a "growling mastiff"). The use of sight, like the use of speech, is a mark of the overcoming of distance, of control and of power. Sight becomes the sign of the imposition of personal will: *my* sight cast upon the other, that is to say, for to *look at oneself* is to turn away from such power. Thus Nabuzardan asks Nabuchodonosor what could be a worse punishment for Sedecie than *to see himself* in his present condition:

> A un Roy? que peut-il endurer d'avantage
> Que de se voir reduit en si honteux servage?
> Que de se voir priver de son sceptre ancien?
> Que d'avoir tout perdu? que de Roy n'estre rien?　　　[2.219–22]

> [For a king? What can he suffer more than to see himself reduced to so shameful a bondage? To see himself deprived of his former scepter? To have lost everything? From having been a King to be nothing?]

Those last two hemistiches toll like the final confirmation of just what is in question. For Sedecie to see himself is to have his power completely negated. This is made quite clear at the end of the tragedy, for the victor will have found the means to deny that very possessive will which is the first mark of his humanity: his means will be by depriving the Jewish king of his sight.

Nabuzardan had advised Nabuchodonosor that he should force ("contraindre") Sedecie to live in his power just because the latter does not wish it ("or qu'il n'en eust vouloir" [2.229–30]), because so to be forced is the sign of the other's absolute power. Nabuchodonosor discovers, in the terms the tragedy prepares for us, the ultimate demonstration of such constraint—as Sedecie is only too well aware:

> *Astres*, qui sur nos chefs eternels *flamboyez*,
> *Regardez* mes tourmens, mes angoisses *voyez*,
> *Mes yeux* ne *verront* plus vostre *lumiere belle*,

Et vous *verrez* toujours ma passion cruelle:
Vous *me verrez* un Roy privé de liberté,
De royaume, d'amis, d'enfans et de *clairté*.
Qui vit si miserable? Autour de ceste masse
Voyez-vous un malheur qui mon malheur surpasse? [5.2093–2100]

[Stars, which flame eternally above our heads, look upon my suf-
ferings, see my anguish, my eyes will never again see your beautiful light, and you will always see my cruel passion: you will see in
me a King deprived of liberty, of kingdom, friends, children and
light. Who else lives so miserable? In all this round world do you
see any misfortune surpassing my misfortune?]

The images of light and the action of seeing are now always to be on
the other side (except in the negative: "mes yeux ne verront plus"):
This discursive subject is obliged to speak of itself as the eternal object
of another's seeing activity. Thus the phrase "ma passion cruelle"
takes on an added emphasis: it is passivity itself which is cruel. "*Je
veux* avoir sa vie," Nabuchodonosor had said of Sedecie (2.224), and
in one sense he has it. Sedecie's only escape at the end of the play will
be that of John the Baptist—to leave the human dimension altogether
in favor of the divine. In *Les Juifves* even that will be *told* to Sedecie
by the prophet. The Jews are presented from beginning to end of the
tragedy as confined within a space that is defined in terms of their acceptance of another's eye (*I*), of a light inflicted upon them from outside. It is not for nothing that Nabuchodonosor had glorified himself
(like Tamburlaine and Faustus) as rival to Jupiter and in terms of the
sun's brightness: he too is Apollo. But he is Apollo in the very specific
sense of an inflicter of light upon what he rules. That is no doubt why
Amital will address him in terms otherwise reserved for the Jews' prayers to God: "Jettez sur nous un *rais* de vos *yeux* pitoyables" ("Cast
upon us a beam from your merciful eyes" [3.1032]). God's eye and
God's glory (or Nabuchodonosor's eye and glory) situate the boundaries of their activity. Sedecie was blind (and deaf) to their limits, as he
was to his own. The present misfortunes of the Jewish people are the
consequence of *his* ignorance of the rules ("ordonnances").
    Until the time of his literal blinding he is caught in that tragic circle
from which ignorance and necessary inefficacy in action prevent his

exit. Indeed his final blinding is precisely parallel to that of Israel at the beginning, adorers of an idol whose open eyes (like Sedecie's empty sockets at the conclusion) see nothing:

> Immolant à un dieu *que toy-mesme t'es fait.*
> Il a des *yeux ouverts,* toutefois *ne voit goutte:*
> Des *oreilles* il a, toutefois il *n'écoute:*
> On lui *voit* une *bouche,* il *ne scauroit parler.* . . .   [2.76–79]

[Sacrificing to a god you made yourself. He has open eyes, and yet sees not at all: he has ears, and yet does not listen: his mouth can be seen, yet he cannot speak. . . .]

The passage indicates the total failure of what is now the self (in this case multiple: the Jewish people) to situate itself in the terms we have been exploring within the tragedy: a turning inward ("que toy-mesme t'es fait"), a lack of sight, a lack of hearing, an inability to speak. They are, the chorus says, like Adam when, having turned his sight away from heaven, "Dieu le bannit de sa veue" ("God banished him from His sight" [1.153]). Amital will pray to God: "Estens sur nous ta veuë,/ Et voy l'affliction . . ." ("Spread your sight upon us, and see our affliction" [2.555–56]), just as the prophet had done from the first: "O Seigneur nostre Dieu, ramolli ton courroux./Rasserene ton oeil, sois pitoyable et doux" ("O Lord our God, soften your anger. Calm your eye, be merciful and kind" [1.7–8]).

The eye of God envelops the Jewish people ("hé, Dieu, vous nous voyez!" exclaims Amital later [2.657]). In becoming blind to it they have offended in just the same way as Sedecie has personally offended against Nabuchodonosor ("nous t'avons offensé," says the priest [1. 9]), and, like Sedecie, they confess their blindness ("nous sommes punissables," [1.10]). Part of their punishment will be the continued inability to *see* throughout the tragedy: for stable relations, as we have seen, the "seeing" must be mutual. That is why the priest begs the Jewish people: "*Retourne-toy* vers luy, peuple fautier, à fin/Qu'à tes calamitez *il veuille* mettre fin" ("Turn yourself back toward him again, sinful people, so that he may be willing to put an end to your calamities" [1.87–88]). This they will *not* do, however, until the very end of the play. Until that time they ask always that the other make the effort; so that just as God "*se monstre* plus doux" to the repentant sinner so should Nabuchodonosor ("monstrez-vous debonnair" [3. 998–99]). They may even do this towards a prospective representative of God, Amital's dead husband:

> Maintenant que tu vis sur les voûtes celestes,
> Regarde de Juda les miserables restes:
> Et si tu as encor des tiens quelque souci,
> Si tes yeux penetrent jusqu'ici. . . .   [3.1135–38]

> [Now that you are living upon the heavenly vaults, look down on the miserable remnants of Juda: and if you still have some care for your people, if your eyes penetrate this far. . . .]

The point made by Father Ong (and others) is well supported by this play: a preoccupation with speaking is indeed being replaced by a preoccupation with vision, which will be characteristic of the neoclassical episteme. What we seem to be seeing here, however, is that it is not so much a "replacement" (i.e., a rupture) that is in question as a gradual *transformation*. We are following a development in the way in which certain problems are confronted and solved, a discursive development that gradually alters both the problems and the solutions. The introduction of the visual paradigm matches other developments: from enunciating subject to self; from activity of enunciation to (for example) psychological or emotional activities; from the difficult situation of multiple subjects using a common discourse to a power confrontation among individuals. We are increasingly in a discourse, therefore, that is becoming a true and systematic representation of a known reality. Vision, which is part of the solution to older difficulties (the overcoming of distance, the discovering of a knowable shape, i.e., meaning, and so on), will be able to become a part of the technique of knowing —and will therefore itself pose a new problem (perhaps the same, in different terms). It is striking that in *Les Juifves* even reflections concerning the proximity of God to the chosen people *in the past* are put in terms of a prevention of blindness (though the comparison itself is to be found in the Old Testament, we are here considering an entire paradigm): "Prenant de son salut solicitude telle/Qu'on a de conserver de ses yeux la prunelle" ("Having such solicitude for their salvation as one has for the preservation of the pupils of one's eyes" [1.37–38]).

That remark directs us straight to the end of the play: Sedecie had

acted blindly, so he will be punished by the sign that he had not taken
the necessary solicitude. The executioners "cernent d'un fer la prunelle de ses yeux" ("surround with an iron his eyes' pupils" [5.2002])
—he is burned by the very light from which he had turned away. The
most serious crime committed by the Jewish people is that they have
adored a *blind* "god." According to Amital, the defeat of the Jews was
due to a complete loss of "tout humain jugement" (2.730). As a result
of this blindness toward the divine order, power over them will be signified by their being forced to see what they do not wish to see: "Helas! je n'eusse veu ce que voir me *faut* ores,/Et que voir me *faudra* si
je survis encores" ("Alas! I would rather not have seen what henceforth
I must see, and what I will have to see if I continue to survive" [2.
671–72]). Indeed the actual defeat of the Jews occurred at a time
when they literally could not see: "le somme enchanteur/Versoit dedans nos yeux une aveugle moiteur" ("bewitching sleep spilled in our
eyes a blind moisture" [2.738]). The flight of the royal family fails
for the same reason: "La nuit estoit obscure, et nos humides yeux/Ne
voyoyent pour conduite aucune lampe aux cieux" ("The night was
dark, and our damp eyes could see no guiding lamp in the sky"
[2.773–74]). The same image marks Sedecie's blindness: "Comme ses
yeux esteints vont decoulant à val/Le sang au lieu de pleurs, par leur
double canal!" ("How his extinguished eyes did spill down blood instead of tears, from out their double canal!" [5.2089–90]).

Tears, then, are a sign of blindness, a sign of failed power: for two
reasons. The first and less important in this tragedy is that they prevent speech. Amital says that at the death of her husband,

> Poussant mille sanglots qui m'estoupoyent la voix,
> Si qu'etreinte de mal je ne luy peux rien dire,
> Sinon entre mes dents son desastre maudire.   [2.406–08]

> [Bringing forth a thousand sobs which stopped my voice, so that
> suffocated with misery I could say nothing to him, except to curse
> his disaster between my teeth.]

But the most important reason is that tears prevent sight. Tears are
both the first reaction to imposition and the sign of it: "Las! tu vois
en cendre/Nostre *lamentable* Cité" ("Alas! you see in ashes our wail-
ing city" [2.291–92]). Egypt *sees*, Jerusalem *is seen* and weeps.

"Tu vois," the Chorus continues, "nostre infortuné Prince / Aujourd-huy sous les fers ployer: / Et nostre fertile Province / Reduitte en deserts, larmoyer" ("You see our miserable Prince now bend beneath the irons and our fertile Province reduced to deserts, weep." [1.95–98]). They have been deprived of all potentiality to action, there is nothing to be seen (*deserts*) even if they could see.

There has been a kind of double negation of the eyes' function. They weep instead of seeing. They shed water and can thus no longer be instruments of the being of fire, Apollo, the sun. In opposition to God and to Nabuchodonosor the Jewish king had sought to manifest his power in the same form, by adoring gold ("le Veau déifié" [2.352]) with "des holocaustes pacifiques" (2.353). That blind (despite its false pretense to brightness) and therefore false power of Sedecie is now extinguished and reduced to ashes (2.291). Thanks to it the chosen people have been led into the desert "par les eaux ameres" (2.357). Amital would like to *drown* herself in "un sombre tombeau" (2.380), while the chorus tells her: "Souspirez, larmoyez nos cruels infortunes, / Comme ils nous sont communs, soyent nos larmes communes" ("Sigh, weep for our cruel misfortunes, since they are shared, let our tears be shared" [2.395–96]). To that she can only reply: "Mes yeux n'ont point seché . . . " (2.397); and she recalls here her husband's, Sedecie's father's, death: "Ce pendant ses deux yeux en la nuit se plongerent" ("Meanwhile his two eyes plunged into darkness" [2.411]). Thus the chorus bewails Israel's misfortunes:

> Il nous les faut plorer, car las! à nos malheurs
> Pour tout allegement ne restent que des pleurs.
> AMITAL: Pleurons donques pleurons sur ces moiteuses rives,
> Puis que nous n'avons plus que nos larmes, captives:
> Ne cessons de pleurer, ne cessons, ne cessons
> De nous bagner le sein des pleurs que nous versons.
> Pleurons Jerusalem, Jerusalem destruite,
> Jerusalem en flamme et en cendres reduite:
> Ne soyent plus d'autre chose occupez nos esprits,
> Ne faisons que douloir, que jetter pleurs et cris
>
> [2.457–66][9]

[We must weep for them, for alas! for our misfortunes only tears remain to provide assuagement. Let us weep then let us weep upon these humid shores, since we have nothing other than our tears, captive as we are: let us not stop weeping, not stop bathing our breast in the tears that we weep. Weep for Jerusalem, Jerusalem destroyed, Jerusalem burning and to cinders reduced: let our minds be occupied with nothing else, let us only grieve, sob and lament.]

Jerusalem under Sedecie has been the imposing vassal of Nabuchodonosor; a word broken, and it is first "en flamme," then "en cendres," now in tears. Night, loss of all light, has fallen upon them: "O trois fois malheureuse nuit, / Que tu nous as de mal produit! / Jamais autres tenebres / Ne furent si funebres!" ("O triply unfortunate night, what misery you have brought upon us! Never were other shades so deathly!" [2.509–12]). The loss of sight was produced at night. It cannot for most of the tragedy be regained. Their sight turns inward, and they see but their memories ("Il me semble encor que je voy" [2.513]). They raise their eyes to heaven (2.537), but are blinded by tears. Even near the end, Sedecie, about to see his children put to the slaughter, cannot overcome this blindness as he "elevoit, pitoyable, / Ses yeux enflez de pleurs vers le ciel implacable" ("Raised, pitifully, his eyes swollen with tears toward the implacable sky" [5.1927–28]).

Only after all this does a change seem to occur in the Jews' situation. The enormity of the executions, the killing of the children before the very eyes of the father, his subsequent blinding, has begun to open the Jews' eyes. Already, as he was about to die, the priest Sarree raised clear eyes to heaven ("eleve au ciel sa veuë," [5.1959]), and now, about to recount the event, the prophet tells his listeners: "Ce mal est incredible, il n'a besoin de pleurs: / Les pleurs et les soupirs sont pour moindres douleurs" ("This misery is unbelievable, it needs no tears: tears and sighs are for lesser griefs" [5.1885–86]). At the same time there is a gain in power, there are hints that the shoe is passing to the other foot: now it is Nabuchodonosor's people who cannot look without weeping: "Ne peurent, sans plorer, regarder ces miseres" ("They could not, without weeping, watch these misfortunes" [5.1932]). It is these spectators who turn away their eyes ("destournoyent les yeux," 5.1933). For Nabuchodonosor has overstepped the bounds of equitable (stable) relationships: he indeed said to Sedecie upon this occasion that "il veut son forfait payer avec usure" ("he wishes to repay his crime with usury"

[5.1944]). I referred to this before as Nabuchodonosor's only mistake, but if mistake it is, it appears very deliberate.

Until this conclusion of the tragedy the victors had always appeared in exactly opposing terms. The queen's share in their general good fortune and in her husband's power is indicated by a kind of hymn to the sun, the expression of her sight of a glorious exterior:

O beau Soleil luisant, qui redores le monde
Aussi tost que la nuit te voit sortir de l'onde,
Rayonnante lumiere, oeil de tout l'univers,
Qui dechasses le somme et rens nos yeux ouvers,
Tu sois le bien venu sur ces belles campagnes,
Bien venu le bonheur de qui tu t'accompagnes:
Ta clairté nous fait voir le desirable fruit
Du sort victorieux, dont nous oyons le bruit.
Nous voyons maintenant les Rois Israelites
Et leurs peuples restez à nos fiers exercites
Amener par troupeaux, miserable butin. . . .   [2.567–77]

[O beautiful shining Sun, you who regild the world as soon as night sees you come up out of the waves, brilliant light, eye of the whole universe, who chase away sleep again and open up our eyes, may you be welcome over these beautiful lands, welcome the happiness of whomever you accompany: your brightness makes us see the desirable harvest of the victorious outcome, whose sound we hear. Now we see the Israelite Kings and their people captured by our proud soldiers brought on in flocks, miserable spoils. . . .]

The exchange of sight and light with the sun marks power: then the sun is on their side. There is, of course, a certain play here, for this sun is also the king: "Tout depend du Roy seul, nul que luy n'a puissance" (Everything depends on the king alone, only he has power" [2.632]), says the queen to Amital.

We have already heard Nabuchodonosor express his power in just these terms. He *is* Apollo: there is no system in which *I* can wield absolute power except in my own, and when he swears he is obliged to do so, in a sense, by himself: "par le Soleil je jure,/Que si mon propre enfant m'avoit faict telle injure . . ." (by the Sun I swear, that if my own child had done me such an injury" [2.247–48]). Yet here the power of the *I* speaker is now maintained in terms of an exterior, for otherwise one has no choice: the other is always a rebel, and one is captive of the same old discursive trap, forcing the speaker back into a fruitless circularity of discourse. Exteriorized, made visible, the power of the *I* requires constant *seeing* (which is why Sedecie must finally be prevented from dying). The relationship now requires the other; without such another there can be no power. Thus, while the opponent is a threat, it is a necessary one and the very revolt can be inscribed as a sign of *my* power. As Nabuchodonosor says:

> Mais ne *les voy-je* pas? les voila *mes* rebelles,
> *Mes* traistres, *mes* mutins, *mes* sujets infidelles:
> Amenez, attrainez: hà rustres *je vous tiens,*
> Vous estes à la fin tombez en *mes* liens.   [4.1371–74]

[But do I not see them? There they are my rebels. My traitors, my mutineers, my unfaithful subjects: bring them, pull them in: ha, scoundrels I have you, you have finally fallen into my bonds.]

It is worth comparing this glorying of the Assyrian victor in his final power to Amital's farewell speech to her grandchildren. Here the use of terms that correspond to those of Nabuchodonosor, but entirely negatively, confirms all I have been saying both about what is necessary to power and about the mark of its failure. I italicize the appropriate terms:

> Or *adieu mes* mignons, *adieu mon* esperence,
> *Adieu* de tant de Rois l'heroïque semence,
> Race du bon David, *je ne vous verray plus,*
> Vous serez *loin de nous* en un serrail *reclus.*
> Puis de mes ans vieillards la trame est achevee,
> Au bout de mes travaux je suis presque arrivee:
> Et long temps *du Soleil, qui me luist ennuyeux,*
> *Les rayons etherez n'esclaireront mes yeux:*
> Aussi que tant de maux ont mon ame outragee,
> Qu'elle affecte *se voir* de son corps desgagee.
> *Adieu* donc *ma lumiere, adieu* pour tout jamais,
> Las! je *n'espere pas vous revoir* desormais.   [4.1711–22]

[Now farewell my dear ones, farewell my hope, farewell heroic seed of so many Kings, descendents of good David, I will see you no more, you will be shut up far from us in a harem. Since the thread of my old years is complete, I am nearly arrived at the end of my labors: and for a long time the Sun's ethereal rays that unwelcome shine upon me, will not brighten my eyes: for so many evils have outraged my soul, that it longs to see itself separated from my body. So farewell my light, farewell forever, alas! I never hope to see you again.]

That is perhaps not the last word. Sedecie and Amital occupy throughout most of the tragedy the tragic space of incomprehension: within the order of which Nabuchodonosor has been, has provided, the limits. Sedecie's attempt to break out of them labels him a false Apollo (worshiper of the golden calf) for whom the Assyrian king is a real sun at its zenith. The attempt leaves Sedecie with the labels of a breaker of his word and "infidelle." But so, too, in another context, is Nabuchodonosor. Twice he is named a "Prince infidelle"—once by Sarree (4. 1339) which, given the priest's situation with regard to power, is perhaps not very significant; and once by the prophet (5.1848), at a moment rather less auspicious for the Assyrian, because it accompanies his own people's tears. It then accompanies the relation of his "excessive" punishment, of the "unjust" (according to his own definition) slaughter of Sedecie's children, and it accompanies the implication that now his own fiery power may be false:

Le Roy, que la fureur embrasoit en dedans,
Comme un bucher farci de gros charbons ardans,
Y entre forcené, monstrant à son visage,
Et à ses yeux affreux, l'horreur de son courage. . . .
[5.1897–1900]

[The King, whom fury burned up inside, like to a bonfire made up with great burning coals, comes in raging, revealing by his face, and by his awesome eyes, the horror of his intentions. . . .]

Thus is prefigured the defeat of Nabuchodonosor, foretold by the prophet: he will fall beneath thunderbolts and lightning (5.2133, 2138), attacked (like Sedecie) by the very light that is the present sign of his power. But then, as we said before, we might rather be inclined to consider Nabuchodonosor the tragic figure (as is Tamburlaine) and not Sedecie. The difference, then, between *Tamburlaine* and *Les Juifves* is that in *Tamburlaine* the system springs from the tragedy itself, whereas that level so far as *Les Juifves* is concerned is outside the tragedy—and works *against* the system composed by the tragedy. It composes one in which Nabuchodonosor's maneuvering is in vain and in which Sedecie must remain utterly passive. In that sense the appeal to a divine system (not surprisingly) works against the new humanity that is being produced, with its new conception of *human* powers and rights and obligations. It is the Tamburlaines, the Faustuses, the Nabuchodonosors of tragedy who are the speakers composing and producing these new conceptions, the new order that *makes* them.

6 Hamlet on Distraction and Fortinbras on Knowledge

emblems of the tragedy's problematic

"Who's there?" asks Bernardo as *Hamlet* opens. It is a question that will reverberate through the tragedy as each of the principal speakers seeks to clarify and define his relationship with each and all of the others. "Nay, answer me," responds Francisco, with a negative that likewise produces an echo lasting the duration of the play. "Stand and unfold yourself." The original question, the negative, the avoidance of reply by casting the question back in the teeth of the original speaker, all are almost emblems of the tragedy's problematic. Bernardo's next reply—"Long live the king!"—is a distinctly indirect way of revealing himself, and Francisco responds with yet another interrogative: "Bernardo?" The sentry, of course, can define himself in terms of his military and social function—as Bernardo has done in crying out, "Long live the king!" Others in the tragedy will be less fortunate.

Something seems out of joint even at the very outset of the play, in the most banal of discursive exchanges and among the very least of the play's speakers. Indeed, Francisco is quite right to rebuke Bernardo with his negative. As sentry on duty Francisco had the right to the first question, and by asking it Bernardo was reversing the accustomed and correct order. Besides which, as officer of the watch, he need scarcely ask the question of the sentry for whose placing he is responsible. When Francisco then remarks that he is "sick at heart" he merely emphasizes what this exchange has already suggested: that something is amiss.

The remainder of the scene indicates just what is amiss. There are two symptoms. The first is the "thing" of which Horatio speaks

162

rather disparagingly and which provides the reason he and Marcellus
are out (1.1.21).[1] The term he uses thus to indicate the ghost emphasizes his disbelief and anticipates an essential problem of knowledge in the tragedy: the credibility of the informant of mischief.
Bernardo will seek to overcome this disbelief by *telling a story*: "Sit
down awhile, / And let us once again assail your ears, / That are so
fortified against our story" (1.1.30–32). The difficulty in this is that
to use the metaphor of "assailing the ears" with a story is a sure way
of implying that such a story is something of a lie. When Horatio
speaks of "the sensible and true avouch / Of mine own eyes" (1.1.57–
58), we may remain in some doubt as to the value of such "true
avouch." In act 3 Gertrude considers the ghost to be "the very coinage of your [Hamlet's] brain" (3.4.138). Hamlet too will doubt the
ghost's testimony and be constrained to seek "grounds / More relative than this" (2.2.584–90). The question then will be whether "The
Mousetrap" will suffice to supply such telling grounds.

Several central problems are posed in the first scene: the individual's
perception of the self; his or her relationship with others; custom and
order; the nature, and certification, of truth and therefore of the
grounds of knowledge and action. Now the ghost enters, and exits
to Horatio's cry: "Speak, speak. I charge thee, speak" (1.1.51). Here
is another opposition marked that will invade the whole matter of
the tragedy. The opposition of speech and silence, or the encounter
of speech with misunderstanding (willful or accidental), constitutes
at one level the entire action of the tragedy—at least until the final
scene. The space of speech is one of disorder, confusion, and distraction. To it will be opposed a sphere of action, as a place of order and
firmness, of reason—and unjust tyranny.

In saying this I am indicating the second symptom of something
amiss, of the prospect of "some strange eruption to our state" (1.1.
69). All of those onstage after the ghost's first appearance assume it
to be connected with the warlike preparations presently in evidence
in Denmark—and it is Horatio who tells the story of "this sweaty
haste," just as it will also be Horatio whom Hamlet asks to tell his
story at the end. Now Horatio tells a tale of war and military action
that falls pat between the first and second appearance of the ghost
and his own first and second cry: "Speak to me. . . . Speak to me. . . .

O, speak! . . . Speak of it. Stay and speak" (1.1.129, 132, 135, 139).

And what is this tale of war? It is surely the story of the attempt to breach an old order and impose a new one. It is the story of a frame imposed by chivalry and now no longer accepted. It is a tale of the confrontation of two concepts of thought and action. Young Fortinbras, who thus threatens Denmark, is a man who no longer accepts the customs of chivalry and who seeks to break the compact between Denmark and Norway, though "well ratified by law and heraldry" (1.1.87), according to which the conquered has become vassal to the conqueror (1.1.80–107). He is a man who replaces such custom (the original battle itself being the result of a properly placed challenge [1.1.84]) with a militaristic land-grabbing: "We go to gain a little patch of ground/That hath no profit in it but the name" (4.4.18–19).

Hamlet admires Fortinbras for his activity, for using the "capability and godlike reason" that is the part of humanity. He admires him for finding "quarrel in a straw/When honour's at the stake." Nonetheless, it is admiration for an "imposthume," an abscess about to burst out of sight, for an example "gross as earth" (4.4.27–56) coming from a man who had bewailed a world now possessed by "things rank and gross in nature" (1.2.136). Hamlet's admiration is mixed with scorn for the ugly militarism of Fortinbras, dependent on heedless slaughter and needless expense—for a "straw," and which, at best, can lead only to the emulation of Osric: "a chough, but, as I say, spacious in the possession of dirt" (5.2.88–89). Hamlet, who needs no such material evidence of outward power and possession ("I could be bounded in a nutshell and count myself a king of infinite space" [2.2.251–52]), is the very essence of that chivalry broken by Fortinbras—as even Claudius admits, while himself helping to destroy it by using it to trap Hamlet in his own magnanimity (4.7.133–35).

But in Hamlet chivalry is clouded already. It is distraction, a remnant that prevents him from acting. Indeed it prevents him from accepting with ease the certainty of any truth, just because its context has been utterly changed ("Our state," as Claudius puts it, is "disjoint and out of frame" [2.2.19–20], though he himself does not take it to be so, arguing only that young Fortinbras *thinks* it is). Fortinbras is right and Claudius is wrong. Fortinbras will be the future and Hamlet the too too solid reminder of the past who would, if he could, bring back his father to rule. What is rotten in the state of Denmark is not just murder and incest, it is not simply that calumny has taken over, it is that one kind of order has decayed to distraction and confusion, to unreason and untruth, to a misuse or disuse of that "such larger discourse" (4.4.36) which should be the mark of humanity. It is to be replaced by something new. Murder, incest, calumny, doubt, confusion, distraction, are symptoms of transformation.

Such is the opposition to be played out between Hamlet and Fortinbras. But it is to be played out not only on the stage: it will also be performed between the stage and the audience. When Fortinbras orders Hamlet's body to be borne "like a soldier to the stage" (5.2. 385) he is placing it both aside and above: Hamlet is being placed *on view*, an object from the past whose story can now be told. A direct appeal is made to the audience. Shakespearean tragedy (and not just Shakespearean, for it is in large part a function of the physical organization of the theatre itself) avowedly presents the spectator with the task of judging the ordering of truth and action. The spectator is obliged to pass through a space of doubt first. In that connection we can, I think, accept with ease the arguments advanced by Mark Rose concerning the way in which a Shakespearean play is tightly organized by means of a particular relationship between the basic scenic units of the play and within these units in terms of their relative proportions and their spatial design and pattern. Such an ordering, by its very nature, would provoke a judgmental reaction on the part of the spectator because of the very juxtaposition of such scenic units: but the spectator is first involved otherwise in the action. According to Rose the two chief designs in Shakespeare would be the "frame scene" and the "diptych scene," the first a matter of containment, the second one of juxtaposition.[2] The latter need not concern us here, for *Hamlet* visibly depends on a successive series of framing producing the embedding that culminates in the central scene of "The Mousetrap."

Now it seems to me that such a process of framing would make a very particular kind of appeal to the spectator, say at the Globe. What is contained in the frame is not in itself the gentle order of clear-cut and identifiable relationships. One cannot conceive of an empathy be-

tween observer and stage character—quite the contrary, all is confusion and unclarity, and in one way the spectator is included in the
confusion. At the Globe there was no distinction of lighting between
the audience and the stage; and there was not always a considerable
difference in noise level either! All kinds of things apparently went
on among the spectators as the play was performed. This was no
occasional accident; it was a consequence of the way in which
theatres were conceived and built, their audiences standing and
their roofs open to the sky.[3]

Moreover, the playwright went out of his way to exploit the special nature of the relationship between stage and spectator: "The
abundant use of asides, eaves-dropping and disguise give depth to action within scenes. Events were perceived not in themselves alone,
but as they were filtered through the words of a commentator or the
eyes of an observer."[4] Brecht several times refers to the Shakespearean theatre as an epic stage. And of all this the great central play-
within-a-play scene of *Hamlet* is perhaps the most resounding example.
However, from the very start of *Hamlet* the spectator is made a particular part of the performance. Bernardo's story of the ghost is
certainly directed as much to the audience as it is to Horatio; and
what are we to make of Hamlet's reply to the ghost but a little later?
"Remember thee?/Ay, thou poor ghost, while memory holds a seat/
In this distracted globe. Remember thee?" (1.5.95–97).

The "globe" in question is not only his head, or the world; it is also
the theatre in which the audience is watching and listening. Frances
Yates has shown how the architectural form of the Globe enabled a
play to produce various levels of the medieval analogical universe as it
was still made use of by the humanists: how, for example, the geom-
etry of the floor plan of stage and auditorium may well have repro-
duced, with the necessary adjustments for the changed overall shape
of the theatrical space, a Vitruvian pattern whose order was symbolic of man in the universe—here informing both stage and auditorium; how the underside of the stage canopy, the so-called shadow,
perfectly visible to the pit, the actors, and certainly the lower levels
of the balconies if not all three, was almost certainly painted with
the zodiac.[5] In this way, the world was symbolized horizontally in
the floor plan, demonstrated vertically in the frequently staged se-

quence of hell (below stage), earth (stage) and "heavens" (the name given, probably, to the upper loft immediately beneath the zodiac-bepainted shadow), and performed by the interaction of stage and audience. If theatrical use was made of some members of the audience being onstage (as opposed to their being considered a mere nuisance, as they were in the Restoration), there would be further reinforcement of this complicated relationship.[6]

However the spectator's inclusion in the total experience of the theatre was reinforced, it seems clear that the play used, and produced, that spectator in a way quite different from the way in which the audience was played *to* in the neoclassical theatre of Restoration England and French absolutism. It is quite different from humanist techniques as well, though the discursive hierarchy I noted in Jodelle's *Cléopâtre* would have an effect (as to the knowledge it names) not altogether different from that of the performed frame in *Hamlet*, though its role and effect is in other ways quite different.

Of course, the number of asides in *Hamlet* is considerable: indeed, every one of Hamlet's soliloquies is an aside. When Polonius applauds his own cleverness in discovering the cause of Hamlet's madness (2.2.passim) the full succulence of the irony depends on the audience's superior knowledge, having earlier (2.5.171–72) been informed of the role Hamlet is to play: "(As I perchance hereafter shall think meet/To put an antic disposition on)." This superiority of the spectator, mocking of the trivial-minded Polonius, becomes serious when it is turned toward Hamlet's dilemma: the revelation Hamlet chooses to read in "The Mousetrap" remains very far from satisfactory for one in his position, but the audience is immediately given an advantage concealed even from Hamlet until the very end—Claudius, alone, confesses the matter (3.3.36–38).

Until this point Hamlet's distraction might well also be that of the entire Globe. After this admission we are only torn between the magnanimous glory of Hamlet's hesitation and the dubious desirability of the activities of Fortinbras, of which we are from time to time reminded (not to mention the similarly sordid maneuverings of Claudius and Laertes). There are, of course, other reminders to the spectator of his presence in a particular theatre at a particular time and place—Hamlet's well-known references in 2.2 to the boy companies, to the "War of the Theatres," to the Globe itself ("Hercules and his load," symbol of that theatre [2.2.353–54])—and of the duration of the performance (when Hamlet remarks, "My father died within's two hours" [2.2.121]),[7] and so on.

The "framing" effect must be considered in relation to this inclusion of the audience in the entire theatrical event. The sentry scene with which the play opens is almost always played on a platform raised above the stage, as is the scene (1.5) in which Hamlet and the ghost converse: "another part of the fortification," suggests the editor of the Pelican Shakespeare; on "the Battlements," says the Signet edition. This is partly because Marcellus later speaks of "the platform where we watched" (1.2.213), but it is also partly because of the feeling that there is some kind of vague threat that is outside the space in which tragedy is to be performed. What is outside is of a different quality from what is inside. It is what is being guarded against—whether the imperialism of Fortinbras or the knowledge that the ghost will strive to bring and whose result is complete change in the state of Denmark. Of course, the danger is in fact as much within as without, and the important thing is not the one or the other so much as the confrontation of the two. The wall is the place where that confrontation occurs, and the entrance of Fortinbras at the end is often played "from above" (for he must get "over the wall" into Elsinore). The suggestion is that all these scenes would be played in the loft.

As in the matter of all Shakespearean staging, there can be no agreement on the matter.[8] But it is not really necessary that there should be. What does seem clear is that the main action of the play is framed off from these opening and closing scenes. The sentry is guarding against some irruption from the outside. Hamlet and the ghost occupy some place "apart," away from the rotten state of Denmark possessed by "things rank and gross in nature" (1.2.136) and "between" it and the "sulph'rous and tormenting flames" (2.5.3) of a somehow purer space containing "thoughts beyond the reaches of our souls" (2.5.56). It is as though, there, a meager (and eventually doubtful) spark of true knowledge were appearing, under whose influence Hamlet for a moment sloughs off his depression in the warmth of a possible active revenge and his "serious hearing" (1.5.5): and that occurs outside the space of nonreason and distraction that will now seize and hold sway over the tragedy. At the end Fortinbras, his army, and the English ambassadors come in from the same "place" and write *finis* to the story of Hamlet.

Between these two moments the audience of the distracted Globe is also caught up in a constant exchange which, as Bertolt Brecht was perhaps right to remark, only the epic theatre style among contemporary kinds of playing could come close to recapturing.[9] This "dialectic" (as I have chosen to call it in hope of indicating the kind of movement that is going on, and not to assimilate it to Brecht's Marxian concept as brought to his theatre), will eventually have to be cut off if a knowledge of (referential and singular) truth is to become possible. Order will thus be imposed from elsewhere: Fortinbras enters.

In Shakespeare, however, the maintenance of such an order remains precarious even at the end, and Norman Rabkin may be quite correct when he argues that each of Shakespeare's best-known plays presents the spectator with two ethical, social, or political solutions to a given dilemma and, far from forcing him to choose between them, makes it impossible for him to do so: they may well appear contradictory even, but each is as valid and as useful as the other, indeed each *needs* the other. In Rabkin's view, therefore, the complexity of the situation for the spectator would by no means be resolved at the end of the tragedy: nor, he suggests, need it be.[10] Even for Rabkin, however, the two complementary responses are *solutions*; they are, that is, based on some knowledge and evidence of such knowledge. And that, of course, is part of our point: in Shakespeare's tragedy of *Hamlet* the audience is brought through distraction to order. It is an order that indicates that *knowledge and action are coextensive*.

We do not have to agree with the kind of thing represented by Claudius, nor even with the desirability of Fortinbras. Our most considerable admiration will surely go to Hamlet as a person, but what we are shown is that inaction in the face of knowledge serves to invalidate that knowledge. We, the spectators, know the truth of the matter, but does Hamlet? Certainly he never acts as though he does, and the final carnage is not his doing, but Claudius's. His killing of the king is more vengeance for what has just taken place than it is revenge for his father. And why? Because the truth produced by "The Mouse-

trap" is only too clearly *made* by Hamlet and because it could only
be confirmed by Hamlet taking action upon it. The consequence
of inaction is to undermine that knowledge—and the spectator obtains certain knowledge not from Hamlet's trick but from Claudius's
confession (the fact that the confession may be provoked by the
trick is of small matter).[11] Hamlet himself never escapes from those
"bad dreams" that prevent his thought from leaping up to infinite
space (2.2.253).

Innumerable commentators have suggested that the main dilemma
in *Hamlet* concerns "the pursuit of truth," as Willard Farnham puts
it in the introduction to his Pelican edition, which then puts in question Hamlet's conception of his own place in society and of the
nature of (his) being. Hamlet, Lawrence Danson has recently written,
is "a man alienated from his society's most basic symbolic modes."[12]
I prefer to say that the symbolic modes of society have lost their
ground for the duration of the tragedy, and that that is precisely
what is indicated in the opening exchange between Bernardo and
Francisco. What the tragedy does is produce new grounds. In rather
different terms, another relatively recent commentator has viewed
Hamlet's situation as a kind of social experiment:

> A man can either consent to finding his real self only in the mar-
> gin of society, in non-official activities and relationships; he can
> sell himself over, alternatively, to the public definition, become as
> he is valued; or he can continue to assert his authentic life and
> risk destruction. In *Hamlet* we find all three experiments tried,
> and they are all inadequate.[13]

All are in fact tried by Hamlet himself, but one wonders whether
they can be termed "inadequate," at least so far as what the tragedy
shows us is concerned. What is inadequate is the failure to *decide*,
given the terms of the situation as they are proposed. *That* failure is
what leads directly to Hamlet's death. Indeed, death and silence ("the
rest . . . ") are its mark: otherwise Hamlet would be telling his own
story and not begging Horatio to remain "in this harsh world" and
tell it for him (5.2.338).[14]

Hamlet is caught by what we saw in earlier chapters as the ultimate
calumny or slander: the enforcing of silence, the production of death,

the attempt to enforce a pattern upon the other that ultimately either prevents all speech or imposes the speech of the enforcer ("He has my dying voice," Hamlet concedes ambiguously in defeat [5.2. 345]). We may do well to recall that Fortinbras goes to and fro through Denmark with the "license" of Claudius (4.4.2), that both Claudius and Fortinbras seek precisely the same advantage for themselves, and that the Norwegian does not permit his sorrow to prevent him from seizing his chance with alacrity: "I have some rights of memory in this kingdom / Which now to claim my vantage doth invite me" (5.2.378–79). It is surely ironically that Horatio notes the opportuneness of the timing of Fortinbras's arrival from the point of view of the latter's ambitions ("But since, so jump upon this bloody question, / You . . . / Are here arrived" [5.2.364–66]). Indeed, he now has achieved all we were told he sought at the very outset— more, in fact. Fortinbras and Claudius are two of a kind, less concerned with speaking than with preventing others from doing so. The offstage plot of Fortinbras provides a conclusion more acceptable (in terms of a "liberal" notion of justice) than Claudius's replacement of his brother that preceded the tragedy, but the accomplishment is strictly identical.

Hamlet is in a different case entirely. "What we watch in Shakespearean tragedy," asserts Danson, "is not only man speaking, but man trying to speak, trying to create the language that can denote him truly."[15] That is what Hamlet never succeeds in achieving and, failing in the attempt, he asks Horatio to do it for him. This request is the final sign of Hamlet's continuing inability to escape from a space in which no meaning can be seized and no truth transfixed once and for all. At the end Hamlet must insist that it be some other who provides such knowledge: Horatio, who will bear the prince's concession into the brave new world of Fortinbras. His friend will oblige by telling the truth and giving knowledge to the world: but the truth and knowledge he will provide concerns the enclosure of chaos and accidental occurrence, the exorcism of confusion and disorder, of untruth and distraction:

> And let me speak to th' *yet unknowing* world
> *How these things came about.* So shall you hear

Of carnal, bloody, and *unnatural* acts,
Of *accidental* judgements, *casual* slaughters,
Of deaths put on *by cunning* and *forced cause*.
And, in this upshot, *purposes mistook*
Fall'n on th' inventors' heads. All this can I
Truly deliver.   [5.2.368–75]

In this almost emblematic piece of discourse, truth and a knowledge
of causes ("let me speak . . . how these things came about," "truly
deliver") *contains* the space of the inexplicable, where all is chance,
perversion, haphazard event. Hamlet could not escape from it, but
now it is to be made merely the memory of an aberrant moment in
the midst of order. Fortinbras is very clear about the necessity for
speed in resolution ("Let us haste to hear it" [5.2.375]) and as to
who should possess the knowledge ("And call the noblest to the audience" [5.2.376]). Horatio is equally clear that the telling (containing) of Hamlet's story must be accompanied equally swiftly by the
naming of Fortinbras to the throne: "Even while men's minds are
wild, less more mischance/On plots and errors happen" (5.2.383–
84). The telling of the story at the end and the installation of the new
order are part and parcel of the *same* action: Fortinbras's power depends upon the ability to set Hamlet's story in order.

The moments in the play when the activities of Fortinbras will be of
concern are thus most strategically placed. The first time we hear of
him will be when Horatio tells us of the old chivalric fight between old
Hamlet and old Fortinbras, whose outcome young Fortinbras is seeking to overturn. This occurs immediately between the two silent appearances of the ghost at the beginning of the tragedy: it is thus one
of the symptoms of the confusion of the times as it is simultaneously
contrasted with the questions raised by the ghost—natural/supernatur-
al, explicable/inexplicable, brute force/gentle persuasion, reason/mys-
tery. Then we are reminded again of Fortinbras after the second silent
appearance of the ghost and with the first appearance of the Court,
whose primary concern here is to settle the matter of Fortinbras's
threat by sending off the ambassadors, Voltimand and Cornelius, to
treat with his uncle. And next we return to the ghost once again, as
Horatio and his companions tell Hamlet what they have seen.

In this way the play opens with an alternation between two different kinds of matter: the demands of force and the effects of distraction. The opposition continues in the same manner. The subsequent
occasion upon which Fortinbras crops up will be after Hamlet's mad
scene with Ophelia, her recounting of it to Polonius, the latter's revelation of the "real" cause of that madness to the king and queen:
when we see the ambassadors' return following the successful accomplishment of their mission (2.2). We learn then that young Fortinbras
will be given the further outlet for his ambitions, permission to attack Poland. Thus it is in violent contrast with Hamlet's choice to
play the role of a madman, to act the "mole" in secret—a decision he
had in fact taken even before he had seen the ghost: "And what-
somever else shall hap tonight,/Give it an understanding but no
tongue" (1.2.249-50); and which he will repeat afterward: "Never
make known what you have seen tonight" (1.5.144). Once again,
then, Hamlet and Fortinbras are contrasted as action and distraction. For a while now the play will be given up to the latter, but its
potential opponent is at hand in the wings—and we may well remember the oath to everlasting secrecy sworn by Horatio to Hamlet
(*"Never* make known") when he arranges at the end to tell the whole
story to Fortinbras.

When next we are concerned with the Norwegian it is to meet him
in person (after the murder of Polonius, that always overtalkative
and distracted old man,[16] and just before our first sight of Ophelia
in her madness), and Fortinbras is about to ask Claudius for his "license" to march his army across Denmark, about to go and "express
[his] duty in his eye" (4.4.6). By saying this young Fortinbras is not
simply marking his acceptance of the suzerainty of the king of Denmark (he expresses himself with a singular lack of submissiveness
and, besides, he is already on his territory with an army)—he is suggesting that their interests are shared. Just as he goes to the "ren-
dezvous," Hamlet comes in. This is the first of the two occasions
when they almost meet (the second being the Norwegian's final entrance just after Hamlet's death). Perhaps they cannot actually meet:
for they represent two quite different spaces of discourse and action
(as did Pentheus and Dionysos).

Hamlet now, talking to Fortinbras's captain, laments the thoughtless militarism he perceives at work "for a fantasy and trick of fame" (4.4.61), yet can admire Fortinbras's energetic use of the "large discourse" given humanity by God, his active imposition of "that capability and godlike reason" (4.4.36–38). He perceives Fortinbras as "with divine ambition puffed" (4.4.49). And that is the very crux of the opposition: that kind of meager ambition for the "possession of dirt" can only be equated with the "bad dreams" that keep thoughts earthbound (2.2.249–60). It is therefore of considerable significance that the "clown" digging Ophelia's grave became a gravedigger on the very day that old Fortinbras was defeated by old Hamlet, and that Hamlet himself was born on the very same day. Thus is Hamlet's birth bound to his death, to the distraction of Ophelia (see 4.5.2), and to the power and activity of Fortinbras. Just before, in Hamlet's remark that the gravedigger throws down a skull "as if 'twere Cain's jawbone, that did the first murder" (5.1.72–73), the spectator is reminded of Claudius's confession: "It hath the primal eldest curse upon't, / A brother's murder" (3.3.37–38). Hamlet, Claudius, and death; Hamlet, Fortinbras, and death.

Fortinbras's ambitions are earthbound and gross, they concern the possession of land and of people, they are grimy, "drossy," and murderous ("the imminent death of twenty thousand men" [4.4.60]). But they are effective: Fortinbras get his way and imposes his will. Hamlet, on the other hand, cannot settle the place of truth and the time for action. For "enterprises of great pith and moment" may well "lose the name of action" if given up to too much thought (3.1.83–88), and yet Hamlet will not be prevented from demanding that a full knowledge be obtained of them first and of all their ramifications. That kind of truth is unavailable to him. There is always a gap, a little flaw, the "vicious mole" or the "bad dreams," to ignore which is to sink to the ambition of a Fortinbras or a Claudius—for that single lack, in Hamlet's view, corrupts entirely:

> Their virtues else, be they as pure as grace,
> As infinite as man may undergo,
> Shall in the general censure take corruption
> From that particular fault. The dram of evil

Doth all the noble substance of a doubt,
To his own scandal. [1.4.33–38]

If one does not ignore it, however, one ends up not acting at all. "The dram of evil" is a necessary thing in man, says Hamlet, and to ignore it by allowing individual free will untrammeled is the mark not of the sage but of the villain. How can one *act* on the basis of truth and knowledge proceeding from a reason that is flawed from within and therefore forever unknowingly? Just as the action of the "vicious mole" is to break down *all* "the pales and forts of reason" (1.4.28), so argues Hamlet, to recognize the presence of that dram of evil without knowing the limits of its effects (which one never can) is to accept truth as unattainable and action as therefore always potentially vicious.

So Hamlet remains within the space of the inexplicable, within the space where discourse ultimately peters out—"The rest is silence," murmurs Hamlet as he dies (5.2.347)—or where the voice must become that of the other; Horatio's, in the tale to be told, Fortinbras's, in the election for which he has Hamlet's "dying voice." In a sense the whole tragedy of Hamlet, to the extent that it is its protagonist's *performance* and not his friend's *telling*, is constituted by Hamlet's attempts to avoid the ultimate "calumny" of being named by the other. The tragedy is that of his struggle to replay, to retell *for himself* the very same act of calumny, of death and silence, whose metaphor is the pouring of poison in the ear of old Hamlet. That act was first told by the ghost, then performed at second hand by the players, perhaps admitted by Gertrude (but of just what does she admit to having knowledge? nothing), and actually confessed by Claudius—but to the audience, not Hamlet. For Hamlet whatever truth there is in *that* story is always "somewhere else." Is the ghost to be believed? Does Gertrude ever admit to anything? What has he really learned from "The Mousetrap"? Is the whole thing not simply a single metaphor for the human condition? Certainly that is what Hamlet himself seems tempted to make of it, with his continual generalizations. Untruth and lies are the very standard of human intercourse: "Be thou as chaste as ice, as pure as snow," cries Hamlet to Ophelia, "thou shalt not escape calumny" (3.1.136–37).

Claudius's pouring of the poison into old Hamlet's ear is simply the literal performance of Gamaliel's metaphor for calumny and false speech (the metaphor for *all* human speech indeed, as the quotation I then made from *Les Juifves* suggests). It is the ghost himself, as a matter of fact, who suggests that the case is that of the performance of a metaphor. Even before telling how he was murdered, how his brother "in the porches of [his] ear did pour/The leprous distilment" (1.5.63–64), he remarks that Claudius has deceived Denmark as to the truth concerning that death: "So the whole ear of Denmark/Is by a forgèd process of my death/Rankly abused" (1.5.36–38).

As a matter of fact, too, the metaphor is constantly recalled throughout the tragedy: "Here is your husband," says Hamlet to his mother, "like a mildewed ear/Blasting his wholesome brother" (3.4. 65–66), to which she responds by ringing up the changes slightly: "These words like daggers enter in mine ears" (3.4.99). Hamlet later notes how incomprehending is Rosencrantz: "A knavish speech sleeps in a foolish ear" (4.2.22–23), while Polonius is unwise enough to make an oblique reference to the same metaphor when telling Claudius how he will eavesdrop on Hamlet and the queen: "And I'll be placed, so please you, in the ear/Of all their conference" (3.1. 184–85).

Hamlet also makes a point of emphasizing the same metaphorical aspect of the matter when answering the king's question: "What do you call the play?—"'The Mousetrap.' Marry, how? *Tropically*" (3.2. 228–29). The name Hamlet first gives the play, "The Murder of Gonzago," (2.2.22) is itself a metaphor—with a play on "trapically," as most editors do not fail to observe. Second, however, the action to be performed in that play is a replica of the one performed (according to the ghost) by Claudius, which is itself the performance of an earlier metaphor for human discourse and original sin (the serpent's poison in the ear of Eve). Third, we are brought here full circle: for what is the trap in which Hamlet hopes to catch Claudius? He aims *to force the King to a speech of his, Hamlet's, making*: "Observe my uncle. If his occulted guilt/Do not itself unkennel in one speech,/It is a damnèd ghost that we have seen . . ." (3.2.77–79).

Hamlet wishes to turn the metaphor around and use it against Claudius. But his difficulty remains that he is too aware that he himself is speaking. Like Gamaliel, like Jean-Baptiste, he "sees himself" in the process of saying and sees all too well that he *makes* the knowledge he claims only to seek: in this he is utterly different from Polonius, from Claudius, or from Fortinbras. For Hamlet truth and knowledge are produced by the speaker. How can that kind of truth be a basis for action against (or even with) others?

For what, finally, is this play that is going to produce the truth about Claudius's actions, that is going to make the king confess? Hamlet is going to put his stepfather to the "question" like the criminal he believes him to be. Thus the tragedy called "The Murder of Gonzago" and by Hamlet named "The Mousetrap" is a quite different sort of instrument from the tragedy of *Hamlet* which contains it. It is a piece of Senecan-type rhetorical tragedy, prepared for by the reciting of the passages concerning the death of Priam (2.2.438–506), and more akin to Garnier or Heywood than to the Shakespeare we are familiar with.[17] That is little cause for surprise, because this tragedy is *the machine that is to provide knowledge for Hamlet.* Thus the prologue to the play (which is all that is actually performed of the spoken part of Hamlet's machine) is almost a parody of sixteenth-century "university" drama: "Full thirty times . . . thirty dozen moons . . . twelve thirties," and so on (3.2.146–49). Both Claudius and the spectator might be as well aware of this as Hamlet himself.

What is perhaps odd about this prologue is that the player queen expresses fear that old age or sickness will carry off her husband, as though Hamlet were continuing to express some doubt about the nature of his father's death. Nor should we be too ready to think such talk of a natural death does not come from Hamlet himself: for not only did the prince choose the play, he also proposed to add lines to it (and we cannot know which ones).[18] In one way, then, Hamlet is writing his own version of the ghost's story—and even offering excuses for Gertrude's behavior as he does so: is "nor 'tis not strange/ That even our loves should with our fortunes change" (3.2.192–93) —sheer sarcasm on Hamlet's part? The prince is retelling the story of the murder just as Horatio will tell his story after the play of *Hamlet.* Indeed, at the very nub of the trap is the fifth "telling" of the murder (if we accept the notion that Gertrude's silence is an admission of knowledge). It is Hamlet himself, and not the players, who now tells it: "'A poisons him i' th' garden for his estate. His name's Gonzago. The story is extant, and written in very choice Italian. You shall see anon how the murderer gets the love of Gonzago's wife" (3.2. 251–54). Having named his own story and written and produced the play, Hamlet now not only gives his source but tells the action.

There lies the difficulty: for Hamlet *knows* it is his own creation: "There is nothing either good or bad but thinking makes it so" (2.2.247–48). Hamlet, in the space of distraction, can see himself making truth, he can see himself as the all-too-exemplary figure who is unable to escape from the limits of discourse itself. But Hamlet has "come through" the personification of the Promethean metaphor that played out that inability (or as Icarus, or as Phaeton: "Not so, my lord. I am too much in the sun," asserted Hamlet at the beginning of his play [1.2.67]). Hamlet plays it out just as the metaphor itself is played out: it invades the entire tragedy. So even Hamlet will finally stop talking and decide that only action can finally "speak the truth"; action will be truth in that it will produce the solution that speech could not. Action does produce truth. It is Hamlet's return and challenge that provoke Claudius and Laertes to their plot, and Hamlet can now cry out his own name at last—"This is I, / Hamlet the Dane" (5.1.244–45)—as he leaps into the grave.

For finally Hamlet's trap reveals itself incapable of *proving* anything: Hamlet wants objective certainty, and all he gets is a forced cry of pain from the king "upon the talk of poisoning" (3.2.279). Hamlet has caught the king, but in a trap of his own making, and even Horatio can give but meager encouragement for the belief in the king's guilt (3.2.261–84). There are too many possible and quite adequate explanations: the king could easily be upset at the mere thought of being suspected of the crime. There is after all no question but that he is the present possessor of the crown and that he is incestuously married to his former sister-in-law (Henry VIII had had to obtain a special papal dispensation to wed Katherine of Aragon, who had previously been married briefly to his brother). He is obviously not free of some guilt therefore.

Hamlet is looking for certainty, so that any doubt whatever is sufficient distraction—as in a court of law. By the time Hamlet has finished his speech in which he relates the plot of his play, the poisoning of a king's brother and the wedding of his ex-wife, it must be evident even to the least sensitive of his audience that he is making a commentary upon the present king and queen. He could not reasonably expect to do anything other than arouse the king's "choler" (3.2.291) and provoke the queen to being "struck . . . into amazement and admiration" at his "behaviour" (3.2.312–13). It is a long step from the justifiable anger of an innocent to a pained admission of guilt. So what is the interpretation to be given to the result of the trap, so far as Hamlet is concerned?

Cléopâtre had escaped Octavian's trap in Jodelle's tragedy because she was able to see it coming, and because he could not act (or there, speak) quickly enough. Here Hamlet's trap "works" (it produces a result), but he is unable to be sure either of the *meaning* of that working or *what it is in the trap* that has produced whatever particular meaning he may choose to read into it. Gertrude admits nothing beyond her incestuous marriage, already known to all, and her betrayal of old Hamlet's memory, already forgiven by Hamlet in the prologue to his play. Hamlet does not hear Claudius's confession. When the queen tells Hamlet that even the ghost itself "is the very coinage of his brain" (3.4.138), she expresses his own very deepest fears.

When Hamlet, immediately after his upbraiding by the queen for his behavior toward the king, accuses Guildenstern of seeking to trap him, Hamlet, of trying to "play upon" him, and casts obloquy on the very notion that such an entrapment should be thought possible (3.2.331–57), he is surely making a commentary upon the ambiguous results of his own attempts to do just precisely that with regard to Claudius. As Hamlet will shortly say, again to Guildenstern: "The King is a thing . . . of nothing" (4.2.27–29); and if, in saying so, he reminds us of his earlier hopeful remarks that "the play's the thing/ Wherein I'll catch the conscience of the king" (2.2.590–91), we may well be inclined to reflect that the king is indeed a nothing—a blank for the stamp of Hamlet's truth. Hamlet has sought to *invent* the king, to incline him to a particular pattern perhaps invented by the ghost, the coinage of his brain, to force him into the mold of some certain knowledge. And Hamlet is unable to know whether it worked as he wanted it to or not.

It surely *has* worked for the audience, however. It provokes the confession of Claudius, and we now see an ongoing series of machinations that confirm the "reality" of the past we have been told several times. It must be a *past*, though, something able to be *told*: by Horatio, not by Hamlet, because the prince is a part of it as the "bad dreams" are a part of the "large discourse" and the "dram of evil" a part of all virtue and reason. For Hamlet all this is still present: "and my father died within's two hours" (3.2.121).[19] For all those present in the tragedy's action this will also be the case. While from now on the audience may grow increasingly aware of all the ramifications of what is occurring, *all* the characters sink ever deeper into distraction and ignorance, with only one exception: Fortinbras, who is barely present on the stage though he is always being recalled to mind. He remains a kind of shadowy presence pacing up and down in the wings, waiting only for his cue to come onstage and impose order.

The king now notes how Hamlet is "loved of the *distracted* multitude" (4.3.4), how "like the hectic in [Claudius's own] blood he rages" (4.3.65). After Polonius, then, in the distraction of a foolish old age (see note 16), the entire populace and the king himself are "distracted"; next Ophelia, in the madness provoked by her father's death and Hamlet's treatment of her; the queen with her "sick soul" (4.5.17); Rosencrantz and Guildenstern in their ignorance of the fate to be brought on by their "sponging." As Claudius puts it, in a kind of summing up:

> first, her father slain;
> Next your son gone, and he most violent author
> Of his own just remove; the people muddied,
> Thick and unwholesome in their thoughts and whispers
> For good Polonius' death. . . .
>
> poor Ophelia
> Divided from herself and her fair judgement,
> Without the which we are pictures or mere beasts;
> Last, and as much containing as all these,
> Her brother is in secret come from France,
> Feeds on his wonder, keeps himself in clouds. . . .   [4.5.79–89]

All this is confirmed by the immediate news that the "multitude" is proclaiming Laertes king. Laertes, however, keeps his head at least until he sees his mad sister: "O heat, dry up my brains; tears seven times salt / Burn out the sense and virtue of mine eyes!" (4.5.154–55). And then he will be used by Claudius, that the king may at last get rid of Hamlet. But is the king aware that in arguing the justice of revenge to Laertes ("No place indeed should murder sanctuarize; / Revenge should have no bounds" [4.7.126–27]), he is justifying any revenge that Hamlet might seek to take on his own person? It would scarcely seem so from the manner in which he speaks. It is as though from now until the end both Claudius and Laertes were becoming increasingly frenzied, a frenzy that culminates in the almost lunatic bombastic squabble between Hamlet and Laertes on Ophelia's coffin in her grave, and finally in the fencing match.

Hamlet, on the other hand, and in stark contrast to the now almost blundering Claudius, immediately notes the similarity of cases and reacts accordingly: "But I am very sorry, good Horatio, / That to Laertes I forgot myself, / For by the image of my cause I see / The portraiture of his" (5.2.75–78). Hamlet is seeming to attain a new tranquillity, a tranquillity not of knowledge but of acceptance of distraction: "Thou wouldst not think how ill all's here about my heart. But it is no matter" (5.2.201–02). Horatio argues that he should follow his intuition and call off the match. Not so, replies Hamlet in one of his more celebrated pieces of dialogue:

> There is a special providence in the fall of a sparrow. If it be now, 'tis not to come; if it be not to come, it will be now; if it be not now, yet it will come. The readiness is all. Since no man of aught he leaves knows, what is't to leave betimes? Let be. [5.2.208–13]

We might add that for Hamlet ignorance of the future is matched by the uncertainty of the present. It is as though he had given up the search not simply for certain knowledge, but for any kind of knowledge whatsoever. This is the "action" he chooses. The "Let be" just quoted is surely the answer to the most celebrated soliloquy of all tragedy: "To be or not to be." The intentional choice expressed in the latter is answered at the end of the play by an almost passive acceptance of whatever may happen. A sort of fatalism is expressed that cuts through the questions as though a time for action had come not because a decision is now possible and essential (as the soliloquy appears to demand) but because all the questions have been shown vain. Hamlet can give no answers: "Had I but time /. . . O, I could tell you— / But let it be" (5.2.325–27), he repeats as he tells Horatio to report him aright. And to whom is Horatio to tell it? To "you that look pale and tremble at this chance, / That are but mutes or audience to this act" (5.2.323–24): to the spectators.

The vanity of Hamlet's distracted questioning meets the frame of the story whose telling is now coming to a close, a close confirmed by the arrival and imposition of Fortinbras's order. It is thus most fitting that Hamlet is given the most inappropriate salute that Fortinbras could have imagined: "and for his passage / The soldier's music and the rites of war / Speak loudly for him" (5.2.387–89). Hamlet has been enclosed in Fortinbras's new and quite different discursive order—and ours. On the other hand, we may well agree with Brecht that Hamlet's activities in the concluding act of the play indicate that he is enclosing himself in such an order. Far from being inappropriate, Fortinbras's salute merely confirms Hamlet's own renunciation of his previous distraction:

> And so, cautiously using the sound of accidental
> Drums and the battle cry of unknown butchers
> By accident set free at last from his
> So sensible and human inhibition
> Running amuck in one horrendous race
> He kills the king, his mother and himself
> So justifying his successor's contention
> That, had he mounted the throne, he surely would have
> Comported himself most royally.[20]

7   The Lear of the Future

Hamlet comes to an unhappy close in the dominance of Fortinbras, whose commiseration for those caught confusedly in the revolutions of time and the change of orders does not too much prevent him from grasping at power: "with sorrow I embrace my fortune." Still, Fortinbras reveals the very "milky gentleness and course" of Albany (*King Lear*, 1.4.332) in comparison with the harsh triumvirate composed of Goneril, Regan, and Edmund (not to mention the early-dying Cornwall). What remains in *Hamlet* but a fitful thunder, a faint forerunning echo of a storm, in *Lear* bursts out in full fury. In *Hamlet* an order distracted ruled the stage and the theatrical event with a kind of dismal glory: the advent of Fortinbras's willful power at least pauses before the telling of Hamlet's story. In *Lear* we are shown a confusion and an inversion that are not simply those of an order that has lost ground, but that proceed from a direct clash of different classes of discourse, of different ways of acting and thinking, of different conceptions of power, of the place of the self and the role of the other. This tends to make the play something of a throwback, though in an altogether modern context.

Sophoclean tragedy, Pierre Gravel suggests, may have been that discourse in Greek antiquity which would have made clear the impossibility of constructing some "thing" which *we* could (later) have called the "subject."[1] Sophoclean tragedy, in this reading, attempted to compose a discourse in opposition to those "systematizing" devices whose eventual function was to erect the psychological and social being of the *Republic.* (This does not, I think, contradict what I argued in the first chapter: taken against other discourses Sophoclean tragedy would be a systematizing attempt that failed, and whose very failure confirms the success of others). Clearly even this last "subject" (that of the *Republic*, for example) is not *our* (individualistic) subject, the concept that was established on the basis of work by Bacon and Descartes, Galileo and Bodin with his notion of human history (already) as the place of "the empire of the will." For us, the idea of the subject, like those of will, possession, power, and even (above all perhaps) action, all share in the same discursive space. Such a subject could never have been constituted by the Greeks, as the work of Gerald Else and Jean-Pierre Vernant has indicated: the very vocabulary is lacking. And certainly no "subject" at all is created in the Sophoclean discourse of tragedy. There is nothing but dispersion, a constant multiplying (proliferation, as Gravel has it) of the impossibility of providing the human with a specific meaning, of placing being in "its" particular relation with the other and with the world. There is nothing but that constant flux of which Frege will write twenty-five hundred years later (and after three centuries of positivism) that to accept it as the necessary condition of our relation with the world would be to condemn ourselves to definitive ignorance—the space of the tragic.

Now this is just what we have seen the tragedy of the Renaissance gradually evolving away from. While Greek tragedy may not have seen the constitution of the subject (unless Euripedean tragedy did so) and may rather have ceded that constitution to philosophy, where the subject will be a function of the state and its morality, Renaissance tragedy does seem to have done so. The impossibility that was performed in Buchanan's two tragedies of situating a subject (the self) in discourse became metaphorized, personified, and finally endowed with some kind of psychological depth. The subject was created there as the very place where meaning is composed. Tragedy will finally be viewed as the systematic discourse, the "machine," that created it. Tragedy will have confirmed the possibility of a certain knowledge and of a certain conception of power and social practice.

Some of Shakespeare's plays, such as *Hamlet*, confirm this constitution; others complicate it considerably, seeming to return to something closer to the experience of Sophoclean tragedy. This is especially so of *King Lear*. Of course, by now the subject is already in place: it is a matter of making it function. *Lear*, that is to say, does not aim to constitute the subject (or to show, perform, its impossibility) but rather to set in motion the operation and confrontation of power. It is here that a certain impossibility will be demonstrated. In the play of conflicting powers no conclusion will be reached: save perhaps the indication that confrontation is utterly inadequate to produce anything new that may be socially or politically useful. For, in the end, *Lear* may be showing us that a new class of discourse cannot spring simply from confrontation—that it can only arise with a quite different, within an *other* (logical or discursive) space, that it can only arise on the basis of a prior—and essential—displacement. Jonsonian tragedy would be indicative; so too the philosophers and scientists just mentioned. (I will return to this at the end of the present chapter.) We must also recognize that even if *Lear* does in some ways rediscover the mode of Sophoclean tragedy, the tragedy's general tendency so far as the functioning of power relationship is concerned is clear enough: as I will seek to show. That tendency, moreover, is apparently viewed with some dismay by the puppeteer.

It is of some interest, then, and not simply anecdotal, that two such different writers as Brecht and Elder Olson—the one a professed anti-Aristotelian, the other a self-proclaimed neo-Aristotelian—should view the problematic of *King Lear* with so like an eye. Brecht does not limit this view to *Lear*, of course. For him the Shakespearean tragedies as a whole show us "a tragic view of the decline of feudalism. Lear, tied up in his own patriarchal ideas; Richard III . . . ; Macbeth . . . ; Antony . . . ; Othello . . . : they are all living in a new world and are smashed by it."[2] In a similar manner Elder Olson treats the actions of Lear as those of a man caught between the demands of feudality and those of the family (which conflict is possible only if the familial demands can be set on a different plane from those of feudalism, a differentation occurring only at a moment of changing standards and the development of the nuclear family unit).

Lear's reasons for relinquishing power are perfectly sound, Olson points out. He feels he is becoming too old to rule and he wishes the kingdom to have its stability guaranteed while he is still alive as sole anointed king; having no male heir, he wishes to make an equitable

division among his female successors and so avoid strife among his
sons-in-law after he is dead. On the other hand, Olson observes, once
he has yielded his regal authority there will no longer be any guar-
antee of his own privilege. If he is to retain any "security and dignity,
he can only trust to their *love*; and his insistence upon their public
profession of it is an attempt to have it warranted and witnessed as a
formal part of the compact of the delivery of property and power."[3]
Lear is a feudal lord, remarks Olson, but he fails to realize that in the
domestic sphere the "laws of feudality do not operate." Lear's act
is that of a feudal lord exacting "fealty from his vassals," without,
however, realizing that once he has abrogated his authority such
fealty no longer holds (p. 203). Whether he realizes his situation or
not, once he has taken the decision he has (for the future good of the
kingdom) he has little choice but to throw himself upon his daughters' love. And this action elicits from Lear an attempt to use
another class of discourse whose effect upon him (and others) is disastrous, because he is inept at it. Why does Lear perform his decision in the manner he does? Olson asks, and replies that "he gives
in this feudal way and demands in this feudal way, for it is the only
way he knows" (p. 203).

Certainly the "strangely formal speeches, with their legal phrasing"
with which Lear replies to his first two daughters' professions of love
confirm Olson's view. To Goneril, he swears:

> Of all these lands, even from this line to this,
> With shadowy forests and with champains riched,
> With plenteous rivers and wide-skirted meads,
> We make thee lady. To thine and Albany's issues
> Be this perpetual. [1.1.63–67]

To Regan her father contracts:

> To thee and thine hereditary ever
> Remain this ample third of our fair kingdom,
> No less in space, validity, and pleasure
> Than that conferred on Goneril. [1.179–82]

Olson is quite right, I think, to observe that "these are the speeches
of a feudal lord, to vassals who have expressed fealty" (p. 203).

Cordelia, on the other hand, seeks to act in familial terms, where things depend on trust and not on forms and contracts. She knows that the "nature of love and affection is that they are inexhaustible" and that they cannot therefore be restricted to any one person as Lear demands: "any profession to that effect is by that very fact a *lie*" (p. 204). Olson's opposition between feudality and family is tenable only if the latter is thought of in its post–seventeenth–century form at the least, and possibly even in its post–Industrial Revolution shape. His point about what Lear is seeking to do is, however, well taken. Still, Lear is confused in a much deeper way than Olson (or Brecht) suggests, for he is not in fact simply demanding a profession of fealty—he is proposing an exchange of sureties. A feudal overlord does not buy fealty with land—he exacts it: the demand for such a profession is the reminder of superior force and power. The very exchange being proposed by Lear reveals that something is amiss: for his activity as a feudal lord is already distorted.

Paul Delany has recently taken the readings of Brecht and Olson a bit further. In his opinion the play represents a stage of transition between "the dominance of the feudal aristocracy and that of the commercial bourgeoisie."[4] In this reading, Edmund, Goneril, and Regan represent the commercial bourgeoisie, Gloucester and Lear the feudal aristocracy: Cordelia is caught in between. Delany argues that the first group represents the wave of the future, though it is shown to be criminal and utterly unsympathetic, while the feudal aristocracy is quite superb but now outmoded, declining, and powerless. At the end we are left only with the "haziness of England's fortunes under Edgar" (p. 436).

What is uncomfortable about this reading, as also about Olson's, is that it projects something from outside the play into it (and in Olson's case something anachronistic: the nuclear family unit). What the play shows is some kind of clash, resolved in general disaster. Nothing in the play actually suggests that Edmund, Goneril, and Regan can be taken as the wave of the future. If anything, for Shakespeare's audience, they would surely be simply an aberration, a criminal conspiracy that is in fact overcome by Edgar's reliance on the feudal, chivalric decision. And that decision is neither ill-prepared, accidental, nor a last-minute deus ex machina: as soon as he sees the

letter addressed to Edmund from Goneril Edgar realizes that he has
the leverage to break his opponents, and both tells us what he intends
to do with the letter and takes pains to keep it safe while he gets his
father to safety (4.6.258–79).

We next see him with it when he gives it to Albany with instruc-
tions to summon the champion capable of maintaining in judicial
combat the accusation the letter reveals (5.1.38–50). Edgar, this is to
say, is preparing to win whatever the outcome of the battle between
the forces of England and France. And when Edmund accepts the
challenge in the last scene of the tragedy he is accepting to return to
an order whose overthrow he had seemed to seek throughout the
action—a return emphasized by his final decision to do "some good
. . ./Despite of mine own nature" (5.3.244–45). Surely Albany is
recognizing the willful nature of Edgar's rehabilitation of the old order when he suggests, otherwise seemingly illogically, that Edgar and
Kent become joint rulers? However "hazy" and uncertain might be
Edgar's rule, if anything is the "future" of the play it is that, and not
the performance of the evil triumvirate.

It is true that certain characters in Shakespeare (Hamlet, Lear,
Othello) do appear to play out the magnificent decline into the unknowing confusion of some order whose time is past and that is confronted to varying degrees by some other order. Nothing yet suggests
that that order is the wave of the future, however—at least, not in
Lear (though Fortinbras's coming to power does suggest it in *Hamlet*). To make so detailed a parallel as Olson and Delany attempt is to
provide the text with a particular meaning because the specific use
it makes of discourse coincides with a particular social development:
that development then becomes the meaning of the text. Delany
makes it coincide with the reading of the decline of feudalism made
by Lawrence Stone. But Stone himself implies that the decline in
question was not so much a cause of anything (let alone literary re-
countings of it), or even a symptom. The decline is simply part of a
general "discursive" change (my term, not Stone's). Speaking specifically of the increased social mobility and the gradual decay of the
particular social hierarchy of feudalism, Stone write that "by 1641
rust was eating into the shackles of the Great Chain of Being."[5] This
is not simply a metaphor. What used to be called the *Weltanschauung*

is changing and every form of practice will show the results of that change. That there is a discursive clash played out in the text is not in question, but that does not make it a representation of one being worked out elsewhere. Each domain of practice will have to work it out in its own terms, though there will certainly be interplay among them.

What we are confronted with is a clash of different ways of using language, of different discourses, of different ways of conceiving the relation of language to the world, to the speaker and the hearers, to meaning and action. If I insist upon the importance of discourse in that development it is because on the one hand it is the sole common denominator and on the other it is the only means for us to find out about such changes—through what and how people spoke (or wrote). *Lear* shows us people trapped between two different conceptions of what language is and does.

For Cordelia language and meaning, language and the world, what one says and what that saying means are *intrinsically* related. For Goneril, for Regan, and for Edmund, language is an instrument for the acquisition of power and possessions, for the imposition of the speaker. Lear conceives of language in the way Cordelia does, but he wants to *use* it as his two eldest daughters do. Seeking to have it both ways he can have it neither, and he falls into a space where his false understanding of the beginning becomes the utter lack of comprehension of his final meeting with Cordelia: "I know you do not love me; for your sisters / Have (as I do remember) done me wrong. / You have some cause, they have not" (4.7.73–75). This in turn becomes the "special horror" (as Brecht puts it)[6] of the gentle but grievous meanderings over the dead body of Cordelia with which the king breathes his last.

This confusion of Lear's is in evidence from the start: "Which of you *shall we say* doth love us most" (1.1.51). Lear is not concerned with any love that may have been shown in the past, he is asking for a future and verbal commitment: and he is saying that that comitment is part of an exchange (for "our largest bounty"). However, if he is not concerned with the past then he is stripping speech of a referent, he is taking its ground out from under it. For he is saying that it creates its sense as it goes along, and he cannot then expect the professions of love to have any meaning but that of the moment of exchange in which they will have been uttered. He himself will treat Cordelia's refusal to profess more than her "bond" in just that way, as a denial of love, refusing to go beyond the particular utterance. But in doing so he denies himself the right to be upset when Goneril and Regan do precisely the same thing: when they demonstrate that for them too an utterance has meaning only for the context of exchange in which it is uttered. And when he cries out in anguish to his daughters: "O reason, not the need," he is reversing his stance and indicting himself for his treatment of Cordelia, though he doubtless does not yet see it.

Of course, such a view of discourse will make any stable social relationships impossible. That that is indeed the case is indicated not only by the treatment meted out to Lear and Gloucester, but also by the tension and decay of the relationships among Goneril, Regan, and Edmund.

At the outset, then, Goneril is quick to seize on her father's proposition:

> Sir, I love you more than word can wield the matter;
> Dearer than eyesight, space, and liberty;
> Beyond what can be valued, rich or rare . . .
> A love that makes breath poor, and speech unable. . . .
> [1.1.55–57, 60]

This claim is utterly self-contradictory. If she did love beyond the power of "word [to] wield the matter," sufficient to make "breath poor, and speech unable," then she could not say so; so to say it is to deny it. Cordelia sees this: "What shall Cordelia speak? Love, and be silent" (1.1.62). Indeed, according to what Goneril has said the greatest love *must be* silent. But that would pose another dilemma, in which Cordelia will in fact place herself: the refusal to speak makes any kind of relationship impossible. Goneril therefore distracts attention from the contradiction by an entirely appropriate use of words of (monetary) value: "dearer," "valued," "rich or rare," "poor." In doing so she appeals precisely to the scale in which Lear is seeking to weigh them. At the same time she commits herself to the same scale: words, she says, are meaningless, but if the possibility of their use as counters in exchange can be indicated then they acquire some usefulness.

Goneril realizes what Lear wants—(or at least what will satisfy him) —and for her speech becomes first and foremost a means to possession: she is exchanging her words for the "shadowy forest," the "plenteous rivers and wide-skirted meads." Words have no intrinsic meaning (as they have for Cordelia); *they mean only what they can be used for*, and what they are to be used for is possession and control. For Goneril the notion that speech can *lie* is a fact of which socialized discourse must make use: for it is *essential.* It is almost as though she were rebuking Hamlet: do not seek to elucidate calumny, use it (which, in effect, is what Fortinbras has done in his final coming to power). As the Fool will say to Lear after the ill-treatment has begun: "Prithee, nuncle, keep a schoolmaster that can teach thy fool to lie. I would fain learn to lie" (1.4.170–71). Then could he function in the same register as Goneril and Regan. The only reality for them is the possessive *I*, and speech for them is no longer merely the guarantor of the "existence" of the enunciating subject (as it was for speakers in earlier tragedies); it is one of the tools of that subject made "self," and provided with an independent existence. For that reason speech has become a mask: it does not *express* the self (as it did in the case of Tamburlaine or of Nabuchodonosor or Sedecie, for example), it is *used* by the self. And Regan picks up that use right on cue: "And *prize* me at her *worth.* In my true heart/I find she *names* my very *deed* of love;/Only she comes *too short*, that I *profess* . . ." (1.170–72). Every term is picked up, and the word *deed* is wonderfully ambiguous: not simply the fact (or act) of love, but the contract of love by which Lear is claiming to facilitate the donation of the "several dowers" (1.1.44).

Cordelia is once again perspicacious in getting at the very nub of the matter. This time she takes up the metaphor of value in her aside: "Then *poor* Cordelia;/And yet not so, since I am sure my love's/More *ponderous* than my tongue" (1.1.76–78). Cordelia is "poor" in words to be used only in exchange. She turns the metaphor around: for Goneril and Regan words are tokens, like money, and like money they have a mass all their own which can make the thing against which they are to be exchanged seem the more valuable: so Lear. For

Cordelia they remain tokens but they have no value at all save inasmuch as they are "a part of," "truly representative of," are "an attribute of" what they "mean." For her, not words but love itself is "ponderous." Her sisters are concerned with exchange values, with interest (gained by fooling the listener into believing the weight they say). Cordelia is concerned with a different kind of value altogether— that value which is certified by the imprint of the prince on the coin. It is "intrinsic" in the sense that it inheres in the coin, in the word, just because this last and what it expresses are part of a whole network of signification and communication.[7] Of course, it is not just words (or coins) that participate in this network: it is the whole of existence, of which words are simply one part. Perhaps Kent expresses this most clearly when he curses Oswald: "Such smiling rogues as these / Like rats oft bite the holy cords atwain / Which are too intrinse t' unloose" (2.2.68-70). And Kent, representative like Cordelia of the old order, is mocked for this conception of totality: "Smile you my speeches, as I were a fool?" he cries (2.2.77).

The order of Goneril, of Regan, of Edmund (who will use writing to deceive Gloucester as the sisters use speech to deceive Lear) uses discourse as an *instrument* for gain.[8] Cordelia (and Kent) remain in that sense thoroughly medieval. Speech and what it says, speech and reality are part and parcel of a same whole. Speech used deliberately to deceive invalidates not only all speech itself but the very relations and emotions it purports to express. Hence Cordelia must remain silent and say: "Nothing." It is in this sense that Elder Olson can assert that she is simply *"persistently candid."*[9] She relies on acts and (as she thinks) known emotions to fill out the rest because they are all one. Unfortunately her father, at this point, does not see things in quite the same light. Cordelia, like Kent (and Edgar later), is caught up in a world where two orders of discourse are meeting head on, and she is unable to change her discourse appropriately. Danson remarks that in this first scene of the play Cordelia is called upon "to make a statement that is both ordinary and extraordinary, hers alone and yet everyone's."[10] In a way one might be tempted to take Cordelia as that very personification of the "impossibility of speaking": if she speaks like Goneril and Regan she will speak the lie that betrays the intrinsic worth of her words and what they are saying, while at the same time she would be accepting the imposition of a discourse that would force her to act like her sisters and acknowledge that discourse is but an instrument to be used against an opponent. If she does not speak then she maintains her integrity in silence: but that prevents all social discourse whatever, and again lays her open to another's domination.

In the event, however, two things happen. First of all she *does* speak. And she speaks by taking up her sisters' challenge. They have said words are insufficient to express their love. Very well, rather than barter ponderous words with Lear she will say nothing. But she will *tell* him that that is what she is doing: so she actually says, "Nothing." For Lear has not in fact asked her how much she loves him. He has asked her how much she can *say* she does in order "to draw/ A third more opulent." Thus Cordelia is saying that she cannot give love for land, but that if it is simply that he wants profession of fealty then he has it in her love "according to [her] bond" (i.e., precisely what is owed to fealty). If he wants an expression of real love, then he has that too, for in saying, "Nothing," she simply agrees with what both of her sisters have said—her love is too considerable for words. But at the same time she refuses the barter he demands.

Perhaps not surprisingly Lear does not understand her. Kent does. And he expresses the choice of the play, the choice Lear is here making, in a short and pithy sentence: "Kill thy physician, and thy fee bestow/ Upon the foul disease" (1.1.163–64). Kent is actually talking about himself, but Cordelia had already offered Lear the means to cure himself, had he only read her response correctly. Actually Kent's two lines can be ascribed equally well to either Kent or Cordelia (and their fate is the same). Lear is condemning them to silence and to the death of silence. Their discourse is to be replaced by one whose only value lies in the use to which it is put for gain and the acquisition of power (the opposition of "kill" and "thy fee bestow" is thus entirely apposite).

The second thing that happens is that in the face of Lear's incomprehension Cordelia is saved by France who, by removing her entirely from the scene of conflict, permits her silence to be a refuge and not a death, even though that situation will be only temporary. France at the same time cuts through the confusion of tongues with a subtle comment on the way Goneril, Regan, and their father are using discourse, with a well-chosen oxymoron: "this uprized precious maid" (1.1.259). Indeed, France's entire speech is just such a commentary on the misdirection of discourse that Lear has imposed and the two eldest sisters adopted with alacrity: "most rich being poor," "most choice forsaken," "most loved despised," "I take up what's cast away," "cold'st neglect/inflamed respect," "dow'rless daughter/Queen."

The real personification of that impossibility of which we have been speaking, the occupier of the tragic space, remains Lear himself, who remains uncomprehending to the end: "He knows not what he says," laments Albany shortly before the king's death (5.3. 294). Lear is torn and distracted from the beginning. On the one hand he is at the top of the feudal order and is very certain of the power of his language in that context. When he divides the map and grants the land to his daughters the division is a literal one: he is speaking the new name of these lands—they are Goneril's and Albany's, Regan's and Cornwall's. The one becomes the attribute, the definition of the other. Lear has in fact *created*, performed the division in just the sense of which J. L. Austin speaks when he argues that the promise (for example) *does* what it says. Here the performative function of language is not generalized, but is the attribute of a particular class of discourse. Later on the Fool will be very clear on this matter. Word and thing are one—they are, as Kent says of marriage, family and feudal bonds, "too intrinse t' unloose." When Lear first goes to make the division he is assuming that kind of intrinsic relation between deed and discourse. Yet on the other hand he sets up the conditions of a barter: he says the division is made, but suggests that the weightier their words the larger the bounty that will be theirs. Lear fails to distinguish (as do all of his daughters, though they choose differently) between exchange value and intrinsic value. He takes them as coincident— "what can you say to draw/A third more opulent than your sisters? Speak" (1.1.85-86)—and contradicts himself again: the question suggests the division has not in fact been decided.

When Cordelia responds with her "Nothing," Lear's choice is clear: "Nothing will come of nothing. Speak again" (1.1.90). Lear is confusing two issues. He divides the kingdom, and the gift of the parts, merely by his statement, would be theirs, because the speech of donation and the act are one and the same thing. In the same way the expression of love or fealty could function. But he cannot (as he does) make the one dependent on the other, at least not if he wants to maintain the same discourse, because then the donation would not be simply donation, nor the expression of love love: Lear is commercializing feudality. As soon as he seeks a quid pro quo ("How, how, Cordelia? Mend your speech a little,/Lest you may mar your fortunes" [2.1.94–95]), as soon as he seeks the speech of love in return for the land and land in return for future honor and dignity, he is entering a domain of confusion. In his view his granting the land is part and parcel with his honor and dignity: the fact that he is in a position to do the one automatically makes the other a part of it—for him the situation is static, nothing changes. But exchange does not work that way: for Goneril and Regan Lear is merely starting an ongoing series of possible transactions, and in their view he is here trying to get two for one. Lear asked for a profession of love in return for a gift of a third of the kingdom: they give it to him. That is the first transaction.

Later Lear reminds them that a certain honor and dignity is owing him because of the transaction:

> Thou better know'st
> The offices of nature, bond of childhood,
> Effects of courtesy, *dues* of gratitude.
> *Thy half of the kingdom hast thou not forgot*
> *Wherein I thee endowed.*   [2.4.172–76]

But that has nothing to do with the case, Regan replies. "Good sir," she cuts in, "to th' purpose." For Regan and Goneril this honor and dignity can only be a second transaction. In their view he is now wanting something for nothing. The Fool asks Lear whether he can make any use of nothing: "Why, no boy. Nothing can be made of nothing." At that the Fool, turning to Kent, pushes home to Lear the lesson he himself tried to teach Cordelia: "Prithee tell him, so much the rent of his land comes to; he will not believe a fool" (1.4.126–28). The only thing he has left to bargain with is his train. If he is to receive the treatment he craves the transaction will have to involve that last possession: he can go with Goneril, "dismissing half his train" (2.4.196–

201), or with Regan, giving up a further twenty-five (2.4.241–44), and he himself still talks in the same terms: "I'll go with thee. / Thy fifty yet doth double five-and-twenty, / And thou art twice her love" (2.4.253–55). Of course, in Lear's eyes his train is a visible mark of his dignity, and to give that up is not to exchange something for something else, it is to barter away his honor entirely.

For Lear continues to think in the terms of the other discourse as well, and to believe that both can coexist. Despite his claims to barter, he also continues to believe that name and thing are one, as he had stated in the "donation" scene: "Only we shall retain / The *name* and all th' addition to a king" (1.1.135–36). He wants to have the use of both processes and the result works to his confusion, as Kent had warned him ("Reserve thy state" [1.1.149]) and as Goneril scorns: "Idle old man, / That still would manage those authorities / That he hath given away" (1.3.16–18). This confusion and lack of comprehension is indicated in several different ways long before he actually gives way to madness.

In the first scene of the tragedy, Kent is banished on the grounds that "he has sought to make us break our vows" (1.1.168). This, however, does not prevent Lear himself from doing otherwise with regard to Burgundy: "I crave no more than hath your Highness offered, / Nor will you tender less," says the latter (1.1.94–95). Oh yes I will, says Lear, nothing at all. And Burgundy feels the importance of this oath-breaking sufficiently strongly to make the complaint again a little later (1.1.241–44). Lear is able to make this difference of Kent's vow and his own because Kent's loyalty belongs in the discourse of "feudality" (understanding by that the set of intrinsic relationships of which we spoke with regard to Cordelia), while his own vow concerned Cordelia, and in Lear's view she is no longer the same as she was, she now occupies a different space: "When she was dear to us, we did hold her so; / But now her price is fallen" (1.1.196–97).

The casting off of Cordelia is thus the mark of an inversion, and it is so perceived by Kent ("Sith thus thou wilt appear, / Freedom lies hence, and banishment is here"), by France ("This is most strange....") and, of course, by Goneril, who has been able to make the most of it: "You see how full of changes his age is." Throughout the period when they are wandering together the Fool will spend much of his time pointing out this inversion to his master: "thou bor'st thine ass on thy back o'er the dirt" (1.4.154); "The man that makes his toe / What he his heart should make / Shall of a corn cry woe, / And turn his sleep to wake" (3.2.31–34).

Lear's confusion is indicated by his inability to see his own place in matters essential to him. He has banished and cursed Cordelia and has cast off the name of father in doing so ("Here I disdain all my paternal care" [1.1.113]). He has thus already cut himself off from nature at a time when he appeals to her in his curse on Goneril ("Hear, Nature, hear; dear Goddess, hear: / Suspend thy purpose...." [1.4.266–30]). Not much later he will cry out against the treatment he is receiving: "The images of revolt and flying off!" (2.4.86), not realizing that he has given away his authority to his daughters and is therefore contradicting himself once again. One can only revolt against the authority in power, and that authority now belongs to Goneril and Regan. In that sense Regan is exactly correct in placing Kent in the stocks, for Kent is at that moment the one who is in revolt. Gloucester seems to sense that this is the case, whatever his own feelings in the matter: "Well, my good Lord, I have informed them so." "Informed them?" queries Lear in astonishment: "Dost thou understand me, man?" (2.4.93–94). Gloucester does indeed, better than Lear himself, knowing that Lear is no longer in a position to give orders, having bartered away the authority. And at this moment Lear seems to realize it too, for it is now that he begins to barter over the number of his retinue.

Those who functioned within the old intrinsic order no longer can. Kent has been forced for his very survival into using language as a mask: "If but as well I other accents borrow / That can my speech defuse" (1.4.1–2), though his ideal would be to come as close to silence as possible ("I do profess ... to converse with him that is wise and says little" [1.4.12–14]). For in this world of changing discourse silence is becoming the only course still open. Cordelia is, of course, absent in her silence; Edgar will perforce play the role of a madman that Lear will play in reality.

Even Albany will later accuse the world of being upside down when he tells Oswald that he and his are responsible for it; though the steward, needless to say, does not realize it at the time when he relates Albany's outburst, for the servant does blindly what his mistress does willfully:

> Of Gloucester's treachery,
> And of the loyal service of his son
> When I informed him, then he called me sot,
> And told me I had turned the wrong side out:
> What most he should dislike seems pleasant to him;
> What like, offensive. [4.2.6–11]

With Albany, the worm has turned, and he is now able to accuse Goneril of having striven to destroy the old order: "Wisdom and goodness to the vile seem vile:/Filths savor but themselves" (4.2.38–39). Humanity, he cries, will become inhuman if the inversion of things is allowed to continue: "Humanity must perforce prey on itself,/Like monsters of the deep" (4.2.49–50). Now Albany is ready to receive the letter that we are shortly to see Edgar obtain from the dead Oswald.

A time has been passed through of decay and degeneracy—social, political, and moral—and all discursive relations have been thrown into confusion. As the fool had said to Lear, things had to get worse before they could return to normality, before "going shall be used with feet again" (3.2.94). The Fool himself will eventually fall quite silent, not speaking again after 3.6, though there is no indication that he disappears altogether—one of those celebrated Shakespearean mysteries, like that of the third murderer in *Macbeth*. One would like to imagine that Lear is playing with him at the point where he is found by Cordelia's gentleman, and still as Lear shouts: "Then kill, kill, kill. . . ." (4.6.184), leaving the audience to decide whether Lear has actually killed him or whether the Fool is simply shamming. No matter, the significant thing is the Fool's silence. And Lear himself, who started the confusion, must sink most deeply into it. As he does so he comes back in some ways to certain elements of the order he has forsaken: "Blow, winds, and crack your cheeks. . . ." (3.2.1), he shrieks at the storm, for he would have it at one with "the tempest in [his] mind" (3.4.12). But the king is joining now with nature in a madness that denies all order and that heralds a new change in discourse, an absorption in singularity and a murmur of unutterable sadness as Lear turns to "mad Tom": "Let me ask you one word in private" (3.4.151). Lear reaches away from the horror of a public discourse that has betrayed him, momentarily toward an older wholeness he forsook by choice ("O Lear, Lear, Lear!/Beat at this gate that let thy folly in. . . ." [1.4.261–62]), and finally toward the voice of Cordelia which "was ever soft,/Gentle, and low" (5.3.273–74).

All of the chief speakers pass along a parallel track—Cordelia, who sees herself and her discourse from beginning to end as part of a totality from which in every other case there has been a falling off; Kent, who as we have seen adopts the mask of language and becomes a country bumpkin, setting himself deliberately against the order represented by Lear's eldest daughters and, at that point, Lear himself;[11] Edgar, closest to Cordelia in role and perhaps spirit (which is why Nahum Tate was to create the love story between them), who must come to terms with nature in a hollow tree and the straw of a hovel; Gloucester, who, however apparently foolishly, sees all occurrences in the universe as related. On the other side, Lear seeks to separate Goneril from nature through his curse as he already had himself through his curse against Cordelia.

The exemplary figure in this connection, though, is Edmund. Edmund sets himself against the laws and customs of society and isolates himself within the universe ("This is the excellent foppery of the world" [1.2.115]). Legitimacy is dependent only upon "the plague of custom" and can be overturned by a letter, just as Goneril and Regan overturned it with spoken discourse. Where for Lear the private voice is a mark of failure and disappointment, for Edmund it is the sign of the aggressive power of the isolated individual: "Let me, if not by birth, have lands by wit" (1.2.176). That "wit" is the use of discourse as a mask, as a mere instrument of gain, whose success depends upon the other's inability to envision discourse as able to be used—as Gloucester cannot, and as Lear fails to do. That is the "wit" that Kent rejoices in not having ("Having more man than wit about me" [3.4.41]), that Edgar loses ("Poor Tom hath been scared out of his good wits" [4.1.57]), and Lear also: "his wits are gone" (3.6. 85). In all three of these last cases the occasion is when each comes closest to becoming Lear's unaccommodated man—Kent in the stocks and mocked; Edgar meeting Gloucester on the heath and realizing "The worst is not yet / So long as one can say 'This is the worst'" (4.1.27–28); Lear, unbuttoned, ragged, holding court in a hovel with poor Tom, the Fool, and honest Caius.

None of the others, save only Edmund, can sustain the isolated use of "wit." Nor can the evil sisters or Cornwall. The duke slain ignominiously by a servant is soon joined by his coconspirators, slain virtually by one another, as a result of their insatiable lust for possession: and let us remember that it is a letter that brings Edmund down, as a letter had been his own ploy against Edgar. I do not see how one can speak of the wave of the future with regard to anyone in *King Lear*. *Lear* is a tragedy wherein everyone fails.

Both Lear and Cordelia themselves fall silent, not even a memory left of those "low sounds" of which Kent speaks with regard to Cordelia at the beginning (2.2.153) and Lear at the end. Certainly they pass together through a moment of speech: "I am a very foolish fond old man" (4.7.59–84), a still, small, and very private center in the storm, a moment of time past recaptured and of a time already but a memory, whose price is death:

> So we'll live,
> And pray, and sing, and tell old tales, and laugh
> At gilded butterflies, and hear poor rogues
> Talk of court news; and we'll talk with them too—
> Who loses and who wins; who's in who's out—
> And take upon's the mystery of things
> As if we were God's spies; and we'll wear out
> In a walled prison, packs and sects of great ones
> That ebb and flow by th' moon.   [5.1.11–19]

Yet the price of opposition is just the same. The four users of "wit" all die. Kent and Cordelia, who strove to remain in a space they thought entire, die. Gloucester and Lear, the pair most caught in the middle, fare just the same. Only will remain Albany, whose activities had been blurred, to put it mildly (for how long had he acquiesced in Goneril's activities, if only through weakness and absence of objection?), and Edgar, who views the future as short and dismal: "we that are young / Shall never see so much, nor live so long" (5.3.325–26).

In this conflict of discourse incomprehension and confusion reign almost to the very end, and at that end the "victory" for those who remain is hollow in the extreme. Even the spectator here, having seen the struggle waged and its terms, can hardly come out satisfied. From that point of view *King Lear* is perhaps unique among modern tragedies (it would have rediscovered the Sophoclean "mode"). Maybe that is why *King Lear* is one of the most tampered with of all Shakespeare's plays, why Charles Lamb was able to write that the tragedy was impossible to stage, and why Dr. Johnson, not especially noted for open displays of emotion, was moved to write that he had been unable to read the last scene of the play for many years after his first reading of it. Bertolt Brecht has written: "Lear's destruction is complete; there is a startling last demonstration of death as a special horror; Lear really and truly dies." [12]

No other person in Shakespeare, and few if any in any other writer, is quite so utterly *destroyed* as Lear, destroyed in his very being. Brecht remarks that it "was a king that lived, a man who dies" (p. 80), and that is no doubt exact in one sense. But in Lear's own view part of what made him a man *was* kingship. That is something he did not realize until too late: for by then he had already relinquished it. Edgar cannot become another Lear: Lear himself has made sure of that by destroying the certainty of a particular class of discourse. But nor can he be an Edmund: for he has destroyed himself, together with the discourse he might have represented. With what then is the spectator left? Indeed, with very little—far less than in the case of *Hamlet*, for example. We hear of the paradoxical "pleasure of tragedy"—not in the case of *Lear*. Perhaps that is because this tragedy lacks the certain knowledge provided by others at their conclusion. There is no "wave of the future" in *Lear*; at best something like the low rumbling of a past already gone by.

Here, in *Lear*, the "future" is not something new, something developing: it is a hesitant repetition of the past, and of a past already blasted. What does *not* work is clear enough. Of all Shakespeare's play's only one other, it seems to me, comes quite so close to the enigma thus presented to its spectator by *Lear*. That other is *The Tempest*, with Prospero's final cynical remark "'Tis new to thee" as Miranda rejoices in her "brave new world," and with the continued presence of the sinister Antonio, who had provoked the original calamity and remains unrepentant. The enigma in both cases places a challenge before the spectator, a question to be resolved. Yet in both cases, too, the play gives the limits within which the question may be posed and within which the "solution" may be decided. It must be somewhere between Cordelia and Edmund, but it cannot lie in the playing of Lear himself, for that leads only to utter confusion: one cannot play both sides against the middle, play with the elements of an already established discourse that has its own finality (assuming "discourse" can have one).

What these plays show us perhaps is that a new discursive order, when the need makes itself felt, cannot proceed from a space of conflict. Our episteme in fact developed out of elements that are internal and proper to it. It developed from certain aims, certain needs, certain logical a prioris that together constructed a social/discursive space not simply out of a conflict with an "older" class of discourse but by a displacement, by creating its own necessities, conscious no doubt of the other (as the mark of certain limits, for example), but conscious also that the future demanded something else. This instauration was accomplished on the basis of a new set of discursive elements. Bacon, for example, repeats that view many times. It is above all what Vico admired in him—the acceptance of the risk of establishing his analyses from a new discursive space, not just of reviewing established ones but of remaking them entirely. It is on the foundation of this development that the bourgeois future was made (centuries-long and quite admirable no doubt, even if we can no longer remain in the same space, even if we must now once again undertake Bacon's work).

What *King Lear* would have shown us is that *this* instauration is impossible if its need and its goals are established simply through confrontation. Once the older order collapses, so does the conflicting one—whose existence had sense and was possible only so long as the older order existed "whole." An order founded on opposition must by definition disappear once its adversary is defeated. To start from confrontation, then, is simply to fall once again into the tragic space, where meaning and the possibility of communication fade altogether into an incapacity for any action and into an agonizing incomprehension:

And my poor fool is hanged: no, no, no life?
Why should a dog, a horse, a rat, have life,
And thou no breath at all? Thou'lt come no more,
Never, never, never, never, never.
Pray you undo this button. Thank you, sir.
Do you see this? Look on her! Look her lips,
Look there, look there—   [5.3.306-12]

The discourse of tragedy, as a whole, is gradually performing the production of a solution to such incomprehension from within its own elaboration, and not merely, as we have seen, by emphasizing one or other of two conflicting discursive "systems." It is producing (dialectically?) a "third" within the very space of confrontation.[13]

8　A New Time and the Glory That Was Egypt

The supreme effort that distinguishes the theatre at the beginning of the seventeenth century, and that was to some degree common to France, England, and Spain, appears to lead gradually into a dead end. England enjoyed the benefit of a generation of genius, of which Shakespeare was but the chief glory, and which produced, as C. Walter Hodges puts it, a "fountain of playwriting" unrivaled "since the days of Periclean Athens."[1] Spain was not much behind England, where Lope de Vega, Tirso, Calderón a little later, produced plays that were performed in a theatrical environment not very different from that of London. Lope in Spain, Shakespeare and his contemporaries in England, Alexandre Hardy in the provinces of France (though he enjoyed the use there of no permanent theatres and was never successful in Paris), put on a kind of "total" theatre that sought to include the spectator in some way in a whole theatrical event. That seems to have suited comedy, pastoral, and tragi-comedy particularly well. It was not so favorable to straight tragedy, though all three countries saw the appearance of that melodramatic style known to critics and historians of the English theatre of the period as "revenge tragedy."

By the 1620s scarcely any tragedies were being written in France, while in England revenge tragedy collapsed into a kind of decadence which, with few exceptions, sought only to provoke a sort of horrified thrill in the spectator. "Decadence," concluded Fredson Bowers, "is too gentle a word for the insane maze of character, plot, and motive in the minor dramatists; tragedy was actually disintegrating. The closing of the theatres was really a blessing in disguise."[2] Bowers has in mind such writers as Sir John Suckling, William Heminge, and Samuel

Harding. But other writers perhaps boded a different future. Lily Campbell, for example, has pointed out from another point of view (from that of the texts themselves) that the break in the dramatic tradition was not altogether absolute. On March 26, 1639, she notes, a royal patent was granted to William Davenant to build a theatre that looks similar in intent to the theatre at the Palais Royal soon to be opened in Paris. She observes too that the continental influence had already long been felt in the English theatre, and increasingly so after the accession of Charles I with his French queen, Henrietta Maria. When Davenant took up his patent again after the Restoration of a monarchy that had spent its years of exile in France it was almost as though the years of the Commonwealth had been but an intermission to provide a moment of repose and recuperation.[3]

For the theatre was already developing in a particular direction, which was merely confirmed by the rupture of the Commonwealth and the departure for France. One might say that an inevitable historical process had already begun to reveal its trend. It seems to me that the experience of a "dialectical" theatre necessarily implied difficulties for the writing of tragedy: it is almost a matter of two opposing concepts of theatre. What distinguishes the dialectical mode of theatre is the continual exchange between stage and auditorium, the fact that as much commotion is going on in the one as in the other. The separation that will be created by curtain and footlights, by the opposition of lighted stage and darkened auditorium, of moving, talking actors and silently seated spectators, the concept of the fourth wall, all this is a neoclassical development. The mixing of the various sign systems used in the theatre (the words not necessarily supporting the action, for example); the avoidance of any attempt to fix a specific and single place before the eye of the spectator (in France the multiple scene was still used as late as the 1640s; on the English stage until the closing of the theatres scene appears to have been only meagerly indicated); the lack of perspective painting (though beginning to come into theatrical use); the constant engaging of the spectator by aside and soliloquy—all of these things indicate a quite particular relationship of stage and spectator.

Tragedy, on the other hand, seems to be developing toward a "demand" that the spectator take his distance and make a judgment upon the systematic ordering of discourse and eventually upon the human affairs whose point of departure and return, whose place of development, discourse is. This may be why Shakespearean tragedy, even in a case as ambiguous as *King Lear*, always concludes with the imposition of a comprehensible and rational order: then judgment is possible. When the spectator is participating in the "unknowing" of the speakers, clearly such judgment is not possible. I am aware that this remark carries with it the implication that for Shakespeare and his contemporaries the stage action was but one part of an overall experience. It was, quite obviously, the principal part, without which the rest could not be (though the architectural space of the theatre building was not less important), but the "unknowing" of the spectator invades not so much the situation of the play as it does his own situation in the world, of which the theatre is proposed as the microcosm: not the stage alone —the *whole theatre*.

At the turn of the century Shakespearean tragedy is capping the space of disorder and distraction with order that is both imposed from without and prepared for from within (as I have sought to suggest in the two previous chapters). But Shakespeare chooses to shift to the so-called romances or problem plays, as though tragedy were best avoided as tending toward the production of a new (and unwelcome) class of discourse. The romances would be essentially conservative in such an interpretation, a kind of experimental attempt to maintain on the stage a kind of total theatrical experience that was becoming ever less possible. After this enormous experiment it will be a time for the neoclassical theatre and a new order entirely. The order of the conclusion of Shakespeare's tragedies will be installed from the beginning of the neoclassical. The disorder and confusion that are endemic in Hamlet's world or Macbeth's are an intrusion from the exterior in later tragedies.

In *All For Love* the love between Antony and Cleopatra that is the very composition of Shakespeare's tragedy has been relegated to a nostalgic past. In Shakespeare, Antony is first seen casting off all mere political and worldly occupations, wholeheartedly given over to the transcendence of that love ("Let Rome in Tiber melt, and the wide arch/Of the ranged empire fall! Here is my space. . . " [1.1.33–34]). In Dryden, we first see Antony alone and contemplating a "double pomp of sadness" (1.204).[4] Antony, as we will see, is already part of a new order over which he himself has no control (and Caesar not too much). Thus, when the Roman seeks to persuade his faithful Ventidius as Hamlet did Horatio: "Wilt thou not live to speak some good of me?/To stand by my fair fame, and guard th'approaches/From the ill tongues of men?" the soldier can respond only that it is not necessary: "our deaths will speak themselves" (5.300–04). They are now, already and always, part of a well-ordered process that needs no other narrative ordering to be understood. In *All For Love* that love which dares all is already an intrusion of the past into a new social and political order.

Of course, things are not quite so simple, and the complex development we are trying to follow is no exception. Shakespeare's *Antony and Cleopatra* is already flanked by two more Aristotelian versions. In 1594 Samuel Daniel published his sequel to the duchess of Pembroke's *Antonie* (1592), her translation of Garnier's *Marc-Antoine*. So restricted is the space of Daniel's *Tragedie of Cleopatra* that he actually has some difficulty in finding sufficient matter to fill it out. He is constrained to begin his play with the announcement of Antony's death, which he does first by having Cleopatra remember it, and then by means of its announcement to Octavian. Since all that preceded his death has already been told in *Antonie*, the love theme is reduced to a minimum and much is made of one Rodon's betrayal of Cleopatra's son, Caesario. The construction of this play is Senecan, the language owes much to Garnier, the rules believed to be Aristotelian are assiduously courted.

In 1626 Thomas May's *Cleopatra* was in all probability performed, according to Bentley, on the public stage. The play follows the lead given by Ben Jonson in his *Cataline* and *Sejanus*, and the historical accuracy and truth of the play are continually affirmed.[5] In turn, Dryden's drama is preceded (by ten months, in 1677) by Sir Charles Sedley's play of plottings and a multiplicity of loves: not only that of the two principles, but that of Photinus, who plots the betrayal of Antony and Cleopatra "for Iras and a Throne" (2.1.80), and that of Maecenas, who wants the war to comtinue until Antony's death because he is in love with Octavia.[6] With Sedley's play we are not very far from Bower's "insane maze."

In his introduction to the New Mermaid edition of *All For Love*, N. J. Andrew affirms that Dryden intended his play partly as a reply to

Sedley's and to the latter's adaption of "French dramatic practice" (p. xix), though it is hard to see what is particularly French about Sedley's tragedy, and Andrew himself chooses rather to view Dryden's play as a refutation of the attack on Charles II that Sedley's play is taken to be (pp. xix ff). All this strikes one as similar to the various never entirely satisfactory attempts to provide exact satiric keys for such plays as Otway's *Venice Preserved*. It is to a degree justified because such plays *do* now purport to be showing a specific representation of external reality, though I do not think that what is specific to neoclassical tragedy is this kind of superficial representation. For there is much in Sedley's play to remind us of revenge tragedy, just as there is much in the whole corpus of early Restoration heroic tragedy to justify Lily Campbell's claim that the Commonwealth did not cause any entire break in the English tradition.

Eugene Waith has argued that the heroic drama of the Restoration is a continuation of a memory of the chivalric ideals that had emerged onto the stage in the late sixteenth and early seventeenth centuries, most notably in Shakespeare's historical plays, and that had then been maintained for the duration of the Commonwealth interlude by Corneille before coming back onto the English stage in the Restoration.[7] Sedley's play, and the other heroic drama, would therefore be the mark of the continuity in the English stage of which Lily Campbell speaks. Eric Rothstein has noted in this connection the disputes that surrounded the heroic plays from the very start of their appearance upon the Restoration stage, and their most celebrated burlesque, the duke of Buckingham's *Rehearsal*, appeared as early as 1671, almost before the heroic drama was a genre at all. Rothstein notes that aesthetic reasons gradually led to the heroic play being considered "a freak, a burlesque of nature."[8] The reasons given for the genre's rejection could all apply equally well to the tragedy of revenge, and it is surely not mere chance that during the period that saw the triumph and fall of heroic tragedy over half of the tragedies performed by the King's and the Duke's Men were tragedies from the period just before the closing of the theatres. Tragedies as a whole composed 23 or 24 percent of the repertoire, and the plays of Fletcher alone made up from 14 to 17 percent of the entire repertoire.[9]

In some ways this suggests that the heroic drama shows us the English theatre's last effort to get out of its system, something it would have voided earlier had it not been for the Puritan pause. Still, even if there is a kind of general muddle in late revenge tragedy, which is perhaps the result of an increasing inability to use to their full effect the characteristics peculiar to the Elizabethan and Jacobean public theatre (as I suggested that Shakespeare was able to, for example), there is also a new element. It is an element that will demand, and get, a quite different stage and auditorium space (already available in the private theatres). It is the element directly conducive to the kind of "representationality" that is specific to neoclassical tragedy (as opposed to the superficial reflections earlier referred to).

Thus, in the introduction of his recent edition of 'Tis Pity She's a Whore, Derek Roper remarks: "It says much for Ford's powers of detachment that he could in his day present incest, not as an incomprehensible abomination, but as a tragic error."[10] When Sperone's Canace, a play dealing with incest and whose circumstances are similar to those portrayed in Ford's play, had appeared in 1546, it had provoked an argument whose chief element was that incest was so incomprehensible an evil as to make its practitioners unpitiable monsters, and therefore no fit protagonists for tragedy.[11] Ford's presentation of incest says less for his powers of detachment than it does about the development of the system, tragedy, and its public. For it, and they, can now cope with an "incomprehensible" sin as a human error practiced by subjects who are in every other way admirable, whose emotions and actions, far from being beyond understanding, are in themselves perfectly familiar, and whose fate is therefore thoroughly pitiable.

If such is the case, why weren't these kinds of subjects dealt with more frequently? Part of the answer is that they were, though not centrally. Incest, rape, fiendishly ingenious murder, and terrifying, revolting revelations of such events frequently—indeed inevitably—form some element of all late revenge tragedy and certain of its French and Spanish counterparts. But they decayed for the most part into the spectacular elements of melodrama, with emphasis not on systematic revelation but on sensational incident. That is what Fredson Bowers has in mind when he conceives of the Commonwealth as sweeping clean the deck and enabling tragedy to pick up (after a heroic interlude) as though the decay of revenge had been but a gloomy and brackish backwater.

It was able to achieve this with some rapidity because the French had taken things up again where Garnier (and perhaps Montchrestien) had left off, and with the benefit both of the experience gained by an Alexandre Hardy and his less prolific contemporaries in public performance and of the advent (in Paris) of an increasingly sophisticated audience. It seems probable, for instance, that there was a sharp decline in the *ballets de cour*, with which the members of the Court had been chiefly entertained so far as theatre was concerned (and in which the more privileged participated, as they did in the English masque). The duc de Luynes, who had for many years been chiefly responsible for organizing them, died in 1621. The consequence of this (although there is a lack of direct evidence) may have been an increase in aristocratic attendance at the public theatres of the Hôtel de Bourgogne and the Marais. A growing class of literate bourgeoisie was also beginning to seek entertainment. Be that as it may, by the 1630s France was beginning to rejoice in its own generation of genius: Pierre Corneille, Jean Rotrou, Jean Mairet, François Tristan l'Hermite, Pierre Du Ryer, Georges de Scudery. Other names could easily be mentioned, but these are the principal writers of tragedy among that generation which started writing around 1630. I will not examine any plays from this period of the development here.[12]

In *Antony and Cleopatra*, what is most startlingly maintained is the sentiment that the love of the two protagonists is in some way out of time, unable to be diminished at all by the onslaught of Roman history. Though he may doubt its effect upon his valor and reputation, Antony never really hesitates about the supreme value of his love for Cleopatra, nor does she ever lose the near lightheartedness with which her love makes her face even Antony's and her death and defeat, turning even final defeat into victory: "I am again for Cydnus" (5.2.228). Before this love even the army of gloomy Caesar, with all it represents, must confess its submission and Caesar their victory:

> High events as these
> Strike those that make them; . . .
>   Our army shall
> In solemn show attend this funeral.   [5.2.358–62]

The ever-celebrated speech made by the rough and often vulgar-mouthed soldier Enobarbus could well be the emblem of Shakespeare's

play: "Age cannot wither her" (2.2.236). Antony and Cleopatra are
an everlasting piece of the universal process: "No grave upon the earth
shall clip in it / A pair so famous" (5.2.357-58).

In *All For Love*, the two protagonists have become readers of their
own story. The moment is one of nostalgia. After a transcendence that
seems to escape even the grasping bonds of Caesar's brave new Roman
world, history has come to claim its *reasonable* rights: "But I have
loved with such transcendent passion, / I soared at first quite out of
reason's view, / And now am lost above it" (2.220-22). It is almost as
though Cleopatra were making a commentary on her Shakespearean
predecessor. But there reason was not so much *opposed* to love as simply irrelevant to it. In the new and colder society of *All For Love*
reason is an opponent to love and Antony and Cleopatra will fall *because* they have none: "But I have lost my reason," laments Antony
to Roman Ventidus (1.293). "Call reason to assist you," cries
Iras to Cleopatra: "I have none, / And none would have. My love's a
noble madness, / Which shows the cause deserved it" (2.16-18). And at
the end the plotter Alexas will continue to bewail:

> Poor reason! what a wretched aid art thou!
> For still, in spite of thee,
> These two lovers, soul and body, dread
> Their final separation. . . .   [5.134-37]

Yet if it has taken the flight of reason to enable them to love as they
are supposed to have done, it has taken the loss of love to bring them
to the present time: "I know him well," asserts Cleopatra, "Ah, no, I
know him not: I knew him once, / But now 'tis past" (2.26-28). As
Antony remarks: "we have loved each other, / Into mutual ruin," (2.
244-45). Or again:

> How I loved,
> Witness ye days and nights, and all your hours
> That danced away with down upon your feet,
> As your business were to count my passion.
> One day passed by, and nothing saw but love;
> Another came, and still 'twas only love:
> The suns were wearied out with looking on,
> And I untired of loving.

I saw you every day, and all the day,
And every day was still but as the first,
So eager was I still to see you more.   [2.281–91]

"'Tis past," says Antony to Alexas as he goes off with Octavia (3. 373). "Why then," asks Myris at the very beginning of the play, "does Antony dream out his hours?" (1.47).

Reason was set aside to make room for love, love itself is now gone— or at least the transcendent love whose protagonists bestride the world in glory. And there is left nothing, a mere emptiness: "She has left him," accuses Ventidius, "the blank of what he was" (1.172–73), "I have been a man, Ventidius," cries Antony (1.291), to which Cleopatra will later supply the complement: "Now he is lost for whom alone I lived" (3.470). Cleopatra, too, views herself as living only in a kind of nostalgic present: "I am, that he has loved me" (3.448). "Egypt is lost," murmurs Alexas to the queen, meaning both herself and the country (3.397). And it is taken up by Serapion at the end when he tells Cleopatra of the joining of the Egyptian fleet with the Roman:

Egypt has been: our latest hour is come;
The queen of nations from her ancient seat
Is sunk forever in the dark abyss;
Time has unrolled her glories to the last,
And now closed up the volume.   [5.71–75]

The reading of a story, the passing of time, the destruction of a nation, all of these are linked with the nostalgia for a love that is now quite gone. Antony was once, in that transcendent love, "next to Nature's God" (1.182), he was "raised the meteor of the world," but now, like Phaeton, "all [his] fires [are] spent" and he has been "cast downward,/To be trod out by Caesar" (1.206–09).

This void is to be filled by Roman Ventidius and something quite different. Antony may try to recapture the rapture of Shakespeare's speaker: "sink the props of Heaven,/And fall the skies to crush the nether world!/My eyes, my soul, my all!" but Ventidius will scornfully crush such nostalgic effusions: "And what's this toy/In balance with your fortune, honour, fame?" (2.424–27). The love of Antony and Cleopatra has its space appropriately reduced to somewhere far more close and personal. In Shakespeare the common soldier can wax lyrical about Cleopatra and their love, the whole of Egypt rejoices in it even to the end. In Dryden such speeches are given only to Antony himself, and celebrations are distinctly out of place (1.135–97). There even their quarrels were joyous and in some way expanding, here we deal only with "inward groans," downcast eyes, falling tears, blushings, "sighs and tears," breaking hearts (2.47–68); we are left with "a faint image of possession still," as Cleopatra puts it (2.31).

The times may be out of joint, but Time is now all-controlling. Passion has been swept away by an inexorable history in which there is no place for Shakespeare's old lovers. Their legendary love now lies all in an irretrievable past: "I have loved," "Egypt has been," "'Tis past," "I was . . . ," "we were. . . ." There once was a past which was no "past" at all in an historical sense, simply because the love that ruled it did transcend any notion of history. Shakespeare had produced the "no-time" of this transcendence, in which the Roman pretension to dominion and its claims to power were an impertinence. Dryden has selected the moment after the fall, when this mysterious unity has been reduced to a rather pathetic political bickering and to vague attempts to regain what *has been*. In *Antony and Cleopatra* love remains ever more magnificent than Roman power. In *All For Love* we are left only with reflections upon the loss of such power, as Alexas remarks: "but since our will/Is lamely followed by our power" (1.73–74). Loss of reason, failure of will, insufficiency of power: these are now Egypt's characteristics.

Thus Antony's hopes for a future victory, spurred on by his shame before Ventidius (a shame whose strength is inconceivable within the "previous" transcendence), are couched all in the terms of his nostalgia:

Oh, thou hast fired me; my soul's up in arms,
And mans each part about me: once again,
That noble eagerness of fight has seized me,
That eagerness with which I darted upward
To Cassius' camp; in vain the steepy hill
Opposed my way, in vain a war of spears
Sung round my head, and planted all my shield:
I won the trenches while my foremost men
Lagged on the plain below. [1.438–46]

To this Ventidius returns the revealing reply: "Ye gods, ye gods,/For such another hour." Time is so strongly felt, its passage, that it almost becomes a "character" in the tragedy, and it is surely not without significance that this should be the very image selected by Antony for himself and Ventidius: "that thou and I, / Like Time and Death, marching before our troops . . ." (1.449–50). But Antony cannot fight in Caesar's terms and, after a momentary victory and regaining of old love (denied by that very fleetingness), which we view at the beginning of act 3, the rest is all toward death and the tomb.

Time belongs to Caesar, and *All For Love* produces a kind of "passage into history." The great love that the cold system of Rome can neither express nor therefore understand lies all before the play. The new history of Rome lies after it. In between lies the crossroads that is the play. Alone of all the plays written on this subject *All For Love* does not once bring Caesar onstage, and it is Egypt (Serapion) and no longer Rome that mourns the passing of the "blest pair." We are left with the sight not of Rome going down on bended knees, but of a new Egypt about to accept Rome's dominion: "Caesar's just entering: grief here has now no leisure. / Secure that villain as our pledge of safety / To grace th' imperial triumph" (5.512–14). The immortal passion of Antony and Cleopatra not only has no place here, but is reduced merely to a sum of tricks and petty quarrels in the hands of Alexas, Charmion, Ventidius, Dolabella, and even Octavia. Cleopatra and Antony themselves do not escape this reduction. Love is no longer a glory, but a relation of master and slave that corresponds precisely to the Roman view of order.

In this way Cleopatra, having just spurned Antony's "respect" from the lips of Charmion, fairly jumps at the welcome notion expressed by Alexas that Antony, in his love for her, "still drags a chain along / That needs must clog his flight," remaining, as the eunuch has said, "a fearful slave [who] shuns his master's eyes" (2.89–92). Lest we be in doubt as to the implications of this, Antony uses the same notion when he accused Dolabella and Ventidius of betraying him by bringing Octavia to Egypt: "And now I must become her branded slave" (3.286). Cleopatra herself uses the image again when comparing herself with Octavia: "When he grew weary of that household clog, / He chose my easier bonds" (3.425–26). However "easier" it may be, the nature of love remains that of a slave chained to a master. It is again Cleopatra who has reminded us of the wider implications of that bond in her own scorning of the "victor's chain" (2.10) that would be the ultimate mark of Egypt's defeat at the hands of Rome.

The heroic and aristocratic superiority of the couple in Shakespeare is reduced to a network of calculations. The hint was already in Shakespeare, when Pompey remarked that "Caesar gets money where/He loses hearts" (2.1.13–14). In Dryden's tragedy Antony remarks of Caesar, "Fate mistook him,/For Nature meant him for an usurer;/He's fit indeed to buy, not conquer, kingdoms" (3.213–15). All Caesar's acts and emotions are reduced to cunning calculation: "Oh, 'tis the coldest youth upon a charge,/The most deliberate fighter!" (2.113–14). Or again: "Oh, he's the coolest murderer!" (3.65). All this, of course, comes from the lips of Antony. But given that he intends such remarks as insults and given the kind of calculation and the kind of network of relations they imply for him, it is of greater significance that he himself is placed both by others and by himself in such a network as he gradually capitulates to Rome. By others first: "Emperor!" —"Friend!"—"Husband!"—"Father!" (3.362–63). No longer the superior individual, Antony falls in with this—and puts his capitulation in the very financial terms he had just used to scorn Caesar:

> I am vanquished: take me,
> Octavia; take me, children: *share me all.*
> I've been a *thriftless* debtor to your loves,
> And run out much in riot from *your stock,*
> But all shall be amended.   [3.363–67]

Of course, we can say that Antony is casting scorn on his own capitulation, as he was when he referred to himself as having to become Octavia's branded slave—except that Cleopatra had viewed her own and Antony's love in the very same terms. Or perhaps Antony is seeking to overcome his own and newly felt solitude: "Stay, I fancy/I'm new turned wild, a commoner of Nature;/Of all forsaken, and forsaking all" (1.231–33). The ex-demi-god who is now Dryden's Antony has been divorced from his space and brought face to face with the mark of reason and an order to which he does not know how to react. In Caesar's new history Antony runs a real risk of being reduced to the blundering matamore of a far from tragic theatre. Antony's challenge to Caesar is now more than a little ridiculous. Antony knows very well that Caesar will refuse it—he has himself already noted the terms in which Caesar operates. There is even a certain hypocrisy in the challenge. The action he is clamoring for lies in a quite different sphere, as his cry of pain is sufficient to attest: "Oh Hercules! Why should a man like this,/Who dares not trust his fate for one great action,/Be all the care of Heaven?" (2.131–33).

That is the entire point. Antony in his solitude, his new-felt solitude, is forced to accept defeat at the hands of Caesar's Rome. However scornfully he may have referred to his (momentary) capitulation to Octavia and Rome in act 3, it will nevertheless be in terms taken from the same discursive domain that at the end he will resume his and Cleopatra's love:

> I was but great for her; my power, my empire
> Were but *my merchandise to buy* her love,
> And conquered kings *my factors*.   [5.270–72]

At the end he sees himself and Cleopatra in Caesar's terms. They "have had" their "clear and glorious day" (5.389), they have lived their "ages" (5.393), now is Caesar entering. Shakespeare's universal destiny has been reduced to the machinations of Alexas, the "villain" who, alone in trying to maintain the love of Cleopatra and Antony, had been most immediately responsible for the latter's death. But their love, as it had been, is already long gone. In Shakespeare it flooded over all social and political considerations; even to the end, when Caesar permits himself to do obeisance to it as something incomprehensibly beyond the sphere of his own acts and ambitions. In Dryden love itself is reduced to a set of familial, social, political, and finally economic relationships: ordered by the off-stage presence of Caesar, whose physical participation is not even necessary.

It is almost as though Dryden had been putting on stage the proof for the claim made in his Epistle Dedicatory to Danby of his own "loathing to that specious name of republic: that mock appearance of a liberty" (pp. 5-6). The republic would be a time of civil strife, or a time of an Antony's personal and tyrannical use of power. The coming to power of a Caesar is that of a well-ordered monarchy (as, says Dryden, is that of contemporary England): "a government which has all the advantages of liberty beyond a commonwealth, and all the marks of kingly sovereignty without the danger of a tyranny" (p. 5). Thus, of course, Caesar's "coldness" is a distinct advantage.

I do not wish to suggest that the play could be provided with a key (Andrew, for example, argues that for both Sedley and Dryden Antony is Charles II, and adds other possible identifications). I wish to suggest that the play, like others of the time, works out a particular concept of truth—in this case political—in the terms of the theoretical discourse appropriate to such truth. In the present case, we are dealing with something whose closest analogue would, I think, be Hobbes's *Behemoth*. Of course, it is no longer necessary to argue the seriousness of Restoration neoclassical tragedy in support of such suggestions:

> The plays deal, even single-mindedly, with the major epistemo-
> logical issue of the day: the relationship of mind and matter. They
> deal with the major political issues of the age: faction, the nature
> of monarchy, the place of the individual in government. They deal
> with moral values. . . .[13]

It is even becoming a critical commonplace to argue that so far as tragedy is concerned Hobbes is a major influence. The Hobbesian villain replays for Restoration tragedy, Geoffrey Marshall asserts, the role played by the Machiavellian in Renaissance tragedy. Eugene Waith argues that *The Conquest of Granada* deals with the "political chaos" of "a Hobbesian state of nature" and its opposition to an "ideal political harmony." James Black has affirmed that the character of Edmund is made the more villainous by Nahum Tate in his *King Lear* by modeling him on Hobbes's "natural man."[14]

All these, however, have been indications of isolated reflections in the tragedies, exactly comparable to the kind of thing that Gillian Jondorf was able to show for Robert Garnier. What I would like to show in the next three chapters, concerned with three of Racine's tragedies as exemplars, is that neoclassical tragedy is frequently (if not always) concerned with placing on the stage the practical demonstration of some theoretical truth concerning social, political, psychological, and moral reality.

In *All For Love* the supreme love of Antony and Cleopatra is now shown as a threat to the order of that truth and to the truth (as working reality) of the order being created by Caesar. It must therefore be at once banished (by death) and reduced to the same order (by Antony himself in this case); just as it had once been necessary to do in the case of the far more elusive absence of meaning in discourse. In this tragedy, "love" is the name (and hypostatization) given to that old threat. In other plays it will be something else—increasingly often an individual person.

9   Social Truth and the Will to Power: Richelieu, Hobbes, *Bajazet*

Neoclassical tragedy will thus be able to function as though the tragic is in some way outside its own system, as though it were a part of life, to refer back to Henri Gouhier's phrase. It plays with a distance between spectator and actor, between actor and world. This external referent will be considered another system whose order is homologous to that of tragedy. The entities that form the variables of the two are different, but their constants are the same. For tragedy is simply one realized manifestation of the ordering of human thought, and human mental order matches the material of the world: or, as Johnson put it, "the nature of things and the structure of the human mind" will necessarily produce one and the same order in literature. The order of what is outside human thinking and its various artificial manifestations ("literature" being one) is therefore recuperable, explicable, knowable —social, political, economic, physical, metaphysical, and all other such orders are a part of the reality outside thought (discourse), of the material, sensible world. They are all reducible to discursive knowledge. The mystery at the core—mystery just because it seemed to require a profundity of treatment with which language was unable to provide it—will have been exorcised, replaced by an object able to be grasped as a real thing. Tragedy performs thought experiments whose terms correspond to certain theoretical treatments of such parts of "reality" as we have just suggested.

Thus, for example, the beginning of Racine's *Bajazet* corresponds rather closely to that moment in the Hobbesian monarchical state when the prince's protection of his individual subjects has been suspended and they find themselves as a consequence returned to the condition of permanent war in which natural law holds sway: the individual must defend and protect himself, must seek the imposition of his own power. In *Bajazet* this is even produced rather schematically. Marion Zons-Giesa remarks quite correctly that *Bajazet* is unique among Racine's tragedies in that its action depends upon the continuing absence of the figure of the ruler.[1] She is, of course, hardly alone in this observation. We will see that that absence is essential to the thought experiment that is being performed in the play (*by* the play).

The political theory of the period (my examples will be drawn from Richelieu and Hobbes) argues that power must be accompanied by will and by knowledge, that real power consists in action, that these elements may be situated in a general field wherein reason is pitted against passion: "passion" will cause the search for power and its practice to be utterly ineffectual (Richelieu). The first act of *Bajazet* puts into play the various elements of power, will, and knowledge. Their various combinations will then be put to the proof of passion, embodied in characters. The fifth act of the play reveals the necessary failure of humankind in a state of war and the necessary installation of a particular kind of state. For the last act will also reveal that the whole experiment was a trap set by the prince, Amurat, and will confirm the necessity for and the victory of the absolute power through which alone the state may survive. *Bajazet* may thus be viewed as a kind of experimental putting to the proof of a "scientific," political discourse and of the conditions of government producible at the time. Its instruments are the psychologically "probable" characters whose actions we follow upon the stage.

Indeed, when we read the political texts of the Renaissance and neoclassicism, and in particular that majority which take the prince as their privileged point of reference, as the point of departure for any discussion of government, we may well be struck by their insistence upon those three essential aspects of human relationships in society just mentioned. Not seldom they are given as the *four* essential elements that bind together individual and society in their relationship of force, and which *any* political constitution must seek to place in equilibrium: power, will, action, knowledge. As we say, power and action are normally considered one and the same thing, at least so far as the prince himself is concerned: " . . . vouloir fortement et faire ce qu'on

veut est une même chose en un prince autorisé en son Etat. . . ''
("strongly to will and to do what one wills is the same thing for a
prince whose rule in the state is authorized").[2] Knowledge is what
permits will to become the action that is power: for to rule well, in
the case of a prince, or to have a proper idea of his rights and duties,
in the case of a private individual, a certain "knowledge" is clearly
essential.

Machiavelli had long since freed the prince and the state of their
supposedly divine origin (so far as theory was concerned) and in doing
so he had shown that the relationships among the various members of
civil society were those of a struggle among the strongest. Having allowed to "Fortune" and "God" their traditional sway over the activities of humankind, Machiavelli proceeds to undermine it:

> Nonetheless, in order not to annul our free will, I judge it true that
> Fortune may be mistress of one half our actions but that even she
> leaves the other half, or almost, under our control.[3]

From then on the history of civil societies was increasingly becoming
the narration of "l'empire de la volonté" of mankind, as Jean Bodin
puts it in his *Method of History*. The entire seventeenth century was
then able to set out to discuss the power, rights, and duties that belong
both to the prince and to the individuals who may be his subjects (and
who, like him, have their free will, their power, their sphere of action),
and to consider the relationships that will have to be maintained within a stable state once the divine has been distanced.

In this chapter and my next two I suggest that certain of Racine's
tragedies (perhaps all, but that will not be of concern for the present)
participate in this elaboration of political theory. (It is obvious in the
light of what I have earlier written that I mean to implicate the mass
of neoclassical and Restoration tragedy in this assertion.) These tragedies seek to mix the production of truths concerning the psychological
relationships of individuals and interpersonal action with a discussion
of truths of a political kind: political in the very widest sense, that of
the power relationships within civil society, so that, quite inevitably,
questions epistemological, moral, economic, and the like will enter into these thought experiments. There is, for example, a considerable
dispute between a contractual form of political order that would be

monarchical and another that would be democratic or republican (considering here the level of theory): it seems to me that some of this argument is played out between the two successive, and last, secular plays written by Racine, *Iphigénie* and *Phèdre*. *Iphigénie* would play out the instauration of a society based upon a balancing of individual wills and powers, equally possessive and equally strong. *Phèdre*, rather more ambiguous, would perform on the basis of an appeal to an almost scientific discourse of linear temporality (human history) the installation of a legitimate monarchical society.

In *Phèdre*, an agreement is established between two equally willful and strong individuals but there is no contract because of the premature death of one of them. As a result of this lack of contract, the establishment of a legitimate social order is cast in considerable doubt. It has to be established virtually surreptitiously by means of the *adoptive* order, Thésée/Aricie. But the very fact that such an order can only be established by Thésée's fiat negates the contractual nature of the order that might have come about had Hippolyte lived. Indeed, that succession bears no fruit since it cannot be supposed to continue after Aricie (save by admitting, in accordance with one of the versions of the myth, the resurrection of Hippolytos—but that is to ignore the play itself). A legitimate succession is established, but the commentary upon the possible functioning of this order, freed of all divine support and established thanks entirely to human decision, is rather on the bitter side. But that will be discussed in chapter 11.

In *Bajazet*, then (performed in 1672), Racine also debated these questions concerning the matter of a legitimate and stable society, of the place of the ruler, of the role of the individual. But instead of experimenting, so to speak, with the end of the process (as in *Iphigénie* and *Phèdre*), we are here at the moment of what *seems* to be an essential turning point in the social and political order: marked in reality, for example, by the death of a prince with no natural or nominated successor, or by his voluntary abdication from power. At the beginning of *Bajazet* we are witnesses (or seem to be) to that situation which, according to Hobbes, presides over the moment of foundation of civil societies, or, perhaps more precisely, to that situation which corresponds to the turning point just mentioned—but the elements of both situations are the same. Indeed, the first is no more than a theoretical abstraction of the second.

The natural condition of man is one of war, prior to the institution of "a common Power to keep them all in awe." In the celebrated phrase used by Hobbes, man exists in "continuall feare, and danger of violent death; And the life of man [is] solitary, poore, nasty, brutish, and short."[4] There is war through the entire duration of *Bajazet*: the prince himself is absent at war, each person in the seraglio is reduced to the role he or she occupies in the power struggle that is the direct result of this absence. Once again according to Hobbes, such an absence, so far as its implications here are concerned, returns to such individuals the right to protect themselves, for they can no longer trust in the prince's protection—which protection is one of the primary reasons for the monarchical contract in the first place.

Civil society, according to Hobbes, is founded as a result of the first two laws of nature where humankind is concerned: that of seeking peace, and that of making contracts. The manner of this foundation is that of the placing of the will and power of each (warring) individual into the hands of a single individual. This first contract lasts for as long as it may have been foreseen at the moment of its establishment, or else until the prince no longer offers protection to the individuals who are his subjects. When either situation occurs then the natural right of every individual to protect himself again comes to the fore.[5] As Acomat will say to Bajazet: "La plus sainte des lois, ah! c'est de vous sauver" ("The holiest of laws, oh! is to save yourself" [2.2: p. 374]).[6]

This is the very moment at which *Bajazet* begins. That is what explains Acomat's freedom of action and Osmin's astonishment:

> Et depuis quand, seigneur, entre-t-on dans ces lieux,
> Dont l'accès était même interdit à nos yeux?
> Jadis une mort prompte eût suivi cette audace.   [1.1: p. 357]

> [And since when, my lord, do you come into this place, access to which was once forbidden even our view? There was a time when such boldness would have been followed by a swift death.]

Indeed, despite all that critics have been able to say about the savagery and ferocity of Turkish custom (a criticism by which Pierre Corneille will not be taken in, precisely as it refers to *Bajazet*), the right of a prince to protect his own interests in such a manner was upheld by the majority of political writers of the time.

What is at stake is the necessity in which the prince finds himself to assert his own power and privilege: power and privilege that he must be visibly acknowledged to possess if he is to retain what Guez de Balzac calls his "*Reputation*." It was precisely in that sense that Balzac was able to justify the rather brutal repression of the Protestant leaders at La Rochelle, arguing that the king "a agi ne plus ne moins qu'agissent le Loix, qui ordonnent des peines et des supplices, sans se mettre en cholère, et ne sont point passionnées, quoy qu'elles soient dures et inflexibles" ("acted neither more nor less than as the Laws act, which order punishments and tortures without anger, and which do not let emotion intervene, though they may be harsh and inflexible").[7] In the same way Gabriel Naudé was able to affirm that certain apparently barbarous actions carried out by princes, with the Saint Bartholomew's Day massacre particularly in mind, are quite justifiable "quand il s'agit d'affoiblir ou casser certains droits, privilèges, franchises et exemptions, dont jouissent quelques sujets au prejudice et diminution de l'autorité du Prince" ("when it is a question of weakening or breaking certain rights, privileges, franchises and exemptions that are enjoyed by certain subjects to the prejudice and diminution of the Prince's authority").[8] Hobbes goes just as far, and even Richelieu appears to come close to such an opinion in his *Dernier Testament*. In his practice we know that he did not hesitate, if he felt a need for such a show of force: witness, for example, Montmorency's execution in 1632.

Now in Amurat's case the "right of the seraglio," as one might call it, is one of the signs of his sovereignty. Thus, what is signaled from the outset is, first, a considerable change in the political situation ("depuis quand"), and second, the fact that this change concerns the absolute power of the prince ("l'accès . . . interdit," "une mort prompte"). That Acomat should be able to treat Osmin's commentary as "discours superflus" immediately afterward is simply a way of underlining this change. On the one hand it indicates that the turnabout is already accomplished, but on the other it appears to suggest that the king's absence leads necessarily to the return of that situation which reigns prior to the establishment of civil society, when what counts is quite simply the strongest power—and that there is no need to talk of the matter.

Indeed, the first scene of the tragedy puts into play a power struggle that is entirely due to the initial absence of the prince. For this absence has the indubitable effect of removing certain subjects from the king's protection: "The Obligation of Subjects to the Soveraign," writes Hobbes, "is understood to last as long, and no longer, than the power lasteth, by which he is able to protect them."[9] We discover that Amurat, far from protecting them, "a juré [la] ruine" of Acomat and has already sent a slave to "demander la tête à son frère" (1.1: p. 359). In addition Amurat has committed, from the point of view of the needs of a stable state, a second and considerable "error." "If a Monarch," asserts Hobbes once again, "shall relinquish the Soveraignty, both for himself, and his heires; His Subjects returne to the absolute Libertie of Nature."[10] Amurat has granted this sovereignty to Roxane, by whom he does not yet even have an heir ("Avant qu'elle eût un fils . . .") and who will later be referrred to as an "esclave attachée à ses seuls intérêts" (2.5: p. 378). In effect this represents a renunciation of his power: "Il a fait plus pour elle, Osmin: il *a voulu* / Qu'elle eût dans *son absence* un *pouvoir absolu*" ("He has done more for her, Osmin: he has *willed* that during *his absence* she should have *absolute power*" [1.1: p. 360]). For reasons that are sufficiently apparent, two persons cannot simultaneously possess absolute power. So far as Byzantium is concerned, therefore, and more especially the seraglio itself, Amurat, an absent power, cannot dominate the present power held by Roxane—as it would appear, at least. That explains why Acomat is able to say to Osmin, from the very outset: "Quand tu seras instruit de tout ce qui se passe, / Mon entrée en ces lieux ne te surprendra plus"("When you have been informed of all that is happening, that I come into this place will no longer surprise you" [1.1: p. 357], and will explain why it will be immediately necessary to "soustraire à son pouvoir / Un peuple" (1.2: p. 363) who cannot be abreast of what is going on. Still, the end of the play will reveal, as I have already implied, that the supposed turnabout in the political situation is false: the entire play will be revealed to have been, in a very real sense, an experiment performed by Amurat.

At the beginning the situation is even more complicated than I have so far proposed. We there find ourselves back in a time when only natural law and a state of war exist, and each individual is given over to the accomplishment of some personal satisfaction: "So that in the first place, I put for a generall inclination of all mankind, a perpetuall and restlesse desire of Power after power, that ceaseth onely in Death." Hobbes goes on to write that power must always seek an increase in power if it is to permit the accomplishment of all the desires of the individual.[11] Acomat, as visir, is made for war and for military power: the janissaries, we are told, miss the time when they fought under this command, "assurés de vaincre," and Acomat is able to speak of his "gloire passée" (1.1: p. 358). The present maneuverings undertaken by Acomat are aimed at recovering this lost power. To this end a certain knowledge (*savoir*) is necessary, a detailed knowledge of the situation and of others' actions and intentions—that is why Acomat had sent Osmin to Amurat's camp. In this case, however, the end of the search for knowledge remains only ignorance:

> . . . comme vous le savez malgré ma diligence,
> Un long chemin sépare et le camp et Byzance;
> Mille obstacles divers m'ont même traversé:
> Et je puis ignorer tout ce qui s'est passé.   [1.1: p. 357]

> [As you know, in spite of my speed, the camp and Byzantium are separated by a long road; furthermore a thousand various obstacles have impeded me: and I may well be in ignorance of all that has gone on.]

This lack of knowledge will prove fatal. Knowledge and power go together, and for the present Acomat finds himself in a particularly ambiguous situation:

> *Il commande* à l'armée; et moi, dans une ville,
> Il me laisse exercer un *pouvoir inutile.*
> Quel emploi, quel séjour, Osmin, pour un visir!
> Mais j'ai plus dignement employé ce loisir:
> J'ai su lui préparer des craintes et des veilles. . . .   [1.1: p. 359]

> [He *commands* the army; and as for me, in a town, he allows me to exercise a *useless power.* What a task, what a place to be, Osmin, for a visir! But I have used this idleness more worthily: I have been able (known how) to prepare some fears and sleepless nights.]

What is a power that can be called *inutile*? Quite evidently none whatsoever. While Acomat's power may remain ineffective—in part

because he cannot free himself from the prince ("il me laisse," admits
Acomat), in part because of Roxane's *pouvoir absolu*—the same
does not apply to the sultana herself. During his absence, as we have
seen, Amurat has willed that she should wield absolute power; a
last will on his part no doubt, because if one individual's power is absolute then the other's will is "empty," and Amurat has effectively
deposed himself. Absent will can have no effect on present power, any
more than can absent power. Not for nothing has there been a rumor concerning Amurat's death: "Peut-être il te souvient qu'un récit
peu fidèle/De la mort d'Amurat fit courir la nouvelle" ("Perhaps
you remember how a false tale caused the rumour of Amurat's death"
[1.1: p. 361]). Now that he is supposed powerless, it is indeed as
though he were dead. To be sure, the falsity of the rumor corresponds
to the fact that there has been *no* loss of power on the sultan's part.
The rumor was a part of the maneuvers attempted by Acomat and
Roxane: we will see at the end that Amurat had caught the sultana in
a trap by "giving" her that "absolute power." In reality she never had
such power because he continued always to spy upon her, to follow
all her movements. As we have already suggested, the whole tragedy is
a power play by Amurat, who thereby reinforces his own power—
Hobbes's "desire for Power after power" in action?—(It is a power play
on the part of the prince, the only individual who can continue to
function in such terms *after* the institution of civil society.) He is to
return victorious from the war, while on the home front he will have
rid himself at a single blow of a dangerous rival in his brother, of
the visir, who was plotting against him, and of Roxane, a sufficiently
weak link (and more) to cause his downfall.

The lack of power on the part of such individuals is like a death.
Thus "l'imbécile Ibrahim," who has neither will nor power and who
"traîne . . . une éternelle enfance," is said to be "indigne également de
vivre et de mourir" (1.1: p. 360). But the man or woman who has
once tasted power will strive to increase it until death intervenes. That
is why Amurat has sought to have Bajazet put to death; Bajazet, who
is born to war and who has already, under Acomat, experienced the
"plaisir" and "gloire" of war (1.1: p. 360).[12]

Into this play of power, will, and knowledge, then, enters another
factor: passion. Acomat tells Osmin how he succeeded in bringing
Roxane onto Bajazet's side:

Je plaignis Bajazet, je lui vantai ses charmes,
Qui, par un soin jaloux dans l'ombre retenus,
Si voisins de ses yeux leur étaient inconnus.
Que te dirai-je enfin? la sultane *éperdue*
N'eut plus d'autre désir que celui de sa vue.   [1.1.: p. 361]

[I pitied Bajazet, I praised to her his charms, which, kept in the
shade by an envious precaution, remained unknown to her though
so near her view. Well, what can I tell you? The sultana was *utterly
lost* and *had no other desire* than to see him.]

So Roxane has (it appears) power, but she has it without the use of
her reason, and that will necessarily lead to failure:

... en effet, si la passion porte une fois au bien, ce n'est que par
hasard, puisque, par sa nature, elle ne détourne tant qu'elle aveugle
ceux en qui elle est. . . .
   Il faut avoir une vertu mâle et faire toutes choses par raison sans
se laisser aller à la pente des Inclinations, qui portent souvent les
Princes en de grandes précipices, si celles qui leur bandent les yeux
les portant à faire aveuglément ce qu'il leur plaît, sont capables de
produire du mal lorsqu'ils les suivent avec trop peu de retenue.[13]

[Indeed, though passion may once have a good effect, that is by
mere chance, because by its very nature it turns such effects aside
while blinding those whom it possesses. . . .
   A masculine strength is needed, and everything must be done by
reason, without allowing oneself to follow the slope of one's Desires. For these often take Princes over great precipices. If those
who blindfold them lead them on to do whatever they please, they
are capable of producing much harm when these desires are followed with too little restraint.]

   The tale that Acomat continues to tell almost amounts to an illustration of this maxim of Richelieu:

Roxane vit le prince; elle ne put lui taire
L'ordre dont elle seule était dépositaire.
Bajazet est aimable; il vit que son salut
Dependait de lui plaire: et bientôt il lui plut.
Tout conspirait pour lui; ses soins, sa complaisance,
Ce secret découvert, et cette intelligence,

Soupirs d'autant plus doux qu'il les fallait celer,
L'embarras irritant de ne s'oser parler,
Même témérité, périls, craintes communes,
Lièrent pour jamais leurs coeurs et leurs fortunes.   [1.1: p. 361]

[Roxane saw the prince; she was unable to keep from him the
command with which she had been entrusted. Bajazet is most fit
to be loved; he saw that his salvation depended on his captivating
her: and soon he had done so. Everything was in his favor; his at-
tentiveness, her willingness, the secret revealed, and the mutual
knowledge, a love that was all the more sweet for having to remain
hidden, the irritating inconvenience of not daring to speak to one
another, the same temerity and dangers, shared fears, (all of these
things) bound together forever their hearts and their destinies.]

This passage shows us the flaw in Roxane's will and power—but also
in Acomat's. In her case it is a matter of passion's blindness. She fails
to see the mutual love borne for one another by Bajazet and Atalide,
and that ignorance takes away from her the essential support of knowledge. In Acomat's case, we have to deal with a different emotion:
that of ambition, the ambition to bind himself to the royal family by
means of Atalide. And the irony is such that he accuses others of ignorance because they believe that Bajazet is in love with Atalide: "Ils
l'ignorent encore; et, jusques à ce jour,/ Atalide a prêté son nom à cet
amour" ("They still know nothing of it; and until now, Atalide has lent
her name to this love" [1.1: p. 361]). And to the ignorance of his passion we may oppose the *reason* (or knowledge, rather) shown by Atalide
and Bajazet: "*Nous avons* su toujours nous aimer et nous taire" ("We
have always been able [have known how] to love each other and keep
silent" [1.4: p. 367]). It is only much later that we will be able to say
that the visir finally has his eyes opened to the truth, when he exclaims,
"Prince aveugle! ou plutôt trop aveugle ministre. . . " (4.7: p. 399).

Roxane knows that she is lacking some essential knowledge, but she
does not understand the full significance of that lack. She needs (and
wants) the sultan's brother, but without knowing whether he "belongs" to her or not she is without effective power (and let us forget
for the moment the previously mentioned threat of the sultan): "*Je ne
puis* dire rien,/ Sans *savoir* s'il m'aime." Atalide reinforces the relationship of knowledge and power by asking: "*Savez-vous* si demain/ Sa

liberté, ses jours, seront *en votre main?*" (Do you *know* if tomorrow his freedom, his life, will still be *in your hands?*" [1.3: p. 364]). She is being perfectly precise when she uses a phrase such as, "Ce que vous avez fait, ce que vous pouvez faire" (1.3: p. 364). Roxane then relates the demand she is going to make upon Bajazet, in order that she may acquire the necessary sure knowledge, that will lead to the desired action (in this case marriage and the consequent fulfillment both of power and of passion). At the same time as she tells Atalide of the demand she is going to make, through Atalide herself, she seeks to remove from the princess a certain *vouloir* (without knowing that the latter has already "succeeded" where she herself has failed), and in doing so emphasizes her own blindness. In relating the demand, Roxane runs through the entire series of elements of which I am speaking:

> J'en reçus la *puissance* [i.e., of sultana] aussi bien que le titre,
>   . . . je me suis bien servie
> Du *pouvoir* qu'Amurat me donna sur sa vie
>
> . . . .
>
> Voilà sur quoi je *veux* que Bajazet se prononce: . . .
> Je ne vous presse point de *vouloir* aujourd'hui
> Me prêter votre voix pour m'expliquer à lui:
> Je *veux* que, devant moi, sa bouche et son visage
> Me *découvrent* son coeur *sans me laisser d'ombrage*; . . .
> Adieu. Vous *saurez* tout après cette entrevue.   [1.3: pp. 365–66]

[I received the *power* (of sultana) as well as the title. . . . I have used well the *power* that Amurat gave me over his life. . . . That is the matter on which I *wish* Bajazet to say where he stands. . . . I do not now push you *to wish* to lend me your voice to explain myself to him: I *want* his voice and appearance, here before me to *reveal* his heart to me and *leave me in no shadow of a doubt*. . . . Farewell. You *will know* all after this interview.]

Atalide's speech, which follows this decision announced by Roxane and brings the first act to a close, epitomized the movement that was begun from the very moment when Acomat and Osmin came on stage. In the past, at the time Amurat's presence and power, everything was stable and well balanced. The phrase "Nous avons su toujours nous aimer et nous taire" marks indeed a moment when there was no difference between knowledge, will, power, and action, because the clause "nous avons su" in fact has all those meanings ("we knew how to," "were were able to," "we did"). This unity has now been broken.

It is as though the prince's absence had led to a complete collapse of recognized order. "Et moi," says Atalide, "je ne puis rien." But she, too, is mistaken with regard to the sultana when she asserts, "Si Roxane le veut, sans doute il faut qu'il meure," because if he does die it will be the realization of Amurat's will, not Roxane's. She may have been the *agent* of that will, but the order itself proceeds from the sultan: a fact that is emphasized at the end by the arrival of Orcan with a second (and twofold) order (5.11: p. 409). This "forgetfulness" on the part of Atalide is general. As I have indicated, it makes us suppose that the entire tragedy is only a simulacrum of reality, fabricated by Amurat at the same time as being an experiment on Racine's part with the situation discussed (for example) in Hobbes.

The first act appears to put into operation a play among *savoir/pouvoir/vouloir* (both the words and the concepts) in such a way that the lack of any one of these elements leads to a complete failure in any intended action. Thus Amurat, absent from Byzantium and the seraglio, would possess a will but neither power nor knowledge (the conditional is necessary here because Amurat is in fact neither ignorant nor powerless: Orcan's arrival, of which we learn in 3.8, and what is related at the end by Osmin of its final result [5.11], tell us that). Roxane has both power and will, but lacks knowledge; Bajazet and Atalide both have will and knowledge but no power; Acomat has will, but neither power nor entire knowledge. These various insufficiencies provide enough indication as to why the state of war that subsists prior to the establishment of civil societies would be permanent. For this there appears to be only one solution, which will be imposed at the end of the tragedy by means that are not altogether gentle:

> The Greatest of humane Powers, is that which is compounded of the Powers of most men, united by consent, in one person, Naturall, or Civill, that has the use of all their Powers depending on his will. . . .[14]

At the end the legitimate sultan's power will have been maintained and will continue. If Acomat flees, if Roxane and Bajazet are assassinated, if Atalide blames herself for the outcome as she commits suicide, all of that results from their fundamental ignorance of the rights of sovereignty and from their failure to situate themselves correctly into the contractual civil society of which that sovereignty is but one of the elements. They have been performing within the space where Amurat has left his trap. For while the member-subjects of the state do have certain freedoms of action within the general legal system known as "civil society," such freedoms are very different from those which individuals take to themselves in the state of nature:

> Nevertheless we are not to understand, that by such Liberty [of the subjects], the Soveraign Power of Life, and death, is either abolished, or limited. For it has been already shewn, that nothing the Soveraign Representative can do to a Subject, on what pretence soever, can properly be called Injustice, or Injury. . . .[15]

The three central acts of the play are situated between the apparent collapse of order which the first act shows us, and which is due to the prince's absence, and its return at the end as a result of the somewhat brutal repression carried out upon the sultan's orders. Even then the players will not be altogether clear as to what is happening: "J'ignore quel dessein les anime tous deux" ("I do not know what intention moves them both to action"), Atalide exclaims with regard to the activities of Roxane and Acomat, but at a time when they themselves no longer know why they are doing what they are doing (5.8: p. 407). Sovereign order is reestablished upon the remnants of a struggle among individuals who were always lacking some element necessary to absolute power. Thus the greater part of the third act consists in a series of misunderstandings: among Acomat, Roxane, and Bajazet (in a meeting that is recounted by Acomat), between Atalide and Zaire, between Atalide and Bajazet, between Roxane and Bajazet. And that continues right up to the arrival of the sultan's "avenger," Orcan, which leads to Roxane's despairing cry at the approach of failure: "Quel est mon empereur?" (3.8: p. 390). The fourth act seems to be a series of indecisive discussions around the matter of Bajazet's execution and the play of Roxane's passions.

But already in the second act the lines of force revealed in the first began to be nuanced; beginning with the supposedly absolute power possessed by Roxane. She herself does not seem altogether ready to believe in it:

Rien ne me retient plus; et je puis, dès ce jour
Accomplir le dessein qu'a formé mon amour.
Non que, vous assurant d'un triomphe facile,
Je mette entre vos mains un empire tranquille;
Je fais ce que je puis, je vous l'avais promis:
J'arme votre valeur contre vos ennemis,
J'écarte de vos jours un péril manifeste;
Votre vertu, seigneur, achevera le reste.   [2.1: p. 369]

[Nothing holds me back any longer; and I can, from this very day,
carry out the plan my love has formed. Not that I assure you of an
easy triumph, and place in your hands a peaceful empire; I do
what I can, as I had promised you: I provide your courage with
arms against your enemies, I remove a manifest danger to your life;
your virtue, my lord, will accomplish the rest.]

Even when she says this she is relying upon a false rumor, invented by
Acomat, according to which the army is leaning toward Bajazet (end
of 1.1, 1.2). If we put this mistaken notion beside her assertions that
Acomat "répond de Byzance" ("assures the support of Byzantium")
and that she herself has the palace entirely in her power, we will appreciate the considerable irony of the lines: "C'est à vous de courir/
Dans le champ glorieux que *j'ai su* vous ouvrir" ("It is up to you to
run in the glorious field I have been able [*known how*] to open up before you" [2.1: p. 369]).

Roxane, then, seems to confess (or be made surreptitiously to confess) that her power is not complete. Bajazet follows close upon her
heels: "Mais aussi voyez ce que je puis,/Ce qu'était Soliman, et le peu
que je suis" ("But just look at what I can do, what Soliman was, and
the little that I am" [2.1: p. 370]). He goes on to renew the protesta-
tions of his lack of power, of his weakness, in a speech that recalls
Atalide's lamentations: "malheurs," "infortuné," "proscrit," "incer-
tain," "misères," and so on. It is quite true that this speech comes
from an effort to mislead Roxane, but in making himself echo Atalide
Bajazet simply emphasizes our awareness of their powerlessness. In
the state of war everyone starts equal. And if Bajazet's only power is
over the two women and proceeds from the fact that he is loved by
them, we may also understand Roxane's reply to his laments as a further confession on her part:

Mais avez-vous prévu, si vous ne m'épousez,
Les périls plus certains où vous vous exposez?
Songez-vous que, sans moi, tout vous devient contraire?
Que c'est à moi surtout qu'il importe de plaire?
. . . .
Que j'ai sur votre vie un empire suprême;
Que vous ne respirez qu'autant que je vous aime?
Et, sans ce même amour qu'offensent vos refus,
Songez-vous, en un mot, que vous ne seriez plus?   [2.1: p. 371]

[But have you foreseen if you do not marry me, the more certain dangers to which you expose yourself? Do you realize that without me everything will become opposed to you? That it is important for you to please me? . . . That I have supreme power over your life; that you have breath just so long as I love you? And, without that very love that your refusal insults, do you realize, in a word, that you would exist no more?]

Roxane appears here as the very epitome of the misguided passion so scorned by Richelieu. What is above all clear, however, is that Roxane's power is limited to the control of Bajazet (and, by that fact alone, though she herself is as yet unaware of it, to control of Atalide as well), and even that is only due to the right given by Amurat and the command she has not yet carried out. Far from being absolute, as Acomat believes (and she herself on occasion), her power is essentially secondary: "Non, je ne veux plus rien" (2.1: p. 371), she exclaims at the very moment of her outcry against Bajazet. It is thus only to be expected that the remainder of this scene is marked by her hesitations between losing and loving Bajazet, before she comes to a "decision" (still wavering) to return to Amurat.

Bajazet, faced with the threat of death, uses the idea of individual liberty to justify his refusal of marriage: he would be forced into it, it would not be the "présent *volontaire*" (2.3: p. 374) that Amurat's love was to Roxane—a justification that does not prevent his asking Acomat to bring him help from outside. Furthermore, however, Bajazet has a completely different conception of the role of a chief of state from what the play seems so far to have proposed. For him reasons of state do not alone suffice: he has a nostalgia for that magnanimity which belongs to an older and more chivalrous age (not so much older actually, for we can still find it in Balzac's *Prince*). Thus, when Acomat reminds him of those fortunate heroes for whom,

> Libres dans leur victoire, et maîtres de leur foi,
> L'intérêt de l'Etat fut leur unique loi;

adding

> Et d'un trône si saint la moitié n'est fondée
> Qur sur la foi promise et rarement gardée   [2.3: p. 367]

> [Free in their victories, and masters of their loyalty, the interest of the State was their only law; and of so holy a throne half is founded only upon promises given and rarely kept.]

Bajazet exclaims in some disgust that they did not seek to save their own life by trickery, that they "ne la rachetaient point par une perfidie" ("did not buy it back by treachery").

The expression of such a sentiment on the prince's part draws forth exclamations of admiration from Acomat, though we may perhaps be inclined to suspect a certain sarcasm on the visir's part; but above all it underscores Bajazet's inaptitude for combat in the new state and indicates that he must be its victim. The struggle to see who can be most magnanimous in the next scene between Bajazet and Atalide (2.5) indicates in effect that they have both renounced the will to power, leaving such bagatelles to the "esclave attachée à ses seuls intérêts" that Roxane is held to be, and have chosen the magnanimous individual glory of the old heroes. This is Jean-Baptiste's retreat placed in a different key. The struggle between Bajazet and Atalide belongs to a time before the beginning of civil societies as that is explored by Hobbes and others, to a time when "intérêts" still belong to the single individual and not to the individual as part of a community of interests. What Roxane and Acomat are seeking on the one hand, Bajazet and Atalide on the other, though very different in spirit, remains essentially the satisfaction of such individual will—as passions of love, ambition, magnanimous glory:

> It is of itself manifest, that the actions of men proceed from the will, and the will from hope and fear, insomuch as when they shall see a greater good, or lesser evil, likely to happen to them by the breach, than observation of the laws, they will willingly violate them.[16]

When individuals act in such a way the order of the state is returning to that of nature: if such individuals can get away with it, as they do for the period of the tragedy of *Bajazet*.

The sign of the small security and lack of certainty offered in the state of nature would be the rapidity with which individuals change their minds and the direction of their activities. For alliances and agreements would necessarily be constantly shifting to adjust themselves to the ever-changing shape of the power conflicts. In such a situation the very word *will*, loses its meaning: "Si Bajazet l'épouse," asserts Atalide, "il suit mes volontés" (3.1: p. 381). Or again: "Je l'ai voulu sans doute:/Et je le veux toujours, quelque prix qu'il m'en coûte./.../Ce coeur ... /L'aime trop pour vouloir en être témoin./ Allons, je veux savoir ..." ("No doubt I willed it; and I still will it, no matter what it costs me. ... This heart ... loves him too much to wish to witness it. Come, I want to know" [3.1: pp. 381–82]). Atalide is utterly disturbed by what she is going through. She circles all around the concept of will at the very moment of its loss, when it loses its grasp, when she can no longer be coherent even with herself.

Throughout the next two acts the others come in turn to the same condition: Bajazet, who will at one moment refuse to save his own life but who will have done so by the following scene, and who will eventually go (unknowingly) to his death protesting the fate of Atalide; Acomat, who will capture the city and maintain his capture even after all reason for doing so is lost, who will offer help to Atalide, futilely, because she will immediately kill herself; Roxane who, having hesitated throughout the entire fourth act, will finally act out of pique, claiming she does so to obey Amurat: "Obéissons plutôt à la juste rigueur /D'Amurat ..." ("Let us obey rather the just severity of Amurat" [4.6: p. 398]). In this affirmation she will even be backed up by Bajazet: "Aux ordres d'Amurat hâtez-vous d'obéir" (5.4: p. 405).

This assertion of obedience is swiftly followed by his execution at the hands of Orcan, who is following the direct orders of the sultan. The entire play occurs between the "brackets" formed by the mention at the beginning of the order to put Bajazet to death (which Roxane had not obeyed) and the final accomplishment of the second similar command. Bajazet's death marks the reestablishment of order, the reaffirmation of the prince's power after the struggle among individual wills.

Racine could not have experimented with the state of nature per se because that is, by definition, chaos: it could only be shown by contrast. At the end of the tragedy we learn that Amurat had always kept an eye on the state of affairs at Byzantium and in the seraglio: he had forseen what might happen. The "brackets" were put there by the sultan himself. Racine's experimental device, then, was not to show the state of nature before the establishment of civil societies, because that would be impossible; it was to show it in the form of the struggle that would occur following the abdication of sovereign power. The concept of the "State of Nature" was an extrapolation from the manner in which the then-familiar forms of civil society appeared to function and from the conditions their establishment seemed theoretically to require. The tragedy of *Bajazet* shows us not simply what conditions would be dominant in such a state of nature, it also shows us, by means of the bracketing, that such conditions are an extrapolation from the existing monarchical order and from the current concepts of human action and psychology (naturally mutually dependent). In *Bajazet* order is reestablished by a princely coup of a type celebrated from Machiavelli to Hobbes, and prepared from the very first scene of the play.

Corneille criticized Racine's play on the grounds that none of the characters possessed the "*sentiments*" that people in Constantinople should and do have.[17] Saint-Evremond made a similar criticism about Corneille's own *Sophonisbe*, when comparing it to Mairet's arguing that Corneille's heroine was too close in spirit to the period when she had actually lived while Mairet's remained close to the period when his play was written and performed.[18] What Saint-Evremond says Corneille *should have* achieved and Corneille himself says Racine *has* achieved is the idea that the theatrical text and its performance should seek to create a certain proximity of feeling between character and spectator, to make possible the emotional identification that both critics and dramatic authors of the second half of the seventeenth century felt to be an essential part of the dramatic experience.

That notion in turn depends on the assumption—and the "identification" itself would make it possible to believe—that what one sees on the stage and what one *feels* in the performance correspond to the real, that the play itself corresponds to reality. Corneille's failure would result from a certain strangeness, a lack of familiarity with the feelings and situations performed onstage; Mairet's success and Racine's, if we take Corneille's remarks seriously, would be entirely due to the idea that the characters and situations played before the audience reproduce life itself and the truly possible reactions of those who are at present spectators, but themselves actors both before and after.

Frank Sutcliffe has remarked about the period that saw the beginnings of Corneille, Balzac, and Richelieu himself that "literature and politics reinforce one another in a common will to invent the new man."[19] Like Lucien Goldmann, Marion Zons-Giesa has more recently shown in Racine the manner in which the structure of the plays corresponds to contemporary sociopolitical configurations.[20] It has been possible to give certain indications as to how *Bajazet* puts into play the elements of a theoretical political analysis. But one should not forget that this analysis, whose elements underlie the play, or rather perhaps, whose elements are isomorphic with the play, are themselves founded in the *practice* of power. They are based in the concrete political operation itself. In his *Prince* Machiavelli relates the deeds and accomplishments of Cesare Borgia; Gabriel Naudé writes the apology for the Saint Bartholomew's Day massacre; Richelieu constantly refers us to the political realities of the centralization of monarchical power in the France of Louis XIII; Hobbes's works is imbued with his awareness of the English revolution and the power struggles that preceded it.

The theatre of this period seeks to make itself into a reproduction of *this* reality, in the same sense as the discourse of political theory would itself be such a reproduction. In Dryden's manifesto *Of Dramatick Poesie*, Lisideius defines a play as a "just and lively image of human nature, representing its passions and humours, and the changes of fortune to which it is subject; for the delight and instruction of mankind." We could find similar claims for the theatre from d'Aubignac and La Mesnardière to Rapin, Bouhours, and the abbé de Pure, from Boileau to Voltaire and Mercier, in Rymer and Dennis, in Pope and Addison. Apparently similar definitions could, of course, be found in times far distant. But what is specific to this period is that the mimetic concern is based principally not upon linguistic or rhetorical preoccupations (as it was, for example, in the Renaissance), but upon ordered psychological and political activities as representations of a social and, more generally, simply human reality.

In Racine, as representative of the tragedy of the period, the combination of a psychological and social realism with what amounts to an experimental commentary and analysis around questions such as relations of power and struggles of will (as they are in the case of *Bajazet*), begins, or better perhaps confirms, the transformation of tragedy into a discourse of truth. It is a discourse whose model is to be found in the development of positivistic science and in the philosophy of knowledge that accompanies and justifies that science.

10 Classicism, the Individual, and Economic Exchange *(Iphigénie)*

That the notion of neoclassicism is coincident in France especially, but to some extent in England as well, with a general conception of an aristocratic literature aimed at a particularly sophisticated and enlightened recipient is attested not least by the general sentiment of superiority that has surrounded its study and propagation. It has its basis in the fact that in both countries the authors of its literature were, for the most part, at least on the fringes of the courtly aristocracy and consciously writing for it.

Apart from this aspect of privilege (and the very concept of "literature" implies a privilege more or less widely shared), the neoclassicism of which we are speaking is characterized by (a) the effort to codify literary form and so provide a scientific (technical) basis for aesthetics and (b) the search for a verisimilitude that would allow the code to be supposed as a precise homologue of external reality. We have been watching tragedy itself develop little by little the possibility of these two propositions by producing the very objects that will compose the reality so codified. Racine gives some further indication of what is in question when he writes that he has not caused Iphigénie to be saved by Diane, a goddess and a theatrical *machine* ("le secours d'une déesse et d'une machine"), because such an outcome would be "trop absurde et trop incroyable parmi nous."[1]

This particular example is perhaps somewhat simplistic, but it serves us well to give some indication of what is in question. The two propositions I mentioned before are complementary, and both are at the bottom of Racine's observation. They suggest that the neoclassical mind (and ours) supposes a human capacity, on the basis of codes conceived as ordering reality (of which codes human language is accepted as the paradigm, its *use*—discourse), or, as Defoe calls them at the start of the English Augustan age, "the Mathematical Engines of Reason,"[2] to possess and use natural and social phenomena external to the perceiving individual. This attitude represents a complete change from that which saw the individual as merely a part of a unified organism operating as a whole, and neoclassicism may with justice be seen, it appears to me, as the first notable aesthetic representation of such an attitude.

Speaking of Racine's *Iphigénie*, Roland Barthes has remarked:

> Voilà sans doute la plus séculière des tragédies de Racine. Le signe en est que les personnages ne sont plus des figures différentes, des doubles, des états ou des compléments de la meme *psyché,* mais de véritables individus, des monades psychologiques bien separées les unes des autres par des rivalités d'intérêts, et non plus liées entre elles dans une aliénation ambiguë.[3]

> [This is no doubt the most secular of Racine's tragedies. The sign of that is that the characters are no longer different figures, doubles, states, or complements of the same *psyche*, but veritable individuals, psychological monads clearly distinguished from one another by conflicts of interest, and no longer linked one to another in some ambiguous alienation.]

Whatever one may think of this characterization of Racine's theatre, the characters of *Iphigénie* do indeed represent individuals whose *aims*, to be sure, are egotistical, but whose very ontological basis lies in the need of individual possession. It is this need and its expression in a whole system of essentially *economic* exchanges that defines their nature as human beings.

All the difference between Rotrou's *Iphigénie* and Racine's version lies in the latter's creation of Eriphile, without whom, he writes in his preface, "je n'aurais jamais osé entreprendre cette tragédie" (p. 476). For the sake of Greece, Euripides' Iphigenia offered herself as victim, and, to a degree, she is justified by her father's love and Menelaus's sincerity when, after his accusations against Agamemnon, he realizes his brother's situation upon the arrival of his wife and daughter:

When I saw tears bursting from your eyes

Tears started in mine and a great pity
Seized me. . . .[4]

The baroque author's Iphigénie finds herself surrounded by individuals concerned only with their own interests and their worldly image. She accepts the role thrust upon her in a play most of whose other characters perform in bad faith (though the term is perhaps ill used of a play a major part of whose problematic may well be viewed as the development of a concept of individuality within a world order from which it is as yet absent). Iphigénie accepts such a role fully, though not unironically, and, we might say, because the part calls for a particular kind of action. In the world of Rotrou, in which all absolute values are absent, or at least unidentifiable and therefore unattainable, worldly success or failure can depend only upon the greater or lesser efficacy of a "mask:"

> Les grandes attitudes d'Agamemnon, les discours éloquents d'Ulysse, de Ménélas et de Calchas n'abusent personne; on assiste véritablement à un spectacle, à une représentation théâtrale dans laquelle chacun des personnages se donne la comédie à lui-même et aux autres sous la direction d'Ulysse qui les rappelle à l'ordre lorsqu'ils oublient leur rôle et commencent à exprimer *leurs* opinions et non celles de leur personnage.[5]

> [Agamemnon's grand attitudes, Ulysse's eloquent speeches, and those of Ménélas and of Calchas take in no one. We are truly present before a spectacle, a theatrical representation in which each of the characters plays a role for himself and for the others under the direction of Ulysse, who calls them to order whenever they forget their role and begin to express *their* opinions and not those of the characters they are playing.]

Not unlike Saint-Genest in Rotrou's play of that name, Rotrou's Iphigénie is transported by her role; she accedes to *being* through acting. In so doing she demonstrates the futility of social relationships that have lost their divine support. Rotrou's gods, even more than those of Euripides, who at least remain the equal of humans, have been reduced to excuses masking the ambition of Agamemnon, the spite of Ménélas, the pride of Calchas. The appearance of the goddess at the end, virtualized practically by Iphigénie's act of will, merely underscores her status of a dea ex machina, a thing of the play. The ambiguity of such a conclusion is further emphasized by Agamemnon's prophecy of victory over Troy and his concluding words: "Puis revenons aux bords de Mycène et d'Argos,/Après un long travail, goûter un long repos" ("Then let us return to the shores of Mycenae and Argos, after a long labor, to taste a long repose").[6]

The creation of Eriphile changes the commentary entirely. If Iphigénie's development served to show the illusory nature of purely social (i.e., nondivine) relationships, Eriphile's certainty tends to set them apart. Rotrou holds out the possibility of transcendence. Racine denies it. If Eriphile is touched with grace, the rest must make do with affirming an entirely social exchange in which they put all their faith and which they affirm in the knowledge that the sociopolitical reality in which they move confirms the value ("valeur") of their humanity. Eriphile denies it, and her removal is also that of a last hesitancy concerning a continuity among the natural, the human, and the divine. Her hatred of, and rivalry with, Iphigénie marks this separation, and although Achille's semidivinity might have been expected to align him with Eriphile (as it had before the time covered by the play), his love for her rival sets him definitively and squarely into the social exchange system: which is why only Eriphile need disappear from the scene.[7]

That it is a question of exchange there can be no doubt: the sacrifice of "une fille du sang d'Hélène" in return for "l'empire d'Asie" (1.1: pp. 480, 481), blood for blood. This forms the very nub of the drama. Moreover, Ulysse has found a way to present the case to Agamemnon as a more than favorable exchange: less blood for more, one individual for an empire. He has argued that *not* to sacrifice Iphigénie would be to upset this balance, reversing the equation, "immolant tout l'Etat à ma fille." Agamemnon would thus himself be overturned, for he would become a "Roi *sans* gloire" and thereby lose both his power and his greatness, as he confesses.

This factor of foregoing *personal* possession is underlined much later in the play by his resentful and spiteful reaction to Achille's threats to save Iphigénie. Such menaces, asserts Agamemnon, have finally convinced him to sacrifice his daughter, since not to do so would reduce his stature as a military leader (4.7: p. 522). Indeed, although he now insists to Arcas that the gods accuse his hesitation in his dreams, it is the economic arguments of Ulysse that have convinced him: ". . . vaincu par Ulysse,/De ma fille, en pleurant, j'ordonnai la supplice" ("overcome by Ulysse, weeping, I ordered my daughter's torment" [1.1: p. 481]). What is the role of Agamemnon in the bargain (". . . vous *devez* votre fille à la Grèce:/Vous nous l'avez *promise*" ["you *owe* your daughter to Greece: You have *promised* her to us"]), and that it is essentially economic, will shortly be recalled by Ulysse himself as he points out that it is a matter of "un peu de sang" serving to "*acheter* tant de gloire" (1.3: pp. 487–88).

While this central exchange remains the main visible concern of the various characters (and of the play), Agamemnon's wavering is caused not by the simple fact of Iphigénie's being his daughter, by her innocence, and the rest, but by the thought of upsetting another exchange in which she becomes a commodity with "mille vertus":

> . . . une amour mutuelle,
> *Sa* piété pour *moi, ma* tendresse pour *elle*,
> Un respect qu'en *son* coeur rien ne peut *balancer*,
> Et que *j*'avais *promis* de mieux recompenser.   [1.1: p. 482]

[a *mutual* love, *her* piety toward *myself, my* tenderness toward *her*, a respect which nothing in *her* heart can *outweigh*, and which *I* had *promised* to *reward* better.]

Agamemnon is a debtor with a promise to pay. By not paying he becomes dishonorable, and he is able to suppose that the oracle is merely testing his commercial honesty: "Tes oracles sans doute ont voulu m'éprouver" ("No doubt your oracles wished to test *me*" [1.1: p. 482])

By sending Arcas in secret to prevent the arrival of his wife and daughter, Agamemnon hopes to save *himself* from the accusation of acting against the interests of society as a whole and of breaking his contracts, principally because if such an accusation can be made he loses his credit. That is why manipulations must be concealed. His relationship with the army is also an essentially contractual one and depends on the fulfillment of an agreed exchange, such that, should his returning of Iphigénie be discovered,

> Ceux même dont ma gloire aigrit l'ambition

Réveilleront leur brigue et leur prétention,
M'arracheront peut-être un pouvoir qui les blesse. . . . [1.1: p. 482]

[Those very ones whose ambition is irritated by my glory will renew their plotting and their claims, will perhaps seize from me a
power which does them harm.]

So far is he from questioning their right to do this that to break that
contract he will lie a second time about Achille's love, as he already
had done about his present desire for marriage in order to hide the fact
that he was breaking his contract with Iphigénie: "D'Achille, qui
l'aimait, j'*empruntai* le langage. . . " ("I *borrowed* a manner of speaking from Achille, who loved her" [1.1: p. 481]).

Here and elsewhere in the tragedy, language has a false transparency.
The relationship of sign to referent is very precisely the arbitrary one
of money to commodity (which we have seen gradually changing with
the development of tragedy). Agamemnon *borrows* from Achille the
sign whose commodity is love in the exchange between Achille and Iphigénie, and he endows it with a different referent by placing it (unknown, necessarily, to Iphigénie herself) within a different set of
exchanges. It obtains its new value from its role in the set Agamemnon/
Iphigénie/empire.[8] Indeed, when Achille learns of this maneuvering
on the part of Agamemnon, his anger is above all aimed not, for example, at the king's treatment of his daughter, but at the abuse of his
own name, of his "coinage": "Quoi Madame! un barbare osera m'in-
sulter." His money would have been debased in the eyes of Iphigénie,
he exclaims, concluding: "Il faut que le cruel qui *m*'a pu *mépriser*/
Apprenne de quel nom il osait abuser" ("The savage who has been
able to *scorn me* ["disprice" me] must learn what name he has dared
abuse" [3.6: pp. 508–09]).[9]

Agamemnon, then, views himself as having entered into two mutually exclusive contractual arrangements, and in order to protect both
he is obliged to lie. Unfortunately such deceit is possible only if the individual is able to suppose himself alone and can act accordingly ("tout
dort, et l'armée, et les vents, et Neptune" ["all is sleeping, the army,
the winds, and Neptune"]). The presence of others forbids it, and there
is no ambiguity in Agamemnon's fear of discovery:

Déjà le jour plus grand nous frappe et nous éclaire;

Déjà même l'on entre et j'entends quelque bruit.
C'est Achille. Va, pars. Dieux! Ulysse le suit!   [1.1: p. 483]

[Already a greater brightness is striking upon us and giving us
light; already even someone is coming in and I hear some sound.
It is Achille. Go, leave. Gods! Ulysse is coming in after!]

With the arrival of both Achille and Ulysse, Agamemnon obviously
risks having all his dishonest dealings brought to light: that that arrival
should occur with the coming of the dawn is certainly no more accidental than any other event in Racinian tragedy. Now the selfish attempts of the supreme king of the Greeks to protect his own interests
in two mutually exclusive contracts must collide with the equally
self-centered efforts of the other two to protect theirs (which is the
cause of Achille's anger). Ulysse's concerns are bound up with
those of the Greek armies and the winning of an empire. Those of
Achille are rather more complicated.

First, there is the agreement of the groom with the bride's father,
and we know from what Arcas has said that the marriage is virtually
accorded and assured.[10] The coinage of this contract has already
been debased by Agamemnon, who has borrowed it from Achille in
order to turn it aside to his own ends. As a result of that manipulation there is the temporary lovers' quarrel at the end of act 2. Second,
there is the contract between the betrothed themselves: that can
clearly not be fulfilled should one of them disappear. Later on Achille
will insist on that fact in much the same terms as those he will use
to express his resentment of Agamemnon's misuse of his language and
name: Agamemnon will resist the hero's objections to the sacrifice of
Iphigénie, and Achille will exclaim, ". . . elle n'est plus à vous:/On ne
m'abuse point . . ." ("she is no longer yours: No one plays tricks upon
me"[4.6: p. 520]). As a reason for not sacrificing Iphigénie this would
be almost ludicrously egotistical on Achille's part—if it were not that
the whole social order depends for its well-being on the series of contracts
in which at this moment Iphigénie herself is considered simply as
one element. Third, there is the fact that Agamemnon's contract with
Iphigénie calls for the fulfillment of both these others.

Against these "local" contracts account must also be taken of the
fact that Achille's glory can only be enhanced by victory at Troy.

He attempts to strengthen his hand with an imaginary exchange supposed to have occurred thanks to Achille, and claims that the Greeks' loss of Helen is balanced by the Trojans' loss of Eriphile:

> les Troyens pleurent une autre Hélène
> Que vous avez captive envoyée à Mécène:
> Car, je ne doute point, cette jeune beauté
> Garde en vain un secret que trahit sa fierté;
> Et son silence même, accusant sa noblesse,
> Nous dit qu'elle nous cache une illustre princesse.
>
> [1.2: pp. 485–86]

[the Trojans are weeping for another Hélène whom you have sent as a captive to Mycenae: for, I have no doubt, this young beauty is keeping in vain a secret which her proudness betrays; and her very silence, bearing witness to her nobility, tells us she is concealing an illustrious princess from us.]

The king is clearly casting around for something with which to save himself. His confusion is apparent: this entire claim is a matter of guesswork on his part. Since the Greeks have had no recent contact with Troy, there can be no knowledge whatsoever as to their reaction to Eriphile's capture; since Agamemnon is merely hoping Eriphile may be of rank equal to Hélène ("je ne doute point") he can hardly say that she is keeping her "secret" in vain; and there could easily be so many reasons for her silence that to suggest that it is eloquent of her high rank is simply a counsel of despair.

It is with some justice, therefore, that Achille brushes aside this specious argument ("Non, non, tous ces détours sont trop ingénieux" "No, no, all these devices are too clever by half" [1.2: p. 486]), yet the fact remains that the king's suggestion prepares the way for a different exchange. For Eriphile is indeed a princess, albeit fitting into a different set of alliances. Yet it is these which will later make possible her substitution for Iphigénie in the exchange that is to be consecrated by the human sacrifice. As for his own death, Achille rejects it as having nothing to do with the present case and as being a fair exchange for immortality in renown. Moreover, the latter is part of the social structure, and as it can be affected by the individual's activity (it is "dans nos propres mains" [1.2: p. 486]), reflects the individual's possession of himself and his solvency. The former is beyond that control and as a counter in society's exchange systems is nonproductive: "Les dieux sont de nos jours les maîtres souverains;/Mais. . . ."

Human activity is a *value* whose *price* may be death, but whose *reward* is glory—in this particular exchange. He adds, at the same time, that in the contract with Agamemnon whose exchange value is Iphigénie, he himself is not yet free of debt:

> Et quand *moi* seul enfin il faudrait l'assiéger,
> *Patrocle et moi*, seigneur, *nous* irons *vous venger.*
> Mais non, c'est en *vos* mains que le destin la [Troie] livre;
> *Je* n'aspire en effet qu'à l'honneur de *vous* suivre.
> *Je* ne *vous* presse plus d'approuver les transports
> D'un amour qui *m*'allait éloigner de ces bords;
> Ce même amour, soigneux de votre renommée,
> Veut qu'ici *mon* exemple encourage l'armée,
> Et *me* defend surtout de *vous* abandonner
> Aux timides conseils qu'on ose vous donner.   [1.2: p. 486]

[And even if *I* had to go and lay siege alone to (Troy), *Patrocle and I*, my lord, *we* would go *to avenge you*. But no, destiny is giving (Troy) into *your* hands; *I* aspire only indeed to the honor of following *you*. *I* no longer push *you* to approve of the ecstasies of a love that was to remove *me* far from these shores; This same love, careful of *your* honor, demands that *my* example should encourage the army here, and forbids *me* above all to abandon *you* to the cautious advice they dare give you.]

After Achille's departure, Ulysse reminds Agamemnon of the bargain into which he has entered with the Greeks, and recalls that the entire campaign against Troy is itself no more than the fulfillment of a more ancient contract sworn among all the Greek leaders—ex-suitors of Helen—and Tyndareus, her father, in accordance with which they owe it to Ménélas to bring Paris to justice. He remarks, in addition, that it is Agamemnon himself who has enforced this oath, the completion of this contract: "Mais sans vous ce serment que l'amour a dicté,/ Libres de cet amour, l'aurions-nous respecté?" ("But had it not been for you, would we, freed of this love, have respected the oath that love dictated to us?" [1.3: p. 487]).

It becomes clear that a whole series of more or less ancient contractual agreements and exchanges forming the very fabric of society are being seriously threatened. A new bargain has been forced upon its members, a bargain indeed external to the society as such, since it has been imposed from without by an unnatural and asocial "divinity." And that "divinity" itself, if we are to believe Achille, is no more than a rather different human society whose priorities can be rendered in terms equivalent to those which cover his own: "Ne songeons qu'à nous rendre immortels comme eux-mêmes" ("Let us think only of making ourselves immortal like them" [1.2: p. 486]).

This new bargain is being demanded of one society by another in complete disregard of the sum of the victim's contractual arrangements upon which the well-being of the body politic depends. As king, Agamemnon's attempts to evade this new contract—but into which he had already entered for the sake of his own glory, and not in the least unwillingly—may thus be seen as an effort to maintain the state. As king, he *is* the state, and his own contracts may be thought to represent those of the state. In falsifying them he is therefore deceiving the body politic, and it is scarcely surprising that Arcas can describe him as he stands before the avenging Achille at the end of the play as "le triste Agamemnon, qui n'ose l'avouer" ("Melancholy Agamemnon, who dares not look upon her" [5.5: p. 531]).

Now in terms of the play's society, Troy represents a kind of promised land, a pathway to immortality, a sort of myth linking the Greek people to the idea of their destiny: it is, as Russell Pfohl observes, a space of myth lying both before and after the tragedy. In that sense it has nothing to do with the contracts of the society whose functioning we are watching for the duration of the play. Hélène herself, as an object from the past, a memory only, and now a distant goal in the future beyond the time of the play, is completely absorbed into this mythical space. It is manifest that unless Iphigénie can transform herself into a link with the mythical, as do both Rotrou's and Euripides', the social individual is quite inadequate (or *inappropriate*) counter in the exchange. What is really needed is a sacrifice that itself exists in the mythical "time out" of human society.[11]

Racine discovers such a sacrific in the person of Eriphile, daughter of Helen and the equally mythical personage of Theseus, who arrives in the company of Clytemnestre and Iphigénie, and who ". . . de son destin, qu'elle ne connaît pas,/Vient, dit-elle, en Aulide interroger Calchas" ("says she is coming to Aulide to question Calchas about her fortune which she does not know" [1.4: p. 489]). She alone, it would seem, accepts the idea of a *destiny*. For Agamemnon the gods are no more than examiners, justicers of his own power and glory. For Achille, they represent mere patterns for emulation. For Ulysse, they become counters in the maneuvers leading to the greater brillance and might of Greece, whose victory will become "l'eternel entretien des siècles à venir" ("the everlasting talk of the centuries to come" [1.4: p. 490]). To all these calculators of social being, Eriphile opposes the idea of some absolute being.

She appears before us immediately as a person with no contractual ties within the structure of social exchanges. Captive of Achille, and therefore no longer a member of the society either of Troy or of Lesbos, unacknowledged daughter of an uncontracted (because secret, and not ratified by society) marriage, she is politically, socially, and in terms of kinship a nonperson. Indeed, not only is she socially a "stranger" ("remise dès l'enfance en des bras étrangers" "placed in a foreign [strange] arms from birth" [2.1: p. 491]),[12] but she feels alienated both biologically and psychologically:

> *Je* reçus et *je* vois le jour que *je* respire,
> Sans que père ni mère ait daigné *me* sourire,
> *J*'ignore qui *je* suis; et, pour comble d'horreur,
> Un oracle effrayant *m*'attache à *mon* erreur,
> Et, quand *je* veux chercher le sang qui *m*'a fait naître,
> *Me* dit que sans périr *je* ne *me* puis connaître.   [2.1: p. 491]

[*I* received and *I* look upon the light air that *I* breathe, without having had a father or mother deign to smile upon me, *I* do not know who *I* am; and as a final horror, a frightful oracle fastens *me* to *my* ignorance, and tells *me*, whenever *I* wish to find out of what blood *I* am born, that *I* cannot know *myself* without dying.]

This speech is remarkable for the fact that *all* its pronouns are first person singular. When the others speak it is almost always in terms of exchange, and the other person is essential to speech, though always subordinate to the self and operative only in terms of the first person.

With Eriphile, no exchange is possible: she views herself as no-person, and she knows that her accession to being will coincide with her death, and cannot come to her through society. All the others, by their very involvement in the system of exchanges, affirm themselves in their *social* being. For them, *being* in a simply existential sense is a matter of no stated concern and of no interest. They define themselves and are defined by others only through their sociopolitical role. Eriphile is cut off from them by her search for some personal identity having nothing to do with others.

The only social contracts into which she could enter, and indeed has entered, are mistakenly one-sided: Iphigénie, says Doris, will protect Eriphile (*"Elle vous l'a promis et juré devant moi"* [2.1: p. 492]), but, as Iphigénie's rival, Eriphile cannot but play this false, for all the legalism of the terms in which it is expressed. This very rivalry supposes the possibility of another exchange: this time between Achille and Eriphile.[13] But once again it is nonexistent, or at best one-sided. That one-sidedness is emphasized by Achille's rape:

> Cet Achille, l'auteur de tex maux et des miens,
> Dont la sanglante main m'enleva prisonnière,
> Qui m'arracha d'un coup ma naissance et ton père,
> De qui, jusques au nom, tout doit m'être odieux,
> Est de tous les mortels le plus cher à mes yeux.   [2.1: p. 492]

> [This Achille, the cause of your misfortunes and mine, whose bloody hand bore me off a prisoner, who at one blow ripped away from me my birth and your father, about whom everything, even his name, must be hateful to me, is the dearest of all mortals to my eyes.]

She herself views this love as socially abnormal. Like the gods to whom she must be joined if she is to know herself, she is unnatural.[14] To love Achille she must hate Iphigénie and the bargain she offers: but this rejection is only the sign of a much more all-embracing one. *For to love Achille, she must reject all the norms that make possible the system of exchanges within society.*

Lacking social identity she can receive her being only from herself, and in this case that will mean through her association with Helen and Theseus in a revelation from the gods. From the time of her very first appearance she is a part of what Mircea Eliade refers to as *illud tempus*: the no-time (or eternity) of myth. As both Barthes and Goldmann have observed, Eriphile represents the *tragic universe*, while the others move in a *providential* or *bourgeois* world.[15] This "tragic universe" is the final hypostatization of that space of nonmeaning within discourse of which I have spoken so much earlier. It gives a name to what escapes society's orders, to what our discourses cannot analyze: it makes it something we can *know* precisely in its very difference. Or rather, perhaps, one should say that we can thereby define both the way in which we cannot know it (because it is not subject to our analytical tools) and the reason we cannot know it (because, for example—in this case—it participates in the "divine").

I would therefore prefer to put the matter rather differently from the two French critics. On the one hand I would say that there is indeed a bourgeois world in which relationships are organized along the axes of a series of exchanges, each one linked with a preceding and a succeeding one: a series that must be endless if the society is to continue. On the other hand there is a universe in which this kind of exchange has no meaning whatsoever. Here what is at stake is something that may be called personal identity—"being in itself" perhaps—and this is confirmed not by activity aimed at possession, but by the assertion of participation in a "timeless" structure of myth. Eriphile does not seek to enter into a contract with Achille—quite the opposite, she refuses to speak with him about such a contract, though she has the opportunity. She rejects the money of society's language. In response to the calculations of the rest, she can offer only obscure feelings: "Une secrète voix m'ordonna de partir." And she comes to Aulide only in the hope of imposing the weight of her universe upon their world, in the hope that "quelqu'un de mes malheurs se répandrait sur eux" ("Some one of my misfortunes would spread over them" [2.1: p. 493]).

Once these two "systems" have been placed in opposition to one another, once the representative of something utterly foreign has been injected into the social process from some strange space outside, it is clear that something will have to give. The link that was possible between the two worlds, forged by Iphigénie's growth to "saintliness," is no longer conceivable. If Iphigénie now accepts the idea of death (and by no means readily), it is not as an assertion of her own freedom of action, of her liberty to decide her own fate—quite the contrary, it proceeds from her recognition of a debt to her father. "Ma vie," she says, "est votre bien" (4.3: p. 515). In accepting death, she remains resolutely within the system of exchanges, and for the benefit of Achille, she recalls the viewpoint of Ulysse: "Ce champ si glorieux où vous aspirez tous,/Si mon sang ne l'arrose, est stérile pour vous" ("That so glorious field to which you all aspire, if my blood does not sprinkle it, is sterile for you" [5.2: p. 526]).

In her own eyes she remains a "malheureux objet," a "victime" (5.3: pp. 528, 529), sacrificed essentially to the possessive ambition of her father (and the other Greek leaders) of whom Achille is not so very wrong when he remarks that he seeks "une illustre victoire/Qui le doit enrichir, venger, combler de gloire" ("an illustrious victory that is bound to enrich him, avenge him, cover him with glory" [3.6: p. 508]). A far cry from the proud demand of Rotrou's heroine:

Laissez-moi du combat porter les premiers coups;
Autrement je croirai que vous êtes jaloux,
Et me voulez priver de la gloire suprême
D'être aux Grecs plus qu'Ulysse et plus qu'Achille même.[16]

[Let me bear the first blows of the battle; otherwise I will believe you to be envious, and that you want to deprive me of the supreme glory of being more to the Greeks than Ulysse and more than Achille himself.]

The distance between Eriphile's universe and that of Iphigénie is suggested by the change of command in the camp. Calchas, representative of the gods, we are told, "seul règne, seul commande" (5.3: p. 528) during the period of sacrifice. But I say "suggested" advisedly, for the gods of Calchas are not the God of Abraham and Isaac. They also participated in a social exchange: "La piété sévère exige son offrande" ("Harsh piety demands its offering" [5.3: p. 528]). Those gods are also very different, of course, from Eriphile's.

We are here, I believe, at the crux of the matter. All along I have spoken of an exchange between the gods and society by contractual agreement; "the very nub of the drama." But it is clear that the very idea of exchange necessitates at least a superficial equality between the two parties involved. Between the gods of a mythical "time" and the members of a society situated very much within, and limited by, the here and now, this condition can evidently not be met. The rule of Calchas is every bit as much that of ambition as Agamemnon's own rule, and Eriphile's objection to his "profanes mains" (5.6: p. 532) is entirely justified. Since this is so, however, it is clear that the interests of society demand that the single (and, as we see, false) contract involving Iphigénie and an empire be subordinated to all those others which *are* the society. The whole of act 4 was taken up by the demonstration of the unnaturalness of this other contract. That Iphigénie is saved not by a theatrical goddess but by Achille defending his own contracts,[17] and that Eriphile accepts her death willingly when she learns simultaneously that she cannot enter (via Achille) this society's exchange processes and that her alliances thrust her into a quite different universe, merely serve once again to emphasize the separation of the two worlds. Eriphile's very presence is a threat that must be rejected.

Her exit from the stage of intersocial exchange is the obverse of her entrance upon it. She had been dragged in by Achille's rape and forced to participate in a situation scarcely understood, the symbol of which remains her memory of the Greek's bloody arm upraised. It is by a lucid but even more brutal self-violation that she rushes off the stage. Marcel Gutwirth has observed that the proposed sacrifice of Iphigénie is "nothing less than a rape with a dagger; Clytemnestre understands it accordingly":

> Un prêtre, environné d'une foule cruelle,
> Portera sur ma fille une main criminelle,
> Déchirera son sein, et, d'un oeil curieux,
> Dans son coeur palpitant consultera les dieux!   [4.4: p. 518][18]

> [A priest, surrounded by a savage crowd, will wield a criminal hand against my daughter, tear open her breast and with his inquisitive eye, consult the gods in her still beating heart!]

Eriphile, who "prend le sacré couteau, le plonge dans son sein" (5.6: p. 532), herself ritualizes this violation and makes of it, in some sense and for herself, a kind of purification of the blood spilled by Achille. Eriphile is utterly out of place in this "new" contractual society and the brutal violence of her entrance and exit merely serves to emphasize the fact. The sword and the knife bracket the presence of Eriphile just as Amurat's order against the life of Bajazet bracketed the state of nature in the earlier play. The difference is that here Eriphile is an intruder into an already (and permanently) established exchange society.

Between Iphigénie/Eriphile[19] and Iphigénie, between the death of the one whose search never exceeds that of her own identity and the life of the other, whose search fits into the social pattern, there can be no hesitation on the part of these practical men. The death of the first, who cannot fit into society, is set against a possessive conquest ("puisque Troie enfin est le prix de sa mort," [5.6: p. 532]). It is only fitting that this should finally be announced by Ulysse, the one person who throughout has had no hesitation in declaring for "possessive individualism." Nor is it any less fitting that it should be "la seule Iphigénie" (5.6: p. 533) who weeps for the loss of Eriphile. Herself unable to attain the sublimity of her predecessors, she nonetheless remained sufficiently aware of its presence, however obscurely (see note 13), and desirous enough to safeguard it as to attempt to protect Eriphile, in whom she recognized it. Reduced at the end to no more than the object that will seal the "auguste alliance" of Agamemnon and Achille, she alone, no longer an agent, appears to understand and be concerned by what is lost.[20]

By separating into two different persons the universe of Eriphile and the altogether more restricted world of Iphigénie, Racine has essentially affirmed (perhaps *à regret*) the victory of economic individualism. The total irrelevance of Clytemnestre's prayer at the end, indeed its misdirection, is the further indication of this—if it were needed. Indeed, that the whole affair should have proceeded from no more than the misunderstanding of a vague oracular pronouncement also confirms the utter lack of pertinence in the notion of the gods represented by Calchas and his ilk. That the misunderstanding was possible in the first place is the sign in this play that the mythical universe has no place in a society of individuals.

From the fact that *Iphigénie* was performed more times in succession than any other of Racine's plays, and from the fact that it was chosen for the celebrations accompanying the entry into France in

1680 of the future Dauphine,[21] we may assume that the play struck a particularly responsive chord among the contemporary theatre-going public. In the political age of Hobbes and Locke and the economic era of Colbert and Petty (the latter a close friend of Dryden, Rymer, and Hobbes, among others), we are perhaps justified in seeking this chord in a concept of possessive individualism that was already beginning to formulate itself at the time when Corneille was writing a tragedy like *Médée.*

   The secularization of tragedy to which Barthes refers can be generalized away from the Racinian canon—indeed, away from tragedy altogether. For neoclassicism itself marks a secularization, and it is not only to Goldmann that we can look for the effect of an unfamiliar distancing from God. The breaking of the chain has thrown the individual back upon his own resources: what Machiavelli did for the statesman and Copernicus or Galileo for the scientist, Cervantes perhaps did for the artist. The hero of myth brought with him a whole universe onto the sixteenth-century stage and did his level best to link that universe with the world of his new public. A century later, the same protagonists are doing their utmost to escape the weight of that universe, and it is not by chance that Racine will choose to present these heroes and their problems anew by a return from the past precisely at the center of his next play, *Phèdre,* or that Eriphile dies after she has unsuccessfully attempted to condemn their escape from the "time" of myth and their entry into a Hobbesian civil society.

   I am not seeking simply to suggest that Racine's play is no more than a commentary on man in the society of his time. I am rather affirming that the impulses that lead to a Hobbesian concept of the political and social contract, based on the idea of individuals acting together in mutual support of their own interests, or to a late-mercantilist idea of the economic exchange, are the same impulses that give us the individual acting in accordance with certain psychosocial rules, the character following certain esthetic laws in neoclassical literature. If these last are relatively easy to express in economic or social terms that is not because the play is simply a commentary on economics or on society, but because the economic and social structures are essentially similar (see, too, note 8) to the poetic ones I have just referred to as "esthetic laws," as they are used, or revealed, in Racine's tragedies.

Rotrou's Iphigénie finally gives herself to a view of humanity as part of a total divine plan, and it is indeed possible to refer to her, as Charles R. Walker does to Euripides' heroine, as "a true saint."[22] Racine removes the irrational, mythical patterns in the person of Eriphile and affirms a completely rational intrahuman system of exchange. In his analysis of "seventeenth-century individualism" it seems to me that C. B. Macpherson has accurately described the nature of the world confronted by Eriphile, and that his description sufficiently accounts for the necessity of her removal:

> Its possessive quality is found in its conception of the individual as essentially the proprietor of his own person or capacities, owing nothing to society for them. The individual was seen neither as a moral whole, nor as part of a larger social whole, but as an owner of himself. The relation of ownership, having become for more and more men the critically important relation determining their actual freedom and actual prospect of realizing their full potentialities, was read back into the nature of the individual. The individual, it was thought, is free inasmuch as he is proprietor of his person and capacities. The human essence is freedom from dependence on the wills of others, and freedom is a function of possession. Society becomes a lot of free individuals related to each other as proprietors of their own capacities and of what they have acquired by their exercise. Society consists of relations of exchange between proprietors. Political society becomes a calculated device for the protection of this property and for the maintenance of an orderly relation of exchange.[23]

That I came across this passage after writing the original version of this chapter seems to afford confirmation of my analysis and many of the suggestions I have been making regarding the correspondence of "systems." Macpherson's analysis gives deeper meaning to the "monades psychologiques," as they are called by Barthes, and provides a broader meaning for the systems of exchange I have suggested as lying at the basis of the play: these systematic processes and the individualistic psychology that accompanies them are the fundamental elements of the new analytico-referential discourse.

For what is significant here is not that one can break down Racine's tragedy of *Iphigénie* into a pattern of exchange which, in itself, has been readily identified by many as providing the basic form of the "linguistic circuit" (and therefore doubtless as at the bottom of any and all discourse), but that this pattern has been made explicit and specifically *named*: Racine has chosen to present it here as an economic and social process. That is to say that the merely available sign system that all language is has been narrowed down to the domain of a singular specification that may then be readily assimilated to and interpreted as some reality *outside* language and discourse, rendered *in* it. Discourse has been given a particular referential fullness, and the system (here, of tragedy) has become a codification of the *real*.

11 From Phèdre to History: The Truths of Time and the Fictions of Eternity

almost emblematic

In the *Spaccio de la bestia trionfante* (1584), Giordano Bruno proclaimed the replacement of the monster of human ignorance by reason, which would lift man above the limits of her mere body (which provides the material for his thinking by resemblances) into the realm of angelic knowledge. Less mystically, but no less optimistically, Francis Bacon proclaimed the same emancipation, and in terms that suggest some acquaintance with the writings of the Italian philosopher (whom he could well have met in person when Bruno was in England in the 1580s).

Bacon prayed:

> Lastly, that knowledge being now discharged of that venom which the serpent infused into it, and which makes the mind of man to swell, we may not be wise above measure and sobriety, but cultivate truth in charity.

Language, then, is no longer to be a calumny, no longer a falsifier of what it relates; it is to be a bearer of truth. That truth will be that of "things themselves," and it will enable man "to command nature in action." For "time is like a river which has brought down to us things that are light and puffed up, while those which are weighty and solid have sunk."[1] The truth had disappeared because "time" had been beyond human control: indeed, beyond human ken.

To make possible the establishment of this new truth and of this new (and "legitimate," writes Bacon) knowledge of things that will permit man to command nature, a new concept of time is need. Time had been an uncontrollable flow, a veritable flood whose relationship with the confusion of speech (at Babel) is no doubt apparent from their very proximity in *Genesis*. Human governance held no sway here. This "time" was unavailable for any human analysis because it represented—indeed, it *was*—the presence of divine providence. Such a concept meant that historiography could only be viewed as interpretation of a divine ordering and history itself could only be the *mise-en-place* of such a nonhuman ordering. The new reason of Bacon, of Hobbes, of Vico, even of Bruno earlier, will thus call for a new concept of time and a new concept of *human* history. It will call for a reordering of logic and of speech—as undertaken in the second half of the century by the logicians and grammarians of Port-Royal. History will have to become a matter of human responsibility.

This division, performed in *Phèdre* even more dramatically than in *Iphigénie*, will be conceptualized a little later by Vico, who establishes an opposition between "an ideal eternal history" and its traversal "in time by the history of every nation in its rise, development, maturity, decline and fall."[2] The ideal history is also common to the divine institutions that precede the birth of human institutions. National developments are instituted in history, divine institutions are beyond "time" and "history." Indeed, the *New Science* presents itself as but a long demonstration of this premise:

> Our new Science must therefore be a demonstration, so to speak, of what providence has wrought in history, for it must be a history of the institutions by which, without human discernment or counsel, and often against the designs of men, providence has ordered this great city of the human race. For though this world has been created in time and particular, the institutions established therein by providence are universal and eternal.[3]

Vico, who refers constantly to Bacon as the founder of true scientific method, is concerned entirely with establishing a "certain history" of the foundation and "continuous sequence or coherence" of the nations, of civil societies according to "scientific principles" (p. 59). This history is coincident with that of the human mind (p. 78, for example), of which the new idea of history is simply one manifestation: but since they do thus coincide, it is apparent that the appearance of historical discourse (in our sense of a human history, for whose sequence or coherence man's free will is responsible)[4] must coincide with a similar development in civil society. The text of *Phèdre* also performs this manifestation.

The new Adam will apply his names to things and as God (as Hobbes puts it) will create a new temporal world. He will "stretch the deplorably narrow limits of man's dominion over nature to their promised bounds"; his concern is with the future he will pass on to his sons.[5] Bacon's *mundus alter*, the world of the mind made manifest as an *otherness*, as the place of things themselves made functional for the benefit of mankind, will permit the father to conduct the son into his new history. The new reason (*nova ratio*), the legitimate science (*modus ille legitimus*) will have to be such as to constitute its own time, its own history: it will institute itself as the only place of truth (hence the title, *The Great Instauration*).

For Bacon this new masculine birth of time, as he calls it, will permit not only a right knowledge of things, but the general acquisition of wealth and possessions, ultimately combined with (and this is the entire aim of *The Great Instauration*), indeed provoking, an equilibrium in the social order. This latter aspect was manifest in *Iphigénie*. Certainly it is the principal goal of Hobbes in his various writings, and it seems useful to resume a few more aspects of this goal in order to provide a more complete context for the analysis of *Phèdre*.

Time, argues Hobbes, is a word by which we mark our perception of a body (for example) "passing out of one space into another by continual succession" (cf. Vico's "sequence"), it is a notion that is found "only in the thought of the mind" (cf. Bacon, above): "TIME *is the* phantasm [=image, idea] *of before and after in motion . . . ; time is a phantasm of motion numbered*."[6] Hobbes is speaking here specifically of time in relation to space, in terms, that is to say, of phenomenal reality—which is thereby marked (for us) by our inability to grasp it as anything but a part of a logical ordering. Time, therefore, in this conception, is the nomination of continuity ascribed by an act of human will to the perception of discontinuous objects in motion. It is this naming, and this naming alone, that makes it possible for us to entertain such notions as those signified by *past*, *present*, and *future*.[7] These terms represent nothing more, or less, than the reintroduction of discreteness into the general idea of time: the naming of any moment in time is the same as that of any object in space, but it represents an inversion. For where it is indeed the perceived object that allows us to have a notion of space, it is time in general, itself an extrapolation from the "phantasm" of motion in space, that allows us to conceptualize the notion of a moment in time as part of a continuous ("historical") flow. Without such a notion of time, the idea of history (and of all institutions connected with it) as it exists for us since the European seventeenth century would be inconceivable.

The idea of time, then, with all its implications—principally social (and ideological) as regards the terms in which I have been speaking— is for Hobbes, as it was for Bacon and as it will be for Vico, a creation of the individual human mind.[8] Indeed, insofar as it represents, with space, one of the primary phantasms of the mind, a logical a priori, the idea of time may be said to perform the presence of that mind within its own systems (cf. again Vico), of which the principal one, for Hobbes and Vico certainly, perhaps for Bacon and possible for the entire Western European seventeenth century, was the sociopolitical. By the end of the century sociopolitical history was viewed as a human invention, to whatever extent it might still be based on divine prerogative. Even when a Bossuet continues to give an eschatalogical cast to history (in the *Histoire universelle*) such a view is conservative for the time, and he, too, notes that the lesson of history is above all that of humanity's possibility of perfecting its own institutions (in the little time it has left, to be sure, but Bossuet is considerably less apocalyptic than earlier religious writers on this subject). Vico, whatever his originality, is far more typical of his age when he marks the opposition *in kind* between divine providence and the temporal sequentiality, the historical coherence, of human institutions.

In this way Isaac Newton strove to deal with a dual notion of temporality in the first *Scholium* of the *Principia*. There is, first of all, a kind of divine time with which we are unable to deal scientifically: "Absolute, true, and mathematical time, of itself, and from its own nature, flows equally without relation to anything external, and by another name is called duration . . ." There is no question in Newton's mind that this "absolute time" is real and it is to be compared, as Jeremy Bernstein has observed, with "relative, apparent and common

time," which "is some sensible and external (whether accurate or un-
equable) measure of duration by the means of motion, which is com-
monly used instead of true time; such as an hour, a month, a year."
This is clearly close to Hobbes's definition: for Newton human time
is but a measure of an absolute temporality beyond human control.
But in effect that measure is the only time available to us: and in that
we can perhaps see the ultimate source of Vico's conception of the
two temporalities. Bernstein goes on:

> In other words Newton attempted to distinguish between "com-
> mon" time as measured by clocks and some sort of "absolute"
> time whose primary existence was in the consciousness of God.
> If pressed on this distinction, as he was in the famous correspond-
> ence between Leibniz and the Reverend Samuel Clarke, chaplain
> to the Prince of Wales and a protégé of Newton, Newton retreated
> to a position of impregnable theological mysticism. As Clarke
> wrote, certainly with the approval of Newton, in his fourth reply
> to Leibniz, ". . . space and duration are not *hors de Dieu*, but are
> caused by, and are immediate and necessary consequences of
> His existence."[9]

Like Newton in the domain of scientific measurement and Vico in
that of nations, Hobbes had conceived of human institutions and their
temporality as having "certainly been made by man, and [as based on
principles] therefore to be found within the modifications of our
own human mind.[10] The historical existence of societies, as the sum
of their institutions, has thus for its origin the human will. This will
takes its point of departure, for Vico (and Newton) as for Bossuet,
though without the atemporal limitations imposed by the latter, in the
divine constitution of nature and natural "man."[11] And time as social history (sequence, coherence, continuity) is manifest *only* in human institutions.

It seems to me that Racine's *Phèdre* (or at least certain of its speakers)
performs the establishment of such an historically oriented society by,
from, individual will. In doing so it renders impossible any subsequent
"tragic," because its very installation (in the form of a specified
origin of human institutions) affirms the explicative power of an ordered discourse. The discourse, whether literary or social, is given
(as we have previously seen) as the result of an act of will. It is the

mythic = asocial Thèdre
sociopol = Aricie

deliberate replacement of a divine, humanly indifferent (and hence uncomprehended and unorganized) nature by a temporal, historical, and social organization. It is significant that Hobbes should choose to refer to such an installation as the replacement of the divine Logos by a human *logos*: in creating "that great LEVIATHAN called a COMMON-WEALTH" art also sets up

> the *Pacts* and *Covenants*, by which the parts of the Body Politique were at first made, set together, and united, [which] resemble that *Fiat*, or the *Let us make man*, pronounced by God in the Creation.[12]

This fiat, however, is an entirely human one.

I am suggesting, once again, that the classical episteme in France, England, Italy—and indeed Europe generally, though the moments and precise modalities of its establishment vary—has as its signature in literary discourse an effort to codify a quasi-taxonomic, classificatory expression of knowledge such that this discourse may be taken as an experimental one instituting a "science" of man on a conscious analogy with the discursive development of the experimental sciences. Literature thus becomes a kind of treasury of such knowledge, and *as such* available to its readers (essentially, by then, the aristocracy and the fast-rising bourgeoisie). Racine's *Iphigénie*, interpreted in this light, argues the very terms of Bacon's discourse, removing the asocial, mythic (providential) element from a society based on an economic and contractual equilibrium, firmly situated in a history whose organized schema permits the continuation of contractual series and which is in turn identified with it, defined by it.

To the extent that the mythic (the presence of Phèdre, for my analysis) and the sociopolitical (name—Aricie) elements are quantitatively inverted, the text of *Phèdre* is a reversal of that of *Iphigénie*. It is therefore revealing that the conclusion should be the same: Aricie, adopted as the daughter of Thésée—an action that in the very last line deliberately negates *all* the "past" of (and in) the play[13]—will install the historical society whose political existence has been the main area of discussion between herself and Hippolyte. Her very adoption by Thésée assures a political and temporal *succession*, as opposed to the lack of its represented (presented) in the triangle of rivalry,

Hippolyte-Phèdre-Thésée. The ambiguity of Hippolyte's position will
be examined hereafter.

Taken together *Iphigénie* and *Phèdre* manifest two opposite tests of
the validity of this particular type of social code as a "true" representation of human reality. As such the history they institute may be
taken as the "correct" basis of a human society: Aricie, the exile
from the noncontractual society of Phèdre, of Thésée, of Hippolyte
(ambiguously), will found the new Greek order. The others mentioned
enter only into such contracts as will allow the satisfaction of a private
desire, and a desire whose project preexists in the will of divine providence ("O haine de Vénus! O fatale colère!"; "Puisque Vénus le veut";
"C'est Vénus toute entière à sa proie attachée"; "Objet infortuné des
vengeances célestes") ("Oh hatred of Venus! Oh fatal rage!"; "Since
Venus wills it"; "It is Venus in single-minded pursuit of her prey";
"Miserable object of divine vengeance"), and while it is true that, at
least in the play, the same argument cannot clearly be made as concerns Hippolyte, yet he does become the victim of such a project to
the extent that Phèdre herself, who curses him and then hounds him
to death, participates in such providence.

It is perhaps a less simply piously motivated decision than has hitherto appeared that after *Phèdre*, Racine, with Boileau, should have become royal historiographer, that he should write of *history* for the *king*:[14]
an idea proposed to Louis before in the 1666 *dédicace* to *Alexandre*.

The play is instituted on a note that sets these ideas in motion right
away. Whatever may have been the criticism heaped upon Hippolyte's
weaknesses (as a person—which shows the effectiveness of the classical installation of a psychological literature as a code of the real), it is
not confirmed by the first line of the play, which names, on the contrary, the presence of an individual will: "Le dessein en est pris: je
pars." Furthermore, the prince's initial concern, by which this willfulness is explained, is with temporality: "Depuis plus de six mois
éloigné de mon père" (1.1: p. 543).

The question of time for Hippolyte is immediately linked with the
absence of the father, as it is also tied up with "agitation" and a
"doute mortel." This initial speech of Hippolyte thus establishes a
quite definite opposition: the awareness of time, the absence of the
father, and a "mortal doubt," against "l'aimable Trézène (where no

266

such agitation was suffered), the presence of the father, and the "heureux temps" (p. 544), where in fact there was no consciousness of temporality: when Trézène was nothing but "ces paisibles lieux si chers à
votre enfance" ("these calm places so dear to your childhood"), as
Théramène puts it. Obviously a psychoanalysis is possible here and, in
the abstract, there may be some identity between the function of
myth and that of the fantasm; as Mauron remarks: "Le recul myth-
ologique dont Racine joue avec tant d'art, glissant subtilement du
mythe à l'histoire, correspond . . . au recul vers des pensèes inconsci-
entes" ("The mythological retreat with which Racine plays with such
art, slipping subtly from myth to history, corresponds . . . to the retreat toward unconscious thought.")[15] Again, I am concerned here
with classical tragedy as a type of discourse, not as representing a
reality of which it would be the transparent medium, but as participating in a network of discourses that will subsequently *set* that
"reality." I wish, therefore, to avoid the temptation of reading for a
sense that preexists the discourse of tragedy in question (of which
the text under analysis is one example)—though I do not deny that
there may be such a sense, or that I may not always have avoided the
temptation.

The initial opposition thus named by Hippolyte is very quickly
generalized. On the one hand it will be manifested in the essentially
political preoccupations represented by Aricie (her first nomination
is in these terms: "cette jeune Aricie,/Reste d'un sang fatal *conjuré*
contre nous" ["this young Aricie, last remnant of a fatal blood which
plotted against us"] —whatever the ambiguity of the last three words
as they apply to Hippolyte), and on the other it will be filled out by
the mythic presence of Phèdre herself. Hippolyte, like the very place
of Trézène, forms the meeting point of this opposition, and we may
note in passing that with the exception of the first, all his famous delayed departures are intended (whatever the psychological reasons
provided by subsequent criticism) for the *political* purpose of winning
Athens for Aricie; and incidentally for himself. Even the last departure of all will be turned by Hippolyte to such a goal—to seek allies in
order to prevent a political defeat for himself and Aricie at the hands
of his stepmother: "Ne souffrons pas que Phèdre, assemblant nos
débris,/Du trône paternel nous chasse l'un et l'autre" ("Do not let us

allow Phèdre, joining together what we have cast off, chase each one
of us from our paternal throne" [5.1: p. 584]).

Phèdre's presence in Trézène is that of an ahistorical network, one
which includes Hippolyte and from which he was already half-detached
by his love for Aricie—the *legitimate* inheritor of a throne, in whom,
as I have suggested, the purely political element is no less important
than any mutual love. Phèdre's presence marks a "time" out of history:
the phrase "Depuis que sur ces bords *les dieux ont envoyé* / La fille de
Minos et de Pasiphaé" ("Since *the gods have sent* to these shores the
daughter of Minos and Pasiphaé"), reflects this. "Depuis" also directly
links past to present and in so doing tends to destroy the passage itself from one to the other. In this light, Hippolyte's lament "Cet heureux temps n'est plus" indicates not so much a passing from time into no-
time as the passage into consciousness—and the prince's first departure
is the mark of a "regression to childhood." Trézène is no longer its
place, and so his initial desire is to "chercher [son] père" (1.5: p.
546).

Hippolyte, then, is placed before a doubly changed situation. By
loving Aricie he is turning against his father and his childhood; and
this activity is immediately politicized ("Mon père la réprouve" ["My
father disapproves of her"] because of her political role) and tem-
poralized ("depuis quelques jours," "tout change"). He has not so
much left behind a past as he has entered "time" by quitting the altar
of Diana and the arts of Neptune. At the same time, however, Hippolyte has been "made conscious" of a fundamental opposition between this temporality and the indifference of Phèdre's presence to
any such institution. Her presence marks a no-time, it is the "presence"
of eternity, and if we can say that the "time" that was "heureux"
was so essentially because it was not marked by consciousness and the
mortality of doubt, we can also say that what Hippolyte leaves implicit is that the notion of historical time itself is contravened by the
presence of Phèdre.

For if Aricie is attached to a political past and the question of a
legitimate succession, Phèdre is attached to myth: in her, "désordre"
is "éternel" (1.2: p. 547), silence is "inhuman" or "éternel" (1.3:
pp. 550, 551), "cris" are likewise "éternels," she sees Hippolyte "sans
cesse" (p. 552), and these are the qualifiers constantly applied to her.

Odette de Mourgues comments on the no-time of Phèdre when she notes
that her "fate is contained in one moment," between the preparation
for death of 1.3 and its consummation in 5.7. Indeed Théramène has
already noted in 1.1 that she is "une femme mourante et qui cherche à
mourir" ("a woman who is dying and who is seeking to die").[16] Phèdre
further resumes in herself the combination of day (Pasiphaé) and
night (Minos), and her love for Hippolyte again places the sun and
"l'ombre des forêts" ("the forest shadows") in an opposition she seeks
to resolve in herself. These oppositions constantly meet in the persons of Phèdre, Thésée, and Hippolyte. From the outset, Hippolyte
has himself placed Thésée on a par with Phèdre: his father's reproof
is "l'obstacle éternel" placed between himself and Aricie (1.1: p. 546).
Later he will say that Thésée is hidden "à l'univers" (2.2: p. 557),
and it is this eternity and this "universality" that oppose the legitimacy of Aricie's claims: "Dois-je épouser ses *droits* contre un père ir-
rité?" (Must I espouse her *rights* against an angry father?" [1.1:
p. 546]). The lack of temporality, the presence of universality, the
union of opposites, these are the elements of providence or myth.

   It is no doubt correct, as Barthes has observed, that Thésée is a
chthonic hero,[17] as he is also the representative of an order. But that
does not place him on the side of Aricie, representative of a "legitimate" political dynasty and descended from a "roi noble fils de la
terre" ("a king and noble son of the earth" [2.1: p. 556). On the contrary, where Aricie—the descendant of Pallas and Erechtheus—poses
a *division* between earth and heaven, between the solar Phèdre and
herself, in Thésée and Phèdre the *union* of earth and sky is continued.
Judd Hubert has observed how Thésée and Hippolyte appear to become at times "a kind of solar personification."[18]

   Mythically each of the three is descended from both the sky and
the earth. Theseus is descended by his father Aegeus from Erechtheus
(and thence Gaia), by his mother Aethra from Zeus (and thence
Uranus); Phaedra is descended by her mother from the sun, while
her father Minos places her in opposition to this descent when he becomes judge in the underworld.[19] Hippolyte, as son of Thésée, maintains the dual descent, though it is already humanized through his
mother Antiope. This is no longer the case with Aricie, who is entirely
of the earth—as she insists.

Phèdre, it may be said, seeks to maintain the union through herself and Hippolyte (a union that would also deny the successivity of generations). The stepson is already, with Aricie, devoted to terrestrial concerns in a rather different way: to legitimacy, to a sequential history of which he and Aricie would be the originators. Thésée's return reinstalls unequivocally, at first, the mythic order represented by himself and Phèdre; and in this sense I cannot help but feel that Mauron is wrong when he places Aricie and Thésée on the same "side" of his structural model of the play. Such may be the case at the end when Thésée accepts Aricie as his successor, but it is certainly not the case at the moment of Thésée's return and from then until the *récit de Théramène*: and indeed the "dominant dramatic situation" that Mauron is supposedly illustrating no longer exists, since both Hippolyte and Phèdre are by then dead (or dying), and this situation is intended to show the lines of force throughout the play.[20]

Whereas Phèdre, Thésée, and Hippolyte are bound by their mythical links, which are manifested in many ways in the play—thus, for example, as Mauron has pointed out, in the manner in which Phèdre's fear of her father, judge in Hades, matches that of Hippolyte toward *his* father, king and judge in Attica—Aricie is utterly free of such links. Indeed, her relation to the mythical block is a mirror image of that of Eriphile to the social block in *Iphigénie*. In order for a sociopolitical history to be installed, Phèdre must go; so too must Hippolyte, and so Thésée. The first two, of course, die, but effectively Thésée also goes: for in choosing to become "father" to Aricie he chooses the earth, the order of society that she and Hippolyte would have installed had the latter lived; he chooses to institute legitimacy (and the concept of legitimacy can only occur in a sociopolitical context).[21]

I shall return to this last question, but some few more words are in order concerning the mythic block; for however much (and quasi-exclusively) previous criticism may have treated it, the present chapter places it in a rather particular overall context. It is here, then, that the whole matter of monstrosity is involved. Besides the monster narrated by Théramène at the end, there are four monsters in the play, and they are the entire block of myth. Phèdre is referred to both by herself and by Aricie as one such, and implicitly by both Hippolyte and Thésée. She is a monster because she wishes to invert the "natural" order, because she accuses an innocent, because she presents the "no-time" of eternity (indeed, for her, time as duration can only be "coupable" [2.3: p. 549]), and because her very presence throws the crossroads of Trézène into disorder. If Phèdre is inhuman it is more than just metaphorically, and she is quick to reject the inexact claims of Oenone, who would place her on a human level: "Mortelle, sub-issez le sort d'une mortelle" ("Mortal woman, suffer the fate of a mortal" [4.6: p. 583]). She is a stranger to the society of humans as an Aricie would conceive of it. In this she is matched by Oenone herself (whom Phèdre will call a "monstre execrable"), who recalls that other outsider, Eriphile: "Mon pays, mes enfants, pour vous j'ai tout quitté" ("My homeland, my children, for you I have left everything" [1.3: p. 550]).

Hubert suggests that Thésée's escape from the "cavernes sombres" (3.5: p. 572) with the help of the gods signifies that for them he is not a monster: but he adds right away that his return to Trézène is only to be present at his family's destruction—of which he is at least partly the cause and for which he is certainly the necessary catalyst.[22] Unwittingly Thésée himself goes considerably further. When all seek to hide themselves from him, he exclaims: "Quelle horreur dans ces lieux répandue / Fait fuire . . .?" ("What horror spread throughout this place makes fly . . .?" [3.5: p. 572]). The immediate cause—horror—is, of course, his own presence. His possibility of descending into Hades and returning, his slaying of monsters, as well as his parentage, all place him alongside Phèdre: at least until the final rupture. Then he will find himself in a position similar to that of Hippolyte at the beginning of the play, for he will remain, given up to those "mortels regrets" (5.6: p. 590) which correspond not a little to the "doute mortel" of his son.

Hippolyte is a monster in the eyes of both Thésée and Phèdre, because he is unable to give himself unequivocally to *their* world, to the world into which he was born by virtue of his father. This world he starts to reject after his declaration of love and his increasing preoccupation with the "legitimate" succession of Aricie. Little by little he is drawn backward however, and this is marked by Phèdre's comment

concerning "ses yeux inhumains" (3.1: p. 566). Confronted by the
fact of his father's return, he requests only to be able to emulate him:
he will fight other monsters, die if need be, and thus "*Eternisant* des
jours si noblement finis,/Prouve à *tout l'univers* que j'étais *votre
fils*" ("*Immortalizing* a life so nobly ended, prove to *the whole universe* that I was *your son*" [3.5: p. 572]). Hippolyte's "silence" in
act 4 is his acceptance of a role in the timeless state of his father;
and when he asks Thésée, "Quel temps à mon exil, quel lieu pre-
scrivez-vous?" he receives the only response possible—no time and no
place: "Fusses-tu par delà les colonnes d'Alcide . . ." ("If you were beyond the columns of Hercules" [4.2: p. 578]). The prince's choice of
the sacred place outside Trézène to consecrate his marriage with Aricie connotes a similar acceptance, for that is the one place where
such a marriage cannot be performed: here are all the gods of his father, and here the final monster of the play will answer Thésée's prayer
to Neptune.

Hippolyte remains, nonetheless, in a continually ambiguous situation: if his exile signals his acceptance of the myth of his father, he
also proposes to use it to go to various other political centers to fo-
ment sedition. He is both human and inhuman. This is no doubt the
reason for his mistaken trust in the gods, of whose "équité" and
"intérêt" he speaks, not comprehending (unlike Aricie) that the gods'
participation in an entirely different order of things makes them
strangers to such concepts of socioeconomic exchange (5.2: p. 584).
Hippolyte is both innocent and guilty (more than one critic has noted
his own acquiescence in his death), and this ambiguity emphasizes
his intermediary position. Destroyed nonsensically by Neptune for a
crime he did not commit, he is the *pharmakos*, the scapegoat whose
expulsion and killing will permit the constitution of a new society.
Yet that he is a monster in the eyes of Phèdre and of Thésée is mark
of his belonging to their world, and signals a justification of his purging.

Hippolyte's incapacity to situate the gods "correctly" is in utter
contrast to Aricie's clear-sightedness in their regard: clearly on "the
other side" she has no illusions as to the rules governing the divine
order (5.2: p. 583; 5.3: p. 587). Her incredulity concerning Thésée's
supposed descent alive into Hades ("Croirai-je qu'un mortel, avant sa

dernière heure,/Peut pénétrer des morts la profonde demeure?" ("Am I to believe that a mortal, before his last hour, can penetrate to the deep dwelling of the dead?" [2.1: p. 555]) and the "bruit mal affermi" ("the uncertain rumor") of his death is the sign of her difference. She occupies a quite other scheme of things from the representatives of myth. Until this point Thésée and Phèdre have occupied an entirely mythic scheme of things (Phèdre's parentage, Thésée's fabulous conquests, his supposed descent into the underworld), while Aricie on the contrary has been an entirely secular concern. Hippolyte's love for her is criminal because she is a *political* "criminal," she represents a political Athens without Phèdre and Thésée. If Phèdre is ruled by Venus and other gods, Aricie is bound only by a "sévère loi" that is an entirely political one (2.1: p. 556). In declaring his love for her, Hippolyte also becomes the *homo politicus* whose entire concern will be to reinstate Aricie in what he conceives as her legitimate patrimony.

As he does so he is not at all the politically powerless prince certain critics have claimed him to be. Jean Gaudon argues that Hippolyte has nothing, "not even the right to succeed his father in Athens," and while the detail is exact the generalization is not, for he does have Trézène.[23] Upon the announced death of Thésée, there is no hesitation—as Ismène informs us: "Et déjà pour son roi [Trézène] reconnaît Hippolyte" (2.1: p. 555). But Oenone had already remarked to Phèdre: "Roi de ces bords heureux, Trézène est son partage,/Mais il sait que les lois donnent à votre fils/Les superbes remparts que Minerve a bâtis" ("King of these happy shores, Trézène is his share, but he knows that the laws give your son the proud ramparts built by Minerva" [1.5: p. 554]).

This last line underscores all the change the proposed machinations of Hippolyte and Aricie would bring about: under the "laws" remarked by Oenone, Athens remains marked by myth, the fortress of Minerva. Ruled over by Aricie and Hippolyte, Athens would change entirely. Indeed, instead of a divine institution, such a rule would be the result of a completely human and political "brigue" ("plot") that is "insolent" (as Panope puts it [1.4: p. 553]) because it sets itself against this divine institution. The choice of the word "insolent" denotes what is against custom (*insolens*), it connotes hubris: but may it not also be read as a going-against the sun (*sol*)?

However far-fetched such additional connotation may seem, that is what is occurring, and in this connection it is significant that we were reminded at the outset not only of the solar origins of Phèdre, but also of the fall of Icarus (1.1: p. 543). In this light, the word "volage" ("flight") applied to the people of Athens who would follow Hippolyte takes on a fuller sense,[24] as, too, does the phrase used by Ismène, underscoring a *political* situation: "Préparez-vous, Madame, à voir de tous côtes/ *Voler* vers vous les coeurs par Thésée écartés" ("Be prepared, Madame, to see from all sides fly toward you the affections set aside by Thésée" [2.1: p. 554]). That it is because of his refusal of or supposed attack upon Phèdre that the latter speaks of Hippolyte's "yeux *insolents*" and that Thésée exclaims, "L'*insolent* de la force empruntait le secours!" ("The *insolent* boy borrowed the aid of force!" [3.3: p. 571; 4.1: p. 574]) takes on similar significance. The crossroads Icarus represents, with his technological failure, is in many ways echoed by Hippolyte, with *his* failure to participate in the instauration of society in history. But both signify the establishment of such new conditions immediately after their deaths: Daedelus escapes, and so too does Aricie (or even Thésée, if we wish to make the analogy precise). Faustus's spectator is now *in* the play.

Brian Vickers points out that in Euripides' *Hippolytus* a parallel of similar effect is drawn between the crash of Phaeton into the sea and the end of Hippolytus in the second stasimon (2.732 ff.). There the unhappy chorus sing that they would like to fly

> Into that deep-blue tide,
> Where their father, the Sun, goes down,
> the unhappy maidens weep
> tears from their amber-gleaming eyes
> in pity for Phaethon.   [2.738–41][25]

But in Euripides the parallel underlines a certain futility in the chorus's (and our) possible intervention in the tragedy, for Phaedra is already "preparing to kill herself (and to slander Hippolytos)."[26] Vickers himself does not seek to follow the parallel elsewhere, but we have already seen how it can function in certain tragedies of the Renaissance as the Phaeton and Icarus metaphors are gradually embodied in a person, as they develop into specifically recognizable names of explicable "failure."

In Racine the comparison is central to the tragedy, and that is "why" it is made from the outset. Hippolyte fails himself to establish the new society, but his activity and departure from the scene help make such establishment eventually possible.

For the insolence of Hippolyte is echoed by Aricie in the same sense: "Reste du sang d'un roi noble fils de la terre, / Je suis seule échappée aux fureurs de la guerre . . ." ("Remnant of the blood of a king and noble son of the earth, I alone escaped the fury of war" [2.1: p. 556]). She is, as suggested, in all ways different from the others. Aricie may be alone, but unlike Eriphile (and Oenone) she is not *étrangère*, she is not cut off from her past. On the contrary, it is because she represents continuity, because she may be inserted in a *succession*, that her "rights" are opposed. That this succession is *legitimate* is not in doubt, and through her entire long speeches to Ismène (2.7: pp. 556–57) she shows her consciousness of this. At the same time she reveals that other aspect of the sociohistorical discourse contemporary with the play: the willful determination of its enunciating *I* to seize the object it predicates. In her, this takes the form of both power and love. Hippolyte can satisfy both demands. She is here, as recent critics have observed, anything but the "demoiselle de pensionnat" of traditional criticism.[27] She is rather the militant imposer of the self:

> *Pour moi, je suis plus fière et fuis la gloire aisée*
> *D'arracher un hommage à mille autres offert,*
> *Et d'entrer dans un coeur de toutes parts ouvert.*
> *Mais de faire fléchir un courage inflexible,*
> *De porter la douleur dans une âme insensible,*
> *D'enchaîner un captif de ses fers étonné,*
> *Contre un joug qui lui plaît vainement mutiné:*
> *C'est là ce que je veux; c'est là ce qui m'irrite.*
> *Hercule à désarmer coûtait moins qu'Hippolyte;*
> *Et vaincu plus souvent, et plus tôt surmonté,*
> *Préparait moins la gloire aux yeux qui l'ont dompté.*
>
> [2.1: p. 557]

[*As for me, I am more proud and fly from the facile glory of seizing vows offered to a thousand others, and of penetrating a heart open upon all sides. But to force an inflexible courage to waver,*

to bring pain into an unfeeling soul, to chain up a captive amazed
to see himself thus in irons, *vainly revolting* against a *yoke* he finds
pleasant; that is what *I want*; that is what excites *me.* Hercules
cost less to *disarm* than Hippolyte; and *defeated* more often, sooner
overcome, brought less *glory* to the eyes that *tamed* him.]

It is naïve to shrug this off as mere preciosity—these phrases are, after
all, not monolithic; they are within the control of the speaker. What is
emphasized here, however, and it is what gives its basic tonality to the
love of Aricie and Hippolyte, is not only the imposition of the *I* of
enunciation, but that such imposition is matched by that of an opposing *I* equally willful, likewise posited as in full possession of the private consciousness it presents.[28] The succession of the future is the result of an *agreement* between equally dominant "individuals," and if
they have appeared weak to classical criticism it is no doubt precisely
because of their contrast in this to the monoliths of Phèdre and Thésée. As Aricie remarks: "On ne m'oppose que trop de résistance"
("Only too much resistance is opposed to me" [2.1: p. 557]). In order to be "overcome," Hippolyte must be *willing,* must see in an agreement his own interests (hence his comment on why the gods should
be just—for *their* own interests). Such, in the following scene, is the
motive of Hippolyte's offer to Aricie of Athens: his interests dictate
this, for not only can he thus "win" Aricie, he can also *defeat* Phèdre
and the "past" of Thésée, and, finally, rule (with Aricie) over Attica.
The later alliances suggested at the departure from Trézène should
not be overlooked: they are conceived as alliances to win the political
advantage the return of Thésée has presently prevented: "De puis-
sants defenseurs prendront notre querell;/Argos nous tend les bras,
et Sparte nous appelle" ("Powerful protectors will take our quarrel;
Argos holds out its arms to us, and Sparta calls us" [5.1: p. 584]).

Hippolyte is not as submissive as he is often claimed to be: he shows
himself a fit counterpart to the imposing Aricie of the previous scene:
"Je puis vous affranchir . . . ,/Je revoque des lois. . . ./Vous pouvez
disposer de vous" ("I can set you free . . . , I revoke the laws. . . . You
are free to do as you will" [2.2: p. 558]), and it is a political suffrage
that he thus announces. Until he adds, immediately, "de votre coeur."
Clearly this constitutes *his* "attack" on Aricie, and he continues right
away to show what *advantage* she can gain from allying herself with

him: he already possesses Trézène, Athens (at present doubtful) would go to her (and him) with his help. This same opportunism is shown at the moment of his final departure: "L'occasion est belle," he says, "il la faut embrasser" ("The opportunity is a fine one, we must take full advantage of it" [5.1: p. 584]). He argues that he can demonstrate his "véritables droits" ("true rights") over his half-brother, who owes his rights to the "caprice des lois" ("laws' capriciousness"). There is a still greater legitimacy to be considered ("un frein plus légitime"—"a more legitimate brake" 2.2: p. 558): her claim. This legitimacy is emphasized by Aricie a little later when she urges Hippolyte: "Partez, prince, et suivez vos généreux desseins:/Rendez de mon pouvoir Athènes tributaire" ("Leave, prince, and follow your generous intentions: make [bring back] Athens submissive to my power" [2.3: p. 561]). The use of the verb *rendre* is at least as revealing as that of the words *mon pouvoir*.

Clearly love and political power go hand in hand here, and Phèdre misplaces (and misunderstands) their love entirely when she situates it in some kind of pastoral idyll (4.6: p. 581). Such a love is inconceivable to the Hippolyte and Aricie of the play. This is why marriage is sufficiently important to be brought up at the weighty moment of departure under Thésée's curse. It is far from frivolous. Marriage is the *legitimate* inception of the new society, by a legally binding mutual *contract*. Without it there could be no societal history, no succession (recognized) in time. To fly *illicitly* would be to repeat the acts of Thésée and of Phèdre—together with the paradigm into which these acts fall (see 5.1: p. 585).

Aricie and Hippolyte seek the installation of a historical society from a mutual contract of individual powers. Phèdre might indeed want satisfaction in a personal idyll; but the new society replaces the *je/il* of Phèdre's speech (e.g., 1:3: p. 552) with the *je-vous* of Hippolyte and Aricie:

Je vous cède, ou plutôt *je vous* rends une place,
Un sceptre que jadis vos aïeux ont reçu

. . . .

Je pars, et vais, pour *vous,*
Réunir tous les voeux partagé entre *nous.*   [2.2: p. 558]

[*I* yield *to you*, or rather *I* give *you* back a place, a scepter that once your forefathers received. . . . *I* am leaving, and for *you* am going, to *reunite* all the voices shared between *us*.]

In this light, it is not surprising that Phèdre, in her celebrated declaration scene, starts with the *je-vous*, but slips into the *je/il* for the declaration itself: "Oui, prince, je languis, je brûle pour Thésée: / Je l'aime, non point tel . . ." ("Yes, prince, I languish, I burn for Thésée: I love him, not at all as . . ." [2.5: pp. 562–63]). This corresponds to the fact that the declaration is made in the fabulous no-time of the slaying of the minotaur.

Aricie understands the system of exchange sufficiently well that she does not herself believe it when she cries, "Vous-même, en ma faveur, vous voulez vous trahir!" ("You yourself wish to betray yourself in my favor!")–she is "étonnée and confuse" *because* she is already aware of the real situation (2.2: pp. 558–59). And Hippolyte is doing anything but yielding "à la violence" as he puts it, his "raison" is by no means absent: the political propositions already made are sufficient indication of that. Indeed, the line "Je vois que ma raison cède à la violence," is strangely contradictory: at this period seeing and reason generally go together–reason is a seeing and seeing a reason. The line would thus seem to indicate that the speaker is in full control of this yielding. The same is true a little later in the line, "Par quel trouble me vois-je emporté loin de moi" ("By what emotion do I see myself carried far out of myself" [2.2: p. 559]). The subsequent oppositions ("Contre vous, contre moi;" "Présente, je vous fuis; absente je vous trouve") emphasize no doubt the ambiguity of Hippolyte's position: as does the use of the verb "je m'éprouve" ("I test myself"), another activity of the austere hunter dedicated to Diana. The "vainement," joined with it here, suggests that Hippolyte is on the point of yielding the *I* of the mythical hero to the contractual *I* of the society of possessive individualism.

Such too is the sense of Hippolyte's complaint, "Moi-même je me cherche, et ne me trouve plus" ("I seek for myself, and no longer find myself"). For what is the self he has lost? That dedicated to Diana, trained by Neptune: the son of Theseus. The words "étrange captif" are not, if we remember the mythical "étrangère partout" that was Eriphile, without significance. Hippolyte wishes to come in from the cold, as it were; and his "langue étrangère" can well be taken in the two senses—that of love to which he is unaccustomed (the superficially "obvious" sense), or that of his mythic place: is it *étrangère* to him, or to Aricie? I suggest that at his death, Hippolyte, however uselessly, has almost emancipated himself from the myth of Phèdre. He, with Aricie, has become responsible for himself, for his own history, and indeed in part for his own death: "*Libres* dans nos malheurs . . . / Le don de notre foi ne dépend de personne" ("*Free* in our misfortunes . . . the gift of our loyalty depends on no one" [5.1: p. 585]). When he affirms "puisque le ciel l'ordonne," he is mistaken, as his death shows, but this erring is why he must be called only "almost emancipated."

For finally Oenone was right. When she suggested that Phèdre could avenge herself by reigning in Athens, though ignorant of the role of Aricie, she had found the way to wound Hippolyte; and Phèdre was correct in her agreement: "Les charmes d'un empire on paru le toucher! / Athènes l'attirait, il n'a pu s'en cacher" ("The charms of an empire appeared to move him! Athens attracted him, he was unable to conceal it" [3.1: pp. 566–67]). This attraction is not simply for the sake of Aricie, as is clear by now, though the two objectives (launching a society and a succession, and obtaining the hand of Aricie) obviously become identical in Hippolyte. Oenone would naturally be the first to notice it. It is she who, in trying to make Phèdre *responsible* for her own history, in trying to give her the political and amorous future (in neither of which goals does she succeed), sets off the tragedy (see Phèdre's accusations in 4.6)—she it is who causes the retreat of myth (for which she will be "payée" by "le ciel"— p. 583).[29]

Weinberg has shown at some length how Théramène's *récit* is a kind of résumé of the themes of the entire play.[30] It marks, I think, much more than that: it is the passage from myth to history. The monster signals the end of a world. If, as Harald Weinrich has suggested, the formula by which certain folk tales change the narrative at its conclusion into a commentary by a final change of verbal tense from past to present risks making the tale's time our own,[31] then what are we to make of the change from past to present (subjunctive) in the last line of *Phèdre*?

In the sustained past (or historical present) of the *récit*, Théramène replaces the indeterminate present of the body of the play (a *monde commenté*, to use Weinrich's terminology) by the past of a distanced narration. History is installed here, and immediately afterward Thésée, by seeking to exclude the play's events from memory, will try to situate these events before this newly installed history. His adoption of Aricie is in this sense a new "masculine birth of time." By the *récit* the no-time of Phèdre is reduced to temporality, and its immediate *visible* "result" is the death of Phèdre herself.

In classical French theatre the *passé simple* can be used only when what is narrated lies before the beginning of the play. All *récits* concerning the *dénouement* whose representation is forbidden by the *bienséances* are therefore in the *passé composé*, the *imparfait*, and/or the *présent historique*.[32] In *Phèdre*, with one exception, the *passé simple* always signifies a quite distant past: "à peine elle vous vit,/ Que votre exil d'abord signala son crédit"; "Trempa-t-elle aux complots de ses frères perfides?" ("Was she mixed up in the plots of her faithless brothers?" [1.1: p. 544]); "Je le vis, je rougis, je pâlis à sa vue" ("I saw him, I blushed, I grew pale at his sight" [1.3: p. 552]). The single exception is the line in the *récit de Théramène* which, apparently, always drew the vocal approbation of contemporary audiences:[33] "Le flot qui l'apporta recule épouvanté" ("The wave that brought it drew back terrified" [5.6: p. 589]). The combining of the historical present with the unaccustomed *passé simple* marks the entire *récit,* and Racine emphasizes it with the metaphor that is the subject of Boileau's commentary.

A distancing is signaled, permitting the installation of a new time. The events culminating in the death of Hippolyte have been relegated simply to a "time" and "place" of *before*. The new time is one in which a different Thésée (already turned from myth: we may note the similarity of a line spoken by him to one of Hippolyte's already remarked as indicating change: "Je ne sais où je vais, je ne sais où je suis" ("I know not where I am going, I know not where I am" [4.1: p. 574]) will for the first time take a woman as a daughter instead of as a lover. In doing so he will establish a new social order, even though, as suggested in a previous chapter, that order here may be implied to have no future. While Phèdre dies by the poison of

280

Médée, and thus remains even at her death in a "time" of myth, in her "eternity," a different order is established, based on exchange: not simply the cynical one of a daughter for a (murdered) son, but one by which Thésée pays for what he can now perceive as a wrong. That, too, is a novel activity for him.

As he installs the daughter in her legitimate place, it is above all in the political terms of Hippolyte and Aricie herself that Thésée is thinking: "malgré les complots d'une injuste famille" ("despite the conspiracies of an unjust family" [5.7: p. 593]). He himself remains in a now oddly politicized past, for their "injustice" is to balance here the "rights" of Aricie in the society to come. It is a "legitimate" society, instituted in a sequential history, formulated by herself and Hippolyte in their struggle against the myth of Phèdre, and installed by Thésée in accordance with his son's "dernière volonté" (5.6: p. 591).

Hegel shrugs the tragedy off on the grounds that Phèdre herself only acts because she is pushed into it by Oenone and because she is motivated by the spite of a woman scorned in favor of another.[34] Such a reading misses the point entirely, I think. The problem played out in *Phèdre* is not a particular one of a triangle among Aricie, Hippolyte, and Phèdre, or even among Phèdre, Hippolyte, and Thésée, though these are both part of a larger problem. Dryden, in the preface to *All For Love,* makes a similar reduction of the Racinian tragedy, reducing it to a kind of ludicrous tragedy of manners. The problem dealt with is a collision between two concepts of human action, two concepts of time, two concepts of society (or, rather, for a man of Racine's age, one of society and one of nonsociety, of chaos). Shakespeare in *Lear* had shown the same conflict, but there no solution was available.

In that sense the kind of conflict involved in Racine's *Phèdre* is every bit as broad as the irreconcilable one between Antigone and Creon in Sophocles' *Antigone,* Hegel's most admired play. The play does indeed deal with such an irreconcilable conflict. It resolves it in the same way as did *Bajazet* and *Iphigénie*: by removing the threat to a stable and legitimate contractual society. The first experimented with human activities in the nearest situation conceivable to the theoretical state of nature, the second experimented with a threat brought against a well-functioning society of possessive individuals that succeeded in overcoming it without any considerable lapse. *Phèdre* succeeds in showing the very moment of installation of such a society, which is also that of history and of technology.

[handwritten annotations:]

how do you call it when people make gratuitous affirmations

– check dates for his references
ex. PISCATOR (Racine, p. 298

– on frames (p. 139)

– triangle means you yourself said it is a triangle on p. 269, 272, 280

– dico's clipp/ Phaedra
Thes. / Th.
Thes. / Hipp.

– ex. when he is critical of critics (p. 269

– you can start with R. Colie's prismatic criticism

– p. 138 good pass for ? tragedy discourse in ? for myself

– very good introduction to the analysis of the play (ex ch. 5, ch 11

12 Tragedy and Truth

One could say there has never really been such an object as tragedy.
No homogeneous literary discourse crossed over the centuries separating us from Aeschylus; simply a series of theatrical attempts to
invent and grasp what a succession of different periods experienced as
the inexpressible. If we speak of tragedy, the first thing to be emphasized is simply that there has been an *event called* tragedy at various moments in the Western tradition and in certain places. What
this book has sought to show is in what sense, despite the apparent
heterogeneity that characterizes its various appearances, the name refers to a similar kind of event in every case.

The periods in which tragedy has appeared have been notable for
a profound reorganization of the political and social order. One thinks
of the formation of the oligarchic *polis* and the struggles that were
brought to a temporary conclusion in the Peloponnesian Wars. One is
reminded of the creation of the modern nation-state through the
religious wars of the sixteenth century, the Thirty Years War on the
European continent, and the years of Commonwealth, Restoration,
and bourgeois monarchy in Britain. One recalls the German romantic
movement and the gradual unification of that country. Each appearance of the discourse called tragedy was accompanied or immediately
followed by the invention of a powerful political-philosophical discourse, destined to provide for some centuries the limits within which
such theory and practice could be conceived: Plato and Aristotle;
Machiavelli and Bacon, Hobbes, and Locke; Kant, Hegel, German ideal-
ism, and Marx.

This complex conjuncture suggests that the discourse, tragedy, plays a particular—and perhaps fundamental—role in the formation of epistemes. I have tried to show tragedy to be that discourse which permits whatever may be the (non-)element escaping the meaningful limits of the discursive class being invented, to be said and thereby grasped as something "understood." It overcomes what threatens the existence of such discourse in its very meaningfulness. Whence its apparent ambiguity: tragedy would enclose the inexpressible, would reduce it to an order of knowledge, at the very same time as inventing the discursive space from which that inexpressible must be excluded. This inexpressible element, this impossibility of meaning must be *shown*, and enclosed simultaneously with the creation of the discursive space whose limits it indicates. Yet none of that can be said *formally* (e.g., in a philosophical discourse), because to be able to do so would presuppose the impossibility of the new discursive order and reveal that one was already "outside" it: which is why philosophy seeks to occult the threat to the meaningfulness of such discourse.

Such an interpretation explains why one cannot speak of tragedy as though one were speaking of the same thing in Aeschylus or in Shakespeare, in Racine or in Hölderlin, in Strindberg or in Brecht (assuming we can speak of something like a "modern tragedy"). Tragedy is not necessarily collective or individual: it may be both. Its role, that is to say, depends on the parameters of the specific context in which it appears. That is why Artaud is wrong, it seems to me, when he speaks of a kind of general and undiscriminated Evil, present in certain tragedies of antiquity as a recollection of the common, but normally unspoken and occulted, condition of mankind. It would then be the constant task of theater, he argues, to make visible this permanent Evil:

> The terrifying apparition of Evil which was produced in unalloyed form at the Eleusinian Mysteries and was truly revealed, corresponds to the dark moments in certain ancient tragedies which all theatre must rediscover.[1]

This is once again the hypostatization of the tragic: tragedy removed from its nomothetic constitutive action and its essentially political role, and transfigured into a metaphysics of morals.

If one tragedy came to an end at the beginning of the Greek fourth

synchronically
isomorphic

the
semiotic ?
context .
of tragedy

century, another appeared at the end of the European sixteenth century, and perhaps yet another in the thirties of the twentieth century. Tragedy fills a certain discursive role, but the precise form that role takes may differ according to its total semiotic context. Insofar as it traces the particular space of a discursive order and the limits of that space, tragedy corresponds to societal practices that may be synchronically isomorphic, but that differ entirely according to the various periods and places in which tragedies appear.

In Western history tragedy seems to have appeared at moments that, retrospectively, are marked by a kind of "hole" in the passage from one dominant discourse to another. This hole, this momentary and impossible absence of meaningfulness that is simply a necessary flaw in codification during the process of its elaboration, will not however be filled by any law created out of tragedy. It is merely papered over, occulted. In our modernity, the late nineteenth century saw it uncovered. Tragedy creates the flaw that it calls "the tragic" and then conceals it—at the same time. Tragedy brings about rationality by showing what can be termed the irrational within that rationality. That is no doubt why all tragedy is thoroughly embroiled in the political, and why to grasp and enclose the tragic, the inexpressible of the discourse being created, is at once an ideological and an anti-ideological activity: the first, to the degree that it hides what is unspoken in the law that is the order of discourse, the second, to the extent that it shows it.

When he banishes tragic poets from his Republic, Plato seems conscious above all of the second; Racine, too, when he experiments with certain Hobbesian theories as though they grasped permanent social *Racine* realities and eternal human characteristics. It is in that connection that it becomes important to remember that both Racine and Dryden became the historiographers of a centralized state power. Indeed, this fusion of tragedy and "legitimate" historiography at the beginning of the modern period can serve to indicate the considerable difference that exists between the tragedy and social order of Greek antiquity, and those of the European monarchies at the outset of the modern era. It is surely significant that Racine and Boileau's predecessor in the post of historiographer royal was Samuel Sorbière (died 1670), close friend and translator of Hobbes (*De Cive*, 1649; *De Corpore Politico*,

1652). That the post was virtually a sinecure in practice does not detract from the theoretical importance of such nominations.

Greek tragedy was a political act—in its very essence. But the meaning of such a statement must be tempered by the realization that the sense of such a "political act" is not ours. It was a form of participation in the total life of the *polis*. Both the *polis* and the totality in question are difficult, if not impossible, concepts for us to comprehend. Today, the various social practices that compose a culture represent just so many different aspects of the way in which the individual participates in the exchange-systems whose sum constitutes what we view as our society. We divide those aspects into different areas that, we believe, obey different rules, are subject to different kinds of expertise, and imply a variety of obligations.

We are told that such a conception of society was utterly foreign to the citizens of the Greek *polis*—or at least of the Athens that was contemporary with the distant origins of tragedy. And whatever may at a different level have been the internal changes in Greek tragedy during the Athenian fifth century, tragedy would seem to reflect throughout this period the forms taken by such a participation in the total life of the city. Bernard Knox is not alone in emphasizing the political aspect of Greek tragedy (in this sense of "political") when he notes the proximity of its performance to the parliamentary assemblies on the Pnyx, and the fact that it is a religious and social occasion performed on the slopes of the Acropolis, the temple area.

If tragedy proposes an ordering structure enfolding that potential absence of meaning which would, if left unremarked, have made impossible the constitution of and participation in the life of the *polis*, then we can easily understand, too, in what way the spectator would become judge of (and party to) the play, as he might of a legal action. Many recent writers on Greek tragedy have insisted on the juridical aspect of the vocabulary and organization of Greek tragedies. And we can also understand why the language of tragedy—another commonplace of modern criticism—poses such a problem. In tragedy it is precisely a matter of inventing the order of a certain use of language, of creating a discourse. It was first of all a matter of articulating truth and opinion, language and action, not at the level of *telling*—where tragedy may very well indicate the continuing tension between such things, but at that of *performing*: tragedy simply shows their mutual articulation.

Mimesis, as it is named and interpreted by Aristotle, would be nothing other than the unfurling of human actions in so far as they are the real components of the life of the *polis*. The very possibility of such mimesis was created by tragedy (which is why the meaning of the term changes through the centuries, with that of tragedy itself). Whether it be actions that are constitutive of the city, actions opposed to one another as two different conceptions of what the city might be, or compromises that permit the life of the city to continue, tragedy always puts the *polis* into play in one way or another. And because they are so essentially bound up with matters human and social, such developments are inevitably dealt with anachronistically by the critics and philosophers who consider them.

In the case of constitutive actions, one thinks of the *Eumenides* and Athene's concluding decision, which replaces the broken familial and patriarchal economy of the *Agamemnon* with the collective law of the city, a law to which all must submit—including the leaders. In the second case (oppositional actions), one thinks of Sophocles, of the confrontation between Creon and Antigone. It is perhaps risky to try and reduce a play like *Oedipus the King* to a similar schema. And yet one can argue that the protagonist's difficulty arises in part at least from the interiorization of this very confrontation: a particular form of a conflict between choice and change. Maurice Merleau-Ponty has remarked:

> It is the nightmare of an involuntary responsibility and guilt by circumstance which already underlines the Oedipus myth: Oedipus did not want to marry his mother nor kill his father but he did it and what he did stands as a crime. The whole of Greek tragedy assumes this idea of an essential contingency through which we are all guilty and all innocent because we do not know what we are doing.[2]

Of course, Merleau-Ponty is arguing that any act—political or otherwise—is a dialectical play between an historical situation to which the actor must submit and an individual choice that plays upon this historical situation. In that sense his reflection bears rather more on a

Brechtian theater than it does upon that of Sophocles. Perhaps such a dialectic may *be shown* for *one* reader or spectator by *Oedipus the King*, but what the play *says* is Oedipus's innocence. The paradoxical tension that is so often a problem for the modern reader of Sophocles is articulated in the play, and what is told is its resolution. Apollo, cries Oedipus, is responsible for the inescapable conflictual situation, and if the protagonist can also exclaim that he himself is responsible for his own blinding, we can say that he is not thereby taking responsibility for the commission of "crimes" that he could not escape, but simply for not having recognized that human knowledge is above all knowledge of its own partiality (in every sense of the word). What Oedipus finally recognizes is the ineluctability of the tension between choice and necessity. Tragedy, here, was the textual machine that allowed that tension to be at once performed and (thereby) released. The recognition that concludes *Oedipus the King* leads to the apotheosis of *Oedipus at Colonnus*, where the protagonist can claim his entire innocence.

Oedipus is rejected from the city in *Oedipus the King* because he had failed to recognize the limits of the discourse on which its existence is based. But the other participants, and the spectators, are able to do so. Tragedy is the system that makes possible that recognition. Such is the case, also, for the third concept of tragedy, that of necessary compromise. One thinks here, for instance, of Euripides' *Heracles*, whose protagonist must force himself to bear arms despite his pain; or one remembers Dionysos's horrible seizure of power over Pentheus at the end of the *Bacchae*, a seizure which is necessary because two different orders of discourse cannot coexist.

These three apparently different conceptions of tragedy appear to indicate a gradual exteriorization of the idea of the city. It is somewhat in this sense that Wagner speaks in "Art and Revolution," when he talks of the "downfall of tragedy," and in "The Art-Work of the Future," when he talks of tragedy as marking "the entry of the Art-Work of the Folk upon the public arena of political life."[3] Wagner is recording with dismay the increasing attention he sees being paid by tragedy to the domain of the political, not as a sphere of popular participation but as a separate domain for commentary. He understands the "political" as the name given to a commentary upon relations of force among individuals and as a representation of those relations. Like Merleau-Ponty, Wagner appears to be thinking of a more modern theater: "We may take its appearance as an excellent touchstone for the difference in procedure between the Art-*creating* of the Folk and the mere literary-historical *Making* of the so-called cultured art-world."[4] This idea was, of course, destined to acquire the weight of a tradition once it had been taken over by Nietzsche. And Artaud carries on the same tradition: Wagner's "downfall of tragedy" marking the moment when ancient tragedies no longer contain the "dark moments" of "Evil" whose permanent presence it is theatre's task to perform.

Every interpreter of tragedy advances upon the terrain in accordance with the discursive norms dominant in his own time. If Wagner reads Greek tragedy in the terms of a neoclassical practice that he condemns, Hegel is not far from a similar reading, despite the authority his interpretations have since acquired with regard to Greek tragedy. Thus, he interprets Oedipus's "acceptance" of his involuntary crimes as evidence of a social condition that is necessary, but at the same time as a sign of a free acquiescence in the responsibilities accompanying this condition and proof of his self-realization: "He adheres simply to all the consequences and makes good his personal responsibility for the whole."[5]

In Hegel's eyes, Oedipus is the exemplary figure of the heroic age. Now what is remarkable about his concept of the heroic age is its apparently unnoticed similarity to the state of nature of which Hobbes makes use in order to legitimize the introduction of the contractual association later called the liberal state. That is to say that Hegel, like Wagner and so many others, is not speaking of Greek tragedy, but of Renaissance and neoclassical tragedy. His Oedipus reveals all the individualistic and unshakable unity of the hero whose acts, says Hegel, are a concrete manifestation of the concept of self—a concept quite foreign to the Greeks.

Yet the difference in reading between a Hegel and a Merleau-Ponty (for example) is revealing: it is a matter of two different concepts of society and the state (as well as of tragedy). Hegel was undermining an ideology current in tragedy as it existed—or developed—after the mid-sixteenth century: that ideology which presupposed an exchange

between individual wills possessing potentially equal power. Merleau-Ponty is echoing a Brechtian theatre which shows, among other things, that liberal discourse merely serves to hide the violence which is necessary to its continued existence: his Oedipus is the paradigm of such a situation.

Tragedy and the political appear at all times to be inescapably linked. If Hegel rejects Racinian tragedy as inferior to that of Sophocles, while praising the latter quite precisely on grounds he might easily have discovered in Racine, this is perhaps because the French drama-tist remains too close to the immediate sources of Hegelian discourse. Hegel accuses Racine of having placed on stage characters whose ac-tivities are too personal, too individualistic, insufficiently "ideal"—and that extreme is nothing but the ultimate consequence of the logic of the contractual state.

Just as he had done for Sophocles, Hegel praises Shakespeare as well, on the grounds that the English dramatist had succeeded in discover-ing that ideal individualism required by tragedy:

> Shakespeare has, for example, selected much material for his tragedies from chronicles and earlier romances, framed upon a condition of life which has not as yet received the impression of a fully articulated social order, but in which the energy of in-dividuals, as emphasized in personal resolve and achievement, is still the prevailing characteristic.

Thus, he argues, Shakespeare was able to find more easily "all that the form of the Ideal requires." Certainly,

> the characters in the Shakespearian drama do not entirely belong to the princely order [and the heroic period] and only partially are taken from mythical sources [unlike Sophoclean tragedy], but they are placed in the era of civil wars, in which the ties of social order and legislative enactment are either weakened or shat-tered, and they secure from such a condition the exceptional independence and self-sufficiency we are looking for.[6]

What Hegel is really speaking about is a development in neoclassical tragedy: which he would look for in vain in Greek tragedies. It is cer-tainly not mere chance that the theme of usurpation becomes so important in Renaissance tragedy, and Hegel would be quite correct to link, at this period, tragedies and a certain idea of the political. But he is wrong in conflating Greek tragedy, Shakespearean tragedy, and the "failure" of French neoclassical tragedy in terms of a common attempt to show what he calls the ideal individual unity; just as Artaud is wrong in making the revelation of evil the common bond of all (tragic) theatre.

Greek tragedy is coincident with the inception of the collective *polis*, and helps make possible the discourse that rules it. Renaissance tragedy helps make possible the discourse of possessive (and progressive) individualism. Tragedy may mark a moment of transition, but it does not necessarily mark the *same* moment. Tragedy may be the machine of a certain kind of discursive experiment, but tragedies exist within very different overall discursive contexts.

It is with such a proviso that we may assert that Renaissance tragedy, too, is bound up at diverse levels with matters political. A tragedy such as Jodelle's *Cléopâtre captive* was apparently performed at least partly for fairly specific political aims: the play celebrates for the court itself the victory won at Metz in January 1553 (n.s.), and thus asserts the power of Henri II—at the same time as indicating the limits of that power. Gillian Jondorf has shown the preponderance of political commentary to be found in Garnier's tragedies (in the form of aphorisms and *sentences*). *Macbeth* was probably written for performance before James I, and in that case almost certainly, at one level, to affirm the divine legitimacy of his supposed descent from Banquo. What else would one see in the mirror held by the eighth and last king in the parade of act 4, scene 1, except the image of James I himself? Particularly so, when one recalls how for such a performance the king is placed in the one position in the auditorium where he is directly in line with center stage and in the most favorable place to be seen by all the members of the audience.[7]

Such elements suggest that the relation between tragedy and the political has indeed changed: but we have not yet arrived at what Hegel proposes. The political may now be just one aspect of a decomposed social life, but it is not yet the prey of an individual will. If tragedy, like other discursive forms, is becoming no longer the mark of a participation but that of a commentary, the commentary in question is not yet a mere representation. If one may be permitted to speak from a retrospective viewpoint, it may be said that Shakespearean tragedy is only preparing the ground for a new class of discourse. Greek tragedy performed the multiple voices of a collectivity; Renaissance tragedy will eventually put on stage, once they are able to be grasped as meaningful, the power relationships that constitute the state in the form Machiavelli had recently been able to demonstrate.

But Renaissance tragedy does not begin there. It must first of all constitute itself as meaningful discourse. Only then will it be able to order the various relationships of enunciation, those of speaker to his utterance, those among speakers, and so on. We have seen how those relations order themselves into power relationships. We have seen how these, at first internal to tragedy, will then be *interpreted* as representing some reality external to that discourse, used as a kind of thought-experiment to test reality. But this neoclassical belief in representation is not yet what rules Shakespearean tragedy.

What is played out in Shakespeare is not—or not simply, as has often been maintained—a confrontation between feudalism and bourgeois capitalism at the moment of the latter's instauration. What is played out in Shakespeare is a discursive confrontation one of whose manifestations elsewhere (in a different discourse) is a political conflict—or economic. . . , or philosophic . . . , or religious. . . . The political domain, I repeat, is but one aspect of a world split into a diversity of elements, lacking the collective or "total" aspect of Athens, or even that of the High Middle Ages (however imaginary it may be). It is, of course, these divisions, this separation that will make possible the very concept of representation: which assumes the practical isomorphism of two semantically different semiotic systems. That is why what was still, in Shakespeare, the particular form taken by a general discursive crisis can become in Racine a commentary upon a social and human reality taken as situated elsewhere than in tragedy itself: tragedy will have become that ordering machine of which I have already spoken.

It is perhaps useful to suggest two further brief examples from Shakespeare, merely in order to indicate their participation in two different orders of discourse between which no choice is possible: to indicate that the moment of *decision* is yet to come. I will put the

292

first in political terms simply as a matter of facility, for if the *fact* of conflict is apparent, the meaning of that conflict is by no means automatic.

Richard III is often entirely explained as a Machiavellian (despite the ambiguity provoked by the theatrical splendor of the role). Such an interpretation must admit that the man of power is entirely responsible for his own discourse or, in other words, for his power and his own "history" (one can easily see, here, that one is speaking again of enunciative relations). Yet it is clear that Richard also participates in an eschatological history. Not only he himself, but Queen Margaret throughout the play and Richmond at the end, see him as that character of the scourge of God who is so common in tragedies of the age: a character who is not responsible in the long run for his discourse, but who destroys and is destroyed for the accomplishment of some divine goal, and who remains blind to the existence of a superior order of discourse that rules his own. In such a system Richard appears more as the devil, and just as to assimilate the name of Machiavelli to that of Satan was a means of recuperating him within an eschatological discourse, so too with Richard. The sentence that Marlowe attributes to Machiavelli—"I count religion but a childish toy, / And hold there is no sin but ignorance" (*The Jew of Malta*, prologue, ll. 14–15)—is precisely the reversal of the principle of an eschatological history. The latter's original sin was knowledge.

Richard III is both that satanic Machiavelli, scourge of God, and Machiavelli the analyst and publicist of a simply human history. The two discourses are simultaneous, and in conflict. Macbeth, caught between the demands of a supernatural, divine order and those of the imposition of a personal power, plays out something of the same inconclusiveness. But in *Troilus and Cressida* the terms are quite different. The possibility of an individual's evaluation of the other, whether represented as a person, a situation, or a combination of the two, is fully put to the test. The outcome is utterly inconclusive. It is Troilus himself who puts the question: "What's aught but as 'tis valued?" (2.2.52). It is Hector who answers it, by noting the partiality (again in every sense) of such a "private" ordering:

> But value dwells not in particular will.
> It holds his estimate and dignity

As well wherein 'tis precious of itself
As in the prizer. [2.2.53–56]

The difficulty, as both Hector and Ulysses see clearly, is that such valuation is necessarily particular in its first grasping of the object. It necessarily performs the imposition of the subject upon a structure of the world able to be subsumed only partially in such a code, whatever the valuation—that of which Troilus is speaking (the beauty and worth of a woman), the truth of a particular knowledge (as it might be in Bacon), the meaning of a word or an utterance (as it will be in Locke), the status of a particular authority and possession (as it will be in Hobbes and elsewhere).

Shakespeare does not permit that imposition to become dominant and disorder ensues, in the sense that the human speaker is unable to determine the status of the objects of his discourse. Or one might say that the systems of communication are subject to too much interference. Less metaphorically, we can say that the act of determining the predicate of discourse remains visible within that discourse, so that the subject of enunciation is in some sense *responsible* for it: what was "simply" the subject of predication is becoming the subject as responsible speaker—though the discursive mark of that responsibility will eventually become occulted, and the discourse of possessive individualism will conceal the violence of the imposition that Merleau-Ponty is at pains to bring back to the surface.

In the case of Troilus the process produces disorder in the subject: his own status is unclear. He is unable to grasp any certain predicate and is left holding only a series of logical contradictions that he cannot allow to constitute the "being" of Cressida. To do so would be to relinquish any knowledge; it would be to accept madness:

If beauty have a soul, this is not she;
If souls guide vows, if vows be sanctimonies,
If sanctimony be the gods' delight,
If there be rule in unity itself,
This was not she. O madness of discourse,
That cause sets up with and against itself:
Bifold authority, where reason can revolt
Without perdition, and loss assume all reason
Without revolt. This is, and is not, Cressid. [5.2.135–44]

There has been utter lack of coincidence between valuation and its object, between the intention of meaning and the status of the thing that is to find expression. Indeed, Cressida appears to stand aloof from any valuation at all. She cannot be *placed*. One might call her a pure vehicle for experience, innocent in an almost prelapsarian sense. Critics who continue to judge her in terms of a moral code they would impose upon Shakespeare only flout the warning of Troilus himself that "discourse" will be both in agreement with and contradictory to its "cause," that received experience is unqualifiable in any determinate way.

To attempt to surmount this "indeterminacy" is merely to impose our will to knowledge and possession upon a world beyond discourse, and it leads to an inevitable distortion: for the "natural" structure, whose existence is neither assured nor in any case available as such to human reason, is then submitted to the ordering (valuation) of each individual *I*. The subject seeks to seal it up within the sequence of "his" own discourse, and then

> Each thing meets
> In mere oppugnancy . . .
> Then everything [would] include itself in power,
> Power into will, will into appetite,
> And appetite, an universal wolf,
> So doubly seconded with will and power,
> Must make perforce an universal prey
> And last eat up himself.   [1.3.110–24]

Such a passage, recalling Albany's words to Goneril, seems almost to express a horror of what may be to come: Hobbes's natural man brought into the Leviathan of a state made to curb the power, will, and appetite in question, but ever at risk of returning to the individual his natural rights should there be a lapse in the prince's attention: a constant fear of the potential barbarism inherent in an individualism that, once created, can never more be alienated. It is hardly accidental that the main focus of both the Greek and the Trojan councils of war, in acts 1 and 2, should be upon the effect of unleashing the individual will upon what is exterior to it: whether, as in the first, to replace nature's order ("degree") with that of the wolfish individual or, as in the second, to impose a personal system of value upon general experience. In both cases, the tragedy proposes, the result is not order but disorder, and it is Pandarus, the orderer par excellence, who yet debases the very notion of order, who closes the play by bequeathing his "diseases" to the audience (5.10.56).

Troilus and Cressida offers a view of power (the Greeks) and of knowledge (the Trojans) as dependent upon a presently unspecifiable relation between natural "degree," the exterior and the interior, the individual's capacity for order and the claims to value. The development of analytico-referential discourse will gradually specify those relations. In *Troilus* the first two relations appear as unknowable, the second two as insufficient at best and destructive at worst. No unambiguous conclusion can be drawn as to a "right" activity in the contexts of power and knowledge, and no resolution is offered by this most open-ended of Shakespeare's plays. That we know the inglorious endings of almost all of the major characters merely emphasizes this inconclusiveness.

Indeed, the only two who can really be said to have their celebrations ahead of them are Aeneas, who participates here only as an ambassador, and Ulysses, the counselor of natural "degree" against the power of the individual's discourse. He counsels what can only be called the assimilation of the individual to a social organization which is itself presented as a small part of the natural order (viz., his remarks during the council, or those to Achilles in act 3, scene 3). One might recall at this point that Ulysses is both man and no-man. He is the perfect counselor because his discourse is that of no particular.

In the earliest tragedies of the Renaissance, the impossibility of making meaning had been a matter of the functioning of discourse itself: it posed a difficulty to the very act of enunciation, of communication, of the expression of knowledge, and, for example, to the creation of any social relations whatsoever. That impossibility now takes the form of an incomplete knowledge on the part of some participant in a scheme of social relationships that is recognizable and, increasingly, able to be defined: no longer is it an impossibility so much as a *human* insufficiency. To be more precise, the impossibility will be so "translated" once the participant in question is no longer viewed as a threat to that (potential) system of relationships.

It is in Shakespeare that the created individual, created out of that very space of meaninglessness, enters for the first time into a genuine conflictual relationship: "genuine" in the sense that the opponents are of equal power. That relationship remains, however, extremely complex, because the development of discourse has been such as to mark the individual speaker, as we saw, with both a "power" and a "fallibility." On the one hand these two elements would appear to be themselves in a necessary conflict with one another, but on the other we saw that each was in fact essential to the other's function- ing: power carried with it a necessary fallibility (something like an awareness of "responsibility") while, at the same time, "true knowl- edge" required the simultaneous functioning of both—as we saw particularly in *Hamlet* and *Lear*. What was only in embryo in Mar- lowe and Garnier comes into full play in Shakespeare. The individual, with all his fallible power, comes into conflict with other similar in- dividuals and, to some extent, with what begin to appear as the needs of society as a whole. One could say that *all* Shakespeare's plays, certainly the later tragedies and the so-called problem plays, are "about" that conflict in one form or another.

One is obliged to recognize that in plays like *Hamlet* and *King Lear, Richard III, Macbeth,* and *Troilus* it is not some kind of ideal in- dividuality that is being performed. Nor is it yet the representation of some so-called and recognizable external reality. What is being per- formed is a confusion of tongues, what is being pursued is some kind of certainty that is either doomed to remain concealed, or else imposed by force at the end. What is being played out is a disorder in the forms of "social" communication; and, on occasion, its resolution at a certain level of knowledge. It is not entirely accurate, therefore, to assert "that the moment of decision has yet to come." Malcolm does learn the limits to trust, and even Macbeth, in his dreadful soli- tude, learns the consequences of the destruction of order; Fortinbras asserts an essentially military dominion, and Sir Pierce of Exton does remove the potential threat of Richard II in accordance with Henry's expressed desire (even though the latter will finally deny it).

On the whole, where Shakespeare is concerned, the disorder is not really resolved: it is simply brought to a close by a final *imposition* of power (*Hamlet, Macbeth, Richard III*), or left open (*King Lear,*

Troilus, possibly *Antony and Cleopatra,* with Caesar's final recognition of something like the superiority of the two title protagonists). In Dryden, Racine, and their contemporaries, the balance seems finally to be found, the tragic disequilibrium once and for all enclosed and exorcised. In his *Troilus and Cressida* (published in 1679), Dryden makes Cressida *in fact* innocent: there is no question but that her behavior is in agreement with Troilus's initial estimate of her "value." Yet Troilus doubts it on the basis of unexplored evidence, and this mistrust of his own evaluation produces a misunderstanding that alone is responsible for their deaths. Misfortune ensues *because* he failed to trust the knowledge he had from the first, and in doing so he fails both himself and Cressida. In Shakespeare she had been simply beyond any such evaluation. Human discourse had been utterly inadequate to reality. Now it is the measure of that reality.[8]

Except schematically, the conflict found in Shakespearean tragedy no longer exists because the exigencies of the individual and those of society are viewed as coincident with one another—society can eventually identify the individuals who threaten its order, whom it *understands* as destructive, and is able to eject them (I am thinking of Racinian tragedy in particular). A person may make a false choice —and so may society—but the point is that the existence of a choice, and of a particular kind of choice, is now clear. What is examined is a society at once creative of and created by the individual. What is experimented with on stage is the economic and political order of possessive individualism and the true relationships of its members. Discourse in itself no longer poses any difficulty, because the self and the other (created from its dilemmas) have discovered a contractual order in which public and self-expression are at one. Language is no longer the responsibility of the individual speaker, it is the property and expression of society. It is in fact to be outside the control of the individual speaker.

The discourse, tragedy, does not, of course, come to an end with Dryden and Racine, with Tate or Rowe, with Addison or even Lillo, Crebillon or Voltaire. Its epistemic role did. Tragedy was now functioning as simply one part of a whole episteme of ongoing truth and knowledge, and it delineates the ignorance that marks the bounds of that knowledge and its truths. It had been tragedy's task to outline and overcome the *hamartia* that traces out the edges of a logical and discursive space. That *hamartia* has been done away with. Were it to burst forth once again, then the episteme itself, the discursive process in which a particular reality was now organized, would have been exploded. The impossibility of providing systemic discursive meaning which we have seen progressively grasped and hypostatized into a specific human and social psychology would have destroyed the claims of progressive knowledge. Possibly in our own time something like that is happening, and tragedy may once again have a role to play. It has none, I submit, so long as an analytico-referential episteme remains dominant.

After Racine tragedy becomes a form of that naturalism of which Piscator will say that it "asserts situations. It reproduces the uniform relationship between literature and the condition of society."[9] The very concept that there *are* real situations to be taken note of once and for all is the consequence of a discursive instauration. It is the mark of a certain form of knowledge. The impossibility of meaning has been enclosed; meaninglessness and ignorance have been expelled from the lawful order, they exist no longer in the new and "legitimate" discourse, as Bacon called it. The "tragic" has been named and classified as the limit of knowledge. Tragedy no longer shows, as it did among the Greeks or in Shakespeare, the ambiguous moment of an order's constitution; it has become the support of such an order. By the eighteenth century the very details of tragedy were becoming fixed—not just the constants of the system, but even its variables. As Raymond Williams puts it: "The conflict of fixed and formal duties of rank and honour had decisively replaced the earlier and more creative tensions."[10] It is not just the eighteenth century that had to cope with an essentially fixed genre of tragedy. Can one really say that the German romantics, who saw tragedy essentially as a system organizing the analysis of a confrontation of forces, put that genre in question? After what we have seen of Hegel's interpretation we may be allowed to doubt it.

I suppose Ibsen is generally thought (along with Strindberg) to be the most likely candidate for consideration as a writer of tragedies in what may be called *our* modernity. Yet in Ibsen the characters (unlike what we still see in Racine) do not *compose* a realm of knowledge, they deal with systematic truths that preexist their activities. The question is no longer one of a constitution but one of choosing among external situations presented to us as diverse but essentially comprehensible orders—even though we may make a bad choice. Racine's characters had actively to create the system within which their activities can make sense: it may always be the same system that wins out in the end, but nonetheless we see it *in the very process of being worked out.* In Ibsen the characters are faced with a *choice* between different kinds of truth, and it is the operation of that choice that matters.

Certainly Ibsen's characters may make the choice while suffering from an incomplete lucidity (in *Ghosts,* for example, Mrs. Alving is barely aware that her decision, encouraged by Manders, is absolutely controlled by an acceptance of certain social norms), but the possession of the necessary lucidity was theoretically possible. The *knowledge*, that is to say, is taken to be available and it corresponds to an idea of *truth* concerning certain individual and social norms. The truth of personal relationships (and the idea that certain normal assumptions will have known and foreseeable consequences) is not given as something the speakers or characters can create or as simply a "manner of understanding," for instance, but as consisting of a series of real facts in a real world that exists independent of human reference. *Ghosts* and *Oedipus* are not, as Francis Fergusson has suggested, the same play.[11] The speakers in *Oedipus* (the title speaker in particular) must discover their truths as they go along. There is no standard and no guideline. *Their* ignorance is genuine, in the sense that the only choice they have (and one can scarcely call it a "choice") is between remaining ignorant and continuing the search for a truth.

In Ibsen the lack of complete knowledge comes from accepting the "wrong" code as truth. It is because of an unrealized acceptance of a particular normative discourse as the absolute and objective truth of things. But the drama functions for the audience on the assumption that there is a truth that can be presented as a known system of ordered knowledge: it is by placing *that* knowledge against the choice made by the characters that the spectator is able to understand the error made. Thus, for example, the collapse of the fortunes of the Alvings is presented in terms that make the reasons behind it available as knowledge to the audience, and as a knowledge upon which they can act. But it was also available to the Alvings. There it is possible to speak of a *wrong* choice ("wrong" inasmuch as it has unwelcome results), in a way impossible with regard to Sophocles, Shakespeare, or even Racine: for in their tragedies the system by which we would have to make such a judgment is the creation of the play itself. *Oedipus* remains a kind of metaphor for the possible formation of codes of truth (of which the Freudian version is but the most exemplary). *Ghosts* presents us with the *truth* of a socio-psychological situation, with a familiar knowledge of a particular form of the human condition. *That* systematization was available from the end of the seventeenth century.

There may be something in the suggestion that we find ourselves once again in a moment of "discursive despair," in a time of crisis when our systems of action have again lost their meaningfulness, when we have again reached the limits of the discursive space that is our episteme. The work of a Beckett or of a Pinter could be taken as the performative signs of that crisis. The researches of such philosophers as Wittgenstein and Derrida would be attempts to demarcate that crisis and to discover a way out. If such is the case then history would suggest that we are again ripe for the development of some form of tragedy. Indeed, Raymond Williams has proposed that Brecht has already recovered tragedy as a creative process for our time.[12] Brecht would be setting on stage the signs of humanity at work rediscovering and remaking the very process of order. If so, it is significant that to do so Brecht found it necessary to reject entirely the implications he found in neoclassical tragedy: become the thoughtless representation of unquestioned authority.

It is with Brecht that the questions that haunt the tragedies of the great era of fifth-century Athens and of Renaissance Europe once again become constitutive—even though he remarks that the "tragic perspective" merely offers us "the most futile" of "lying illusions": "a certain kind of knowledge (or rather an uncertain kind) which is of a practical order."[13] Like his predecessors and large numbers of our contemporaries, Brecht was thinking here of tragedy as a type of representational theater. What it represented was the struggle of individuals, themselves taken as representing a permanent human condition, caught in situations whose parameters could be known once and for all: Brecht called it the Aristotelian theater.

Yet in his theatrical practice Brecht seems rather to rediscover tragedy as the sign of the necessary creation of discursive order at a moment when such order has been overthrown. Raymond Williams could assert that "the major achievement of Brecht's mature work is his recovery of history as a dimension for tragedy."[14] For Brecht history must be constituted by means of a certain kind of "reading," that reading itself being anchored in turn in the history that precedes (and produces) it.

The concept of history thus becomes that of a permanent crisis in human action. "History" is the place of a fundamental ambiguity, which comes from the fact that such action must create its own meaningfulness. History and social action invent one another simultaneously and mutually. Once again theatre becomes creative of a discursive order, at length perhaps the invention of a new form of practice of what would previously have been called "knowledge." Brechtian theatre can be taken as having rediscovered the ambiguous collective participation in the invention of social history. That is precisely why, when Sartre asserts that the efficacity of a Brechtian theatre depends on the existence of a nonbourgeois public, he displays a major misunderstanding—at the same time as confirming the role played by such theatre. Brecht does not set out to convince. Together with his public he sets off on a collective search for an eventually useful order. That, too, is the role played by a character like that of "Marx" in Peter Weiss's *Hölderlin*: who destroys the old myths so as to remake and recreate the concrete reality of the society in which he wishes to place himself.

Yet what is perhaps above all sad in this play within and before history (sad, but not tragic) is that any so-called "revolutionary" questioning, any attempt to place the established order in crisis must depend on that existing order for its performance: it always runs the risk of recuperation, of being deflected toward goals that are not its own. Tragedy would first of all have marked a certain lack of meaning, it would have *said* that absence which will later be called the tragic. But to reach a public it risks adopting the familiar order of that public, confirming therefore established forms of knowledge and truth.

Such would have been the case from Racine to Ibsen. One could also refer to Emile Copfermann's anecdote concerning a performance by the National Theater of Belgium of *The Threepenny Opera* which, as he remarks, shows among other things that "the commercial organization of thieves bears a relationship more than of simple analogy to the institution of banking." The performance in question was made possible by the Caltex Foundation and, moreover, "the programme offered the spectator a cultural competition whose prize was provided by the Banque Lambert."[15] The point is that the aim is deflected toward what Wagner called "the literary-historical Making of the so-called cultured art-world." Tragedy, like any other discourse potentially constitutive of a (new) order, inevitably confronts such recuperation.

If Brecht rediscovered tragedy, it is in the sense that he shows how the "hole" of meaningfulness must manifest itself, how the search for a new order of meaning must be made through the confrontation with a preexistent order. Neither the one nor the other can appear or be elaborated except under such conditions. Tragedy, therefore, always runs the risk of being caught in a trap and becoming the support of the previous order. Tragedy would be the discourse that at once accepts and questions the nomothetic discourse of society. That is so simply because tragedy marks the moment of the creation of such discursive order, the moment when the impossibility of law is enclosed and rejected beyond and outside the limits of what can be said. It marks the moment when the order of what can be said (i.e., the logical or discursive space of a given culture) is itself asserted. Tragedy escapes from, but installs, the political. Tragedy is at once the moment of crisis and its resolution. Tragedy is simultaneously the invention and the exile of the tragic, indicating the difficulty but also the necessity of the political. It installs a discourse permitting the elaboration of interpersonal relations of force within society, whatever may be the diversity of such discourse according to the different times and places where it appears.

Notes

Chapter 1

1 Henri Gouhier, "Tragique et transcendance: introduction à un débat général," in "*Le Théâtre tragique*, ed. Jean Jacquot (Paris, 1962), p. 479.

2 For more precision on this, see my articles: "Cartesian Discourse and Classical Ideology," *Diacritics* 6, no. 4 (winter 1976), passim; "The *concevoir* Motif in Descartes," in *La cohérence intérieure. Etudes sur la littérature française du XVIIe siècle, présentées en hommage à Judd D. Hubert*, ed. J. Van Baelen and David Lee Rubin (Paris, 1977), esp. pp. 203–04; "Espaces de la pensée discursive: le cas Galilée et la science classique," *Revue de synthèse* 85–86 (Jan.–July 1977): 5–47; and "Du système de la critique classique," *XVIIe siècle*, 116 (1977): 3–16.

3 The "system of signs" obviously need not necessarily be linguistic. I put it that way here simply because that *is* the system with which I will be dealing.

4 I do not suggest necessarily that it is alone in accomplishing this, but simply that the way in which it does it is peculiar to tragedy.

5 "A proposition *shows* how things stand *if* it is true. And it *says* that they do so stand" (*Tractatus Logico-Philosophicus*, tr. D. F. Pears and B. F. McGuiness, intro. Bertrand Russell (London, 1961), 4.022). Tragedy *shows* the overcoming of the impossibility of making meaning, and it *says* that that impossibility is overcome. The showing occurs through a "syntax" that makes analysis possible, the saying corresponds to the notion of referentiality.

6 Samuel Johnson, "Dryden," in *Lives of the Poets: A Selection*, ed. J. P. Hardy (Oxford, 1971), p. 194.

7 Thomas Rymer, *A Short View of Tragedy: Its Originall, Excellency, and Corruption. With Some Reflections on Shakespear, and Other Practitioners for the Stage* [1692], in *The Critical Works*, ed. Curt A. Zimansky (New Haven, 1956), p. 86. I have myself earlier studied some aspects of this "dialectical" stage with regard to its development in early seventeenth-century France, albeit in a rather different overall context from the present, in *Toward Dramatic Illusion: Theatrical Technique and Meaning from Hardy to "Horace"* (New Haven and London, 1971), chaps. 1–3. It is in just these

terms that Nahum Tate explains his reworking of *King Lear*: "I found the whole [Shakespeare's play] to answer your account of it, a heap of jewels, unstrung and unpolished, yet so dazzling in their disorder that I soon perceived I had seized a treasure. 'Twas my good fortune to light on one expedient to rectify what was wanting in the regularity and probability of the tale, which was to run through the whole a love betwixt Edgar and Cordelia, that never changed word with each other in the original. This renders Cordelia's indifference and her father's passion in the first scene probable. It likewise gives countenance to Edgar's disguise, making that a generous design that was before a poor shift to save his life. The distress of the story is evidently heightened by it." Nahum Tate, dedication to Thomas Boteler, *The History of King Lear* (1681), ed. James Black (London, 1976), pp. 1–2.

8 Raymond Williams, *Modern Tragedy* (London, 1966), p. 53.

9 John Dennis, *The Impartial Critick: or Some Observations Upon a Late Book, Entituled, A Short View of Tragedy, Written by Mr. Rymer* (1693), in *The Critical Works*, ed. Edward Niles Hooker, 2 vols. (Baltimore, 1939), I: 39. Such remarks as this are common in the period.

10 Johnson, "Dryden," p. 162.

11 See, e.g., Dennis, *Impartial Critick*, I. 11.

12 John Dryden, *Selected Criticism*, ed. James Kinsley and George Parfitt (Oxford, 1970), p. 165. Cf. R. P. Brumoy, *Le theatre des Grecs*, 3 vols. (Paris, 1730), 1: viii–ix.

13 Dryden, *Selected Criticism*, p. 25.

14 Ibid., pp. 30–48.

15 Ibid., p. 71.

16 Thomas Rymer, *The Tragedies of the Last Age Consider'd and Examin'd by the Practice of the Ancients, and by the Common Sense of All Ages, in a Letter to Fleetwood Shepheard, Esq., Critical Works*, p. 32.

17 Gerald F. Else, *Aristotle's Poetics: The Argument*, 2nd. ed. (Cambridge, Mass., 1963), p. 13.

18 Dryden, *A Defence of an Essay of Dramatic Poesy* (1668), *Selected Criticism*, pp. 80, 85. This view is echoed by Pope in the *Essay on Criticism* (1711).

19 Thora Burnley Jones and Bernard de Bear Nicol, *Neo-Classical Dramatic Criticism, 1560–1770* (Cambridge, 1976), p. 91. Such views lead directly to those of Johnson and Sebastien Mercier, for whom "real tragedy will concern all citizens, will be in touch with current politics, will unfold to the people their true interests, encourage an enlightened patriotism and love of country." Ibid., p. 164, paraphrased from chap. 2 of Mercier's *Du théâtre ou nouvel essai sur l'art dramatique* (Paris, 1773). This ideal had many representatives in English tragedy a century earlier: one thinks of various tragedies by Crown, Lee, Banks, Dennis, and Addison.

20 See chap. 11 on *Phèdre* for some further remarks on this, with particular reference to Hobbes and Vico.

21 Rymer, *Tragedies of the Last Age*, p. 75.

22 Walter Kaufmann, *Tragedy and Philosophy* (New York, 1968, rpt. 1969), p. 153.

23 Lawrence Danson, *Tragic Alphabet: Shakespeare's Drama of Language* (New Haven and London, 1974), p. 50.

24 Cf. Geoffrey Brereton, *Principles of Tragedy: A Rational Examination of the Tragic Concept in Life and Literature* (Coral Gables, Fla., 1968), pp. 3–20. See also Williams, *Modern Tragedy*, pp. 13–15.

25 Kaufmann, *Tragedy and Philosophy*, p. 59.

26 In his long commentary on the *Poetics* Gerald Else continually emphasizes that the text as we have it is constituted of notes (often corrupt) *on the art of composing tragedies.* One of the most useful modern discussions of tragedy is also the only modern treatment to attack the matter from the view of the artisan of tragedies. Elder Olson, *Tragedy and the Theory of Drama* (Detroit, 1961).

27 George Steiner, *The Death of Tragedy* (London 1961), p. 8. Kaufmann (pp. 96–97) notes the centrality of catastrophe in tragedy, but in the context of an opposition to the novel. He notes that it is essential to all tragedy, but does not confuse catastrophe with a bad ending: "It may fill the middle of the play and be averted at the end."

28 *Poetics*, 1454a. When earlier (1453a) Aristotle praises Euripides as the most tragic of playwrights it is not clear whether he is referring to his use of the traditional stories around the few families of horror or to the unhappy endings he gives to "many" of them. On the other hand there is no doubt as to the particular situation Aristotle calls "best of all": a deed of horror contemplated in ignorance of certain relationships that causes considerable suffering but is averted in time to prevent the final consummation by means of peripety and recognition.

29 Richard B. Sewall, *The Vision of Tragedy* (New Haven and London, 1959), p. 29.

30 Else, *Aristotle's Poetics*, pp. 378–85.

31 I will not detail this remark. It has been done, for example, by both Kaufmann and, more extensively, Brian Vickers, *Towards Greek Tragedy: Drama, Myth, Society* (London, 1973), esp. pp. 4–43.

32 The term *hamartia* occurs only twice in the *Poetics, catharsis* once. But the terms matter because they have become an integral part of the legacy of the interpretations of tragedy. Aristotle is talking of an integral part of the *structure* of tragedy. Subsequent writers view the latter at least as an essential *effect* of tragedy.

33 Else, *Aristotle's Poetics*, pp. 437–38. The term is here discussed at some length (pp. 423–47) and the argument seems persuasive. He remarks earlier (p. 231) that the *pathematōn* on which catharsis operates are "painful or fatal acts" rather than emotions (p. 231).

34 Such a need seems to have been felt obscurely by the many writers who have expressed complete mystification as to how catharsis as a purging of the spectator's emotions might be supposed to work and have dismissed the whole supposed operation with profound incredulity.

35 A situation akin to this is already apparent in Homer, for the poet in his description of events always knows which of the gods is responsible and when, while those who within the poem relate their own experiences are

always in ignorance of such identity. They speak "vaguely of a god, of a *daímon,* or of the gods in general." Even the chief of the gods is generalized for these protagonists to such a degree that his name comes to indicate little more than an imprecise divine intervention. The counterpoint of the heroes' ignorance is the knowledge the poet possesses thanks to the ordering of his discourse. Cf. Martin P. Nilsson, *Greek Piety,* tr. Herbert Jennings Rose (New York, 1948; rpt. 1969), pp. 59-60.

36 *Poetics,* 1450a; 1452a-b. Cf. Else, *Aristotle's Poetics,* pp. 343-55.

37 Else, *Aristotle's Poetics,* p. 230.

38 Michel Foucault, *Les mots et les choses* (Paris, 1966), pt. 1. For the Hesiodic rupture, Marcel Detienne, *Crise agraire et attitude religieuse chez Hésiode,* Coll. Latomus, 48, Brussels-Berchem, 1963.

39 Francis Macdonald Cornford, *From Religion to Philosophy: A Study in the Origins of Western Speculation* (New York, 1912; rpt. 1957), pp. 7-39. Cf. Jean-Pierre Vernant, *Mythe et pensée chez les Grecs,* 2nd ed., 2 vols. (Paris, 1971), 2: 95-124; and Bruno Snell, *The Discovery of the Mind,* tr. T. G. Rosenmayer (Cambridge, Mass., 1953).

40 T. B. L. Webster, *From Mycenae to Homer* (New York, 1958; rpt. 1964), pp. 42-43. My italics.

41 Detienne, *Crise agraire,* p. 41. One must remember, of course, that Detienne is referring to an already ordered discourse (that of Hesiod) and cannot speak of an experience not already "reduced" by commentary.

42 Ibid., p. 63; cf. Cornford, *Religion to Philosophy,* pp. 40-123.

43 Ibid., pp. 28-31, and passim.

44 Webster, *Mycenae,* p. 143; cf. Vernant, *Mythe et pensée,* 2:114-18.

45 Cornford argues that the development of Milesian science in the sixth century is precisely analogous to the process followed by religion on its way to complete anthropomorphism. *Religion to Philosophy,* p. 39.

46 Webster, *Mycenae,* p. 292. Cf. Cornford, *Religion to Philosophy,* and Snell, *Discovery of the Mind.* The same is the case for the increasingly complex linear formalization that can be followed between Mycenean and Geometric art, and its "termination" in a classical art where schematization and individualization are combined in a formula that is also quite analogous to what can be seen in tragedy. This same synthesis is visible in theatrical masks: according to the painted artifacts of the period, the totally stylized mask that we are sometimes prone to envisage did not exist throughout the fifth century. There was, on the contrary, a certain "realism" combined with the rigid effect of the mask: see H. C. Baldry, *The Greek Tragic Theatre* (New York, 1971), pp. 56-59, and John H. F. Jones, *On Aristotle and Greek Tragedy* (London, 1962), pp. 45-46. Of course, one must beware of taking such artifact painting as directly representative of what a theatrical performance might have shown, for such painting also involves an ordering process of its own. For the artifacts see Louis Séchan, *Etudes sur la tragédie grecque dans ses rapports avec la céramique* (Paris, 1926); T. B. L. Webster, *Monuments Illustrating Tragedy and Satyr Play,* 2nd ed. (London, 1967); A. D. Trendall and T. B. L. Webster, *Illustrations of Greek Drama* (London, 1971).

47 Steiner, *Death of Tragedy*, p. 8.

48 Thucydides, *Peloponnesian Wars*, 2: 82.4 ff.

49 Tragedies certainly continue to be both written and performed. But things are utterly changed: it is now normal for an Agathon to invent his own plots (Aristotle, *Poetics*, 1451b), the plays are no longer restricted to a couple of particular festivals but are performed everywhere and anywhere, actors have become more important than writers. However, no complete texts are available and commentary is not possible.

50 Jean-Pierre Vernant, "Le moment historique de la tragédie en Grèce: quelques conditions sociales et psychologiques," in Vernant and Pierre Vidal-Nacquet, *Mythe et tragédie en Grèce ancienne* (Paris, 1972), p. 15.

51 Vernant, "Tensions et ambiguités dans la tragédie grecque," *Mythe et tragédie*, pp. 24–25.

52 Vernant, "Oedipe sans complexe," *Mythe et tragédie*, p. 81. My italics.

53 See, e.g., Gerald F. Else, *The Origin and Early Form of Greek Tragedy* (New York, 1965; rpt. 1972), pp. 21–26.

54 Gilbert Murray's views were long ago refuted by Arthur W. Pickard-Cambridge, *Dithyramb, Tragedy and Comedy* (Oxford, 1927), pp. 185–208.

55 Friedrich Nietzsche, *The Birth of Tragedy*, in *The Birth of Tragedy and the Genealogy of Morals*, tr. Francis Golffing (Garden City, N.Y., 1956), p. 54.

56 Else, *Origin*, p. 3. This view is also that of Vickers, *Towards Greek Tragedy*, p. 36.

57 Else, *Origin*, pp. 32 ff.; H. D. F. Kitto, *Form and Meaning in Drama: A Study of Six Greek Plays and of "Hamlet,"* 2nd ed. (London, 1964), pp. 219–20.

58 Vernant, "Le moment historique," p. 14; cf. "Tensions et ambiguités," p. 27. Speaking of the mask, Jones has similarly remarked that for Aristotle "the actor-mask is not a portrait, not a likeness; it presents, it does not re-present; it gives us King Oedipus" (*On Aristotle*, p. 59).

59 Cf. Octave Mannoni, *Clefs pour l'imaginaire, ou l'autre scène* (Paris, 1969), pp. 9–33.

60 T. B. L. Webster, *Greek Theatre Production*, 2nd ed. (London, 1970), p. 2.

61 Adolphe Appia, *La musique et la mise en scène (1892–1897)* (Berne, 1970), p. 38.

62 See Albert B. Lord, *The Singer of Tales* (Cambridge, Mass., 1960).

63 I have in mind here the distinction *tragoïdos/hupokrités* indicated by Else, *Origin*, pp. 56–59; *Aristotle's Poetics*, pp. 167–68.

64 Kaufmann, *Tragedy and Philosophy*, p. 43; cf. pp. 90–93. Pierre Gravel, "Aristote et la poétique (de l'oubli et du travail de certains reminiscences)," *Etudes littéraires* (Dec. 1976), pp. 555–56, n. 1: "La 'mimésis' est reprise, faire paraître, manifestation, dévoilement, évocation."

65 *Poetics*, 1453b.

66 Else, *Aristotle's Poetics*, p. 12. When Rymer and Dennis were arguing about the suitability or nonsuitability of Greek forms for Restoration tragedy they were, therefore, arguing in Aristotle's sense over the wrong thing. Performance is entirely dependent on convention; the order of action, on the other hand, is supposed to correspond in some way to that of the permanent real (in disregard of the fact that such "real" is the product of a given discursive logic).

67 Cf. Else, *Aristotle's Poetics*, pp. 70–71; Daniel Heinsius, *On Plot in Tragedy* (1611), tr. Paul R. Sellin and John J. MacManmon, ed. P. R. Sellin (Northridge, Calif., 1971), p. 20: "Tragedy . . . is an imitation not of men but of actions and human life. That is to say, it imitates not men as men, but men insofar as they act."

68 Jones, *On Aristotle*, p. 29 (my italics); cf. pp. 24–29, 41, 161–62, and passim. Vernant also writes of tragedy as a "model" ("Ambiguités et renversement. Sur la structure énigmatique d'*Oedipe-Roi*," *Mythe et tragédie*, p. 130), and Kitto writes: "Life is represented not by an inspired aggregation of particulars, so chosen and so disposed that they suggest the inexpressible Whole [as he claims of Shakespeare], but by a rigorous selection followed by a significant disposition which illuminates, as in a living diagram, the very structure of human life [the case of Aeschylus and Sophocles]": *Form and Meaning*, p. 225.

69 Else, *Aristotle's Poetics*, p. 263.

70 Vernant, "Tensions et ambiguités," pp. 35–36; but above all, see Vernant's various writings on *Oedipus the King*.

71 Bernard M. Knox, *Oedipus at Thebes* (New York, 1957), pp. 116–38. The phrase "straight linear motion" used here refers to the opposition emphasized by Lévi-Strauss and others between the linearity and diachronicity of analytical thought and the nonlinearity, synchronicity of "mythical thought." The phrase also refers to a certain idea of knowledge and power.

72 Bernard M. Knox, *The Heroic Temper: Studies in Sophoclean Tragedy* (Berkeley and Los Angeles, 1966), p. 146: Oedipus "was a demonstration, through his predicted destiny and his heroic action, that man's keenest sight is blindness, his highest knowledge ignorance, his soaring confidence and hope an illusion." This is very close to George Steiner's claims.

73 Ibid., p. 147.

74 Ibid., p. 9.

75 Knox, *Oedipus at Thebes*, pp. 42–43.

76 Knox, *Oedipus at Thebes*, pp. 147–48. Cf. Jones, *On Aristotle*, pp. 212–13; Kitto, *Greek Tragedy: A Literary Study*, 3rd ed. (London, 1961), pp. 171–86.

77 Kitto, *Form and Meaning*, pp. 208, 217–18. Else also emphasizes the constructive nature of Aeschylus's tragedies: *Origin*, p. 83.

78 *Heracles*, tr. William Arrowsmith, in *The Complete Greek Tragedies*, ed. David Grene and Richmond Lattimore (Chicago and London, 1953–59), *Euripides*, vol. 2, p. 112, line 1385.

79 *Complete Greek Tragedies, Euripides*, vol. 1, p. v.

80 *Iphigenia in Tauris*, tr. Witter Bynner, *Euripides*, vol. 2, p. 145, lines 570–72.

81 William Arrowsmith, introduction to *Hecuba, Euripides*, vol. 3, p. 6.

82 Baldry, *Greek Tragic Theatre*, p. 15, cf. pp. 19–35; Else, *Origin*, p. 101; Knox, *Oedipus*, pp. 107, 159–60, 168, and passim.

83 Kaufmann too views tragedy as ultimately "optimistic." *Tragedy and Philosophy*, p. 227.

84 Of this slowly developing knowledge, Vernant writes: "In order to explain the changes in the cosmos, appeal is made increasingly to models provided

by technical ingenuity, instead of by reference to animal life or the growth of plants. Man understands better, and differently, what he has himself constructed": *Mythe et pensée*, 2: 103.

85 Comedy can (and no doubt should) be examined in these terms. I have made certain suggestions in a short text on Corneille's *Le Menteur* (*Romance Notes*, 15, no. 2 [1974]: comedy appears to put socialized discourse into question, into crisis, in such a way as finally to allow its affirmation as a visible order. Tragedy creates the discourse, comedy takes it already created: which is perhaps why the eighteenth century is essentially one of comedy.

86 Williams, *Modern Tragedy*, p. 15.

87 On the notion of *occulted individualism*, see the articles mentioned in note 2, particularly the first.

88 Quoted by Williams, *Modern Tragedy*, p. 33.

89 On this question of "willfulness," see Vernant, "Ebauches de la volonté dans la tragédie grecque," *Mythe et tragédie*, pp. 48–54; Else, *Aristotle's Poetics*, p. 380.

90 In the same way, were we to conceive of a present-day production and development of the discourse, tragedy (supposing it *necessary*), it would be as once again performing that same role, but the manifestation of that performance would be ruled by a third very different socio-discursive conjuncture. There are a few remarks on this at the end of my concluding chapter.

Chapter 2

1 *La deffence et illustration de la langue françoyse*, ed. Henri Chamard (Paris, 1970), p. 126. Cf. Donald Stone, Jr., *French Humanist Tragedy: A Reassesment* (Manchester, 1974), pp. 11, 16–17.

2 Robert Garnier, *Oeuvres complètes (théâtre et poésies)*, ed. Lucien Pinvert (Paris, 1923), pp. 9–13, 92.

3 Vauquelin de la Fresnaye, *L'art poétique . . .*, ed. Georges Pelletier (Paris, 1885), p. 121: 2:1053–56. For the comments concerning the dates of this text, see pp. xxxii, xxxiv, and xxxv–vi.

4 Stone, *Humanist Tragedy*, pp. 61–75, 79 ff.

5 Roger Ascham, *The Scholemaster*, in *The English Works*, ed. William Aldis Wright (Cambridge, 1904), p. 276.

6 Thomas Sebillet, *Art poétique françoys*, ed. Félix Gaiffe (Paris, 1910), p. 18; Estienne Dolet, *La maniere de bien traduire d'une langue en autre, d'avantage de la ponctuation de la langue françoyse, plus des accents d'ycelle* (Lyon, 1540); Jacques Peletier du Mans, *L'art poétique (1555)*, ed. André Boulanger (Paris, 1930). The preface to the *Art poëtique d'Horace traduit en vers françois* is in the appendix.

7 Jacques Grévin, the "Brief discours," preceding *César*, the "Avant jeux" of *La trésorière* and *Les esbahis*, in *Théâtre complet et poésies choisies*, ed. Lucien Pinvert (Paris, 1922), pp. 7, 52, 116; Etienne Jodelle, *Oeuvres complètes*, ed. Enea Balmas, 2 vols. (Paris, 1965–68), 2:12; *La tragédie du*

sac de Cabrières, ed. Fernand Benoît and J. Vianey (Marseille, 1927). According to the editors, this last play may be dated between 1566 and 1568.

8 Alexander Pope, prologue to Joseph Addison's *Cato*, in *Eighteenth-century Plays*, ed. John Hampden (London, 1928; rpt. 1964), p. 5.

9 Boileau is quoted in the Pléiade edition: *Oeuvres complètes*, ed. Françoise Escal (Paris, 1966), p. 169.

10 Boileau, ibid., pp. 266, 377. Cf. Jules Brody, *Boileau and Longinus* (Geneva, 1958), p. 122.

11 For this aspect of Corneille's theatre and of the drama immediately preceding it see my *Toward Dramatic Illusion: Theatrical Technique and Meaning from Hardy to "Horace"* (New Haven and London, 1971).

12 Michel de Montaigne, *Oeuvres complètes*, ed. Albert Thibaudet and Maurice Rat (Paris, 1962), p. 1046.

13 Louis Marin, *Critique du discours: sur la "logique de port-royal" et les "pensées" de Pascal* (Paris, 1975). See also my commentary, "Sailing to Byzantium: Classical Discourse and Its Self-Absorption," *Diacritics* 8, no. 1 (Spring 1978): 34–46.

14 Jean Paris, *Rabelais au futur* (Paris, 1970), pp. 49–94, and passim.

15 Buchanan's political and religious associations throughout Europe were considerable, but are not really our concern here. His relations with French men of letters in particular are considered by I. D. MacFarlane, "George Buchanan and France," in *Studies in French Literature Presented to H. W. Lawton by Colleagues, Pupils and Friends*, ed. J. C. Ireson, I. D. MacFarlane, and Garnet Rees (Manchester, 1968), pp. 223–45. Buchanan's movements at this period are not well known, but he was in Bordeaux from 1539 to 1542 or 1543, in Paris until 1547, in Portugal from 1547 until 1552, again in Paris until 1561, at which date he returned to Scotland. See P. Hume Browne, *George Buchanan: Humanist and Reformer. A Biography* (Edinburgh, 1890); J. M. Aitken, *The Trial of George Buchanan Before the Lisbon Inquisition* (Edinburgh, 1939). MacFarlane has announced a full-length intellectual biography, not yet published.

16 *Baptistes sive Calumnia; Jephthes sive Votum*. All quotations are taken from Georgii Buchanani . . ., *Opera Omnia, Historica, Chronologica, Juridica, Politica, Satyrica et Poetica . . .*, curante Thoma Ruddimano . . . et . . . Petr[o] Burmann[o], in duos tomos distributa (Lugduni Batavorum, 1725). Both plays are in the second volume. I will discuss them here in the order of their composition rather than that of publication (*Jephthes* in Paris in 1544, *Baptistes* in London in 1577). Buchanan writes in his preface to *Baptistes*: "quod meus, quamquam abortivus, tamen primus est foetus" (2: 217). The date of their composition was between 1541 and 1544, according to Raymond Lebègue, *La tragédie religieuse en France: les débuts, 1514–1571* (Paris, 1929), pp. 206–44. The English translations of both plays are my own and are intended to remain as close as possible to the original without sacrificing readability. A French translation of *Jephthes* by Florent Chrestien appeared in 1587, two others were made in 1590 and 1614; there was one of *Baptistes* in 1613. An English translation of the latter was published in

1642 by order of "the Committee of the House of Commons concerning
Printing," presumably as a commentary on the political situation in England.
This version was later republished as being the original work of John Milton
by Francis Peck in his *New Memoirs of the Life and Poetical Works of Mr.
John Milton* (London, 1740), pp. 265–428. The translation has been more
exactly reprinted by John T. T. Brown, "An English Translation of George
Buchanan's *Baptistes* attributed to John Milton," in *George Buchanan:
Glasgow Quatercentenary Studies, 1906* (Glasgow, 1907), pp. 61–173. This
translation is insufficiently close to the Latin for my purpose.

17 Emile Benveniste, *Problèmes de linguistique générale* (Paris, 1966), pp.
    253–54, 255–56.

18 Robert Garnier, *Les Juifves, Bradamante, Poésies diverses*, ed. Raymond
    Lebègue (Paris, 1949), 1: 115–26.

19 Ben Jonson, *Timber, or Discoveries*, in *Ben Jonson*, ed. C. H. Herford and
    Percy and Evelyn Simpson (Oxford, 1925–52), 8: 580, lines 539–40.

20 Richard Griffiths, *The Dramatic Technique of Antoine de Monchrestien.
    Rhetoric and Style in French Renaissance Tragedy* (Oxford, 1970), p. 73.
    Cf. Wolfgang Clemen, *English Tragedy Before Shakespeare: The Develop-
    ment of Dramatic Speech*, trans. T. S. Dorsch (London, 1961), p. 12; and
    the whole of Stone, *Humanist Tragedy*, esp. pp. 94–96, and more generally,
    pp. 84–131.

21 One thinks here of certain formulae in Seneca: for example, "I Syster of the
    Thunderer . . ." with which Juno begins *Hercules Furens*: Seneca, *His Tenne
    Tragedies. Translated into English*, ed. Thomas Newton, intro. T. S. Eliot
    (Bloomington and London, 1927; rpt. 1964), p. 9.

22 Cf. Kitto, *Greek Tragedy*, pp. 38–40.

23 Lebègue, *Tragèdie religieuse*, p. 238.

24 Benveniste, *Problèmes*, p. 254.

25 On the *ergo* and the discursive space it creates see articles of chap. 1, n. 2.

26 Michel de Montaigne, "Du repentir," *Oeuvres complètes*, p. 782; trans.: *The
    Complete Works. Essays; Travel Journal; Letters*, tr. Donald M. Frame
    (London, n.d.), pp. 610–11.

27 "De Democritus et Heraclitus," p. 290; Frame trans., p. 220.

28 Hugo Friedrich, *Montaigne*, tr. Robert Rovini (Paris, 1968), p. 171.

29 "De la vanite des paroles," p. 294; Frame trans., p. 223.

30 "De la force de l'imagination," p. 104; Frame trans., p. 75.

31 "De Democritus et Heraclitus," p. 291; Frame trans., p. 221.

32 "De l'institution des enfans," p. 146; Frame trans., p. 108.

33 Montaigne writes: "I played the leading parts in the Latin tragedies of
    Buchanan, Guerente, and Muret, which were performed with dignity in our
    Collège de Guyenne. In this matter, as in all other parts of his job, Andreas
    Goveanus, our principal, was incomparably the greatest principal in France:
    and I was considered a master craftsman. [This] is an exercise that I do not
    at all disapprove of for young children of good family" (Frame trans., pp.
    818–19; I: 26: "De l'institution des enfans," p. 176). On the educational
    role of humanist tragedy in France, see esp. Stone, *Humanist Tragedy*,
    pp. 29–36, 84–131. Stone notes that the tragedies very often specify in title,

prologue, or even margin the particular ethical instruction being imparted
(p. 88). He remarks of the "intentions" of humanist tragedy that the "desire
to teach—overtly and incessantly—must share the limelight in this connection with an intense fascination for words" (p. 160). This educational role
of theatre is no less the case in England and Italy, as Lily B. Campbell has
pointed out (*Scenes and Machines on the English Stage During the Renaissance: A Classical Revival* (New York, 1923; rpt. 1960), pp. 83–98. Cf.
her *Shakespeare's Tragic Heroes: Slaves of Passion* (London, 1930; rpt.
1977), pp. 25–38.

34 Two brief but extremely important indications: Ascham's praise of *Jephthes*
in *The Scholemaster* (written c. 1563, published 1570), *English Works*,
p. 284; Sidney's remark that only "the Tragedies of *Buchanan* do iustly
bring forth a diuine admiration," *An Apology for Poetry* (written c. 1583),
in *Elizabethan Critical Essays*, ed. G. Gregory Smith, 2 vols. (London, 1904),
p. 201.

35 René Radouant, "L'Union de l'éloquence et de la philosophie au temps
de Ramus," *Revue d'histoire littéraire de la France* 31, no. 2 (avril–juin
1924): 162. Cf. Walter J. Ong, S. J., "Fouquelin's French Rhetoric and the
Ramist Vernacular Tradition," *Studies in Philology* 51 (1954): 141.

36 Jacques Derrida, *L'Ecriture et la différence* (Paris, 1967), pp. 85 ff.

37 Ibid., p. 64.

38 Ibid., pp. 63–64, and "La pharmacie de Platon," in *La dissemination* (Paris,
1972), pp. 70–197.

Chapter 3

1 Estienne Jodelle, *Oeuvres complètes*, ed. Enea Balmas, 2 vols. (Paris, 1965–
68), 2: 91–147. All references are by act and page to this edition.

2 Edmond Huguet, *Dictionnaire de la langue française du seizième siècle* (Paris,
1925–67, 4: 53–54. The two meanings given are (1) protector, partisan, etc.
(i.e., one who is favorable), and (2) one who makes an error. According to
Littré, the word had only the second, pejorative, sense by the end of the
seventeenth century.

3 For these dates, etc., see Balmas's notes, 2: 444–46. There was at least one
other performance of the play, shortly after the first, at the Collège de Bon-
court for the benefit of teachers and scholars. I say "in effect if not in
chronology" because though the 1552 performance had been a considerable
event, the play was not available to a reading public until its publication
in 1574.

4 We should remember here that stage spectacle played rather a small part in
this theatre. No doubt the play would appear to us more like a dramatized
play reading (like *Baptistes* or *Jephthes*). I mean this as a statement of fact,
not as a value judgment.

5 The matter has been discussed by Georg R. Garner, "Tragedy, Sovereignty,
and the Sign: Jodelle's *Cléopâtre captive*," *Canadian Review of Comparative
Literature* 5, no. 3 (Fall 1978): 245–79. Garner is currently completing a
doctoral thesis at the Université de Montréal that deals with the same
matter over a broader corpus and a greater period of time.

6 Cf. also the reason he gives for not refusing Cléopâtre's treasure: "le bon heur/D'estre du tout en la terre seigneur."

7 This *control* over time will be a later part of the development. For the moment, time, given as a reality outside discourse, is clearly perceived as menacing: it is a power ranged against human activity. In this aspect it is similar to what is experienced in Greek tragedy. Jacqueline de Romilly remarks: "Time is generally thought of as a threat, not as a continued evolution." *Time in Greek Tragedy* (Ithaca, N. Y., 1968), p. 25. For its later development see my extended comments in chapter 11.

8 The implications of Cléopâtre's offer of gold is considered at length by Garner, "Tragedy, Sovereignty, and the Sign," 267–73.

9 Balmas, 2: 443, notes.

10 Each of these, as I said earlier, both permits and contains the "meaning" of the one next to it, but also depends on the others for its continuing process.

Chapter 4

1 In discussing the play I will be following those writers who treat the two parts of *Tamburlaine* as a coherent whole: there is little point in mentioning them all here. The study that comes closest to my own preoccupations is an article dealing only with part 1: David Daiches, "Language and Action in Marlowe's *Tamburlaine*," reprinted in Irving Ribner, ed., *Christopher Marlowe's Tamburlaine Part One and Part Two: Text and Major Criticism* (Indianapolis and New York, 1974), pp. 312–40.

2 J. B. Steane, ed., Christopher Marlowe, *The Complete Plays* (Harmondsworth, 1969).

3 Judith Weil, *Christopher Marlowe: Merlin's Prophet* (Cambridge, 1977), pp. 107–08.

4 Daiches, "Language and Action," pp. 313–14.

5 J. B. Steane, *Marlowe: A Critical Study* (Cambridge, 1964), p. 115.

6 Weil, *Merlin's Prophet*, p. 118.

7 All italics in Marlowe's text are my own; as they are in the text of all subsequent tragedies discussed.

8 Steane, Introduction to *The Complete Plays*, p. 18.

9 Daiches, "Language and Action," p. 333.

10 Ibid., p. 318.

11 Ibid., pp. 332–33.

12 The word *exhalation* is used, I think, twice in *1 Tamburlaine*, the second time referring to lightning, the "fiery exhalation" that will "make the welkin crack" and is likened to Tamburlaine's sword (4.2.43–45).

13 A similar remark is made at 5.2.121–24.

14 Something similar is played out on many occasions. One example is when Tamburlaine, about to go into battle against Bajazeth and leaving Zenocrate and Zabina on thrones side by side, says to Zenocrate: "Manage words with her, as we will arms" (3.3.131). And it is just that that we *see*, while the military battle is going on elsewhere. It is as Zenocrate concludes with the words "he lives and will be conqueror" (3.3.211), as she

thus signifies her verbal victory over Zabina, that Tamburlaine enters with the defeated Bajazeth.

15 Part 2, 3.5.134: Almeda says to Tamburlaine, on being offered a crown by Callapine and urged on by Orcanes: "Good my lord, let me take it." Callapine had earlier shown his lack of understanding of discursive power: "Ah, were I now but half so eloquent/To paint in words what I'll perform in deeds" (part 2, 1.3.9–10). What he does not understand is that he cannot have the one without the other. So at the end of the play Callapine will speak of "our mighty host" (part 2, 5.2.1) at a time when those words have been emptied of meaning: even when he was accompanied by all the other kings they had had to go twice through the numbering of their forces, as though to convince themselves of their might (part 2, 3.1.; 3.5)—three times if we include the first scene with Sigismund, when Callapine was not yet with them. Now he is soon forced to concede that "but one host is left to honour thee" (part 2, 5.2.27), and will shortly be doubting that they can defeat Tamburlaine, whose force "is great,/His fortune greater, and the victories/Wherewith he hath so sore dismay'd the world/Are greatest to discourage all our drifts" (5.2.42–45). They all flee, of course, when confronted with Tamburlaine (5.3.116).

16 A little later, Theridamas will suggest bits for the kings who are not at the moment pulling Tamburlaine's chariot, chiefly because they "pass their fixed bound" of speech (part 2, 4.3.43–47). The ineffectiveness of the speech of those around Orcanes is suggested by Oribassa's statement congratulating themselves on their treaty with Sigismund, whose irony is immediately demonstrated with some force: "Methinks I see how glad the Christian king/Is made for joy of our admitted truce,/That could not but before be terrified/With unacquainted power of our host" (part 2, 2.2.20–23). Whereupon a messenger comes racing in to exclaim that Sigismund has broken the truce and is now marching against them.

17 Susan Richards has pointed out another covert reference to Babel in this acting out of Tamburlaine's falling: "For there my palace royal shall be plac'd,/Whose shining turrets shall dismay the heavens,/And cast the fame of Ilion's tower to hell" (part 2, 4.3.111–13). She writes: "The echo here of the Judaeo-Christian tower of Babel is subtle and fits in quite neatly with the classical allusion to 'Ilion's tower,' especially in the notable irony that both of them fell." "Marlowe's *Tamburlaine II*: A Drama of Death," in Ribner, *Marlowe's Tamburlaine*, p. 306. In my reading, of course, this "irony" is only one aspect of the relationship of Tamburlaine to the entire metaphor of hubris and failure in which he is now caught.

18 In chapter 2 (and it will arise again in chapter 6) I suggested a similar metaphoric passage from nomination (though in the former case it is only hinted at) to stage performance in the case of the poison poured in the ear: verbal slander to the silence of death, the one emphasizing the limitations of discourse, the other a "real," physical death. The impediment of all discourse becomes embodied in a particular metaphor and in turn performed as a "generalizable" and comprehensible human activity. Such is the passage from *Baptistes* to *Hamlet* through, for example, *Les Juifves*.

19 Susan Richards suggests four other levels of operation and meaning for this "appearance in the king-drawn chariot": the ritual role of "the conquering Greco-Roman or Asiatic hero": the dramatic role of showing "the progression of the plot"; the role in characterization of "displaying Tamburlaine's flamboyance," etc.; and the symbolic role embodying "the meaning of the play and the figure of Tamburlaine in his universal sense—the human figure who strives to seek godhead by his deeds and is limited by his very nature, his earthliness, who thinks to climb heaven in a chariot drawn by the symbols of his very earthly power, his captive kings," "Marlowe's Tamburlaine II," 309–10. I maintain, of course, that this last "understanding" of the play is precisely that made possible by the growth of the Phaeton metaphor, undermining all the other "levels."

20 Wolfgang Clemen, *English Tragedy Before Shakespeare: The Development of Dramatic Speech*, tr. T. S. Dorsch (London, 1961), p. 116.

21 See my "Espaces de la pensée discursive" (ref., chap. 1, n. 2).

22 We need hardly be reminded that they are the last words of Christ on the cross, and that is specifically recalled at the end by Faustus's celebrated cry of anguish: "See, see, where Christ's blood streams in the firmament" (5.2.156).

23 Max Bluestone, "*Libido speculandi*: Doctrine and Dramaturgy in Contemporary Interpretations of Marlowe's *Doctor Faustus*," in *Selected Papers from the English Institute: Reinterpretations of Elizabethan Drama*, ed. Norman Rabkin (New York and London, 1969), p. 50.

24 Friedrich Nietzsche, *Birth of Tragedy*, p. 28 (ref., chap. 1, n. 55).

25 Ibid., pp. 30–31.

26 Weil, *Merlin's Prophet*, p. 21.

27 Ibid., p. 176.

Chapter 5

1 Quotations are by act and line from Robert Garnier, *Les Juifves, Bradamante, Poésies diverses*, ed. Raymond Lebègue (Paris, 1949).

2 Amital's words here are chiefly aimed at the Prevost, who tried to play out the same device at length (4.1591–1764). However, a dependent so far as his discourse is concerned, he does indeed lie—"vostre mal a prins fin" ("your misfortune has come to an end")—before he goes on to play out the trick without openly lying. Sedecie will not die now but will live to see many others die before him; they will be going home, the children are required as hostages. But there he lies again, when he affirms that they will be in the king's court and cherished (though *who* exactly will be cherished is left deliberately ambiguous), eventually becoming rulers themselves. Unlike Nabuchodonosor, he goes too far. By now the queens are openly distrustful, in a way that Amital was not when confronted with the Assyrian king. Once again she appears to let herself be tricked, saying, "sa parole est vraye, et sa promesse sainte" ("his word is true, and his promise sacred" [4.1688]). At the end, however, she says her farewells as though she knew they were indeed her last.

3 This point is well made by Gillian Jondorf, *Robert Garnier and the Themes of Political Tragedy in the Sixteenth Century* (Cambridge, 1969), pp. 113–21.

4 The beginning and end of her passage into this "higher" discourse are clearly marked in the discussion: "Hà, Monsieur, je vous prie ayez propos plus sains" ("Ah, sir, I beg you to use a safer form of speech" [3.929]). Then Nabuchodonosor says: "Laissons-là ce discours, il est plein de tristesse," to which the queen responds: "Laissons-le, mais aussi laissez toute rudesse" ("Let us leave off this manner of speech, it is full of gloom"; "Let us leave it off, but quit all brutality as well," 3.947–48).

5 Later Sedecie says the same thing to Sarree: "Je desire mourir . . . / C'est mon port de salut" ("I want to die . . . / It is my haven of safety" [4.1305–07]). Lebègue is "wrong" to speak of Sedecie's "courageuse attitude" (Garnier, *Les Juifves*, p. 275). Death would be an escape for him, and Nabuchodonosor is now well aware of it. The force of these lines is precisely that *we* now *know* that Sedecie cannot escape and why, though Sedecie himself remains ignorant (like Amital). That difference is a consequence of the system, tragedy, well on the way to its stable establishment.

6 If my interpretation of these two lines seems long and far-fetched (it was once even longer), I will remark that without such an interpretation Sedecie's question would be either frivolous or meaningless. The seriousness with which the Assyrian responds suggests that it is neither.

7 Says Nabuchodonosor to Sedecie: "Je t'ay baillé leur sceptre en t'obligeant à moy" ("I granted you rule over them and thus bound you to me in gratitude" [4.1438]).

8 This too, of course, refers us to Seneca: Atreus declaims, "He could not taken bee, / Except himselfe would take: but now my kingdomes hopeth he. / For hope of this he woulde not feare to meete the mighty Jove, / Though him he threatned to destroy, with lightning from above." *Thyestes*, trans. Jasper Heywood (1560), act 2, in Seneca, *His Tenne Tragedies*, p. 64. I will not indicate further such reminders of the formal system of tragedy: they are constant.

9 Amital likewise wishes to use tears to sway Nabuchodonosor's decision: "Approchez donc mes Brus, laschez la bonde aux larmes, / Souspirez, sanglotez . . ." ("So come close my dears, let your tears be unleashed, / Sigh, sob . . . " [3.979–80]).

Chapter 6

1 Quotations are from the *Complete Pelican Shakespeare*, gen. ed. Alfred Harbage (New York, 1969).

2 Mark Rose, *Shakespearean Design* (Cambridge, Mass., 1972), pp. 7–26. On *Hamlet* particularly, see pp. 95–125.

3 On the Globe (and Elizabethan public theatre design generally), see Bernard Beckerman, *Shakespeare at the Globe* (New York, 1962); Sir Edmund K. Chambers, *The Elizabethan Stage*, 4 vols. (Oxford, 1923), 2:414–34, 3:103–54; C. Walter Hodges, *The Globe Restored: A Study of the Elizabethan*

Theatre, 2nd edition (London, 1968); A. M. Nagler, *Shakespeare's Stage* (New Haven, 1958); Irwin Smith, *Shakespeare's Globe Playhouse* (New York, 1956); Frances A. Yates, *Theatre of the World* (London 1969). The nature of the audience has been dealt with especially by Alfred Harbage, *Shakespeare's Audience* (New York, 1941), and *As They Liked It* (New York, 1947).

4 Bernard Beckerman, "Shakespeare's Theatre," in Harbage, *Complete Pelican Shakespeare*, p. 28.

5 Frances Yates's *Theatre of the World* is controversial, and there are many who refuse to give the weight she does to Robert Fludd's memory theatre and to the supposed contacts between James Burbage and John Dee. But many of her arguments must be well taken as to their principle, if not to their details.

6 There is, however, some doubt as to this. Hodges speaks of a part of the audience being "allowed to sit smoking and playing cards on stage" (*Globe Restored*, p. 8), while Irwin Smith denies categorically that such was ever the case at the Globe. Indeed, in his view it is one of the differences between the public and private theatres: "The Blackfriars Playhouse permitted gallants to sit upon the stage during performances, in spite of the actors' and the dramatists' dislike of the practice. The Globe did not." *Shakespeare's Blackfriars Playhouse: Its History and Its Design* (New York, 1964; London, 1966), p. 220.

7 Irwin Smith (among others) notes the duration of performances as between two and three hours (*Blackfriars Playhouse*, pp. 260–61). See also my note 19.

8 Actually the upper stage is not really required here by the action, and the audience of the Globe would almost certainly not need the indication of a particular place for any of these scenes: the dialogue itself contains sufficient indication. Furthermore there would seem small justification (or stage logic) for the ghost's being "under the stage" (1.5.149) if Hamlet, Horatio, and Marcellus were on the upper stage—though Hamlet could have remained above while the other two came in on the main stage. It would make for an awkward conversation, particularly one so intimate. Chambers also denies the need of the upper stage for these scenes. *Elizabethan Stage*, 3:116.

9 Bertolt Brecht, in *Brecht on Theatre*, ed. and trans. John Willett (New York, 1964), pp. 218, 225, and especially, *The Messingkauf Dialogues*, trans. John Willett (London, 1965; rpt. 1977), "The Second Night," pp. 57–63.

10 Norman Rabkin, *Shakespeare and the Common Understanding* (New York, 1967).

11 I am, of course, speaking not of what *Hamlet* "is" (i.e., of the many meanings one may wish to read into the play) but of what the play *does*. What it does is oppose action and inaction, knowledge and distraction; what it *is* will have to do with our attitudes toward the representatives of those "sides" and suchlike.

12 Lawrence Danson, *Tragic Alphabet: Shakespeare's Drama of Language* (New Haven and London, 1974), p. 33.

13 Terence Eagleton, *Shakespeare and Society: Critical Studies in Shakespearean Drama* (London, 1967), p. 52.

14 The idea that *The Tragedy of Hamlet, Prince of Denmark* is the story told
    by Horatio in accordance with the request made by Hamlet himself at the
    end has become of late something of a critical commonplace. See, e.g.,
    Danson, *Tragic Alphabet*, p. 49; Northrop Frye, *Fools of Time* (Toronto,
    1967), p. 31.
15 Danson, *Tragic Alphabet*, p. 2.
16 There are many indications of this "distraction" in this man who never
    speaks to the point. He tells Laertes to be above all true to himself (1.3.78),
    where the whole play tells us that such a demand is meaningless: one is as
    one does (though no one can say which comes first), as others see one, or
    outside human relationships altogether. "I have found out," he says, "the
    very cause of Hamlet's lunacy" (2.2.48–49), when we know that (a) Hamlet
    is not mad, and (b) the cause of his pretense is not what Polonius claims it
    to be. He tells Ophelia incorrectly that Hamlet's love is false, he asks the
    audience to accept his mistaken judgment of Hamlet's mocking treatment of
    him ("How say you by that" [2.2.185–90]), he asks Claudius if he has ever
    known him, Polonius, to be wrong (2.2.153–55). In short, right up until
    his death he has misunderstood everything—including, and in that his atti-
    tude is shared by Gertrude, his ignorance of the king's crime and his com-
    placent acceptance of incest. Unlike the Jephtha of the Bible, of the
    popular ballad (apparently), and of Buchanan's play, Polonius will sacrifice
    his daughter through ignorance, not through strength (by telling her to
    refuse Hamlet's love and then using her to bait a trap for the prince)—
    though it is true that Buchanan's Jephthes did not understand the limits of
    his strength. But that ignorance on Polonius's part is surely what provokes
    Hamlet's mocking cry to the old man: "O Jephthah, judge of Israel, what a
    treasure hadst thou!" (2.2.393). The worst thing about Polonius remains
    his unwavering conviction that his ignorance is knowledge.
17 Cf. the way in which Thomas Nashe speaks of an earlier *Hamlet*: "Yet
    English Seneca . . . yields many good sentences . . . and if you entreat him
    fair in a frosty morning, he will afford you whole *Hamlets*, I should say
    handfuls of tragical speeches," from the preface to Robert Greene's *Mena-
    phon* (London, 1589), quoted by Edward Hubler in the Signet edition of
    Hamlet (New York and Toronto, 1963), p. 184. In a certain sense, then, Ham-
    let is using the style of an earlier *Hamlet* as a trap for a king who earlier per-
    formed the crime.
18 Perhaps an earlier *Hamlet* is recalled here too. It seems probable (according
    to critical reconstruction) that the rumor there spread was not that the
    king had died the unnatural death of a snake bite (with all its metaphorical
    overtones) but the natural one of an apoplexy. Again, the spectator might
    well know this.
19 As I suggested earlier, this may also be a reference to the duration of the
    play, and so a remark made not only to Ophelia but also to the audience.
    The comment is deliberately ambiguous: it can also refer to the length of
    time old Hamlet took to die.
20 Bertolt Brecht, *Collected Plays*, ed. Ralph Manheim and John Willett (New
    York, 1971–), 6: 351. The passage is among the *Practice Pieces for*

Actors (trans. Ralph Manheim), and is the "Concluding Report" to be performed while rehearsing *Hamlet*.

Chapter 7

1 Pierre Gravel, *Pour une logique du sujet tragique: Sophocle* (Montreal, 1980).
2 Bertolt Brecht, *The Messingkauf Dialogues*, trans. John Willett (New York, 1964), p. 59.
3 Elder Olson, *Tragedy and the Theory of Drama* (Detroit, 1961), p. 201.
4 Paul Delany, "*King Lear* and the Decline of Feudalism," *PMLA* 92, no. 3 (May 1977): 429.
5 Lawrence Stone, *The Crisis of the Aristocracy, 1558–1641*, Abridged edn. (London, 1967), p. 21.
6 Brecht, *Messingkauf*, p. 81.
7 The details of this relationship can easily be found. Cf. the introduction, notes, and bibliographical references of Timothy J. Reiss and Roger H. Hinderliter, "Money and Value in the Sixteenth Century: the *Monete Cudende Ratio* of Copernicus," *Journal of the History of Ideas* 40, no. 2 (April, 1979): 293–313.
8 One wonders if *deceive* is the right word: like Lear, Gloucester *wants* to believe that the exchange value and the "intrinsic value" (use value) of words are the same. Hence Gloucester makes no real effort to listen to Edgar. For him, like Lear, it is sufficient that a statement has been made.
9 Olson, *Tragedy and the Theory of Drama*, p. 209.
10 Danson, *Tragic Alphabet*, p. 165.
11 In fact it must be said that Kent is not successful in masking himself: which explains why he lands in the stocks. He and Cordelia do not build "themselves" as subject, as individual self: they are constituted in and by their participation in the network of the intrinsic. Lear's end will of necessity be theirs as well.
12 Brecht, *Messingkauf*, pp. 80–81.
13 In an article that appeared only after the present volume was in proof, Michael Hays argues that this "third" is already presented in the play ("Reason's Rhetoric: *King Lear* and the Social Uses of Irony," *Boundary 2* 7, no. 2 (Winter 1979): 97–116. He suggests that Edgar succeeds in combining Lear's "theatricality" with Edmund's "self-consciousness," that he reacts out of a recognition of their limitations, on the basis of the "rational analysis" of a situation imposed upon him from without and for which he is not at all responsible (and therefore quite differently from almost all the other characters in the tragedy). "His passage through the play," writes Hays, "marks the process of wedding poetic imagination with rational social action" (p. 105). He finds similarities between Edgar and Kent, both with regard to their initial reactions, and inasmuch as they "prepare the way for a justice based on law at the end of the play" (p. 109), for "a larger social vision based on real experience" (p. 113), and for "an integrated vision of creative individuals operating together within the confines of a rational social compact" (p. 116). I find Hays's arguments partly

convincing: there is perhaps rather more in Edgar's future England than a mere grumbling of the past. Though I cannot ascribe to it the certainty Hays infers, there would certainly appear to be more than a hint of a different (future?) discourse from those others proffered in the play.

Chapter 8

1 C. Walter Hodges, *The Globe Restored: A Survey of the Elizabethan Theatre,* 2nd edn. (London, 1968), p. 2.
2 Fredson Thayer Bowers, *English Revenge Tragedy, 1587-1642* (1940; rpt. Gloucester, Mass., 1959), pp. 283-84.
3 Lily B. Campbell, *Scenes and Machines*, pp. 210-19 (ref., chap. 2, n. 33).
4 Quotations are by act and line from the New Mermaid edition: John Dryden, *All For Love*, ed. N. J. Andrew (London and Tonbridge, 1975).
5 See Gerald Eales Bentley, *The Jacobean and Caroline Stage*, 7 vols. (Oxford, 1941-68), 4:834-35. Thomas May's *The Tragedy of Cleopatra Queen of Egypt* was published in 1639.
6 *Antony and Cleopatra: A Tragedy,* in *The Poetical and Dramatic Works of Sir Charles Sedley,* ed. V. de Sola Pinto, 2 vols. (London, 1928), 1:187-263.
7 Eugene M. Waith, *Ideas of Greatness: Heroic Drama in England* (London, 1971).
8 Eric Rothstein, *Restoration Tragedy: Form and the Process of Change* (Madison, Milwaukee, London, 1967), p. 31.
9 Ibid., pp. 51-52.
10 John Ford, *'Tis Pity She's a Whore*, ed. Derek Roper (London, 1975), p. xliii.
11 Ibid., pp. xxxiii, xlii.
12 See Timothy J. Reiss, *Toward Dramatic Illusion: Theatrical Technique and Meaning from Hardy to "Horace"* (New Haven and London, 1971), esp. chaps. 2 and 3.
13 Geoffrey Marshall, *Restoration Serious Drama* (Norman, Okla., 1974), pp. 70-71.
14 Ibid., p. 27 and ff.; Waith, *Ideas of Greatness*, p. 221; James Black, "The Influence of Hobbes on Nahum Tate's *King Lear*," *Studies in English Literature: 1500-1900* 7, no. 3 (Summer 1967): 378-79 and ff.; Rothstein, *Restoration Tragedy*, pp. 8-9ff. For the more general intellectual context see Louis I. Bredvold, *The Intellectual Milieu of John Dryden: Studies in Some Aspects of Seventeenth-Century Thought* (Ann Arbor, 1934; rpt. 1966); and Anne T. Barbeau, *The Intellectual Design of John Dryden's Heroic Plays* (New Haven and London, 1970).

Chapter 9

1 Marion Zons-Giesa, "*Racine: Dramatische Dialektik und die Ende der Tragödie,*" *Freiburger Schriften zur Romanischen Philologie* 34 (Munich, 1977).
2 Cardinal de Richelieu, *Testament politique*, ed. Louis André (Paris, 1947), 2:2, p. 327. The passage continues: "Le Gouvernement des Royaumes

requiert une vertu mâle et une fermeté inébranlable . . ." ("The Government of Kingdoms demands a masculine force and an unshakable firmness").

3 *The Prince*, in Niccolo Machiavelli, *The Chief Works and Others*, trans. Allan Gilbert, 3 vols. (Durham, N.C., 1965), 2: 90 (chap. 25).

4 Thomas Hobbes, *Leviathan*, ed. C. B. Macpherson (Harmondsworth, 1968), 1:13, pp. 185, 186. A few dates may be helpful here: Hobbes published the *De Cive* (the second version of what will eventually become *Leviathan*) in Paris in 1642. At that time he was living in Paris and was very close to the group around Pierre Gassendi, to the polymath (and close friend of Descartes) Marin Mersenne, and others. The first French translation of the *De Cive*, made by Samuel Sorbière, was published by Blaeu in Amsterdam in 1649, two years before the English translation made by Hobbes himself. The French translation went quickly through a number of editions, and there was even a second (abridged) translation made by François Bonneau and published in Paris in 1660. *Leviathan* appeared in 1651, followed by its translation into Latin, chiefly the work of Hobbes, published in Amsterdam in 1668.

5 Thomas Hobbes, *De Cive or The Citizen*, ed. Sterling O. Lamprecht (New York, 1949), 1.1.7, p. 27: "The first foundation of natural right is this, that every man as much as in him lies endeavour to protect his life and members." *Leviathan*, 1: 14: "THE RIGHT OF NATURE . . . is the Liberty each man hath, to use his own power, as he will himselfe, for the preservation of his own Nature . . ." (p. 189); 2: 21: "If a Monarch shall relinquish the Soveraignty, both for himself, and his heires; His Subjects returne to the absolute Libertie of Nature . . ." (p. 273). Cf. *De Cive*, 2:7:18, pp. 98–99; 2:6:3, p. 72.

6 Jean Racine, *Bajazet*, in *Théâtre complet*, ed. Maurice Rat (Paris, 1960).

7 Jean-Louis Guez de Balzac, *Le Prince*, in *Oeuvres*, ed. L. Moreau (Paris, 1854), 1:22, 31.

8 Gabriel Naudé, *Considérations politiques sur les coups d'estat*, sur la copie de Rome, 1667, p. 155.

9 Hobbes, *Leviathan*, p. 272 (2:21).

10 Ibid., p. 273 (2:21).

11 Ibid., p. 161 (1:11).

12 The other last will of Amurat concerning his brother should be mentioned in the present context: "Il partit, et voulut que, fidèle à sa haine,/ Et *des jours de son frère arbitre souveraine,*/ Roxane, *au moindre bruit*, et *sans autres raisons,*/ Le fît sacrifier à ses moindres soupçons" ("He left, and he willed that Roxane, true to his hatred, and sovereign judge of his brother's life, should, at the slightest rumor, and with no other justification, sacrifice him to her least suspicions" [1.1: p. 360]). This demand is very close to the counsels of *Realpolitik* common to many writers of the period. Cf. in Machiavelli, *The Prince*, chap. 7; *Discourses*, 1.9; Naudé, *Considérations*, p. 191, and many others.

13 Richelieu, *Testament*, 1.6, pp. 271, 276.

14 Hobbes, *Leviathan*, 1:10, p. 130.

15 Ibid., 2:21, pp. 264–65. This view is, of course, quite general.

16 Hobbes, *De Cive*, 2.5.1, p. 63.

17 *Segraisiana* (Paris, 1723), mentioned by Maurice Rat, Racine, *Théâtre Complet*, p. 353.

18 Charles de Saint-Evremond, *Oeuvres mêlées*, ed. Charles Giraud (Paris, 1865), 2:300.

19 F. E. Sutcliffe, *Guez de Balzac et son temps: littérature et politique* (Paris, 1959), p. 9.

20 Lucien Goldmann, *Le Dieu caché: etude sur la vision tragique dans les "Pensées" de Pascal et dans le théâtre de Racine* (Paris, 1955); Zons-Giesa, *"Dramatische Dialektik,"* 314 and passim.

Chapter 10

1 Jean Racine, *Théâtre complet*, ed. Maurice Rat (Paris, 1960), p. 476.

2 Daniel Defoe, *An Enquiry into the Case of Mr. Asgil's General Translation* (London, 1704), p. 8, quoted in Maximilian E. Novak, *Defoe and the Nature of Man* (Oxford, 1963), p. 10. It is with deliberation that I insert here the name of the author of *Robinson Crusoe*.

3 Roland Barthes, *Sur Racine* (Paris, 1963), p. 109.

4 *Iphigenia in Aulis*, tr. Charles R. Walker, *Complete Greek Tragedies*, 9 vols., *Euripides*, 4:237, lines 476–80.

5 Jacqueline Van Baelen, *Rotrou: le héros tragique et la révolte* (Paris, 1965), pp. 122–23.

6 Jean Rotrou, *Iphigénie en Aulide, Tragi-comédie*, in *Oeuvres*, ed. Viollet-le-Duc (Paris, 1820), 4:338:5.3.

7 Russell Pfohl argues that the full effectiveness of Racine's tragedy depends on our awareness that it is a retelling of the story: each character "rehearses" the emotions, relationships, and activities of their literary predecessors, in a way perhaps not altogether different from Hamlet's "rehearsal" of his father's murder and Horatio's of Hamlet's own story (*Racine's "Iphigénie": Literary Rehearsal and Tragic Recognition* [Geneva, 1974]).

8 The relationship is quite precise: between money (the signified) and money-of-account (the signifier) the relation fluctuates according as the controlling order (the "State," "Law or Custom") changes the signified (J. M. Keynes, *A Treatise on Money*, 2 vols [London, 1950], I:4). The two together represent a sign whose referent is the goods whose "value" in exchange it denotes. In a period of economic primitivism such as the late Middle Ages in Europe, this discursive sign was hardly perceived as such, or rather, money entered into the same relation with goods as words did with phenomena: they were associated by being possessed of a value equally inherent in all things. That, of course, is what I viewed as Cordelia's attitude toward discourse (see, e.g., E. Heckscher, *Mercantilism*, 2 vols. [London, 1935]; R. H. Tawney, *Religion and the Rise of Capitalism: A Historical Study* [New York, 1926]). The crisis of the great debasement in England in 1550 was the result of a new awareness that money was no more than an arbitrary sign, it showed that the value of money was not inherent but a consequence of human decree: "the rule of custom was overthrown by the alteration of

customary equivalents; each man had to fend for himself and try to maintain his position against the rising price-level" (H. M. Robertson, *Aspects of
the Rise of Economic Individualism: A Criticism of Max Weber and His
School* [Cambridge, 1933], pp. 181–82. Agamemnon is using a fact of this
kind to his own ends, and Achille is understandably bitter when he learns of
it. This is by no means the only time. To Ulysse, for example, Achille comments on a similar disparity between word and thing: until the actual
battle for Greece, "Vous pouvez *à loisir* faire des voeux pour elle" ("You
can make vows on her behalf [that of Greece] with ease"[1.2: p. 484]).
One could pick out innumerable such moments.

9   Commentary upon the "abuse" of names has been a constant of criticism of
Racine's *Iphigénie*. See, e.g., Pfohl, *Racine's "Iphigénie,"* pp. 165–68.

10   Besides, Clytemnestre will protest later, believing Iphigénie jilted by
Achille: "Moi-même, de l'ingrat approuvant le dessein,/Je vous l'ai dans
Argos présenté de ma main;/Et mon choix, que flattait le bruit de la
noblesse,/Vous donnait avec joie au fils d'une déesse" ("Myself, approving
the ungrateful man's intention, I presented him to you with my own hand
at Argos; and my selection, encouraged by the nobles' approval, joyfully
gave you the son of a goddess" [2.4: p. 498]). This statement itself shows
the queen's egotistical motives in her forging and accepting of the contract.

11   Not only is Iphigénie "inadequate" in these terms, but her sacrifice would
defeat its own object, by destroying the very fabric of the society whose
wholeness is to be confirmed by victory at Troy.

12   Later she will call herself "etrangère partout" (2.3: p. 496).

13   That Iphigénie also supposes this possibility is revealed by the lovers'
quarrel and her bitter words to Eriphile: "Vous triomphez, cruelle . . ." She
cannot quite understand Eriphile, and can only see her in the light of her
own social system. Small wonder that Eriphile should express surprise, she
who cannot understand the working of exchange, let alone engage in one
herself.

14   Cf. Barthes, *Sur Racine*, p. 110.

15   Ibid., pp. 109 ff.; Goldmann, *Le Dieu caché*, p. 403.

16   Rotrou, *Iphigénie, Oeuvres*, 4:334:5.3.

17   His glory depends on his going to Troy, his honor *now* depends on his
doing so only after saving Iphigénie as he had promised. He is going to
Troy, we have seen, in fulfillment of a bargain drawn up with Agamemnon,
in which Iphigénie herself is the price. But the contract with Iphigénie herself cannot be for nothing, as he insisted when she had refused to escape
with him: "Songez-vous quel serment vous et moi nous engage?" ("Are you
thinking of what a vow binds us together, you and I?" [5.1: p. 525]).

18   Marcel Gutwirth, *Jean Racine: un itinéraire poétique* (Montreal, 1970),
p. 65, n. 7.

19   For Eriphile's real name is Iphigénie, Calchas proclaims (5.6: p. 532).

20   Pfohl argues that Iphigénie is the "truly tragic" figure in the play, because
alone of all the characters she finds herself at the end without a future:
her place has been taken by Eriphile. We know what the future holds for
Agamemnon, Achille, Ulysse, and Clytemnestre; only Iphigénie's "breaks

off into nothingness" (p. 198). Inasmuch as such an assessment suggests that tragedy is at an end in the sense I have indicated, I would agree: her future is not even Nabuchodonosor's potential tragic space outside the tragedy of *Les Juifves*. In Pfohl's reading the system is continually creating and explicating itself. Tragedy would therefore be capable of writing itself out of existence—and does so (though this is emphatically *not* Pfohl's view).

21 Maurice Rat, preface to *Iphigénie*, p. 473.
22 *Euripides*, 4: p. 210. Cf. Pfohl's view of these two versions.
23 Crawford Brough Macpherson, *The Political Theory of Possessive Individualism: Hobbes to Locke* (Oxford, 1962; rpt. 1964), p. 3.

Chapter 11

1 The phrase "things themselves" recurs throughout Bacon's writings; the other quotations are from the Preface and Plan of *The Great Instauration*: Francis Bacon, *The New Organon and Related Writings*, ed. Fulton Anderson (Indianapolis and New York, 1960), pp. 15, 19, 20.
2 *The New Science of Giambattista Vico*, Revised Trans. of the Third edition (1744), by Thomas Goddard Bergin and Max Harold Fisch (Ithaca, N.Y., 1968), p. 104, §349; cf. pp. 79, 88, 124, §§245, 294, 393. The first edition of the *New Science* appeared in 1725, the first performance of *Phèdre* was fifty years before, on January 1, 1677. In October 1677 Racine and Boileau became royal historiographers.
3 Vico, *New Science*, p. 102, §342. For Vico "eternal history" is supposedly a *history* in "our" sense, but in fact it is made "timeless" because it is (for us humans) a tracing of the "mental language common to all nations" and to all "human social institutions" (pp. 67, 106, 161–62, 355), the permanent deep structure of human "thinking" which is one with "divine providence" (e.g., pp. 103, 345).
4 Cf. "L'empire de la volonté" of Jean Bodin, *Méthode pour faciliter la connaissance de l'histoire*, in *Oeuvres complètes*, ed. Pierre Mesnard (Paris, 1951), 1:287. In this context it is significant that Descartes presents his methodical scientific discourse as the imposition of an enunciating *"I"* and as a history: an intellectual sequential development leading necessarily to a *right* method and legitimate science ("ne proposant cet écrit que comme une histoire," *Discours de la méthode*, part 1).
5 Bacon, *Temporis Partus Masculus* c. 1603, in *The Works of Francis Bacon*, ed. J. Spedding, R. L. Ellis and D. D. Heath (Boston, 1863), 7:17. The work is translated in Benjamin Farrington, *The Philosophy of Francis Bacon: An Essay on Its Development from 1603 to 1609*, with new translations of fundamental texts (Chicago, 1964; rpt. 1966), pp. 59–72.
6 Thomas Hobbes, *De Corpore*, chap. 7, §3, in *Body, Man, and Citizen: Selections from Thomas Hobbes*, ed. Richard S. Peters (New York, 1962), pp. 95–96. Cf. *Leviathan*, p. 97.
7 See the commentary on time and numbering in Hobbes, *Leviathan*, pp. 104 ff.; *De Corpore*, chap. 1, §3, chap. 2, §14.

8 For Hobbes this is true of all knowledge: true "science" for him is always "Conditionall" (*Leviathan*, p. 131).

9 Jeremy Bernstein, *Einstein* (London, 1973), p. 73. See Sir Isaac Newton, *Mathematical Principles of Natural Philosophy and His System of the World*, trans. Andrew Motte, ed. Florian Cajori, 2 vols. (Berkeley and Los Angeles, 1934; rpt. 1966), 1:6.

10 Vico, *New Science*, p. 96, §331.

11 The quotation marks are necessary because for Vico *man* does not exist prior to his institutions. We may bear this in mind as regards *Phèdre* and its "*monstres*," the creatures that precede *history* and its accompanying *legitimate* institutions.

12 Hobbes, *Leviathan*, pp. 81–82.

13 "Que . . ./ Son amante aujourd'hui me tienne lieu de fille!" ("May his mistress now take the place of my daughter!" [5.7: p. 593]).

14 Both protested their innocence in such matters. Evidence suggests that Racine, at least, devoted considerable time and effort to the work (see his letters to Boileau). That there is little tangible evidence of actual production is due to the fire that in 1726 destroyed Valincour's library, destroying all the mss. there. Valincour several times wrote of the accumulated mass of papers. It is of more than simply antiquarian interest that in England at this time the posts of poet laureate and historiographer royal were combined in a single officeholder. Until 1666 James Howell held the latter post alone. Dryden was laureate from 1668, and historiographer royal from 1670. He held both posts until 1689, at which time Shadwell was installed. After Shadwell's death in 1692, Thomas Rymer became historiographer (and edited the *Foedera*) and Nahum Tate became laureate. Until Rymer held it, the post of historiographer was a sinecure, but the fact remains that there are certain theoretical implications involved in the combination. The Court of Charles II had, of course, spent its years of exile at that of Louis XIV: it is with the (elected) reign of William III that the two posts are again separated. That situation seems to reinforce what I am here implying with respect to Racine.

15 Charles Mauron, *Phèdre* (Paris, 1968), p. 120.

16 Odette de Mourgues, *Racine, or the Triumph of Relevance* (Cambridge, 1967), p. 13; cf. Bernard Weinberg, *The Art of Jean Racine* (Chicago and London, 1963), pp. 256–57.

17 Roland Barthes, *Sur Racine* (Paris, 1963), pp. 119–20.

18 Judd D. Hubert, *Essai d'exégèse racinienne: les secrets témoins* (Paris, 1956), pp. 212–13.

19 Since it is after his death that Minos is transfigured, Phaedra might be viewed as entirely "heavenly" (Minos was the son of Zeus), but in the play he is already judge in Hades: "mon père y tient l'urne fatale" (my father holds there the fatal urn" [4.6: p. 582]).

20 Mauron, *Phèdre*, p. 31.

21 The establishment of legitimacy is not a "return" to order (Lucien Goldmann, *Le Dieu caché: étude sur la vision tragique dans les "Pensées" de Pascal et*

   dans le théâtre de Racine [Paris, 1955], pp. 427–28: Jean Gaudon, " 'Par vous aurait péri le monstre de la Crète,' " *Romanic Review* 63, no. 4 [Dec. 1972], p. 260). The historical order of society does not exist in the text of the play nor prior to it: there is a *passage* from "myth" to history *in* the play.

22 Hubert, *Essai d'exégèse racinienne*, p. 207.

23 Gaudon, " 'Par vous aurait peri . . . ,' " p. 255. John Lapp is also mistaken in calling Phèdre "all powerful at Troezen" (*Aspects of Racinian Tragedy* [Toronto, 1955], p. 22).

24 "Et l'on craint . . . /Qu'il n'entraîne après lui tout un peuple volage" ("And it is feared lest he draw behind him an entire flighty populace" [1.4: p. 553]).

25 *Hippolytus*, trans. David Grene, *Euripides*, 1.

26 Brian Vickers, *Towards Greek Tragedy*, p. 19.

27 With this phrase Thierry Maulnier merely gave ironic verbalization to a generally received tradition: even Goldmann accepted it. I will come later to the question of legitimacy that provokes the passage.

28 This may be contrasted with Phèdre's case: "Cet aveu si honteux, le crois-tu volontaire?" ("Do you think this utterly shameful admission is voluntary?") [2.5: p. 564]). Or earlier: "les Dieux m'en ont ravi l'usage" ("the Gods have stripped me of their use" [of "reason" and "will"]), when she laments that she acts "malgré moi" ("in spite of myself" [1.3: p. 548]). Shortly she will bewail an entire loss of control: "Moi, ranger un Etat sous ma loi,/Quand ma faible raison ne règne plus sur moi!/Lorsque j'ai de mes sens abandonné l'empire!/. . . *Je ne le puis* quitter" ("Me, place a state under my command, when my weak reason no longer rules over myself! When I have abandoned control of my senses! . . . *I cannot* leave him" [3.1: p. 566]). It is just after this admission that she adds: "Il n'est plus temps" ("It is too late," but also "There is no more time"). In this no-time, far from imposing herself, the place imposes itself upon her: "Il me semble déjà que ces murs, que ces voûtes/Vont prendre la parole . . ." ("It already seems to me that these walls, these vaults, are going to speak" [3.3: p. 569]); or again, "Je ne puis rien pour moi" ("I can do nothing for myself" [5.3: p. 571]).

29 She makes of Phèdre's silence a tool "dont la vie est [le] prix" ("of which the price is life" [3.3: p. 570]), honor is a "trésor" (3.3: p. 571).

30 Weinberg, *Jean Racine*, pp. 277–79.

31 Harald Weinrich, *Le Temps: le récit et le commentaire*, trans. Michèle Lacoste (Paris, 1973), p. 47.

32 Ibid., pp. 295–96.

33 According to Boileau in the *Réflexion XI* on Longinus: "une espèce d'acclamation" ("a kind of acclamation") *Oeuvres complètes*, p. 560.

34 G. W. F. Hegel, *On Tragedy*, ed. Anne and Henry Paolucci (New York, 1962; rpt. 1975), pp. 159, 326.

Chapter 12

 1 Antonin Artaud, "Theatre and the Plague," in *Collected Works*, tr. Victor

Corti (London, 1974–), 4:19. I have brought the English text closer to the French original.

2 Maurice Merleau-Ponty, *Humanism and Terror: An Essay on the Communist Problem*, tr. John O'Neill (Boston, 1969), p. xxxix.

3 Richard Wagner, *Prose Works*, tr. William Ashton Ellis, 8 vols. (New York, 1966), 1:35, 135. Both works mentioned appeared in 1849.

4 Wagner, "Art-Work of the Future," *Prose Works*, 1:135.

5 Paolucci, ed., *Hegel on Tragedy* (New York, 1975), p. 102.

6 Paolucci, ed., *Hegel on Tragedy*, pp. 105, 107–08.

7 See, e.g., Stephen Orgel, *The Illusion of Power: Political Theater in the English Renaissance* (Berkeley, Los Angeles, and London, 1975), passim.

8 John Dryden, *Troilus and Cressida*, in *The Works*, ed. Sir Walter Scott, revised and corrected by George Saintsbury, 18 vols. (Edinburgh, 1883), 6:241–391.

9 Erwin Piscator, *Das Politische Theater* (Berlin, 1968), pp. 29–30: "Der Naturalismus stellt Züstande fest. Er stellt die Kongruenz zwischen Literatur und dem Zustand der Gesellschaft wieder her."

10 Raymond Williams, *Modern Tragedy* (London, 1966), p. 93.

11 Francis Fergusson, *The Idea of a Theater: The Art of Drama in Changing Perspective* (Garden City, N.Y., 1953), p. 164.

12 Williams, *Modern Tragedy*, pp. 190–204.

13 Bertolt Brecht, Über das Unterhaltungsdrama," in *Gesammelte Werke*, 15: *Schriften zum Theater*, 1 (Frankfurt a/M., 1967), p. 43.

14 Williams, *Modern Tragedy*, p. 202.

15 Emile Copfermann, *Le théâtre populaire, pourquoi?* (Paris, 1969), p. 103.

Index

In the absence of a general bibliography, the following index provides footnote references for the first occurrence of a work (i.e., for its full bibliographical description). Other footnote references are discursive.